INDUSTRIAL RELATIONS
THEORY

Its Nature, Scope, and Pedagogy

Industrial Relations Theory

Its Nature, Scope, and Pedagogy

edited by

Roy J. Adams and Noah M. Meltz

*Institute of Management and Labor Relations
Series, No. 4*

*HD
6961
I5594
1993*

IMLR Press / Rutgers University

and

The Scarecrow Press, Inc.

Metuchen, N.J., & London

1993

British Library Cataloguing-in-Publication data available

Library of Congress Cataloging-in-Publication Data

Industrial relations theory : its nature, scope, and pedagogy / edited by
  Roy J. Adams and Noah M. Meltz.
        p.   cm. — (Institute of Management and Labor Relations
  series : no. 4)
      Includes bibliographical references.
      ISBN 0-8108-2678-X (alk. paper)
      1. Industrial relations—Methodology. 2. Industrial relations—
  Study and teaching. I. Adams, Roy J. II. Meltz, Noah M. III.
  Series.
  HD6961.I5594 1993
  331—dc20   93-9898

Contents

Understanding, Constructing, and Teaching Industrial Relations Theory

Roy J. Adams

Industrial relations is a field of social science inquiry which has taken shape only during the past 50 years or so. The central focus of the field is labor: labor as a movement, labor as a commodity for which there is a market, labor as a workforce to be managed and labor as working people seeking security, challenge and self-fulfilment. As a field, industrial relations (IR) is composed of scholars—some of whom were trained in, and continue to identify with, traditional disciplines such as economics, history, law, and sociology and others whose identification is entirely with industrial relations. In the last several decades, as the result of the establishment of programs granting Ph.D. degrees in IR, the field has begun to take on more of a disciplinary status. The changing makeup of the field is indicated by the composition of professional organizations such as the American-based Industrial Relations Research Association. As indicated in my article, three decades ago most members of the IRRA were also affiliated with one of the traditional disciplines; today the plurality of academic members identify industrial relations as their primary discipline.

One of the defining characteristics of most fields is its theory. Industrial relations, however, has been something of an exception. As noted by Jack Barbash in his essay for this volume, the field was founded by pragmatists seeking to understand and solve labor problems. Staying close to the real world has remained an important value and, towards that end, many industrial relationists have

spurned abstract theory. Not only have they foregone theory building as a core intellectual activity, many prominent industrial
relationists hold that there is no such thing as IR theory (Adams
1988). As a field of inquiry, it is asserted, IR is an atheoretical,
practical endeavor. Instead of pursuing elegant, all-encompassing
explanations for patterns of social interaction, the objective is
simply to solve current, pressing problems by drawing on more
basic work in the traditional social sciences, as necessary.

Despite such assertions, many articles have been written on IR
theory, and graduate programs in IR frequently (even if less so than
economics programs as Paula Voos notes) require a course in IR
theory. In short, the existence of IR theory, its nature, its content,
and its bounds are all problematic. There is little consensus about
what the term means or about the empirical phenomena to which it
is intended to refer. This absence of clarity tends to frustrate
meaningful discussion about the state and progress of the field. One
of the major purposes of this book is to help clarify the term and
thus, hopefully, to assist meaningful discussion about the strengths
and deficiencies of the body of thought to which it refers.

Another defining characteristic of traditional academic disciplines is that they are global. They seek, at least, to make "if then"
statements which are universally valid. Industrial relations, however, has been more nationalistic in nature. American scholars have
been concerned primarily in solving American problems, rather
than in discovering or creating universally valid propositions. There
has, nevertheless, been some cross-national fertilization. Theory
developed in the United States and Britain has been studied and
applied in other English-speaking countries, not always with the
best results as indicated in the essay by Kevin Hince. One premise
of this volume is that industrial relations is a multinational field
whose disciples should be seeking principles which apply over the
broadest span of time and space.

In the mid-1980s, on the initiative of Jack Barbash, the International Industrial Relations Association established a study group
on Industrial Relations Theory and Industrial Relations as a field.
In meetings held in Hamburg, Brussels, and elsewhere it was
evident that there was a good deal of interest in this subject. In 1989,
Noah Meltz and I assumed co-chairmanship of the group. One of
my first projects, as co-chairman, was to collect outlines of courses
on IR theory with a view towards helping to clarify the nature of

the subject. My "theory" was that if psychology could be defined as whatever psychologists do professionally (Marx and Hillix 1963), then IR theory might be defined as that which IR theory teachers teach. During 1990, 16 outlines were collected. An analysis of their contents suggested an ideal theory course in which several themes are discussed:

1. The nature and scope of industrial relations as an academic field.
2. The relationship of industrial relations to other fields such as economics, psychology, sociology, history, and law which also focus to some extent on labor.
3. Paradigmatic approaches to industrial relations including institutional analysis, marxist analysis, the managerial perspective, and the market framework, and
4. The techniques of theory construction and assessment.

The extent to which these four themes were stressed (or even covered) varied from course to course. All four are addressed in this volume.

Two of the 16 teachers who provided outlines in response to my request contribute essays to this volume on the scope of their course and the logic underlying it. The course now taught by Paula Voos at the University of Wisconsin has a rich history. It was first introduced by Jack Barbash around 1970 and has been taken by many of the most active researchers in the field at present. Of those contributing to this volume, Tom Kochan, Hoyt Wheeler, Steve Hills, and myself are graduates of this course. If one were to construct a model course based on those currently being taught, it would include reference to most of the subjects covered by Paula Voos at Wisconsin. She begins with Marx and then traces the thought of three generations of American "institutionalists," reviewing all of the major paradigmatic approaches to labor problems while drawing on, and contrasting work done in, several of the traditional disciplines. She notes some of the problems of the industrial relations theory teacher. The students may have diverse backgrounds and thus the instructor may have to teach them basic concepts from several disciplines (e.g., anomie from sociology, transaction costs from economics, self-actualization from psychology, bargaining unit from law). The challenge of doing so places a considerable burden on anyone who would become sufficiently competent in the requisite range of theory to be able effectively to teach a graduate course in IR theory. It also, of course, poses a challenge to all students of industrial relations. As Kochan notes in his essay, pressure is on the industrial relationist not only to integrate learning from several fields but to do it "at a sufficient depth to gain the respect of those working on the same issues within [any specific] discipline."

The Wisconsin course also has a legacy. Joel Cutcher-Gershenfeld, who discusses the theory course which he now teaches at Michigan State University, is a student of Tom Kochan. His course is a modified version of the one he took from Tom at MIT. Although he uses different terminology, the themes covered in Cutcher-Gershenfeld's course are similar to those addressed by Voos. The major portion of the Michigan State course is divided into three sections. Each section looks at a body of literature which treats "conflict" in a different way. One body (the radical literature) is predicated on the assumption or assertion that relations between labor and management are fundamentally conflictive within capitalist society. A second body of literature, variously referred to as management, human relations/human resource management, and unitarist, proceeds on the assumption that the interests between employers and employees are essentially the same and that if properly managed no conflict need arise between labor and management. The third body of literature Cutcher-Gershenfeld refers to as mixed-motive. Contributors assume that, even though labor-management conflict may be inherent in industrial society, employees and employers also have many interests in common. Institutional-pluralists, who embrace the mixed-motive outlook, assert that conflict, while fundamental, still may be channeled and controled to the benefit of both sides.

In recognition of the multidisciplinary roots of industrial relations, Cutcher-Gershenfeld also reviews research on labor done from the disciplinary perspectives of economics, sociology and history, especially the "New Labor History," which focuses less on trade unions and political parties and more on the day to day experience of working people in history. Finally, Cutcher-Gershenfeld finishes his course by addressing current debates. In the United States during the 1980s, perhaps the most widely discussed and debated "theory" was the "Transformation of Industrial

Relations" thesis developed by Tom Kochan, Peter Cappelli, Harry
Katz and Bob McKersie (Kochan, McKersie, and Cappelli 1984;
Kochan, Katz, and McKersie 1986). Being a U.S.-based course, this
issue is of great interest to contemporary American students.

If what appears on IR theory course outlines is indicative,
industrial relations theory is theory about labor, and relations between labor and management and labor, management, and the state.
The term *industrial relations theory* incorporates economic, sociological, psychological, and legal theory, which is designed to explain labor phenomena. Such theory is both economic theory and
industrial relations theory. The term also incorporates theory such
as the Dunlopian systems framework, the convergence hypothesis,
bargaining theory, and the transformation thesis, which are not so
clearly associated with any one of the traditional disciplines. As
Paula Voos notes, IR as a field is not dominated by any overriding
theoretical scheme. Instead, the field is characterized by "competing paradigms." In this regard it is quite different from contemporary economics which has overwhelmingly embraced neoclassical
theory. On the other hand, economics is not really exemplary of the
general situation in the social sciences. Paradigmaic diversity rather
than unity is characteristic of psychology and sociology for example.

Another insight into the nature of the subject is provided by
Jack Barbash, who reviews the basic ideas of the people he consid-
ers to the be the "Makers of Industrial Relations": Karl Marx, Max
Weber, Frederick Taylor, Elton Mayo, Beatrice and Sydney Webb,
John R. Commons, Selig Perlman, Sumner Slichter, and Robert
Hoxie. One finds most of these authors (Marx, Taylor, Mayo, the
Webbs, Commons, and Perlman) discussed in theory courses ev-
erywhere. Slichter and Hoxie, however, are more local "American"
heroes rather than international ones and it is unusual to find their
work discussed in courses taught outside of North America. In
British courses one nearly always finds the work of Clegg (1976),
Flanders (1965), and Fox (1971, 1974) discussed. Their work is
also not uncommonly discussed in other countries as well. Work by
all three, for example, appears on the outlines of Voos and Cutcher-
Gershenfeld.

Max Weber is a problematic figure for industrial relations. As
Barbash notes he "was not a labor reformer nor was labor his
paramount interest." Of major relevance to industrial relations,

however, is his work on management and particularly his theory of bureaucracy. Barbash considers it to be a necessary corrective to Marx's refusal "to accept the legitimacy and efficacy of a management function to economize on labor resources, which later proved to be one of the flaws that eventually brought down Soviet-style socialism."

Although industrial relations is characterized by competing paradigms, Barbash suggests that competition is not the whole story. If one looks for a common thread running through the interests of those scholars who consider themselves to be industrial relationists, one finds (in contrast especially to economics from which IR emerged as a field) a concern with both efficiency (the dominant focus of economics) and with equity—understood broadly to include concern with justice, fairness, dignity, security, and democratic participation.

One of the key subjects discussed in industrial relations theory courses is the theory of the labor movement. Indeed the trade union and its allied institutions (e.g., labor/socialist political parties, cooperatives, works councils) has been a dominant focus of research by industrial relationists. Trade union theory was developed in the 19th and 20th century by thinkers in Europe and North America, who reflected on the experience in their part of the world. Nevertheless, that theory is generally discussed as if it had universal validity. One result of the assumption is that writers in Australia and New Zealand, Asian countries dominated by Anglo-Saxon language and culture, have naturally attempted to apply Euro-American trade union theory. In this volume, Kevin Hince argues that the fit has always been awkward. Drawing on the work of Howard, he outlines and provides evidence for a theory of trade unions as institutions whose existence and behavior are largely functions of government policy. Most contemporary unions in Australia and New Zealand, he argues, did not emerge naturally from problems perceived independently by working people. Instead, they were created to take advantage of national arbitration laws and thus were creatures of those laws.

Although Hince wishes to do no more than illuminate the character of unions downunder, the thesis, in fact, may have much wider applicability. Unions in North America, although they may have emerged out of perceived needs of workers, have over time become addicted to the procedures and behavior elicited by the

North American legal framework. In the United States that framework has been applied in a manner much less favorable to organized
labor than it was in past decades. As a result, the fortunes of
organized labor have turned dramatically downward. Moreover,
although unions may function outside of the legal framework, they
have shown little capacity to do so, despite a decade or more of
apparent efforts in that regard.

The idea of the union as a instrument of something other than
the wishes of its members has also been pursued in a recent book
by Ross Martin (1988). Unions as autonomous worker-controled
institutions exist in only a minority of the world's nations. Consistent with Hince, Martin argues that many union movements (and
particularly those in the communist and ex-communist countries)
are instruments or creatures of the state. Still others, he suggests,
are tools, not of their members but rather of political parties. The
time seems ripe for a new debate over "The theory of the labor
movement."

Although Western theorists tend to assume or imply that their
theories are universal in scope, in fact very few theorists have made
efforts to construct theories explicitly intended to explain "facts"
gathered from around the globe. Michael Poole is one of the few
major exceptions to that observation. His book *Industrial Relations,
Origins and Patterns of National Diversity* (1986) was a daring
attempt at making coherent sense of observations drawn from the
four corners of the earth. In this volume, his article assesses the
current state of "the convergence hypothesis," the proposition
(developed by institutional labor economists but considered to be
fundamental to the theoretical base of both industrial relations and
comparative industrial sociology) that patterns of interaction between labor, management, and the state are becoming increasingly
similar, due largely to the exigencies of technology. Recent events,
especially the fall of the unitary communist regimes of East and
Central Europe and their replacement with pluralistic political and
industrial relations systems more similar to those in the West, have
given new credence to this thesis. Not only technology but also the
globalization of markets and the internationalization of knowledge
and production are forces driving industrial relations in a common
direction. Arrayed against the forces for convergence are continuing powerful forces for diversity, including differences in cultural
values, ideology, political and economic conditions, and institu-

tional arrangements. Poole notes that once established institutional arrangements tend to persist even against very powerful environmental forces.

Poole also reviews three major recent developments which, if not uniform globally, still represent significant international trends:

1. The embracing by corporate managers of a new pro-active policy of labor management commonly referred to in North America as "the new human resources management" and in Britain simply as "human resources management."
2. The widespread decline in trade union membership and power, and
3. The broad movement by governments towards privatization, deregulation, and the declining use of economic planning in favor of free-market forces.

While widespread, these trends are not universal, and even where they are evident, action taken by the actors in response to them have been diverse. Poole concludes that significant variation in industrial relations systems is likely to continue "well into the twenty-first century."

As noted previously, most IR theory courses contain a section on the development of IR as a field of inquiry. That theme is taken up here in my essay, which focuses on the development of the field in North America, Britain, and Australasia. Although it is now being taken up in several countries, IR was at first largely an Anglo-Saxon phenomenon and it is, at present, still most well established in English-speaking countries.

The research reported in "All Aspects . . . " indicates that industrial relations in all of the countries under consideration emerged from economics. It also suggests that industrial relationists, while paying lip service to the goal of achieving understanding, prediction, and control over all aspects of employment, in practice tend to focus most of their attention on unions, collective bargaining, and miscellaneous labor market issues. The American Industrial Relations Research Association, established in 1946, was an attempt to bring together scholars from a wide variety of disciplines interested in labor but it was not very successful in doing so. In particular, it failed to hold together in a single community of scholars the interdisciplinary specialists in the closely related fields of labor relations, personnel/human resources management, and organizational behavior. Instead of coalescing into a single discipline, these three specialties have developed separate literatures and separate identities, even though many industrial relations institutes offer coursework and carry out research in all three areas and permit graduate students to specialize in any of the three.[1]

Not only has IR failed 1) to provide an institutional vehicle for bringing together scholars from several disciplines interested in labor issues and 2) to knit together organizational behavior, human resources management, and labor relations, but also many competing interdisciplinary fields have been established in disregard of IR's offer to be the assimilating vehicle. Does all of this mean that IR has been a failure? Despite its shortcomings, evidence at this point does not lead to that conclusion. In its own right, IR has attracted a growing following in recent decades. Membership in most IR associations has expanded and scholars in a larger range of countries are carrying out research in the IR tradition.

For those who joined IR because they wanted to study labor broadly and holistically, the greatest challenge at present is to find ways of bridging the gaps between the many isolated labor researchers, both disciplinarians and interdisciplinarians. Perhaps the greatest threat to the future of IR as a field is the current expansion of human resource management (HRM). Scholars who receive Ph.D degrees from IR institutes usually accept academic jobs at either other institutes or at business schools. During the 1980s, student interest in HRM has expanded significantly, while in many places interest in labor relations has waned. As a result, various departments and even some institutes have been dropping industrial relations from their title and adding human resources management. In short a scenario in which HRM supplants IR is not entirely fanciful. HRM, however, is more limited in scope. Unlike IR, it never has had the ambition to understand "All Aspects of People at Work." Its focus is almost exclusively on the management of labor (Dowling and Schuler 1990).

Noah Meltz' essay explicates the industrial relations systems concept, first put forth by John Dunlop in 1958, by assimilating the strategic choice framework of Tom Kochan and his collaborators. It is an attempt to provide a scheme which will have the ability to subsume various approaches to the study of labor and labor management. IR systems is the framework most commonly utilized by teachers of industrial relations to organize courses and textbooks, but it has been accused of biasing the user towards focusing on union-management relations from a conservative, pluralistic point of view. Meltz argues that his revised framework indicates how various approaches to employment relations relate to each other, and thus it provides a useful conceptual map to the whole universe of labor and labor management.

Since its appearance in the late 1950s, the Dunlopian framework or variants of it has been the primary conceptual structure utilized by industrial relations teachers and researchers to organize books and courses. To some extent, the Marxian framework of two classes locked in struggle has also been used, more so in the United Kingdom, Canada, and Australia than in the United States. Steve Hills in his essay for this volume puts forth a new conceptual framework which has been designed specifically as a vehicle for assimilating the contributions of the various social sciences to the study of labor. He argues that any society must create institutions capable of developing, allocating, utilizing and maintaining human resources. In developing such institutions, it has choices in terms of where it places the locus of control over these functions. Some societies (communist countries) concentrate control in the government; others (early 19th century Britain) foster market control, and still other nations provide enterprises with considerable power to make decisions with respect to the requisite functions. Whichever direction this policy plane may tilt, negotiations between labor, management, and the state with respect to these functions are continually in progress. Hills demonstrates how followers of alternative approaches to policy development proselytize different policy plane tilts. Marxists traditionally have argued for a strong tilt in the direction of the state; liberals push for market dominance.

Despite the fact that relations between employers and employees have enormous consequences for the politics of any nation, industrial relations has been the traditional province first of economists, then of management theorists, and then of law scholars, sociologists, and historians. Political scientists, however, have contributed very little to knowledge about people at work and as a result very little "positive" research has been carried out on the role of the state in industrial relations. Braham Dabscheck in his essay for this volume takes a step in the direction of changing that situation.

Drawing on "regulation theory," a body of literature developed to explain the behavior of government regulatory agencies, he analyzes the course of wage regulation in Australia during the 20th century. His technique is suggestive of how theories drawn from political science might be usefully applied to acquire a better knowledge of the motivation and behavior of the state in industrial relations. It is my belief that during the next decade there is likely to be a significant expansion of research on the nature of the state in IR, and regulation theory is one resource which may be utilized in that quest. The essay contributed by Craig Littler to this volume, discussed in more depth below, is also relevant to this issue.

In their widely read book on social science research, Burrell and Morgan (1979) classified such research along two dimensions: radical/regulationist and subjective/objective. In their essay contributed to this volume, Audet and Larouche review "158 theoretical articles, chapters of books and other material (published between 1897 and 1988) which significantly focused on 'what industrial relations is . . . '" They find that the preponderance of IR thought has been (and continues to be) objective and regulationist. Almost all of it falls into the inquiry paradigm, which has been labelled "positivism" or "logical positivism." Under this form of inquiry the object is to discover uniformities in nature. To do so, one begins with questions or hypotheses stated in advance in propositional form and subjects those propositions to empirical tests under carefully controled conditions (either physically or statistically). The more quantitative the data and the more sophisticated the analytical technique used to assess the data the more credible the resultant argument. The professional inquirer is expected to adopt a neutral unbiased attitude toward the data. An implicit assumption is that knowable regularities exist in nature.

Only a small minority of IR researchers have attempted to make use of radical frameworks for inquiry. Radical researchers do not adhere to all of the tenets of logical positivism. In particular, they do not adhere to the proposition that the researcher must adopt an unbiased attitude. Indeed they claim that unbiased research is impossible. All researchers, they assert, are captive to their own values and thus the responsibility of the researcher is not to conduct unbiased research but rather publicly to reveal the values on which the research is based. Nor do radical researchers accept that the function of the researcher is dispassionately to discover regularities of nature. Instead, the subject matter of social science research is people and the proper function of the social science researcher is to strive to make the world a better place for people to live in. One way to do this is to reveal misconceptions about the nature of social relations. Thus, Marxists strive to demonstrate that, although Western society appears on the surface to be pluralistic, a deeper analysis reveals that it is really composed of two antagonistic classes. The feminist attempts to show that, although a surface analysis might lead one to conclude that both men and women have equally important roles in society, in fact women must work harder and longer and have less power and prestige.

According to the research of Audet and Larouche, industrial relations researchers have completely ignored subjective approaches to the acquisition of knowledge about human behavior. This type of inquiry has been growing throughout the social sciences since the publication of Thomas Kuhn's *The Structure of Scientific Revolutions* (1962). That book deflated some of the haughtiness of the logical positivists by demonstrating convincingly that research in many fields has not moved in the cumulative fashion proposed by the positivists. Nor has the application of positivistic methods produced knowledge objectively superior to knowledge acquired by other methods.

Among the approaches alternative to logical positivism are hermeneutics, social action theory, naturalism, and postmodernism. Guba (1990) has suggested the generic term "constructivism" to encompass various approaches diametrically opposed to logical positivism. According to constructivism if an objective reality guided by laws of recurring behavior does exist, it is not knowable by human beings. Instead human inquiry always begins with the choice or construction of concepts which order perceived reality. As a result "'reality' only exists in the context of a mental framework (construct) for thinking about it" (Guba 1990, 25). Thus "empirical tests" cannot be "valid as arbiters of propositions (hypotheses and questions) put to nature by inquirers" because "theoretical and observational languages" are not independent. By choosing a theory one organizes reality. For example, labor is not a commodity in nature. It only takes on that characteristic when one utilizes classical (or neoclassical) economic theory to order perceptions. Societies do not "naturally" and objectively split into two classes (or many classes) but those classes appear to the researcher who approaches social research from a Marxist perspective. Without a theory, perceptions are no more than chaos. The choice of theory provides order to perceived reality.

Because nature may only be engaged with the aid of a theoretical framework and because the choice of the framework is up to the researcher, the research process is necessarily subjective and cannot be value free. All theories have value positions embedded within them. As a result, when one chooses a theoretical framework, one also chooses a value position from which to conduct research. Because one may interpret any situation utilizing alternative theories and thus alternative value positions, there is no "ultimate truth or falsity." There is no "foundational" yardstick against which research may be assessed to determine its goodness, badness, or prestige. Knowledge is relative and the key to progress lies in openness and continual dialogue.

At present there is no consensus in the social sciences about the proper approach to social research. There is, however, an emerging consensus (one that has yet had little impact on IR) that logical positivism should no longer be accorded a position of unchallenged pre-eminence. Indeed, new techniques for "decentering" arrogant claims to intellectual dominance have been invented and have been utilized increasingly in social scientific work. Of particular note is the "deconstruction" technique pioneered by Derrida (1978, 1981, 1982, 1987) and the critical historical work of Foucault (1967, 1970, 1977, 1980, 1981). In this volume, John Godard reviews several strands of subjectivist inquiry and their implications for IR theory and practice.

Craig Littler takes a look at the critical literature, especially its recent evolution and likely future direction. He notes that "political economy" in its recent form arose in reaction to the "exchange paradigm," which "treats the mutual trading of money and services between employers and employees as a subset of the more general category of transactions between buyer and seller." The exchange paradigm thrusts economic relationships to the fore and de-emphasizes the political nature of the employment relationship. Political economy has grown as a corrective to that development. In his essay, Littler focuses on two streams of political economy research: labor process and "the regulation programme of research." The first body of literature "starts from the management end of the spectrum: it is concerned with a critical analysis of managerial process." A major effort of this group of researchers is to identify managerial systems types (e.g., Taylorist, Fordist, Post-Fordist, flexible specialization) and to investigate their implications for labor-management relations. Unlike the human resources management literature, the objective of labor process theorists is not to provide management with insights and tools to enable it better to achieve its objectives. Instead, the object is to reveal the true nature of managerial behavior with a view towards changing social relations to bring them into closer line with radical values.

Littler notes that, in part because of its focus on labor-management relations at the shop-floor, "labor process writing tends to neglect the role of the state." Regulation theory (originally identified as French Regulation Theory, this is a body of theory entirely different from the work reviewed by Dabscheck) incorporates more macro considerations. It "involves an attempt to recast the logic of capitalist power relations on a nondeterminist basis." It posits that capitalist labor relations have evolved through a series of "modes of regulation" (which include managerial strategies and industrial relations institutions) and that the current period is one of crisis in which old patterns are being challenged by new ones. Littler reviews three analyses of the generation, nature, and likely conclusion of the crisis: the [French] regulation thesis, flexible specialization, and Japanisation. Of the three, he feels that "it is an in-depth analysis of Japanese management practices which will provide keys to understanding the political economy of the 1990s and beyond."

If they are to have an impact of any size on the field and the world, students of industrial relations must not only be well versed in existing theory but also be capable of building new theories. It was with that end in mind that I wrote the essay on theory construction for this volume. Theory building is not an easy skill to learn and one who is not versed in theory assessment may be lulled into acceptance of specious arguments. Unfortunately, method courses in the social sciences spend much less time on theory building than on data gathering and analysis.

Note that my essay is written entirely from a logical positivist perspective. As an assessment technique, the "checklist" is "foundational" in nature. It supposes that there are objective criteria against which theories may be assessed in order to reach an unbiased assessment of their quality. It was not my attention in writing the essay to assert the primacy of the logical positivist approach.

However, I do believe that a sound grounding in the techniques of logical positivism is an invaluable base for the effective use of alternative paradigms.

The two final essays, those by Kochan and Wheeler, provide some insight into the art of the theorist at work. Kochan and his colleagues at MIT have had a very major impact on IR thought, research and practice. Kochan tells us how his thinking evolved, especially with respect to the creation of the widely discussed strategic choice framework. Hoyt Wheeler's integrative theory of industrial conflict (1985) has been called one of the most creative efforts at industrial relations theory building over the past several decades. Wheeler's work, it would seem, was precisely what the founders of the IRRA hoped would result from the offering of interdisciplinary studies at the graduate level.

Notes

1. This theme is also developed in some detail in Bruce Kaufman, 1993.

Works Cited

Adams, R. J. 1983, "Competing Paradigms in Industrial Relations," *Relations Industrielles,* vol. 38, no. 3, pp. 508-529.

_____. 1988, "Desperately Seeking Industrial Relations Theory," *International Journal of Comparative Labor Law and Industrial Relations,* vol 4, no. 1, pp. 1-10.

Burrell, G., and G. Morgan. 1979, *Sociological Paradigms and Organizational Analysis,* London: Heinemann.

Clegg, H. 1976, *Trade Unionism Under Collective Bargaining: A Theory Based on Comparisons of Six Countries,* Oxford: Basil Blackwell.

Derrida, J. 1978, *Writing and Difference,* Chicago: University of Chicago Press.

_____. 1981, *Positions,* Chicago: University of Chicago Press.

_____. 1982, *Margins of Philosophy,* Chicago: University of Chicago Press.

_____. 1987, *The Post Card,* Chicago: University of Chicago Press.

Dowling, P., and R. Schuler. 1990, "Human Resource Management," ed. R. Blanpain, *Comparative Labor Law and Industrial Relations in Industrialized Market Economies,* vol. 2, Industrial Relations, Kluwer: Deventer.

Flanders, A. 1965, *Industrial Relations, What Is Wrong with the System?* London: Faber.

Foucault, M. 1967, *Madness and Civilization,* London: Tavistock.

_____. 1970, *The Order of Things,* London: Tavistock.

_____. 1977, *Discipline and Punish,* London: Allen Lane.

_____. 1980, *Power/Knowledge: Selected Interviews and Other Writings 1972-1977,* New York: Pantheon.

Fox, A. 1971, *A Sociology of Work in Industry,* London: Collier-Macmillan.

_____. 1974, *Beyond Contract: Work, Power and Trust Relations,* London: Faber.

Guba, E. G., ed. 1990, *The Paradigm Dialog,* Newbury Park, CA: Sage.

Kaufman, Bruce E. 1993, forthcoming, *The Origin and Evolution of the Field of Industrial Relations in the United States,* Ithaca, NY: ILR Press.

Kochan, T. A., R. B. McKersie, and P. Cappelli. 1984, "Strategic Choices and Industrial Relations Theory," *Industrial Relations,* vol. 23, no. 1, pp. 16-39.

Kochan, T. A., H. C. Katz, and R. B. McKersie. 1986, *The Transformation of American Industrial Relations,* New York: Basic Books.

Kuhn, T. 1962, *The Structure of Scientific Revolutions,* Chicago: University of Chicago Press.

Martin, R. M. 1988, *Trade Unionism, Purposes and Forms,* Oxford: Clarendon Press.

Marx, M. H., amd W. A. Hillix. 1963, *Systems and Theories in Psychology,* New York: McGraw-Hill.

Poole, M. 1986, *Industrial Relations, Origins and Patterns of National Diversity,* London: Routledge.

Wheeler, H. 1985, *Industrial Conflict: An Integrative Theory,* Columbia, SC: University of South Carolina Press.

Designing an Industrial Relations Theory Curriculum for Graduate Students

Paula Voos

It is useful to reflect periodically on the pedagogy of one's field. Such an exercise can improve teaching and learning, while facilitating the exchange of ideas among universities. And because industrial relations (IR) theory is essentially defined by what is included in university curricula, examining those courses of study critically gives us a better understanding of what is currently meant by industrial relations theory, and how IR theory is changing as industrial relations itself evolves within our economic system.

This chapter makes several major points. The first is that industrial relations theory is extremely varied both ideologically and in terms of the great range of questions considered by different IR theorists (see also Adams, this volume). This great range is made evident by contrasting the role of industrial relations theory in the field of IR with the role of economic theory in the field of economics. Secondly, I contend, this diversity of IR theory is primarily due to the multidisciplinary origin of industrial relations as well as the great variety of ideas in the contributing social science disciplines. Third, this wide range of theoretical discourse in industrial relations

Comments from several persons were most helpful in formulating the ideas in this chapter. I would especially like to thank Roy Adams, Jack Barbash, Glen Cain, W. Lee Hansen, Stephen Hills, and Lois Shawver.

creates problems for the structuring of courses in IR theory. I will explore these problems and explain how this can be remedied to some extent by focusing on the dominant institutionalist tradition. The graduate-level IR theory course which I teach at the University of Wisconsin is discussed in some detail as an example of this strategy. Finally, I conclude by considering a variety of dilemmas which face the instructor of a course in IR theory, including those stemming from declining unionization in the U.S.

The Place of Theory in the Field of Industrial Relations

There is a wide range of theoretical discourse in industrial relations, but at the same time, abstract theory per se does not play a dominant, or even a particularly central role, in our field. The contrast with economics is instructive on both counts.

In the discipline of economics, at least within the United States, there is one central theoretical paradigm—neoclassical economics—that forms the basis of almost all graduate curricula, of most applied research, and of usual economic policy discussion. Of course, neoclassical theory has a number of contemporary critics and detractors, including those operating in institutional or Marxist frameworks.[1] Nonetheless, these alternative approaches tend to be peripheral within contemporary American economics. The intellectual rule of neoclassical economics has been insured in part by its extensive modification over the years, including the development of Keynesian macroeconomics, the elaboration of the concept of externalities, and the theory of the second best. As a result, *laissez faire* is not the inevitable policy prescription of the economically sophisticated; the very flexibility of the neoclassical paradigm in this regard has contributed to its overwhelming dominance of the field of economics.

To understand the contrast between the role of theory in economics and its role in IR, we need to notice not only the hegemony of a generally accepted theory in economics and the absence of such a single paradigm in IR, but also the centrality of theory in the training of economics graduate students and the relatively lesser importance of theory for IR graduate students. Virtually all programs which train economists at the graduate level require students to take an economic theory sequence as they enter graduate study.

This sequence is considered to be at the heart of the graduate curriculum. Moreover, economic theory forms the basis for much of the later material studied in the applied fields of economics. In contrast, industrial relations theory per se is required in only 38 percent of the IR Masters programs in North America (Wheeler 1989). IR Theory is seldom regarded as the central vehicle for training students new to the field. Where it is required, students often register for it in the second year of graduate study. Nothing could be more indicative of the relatively lesser role theory plays in the field of industrial relations than this comparison with economics.

The lesser role accorded theory in industrial relations stems largely from two factors. First, graduate programs in industrial relations are oriented less towards training future academics and more towards training practitioners than are graduate programs in economics. We train more masters students than Ph.D.s, unlike economics departments. Consequently, courses are more practical and less focused on theoretical abstractions.[2] Second, industrial relations has traditionally eschewed mathematically elegant, abstract theory in favor of "middle-level" conceptualization that is more useful for the "practical, applied problems of labor and management," (Kochan 1980). The key concepts of industrial relations have often been developed within its applied fields of collective bargaining, labor law, human resource management, and so forth. The theory of industrial relations is often the theory of its contributing social science and management disciplines, applied to the employment relationship. Consequently, we tend not to have one theoretical paradigm, but many. In short, in comparison to the situation in economics, theory in industrial relations has a lower status and a much greater range of ideas.[3]

The Origins of Diversity in IR Theory

Diversity in IR theory results from a number of factors. One is the multidisciplinary nature of our subject. Depending on one's frame of reference, industrial relations is either a field of study in which multiple disciplines apply their separate insights and in which scholars from disparate backgrounds join together in interdisciplinary applied research, or industrial relations is a new, emerging field, with origins in several of the social sciences. In either event, industrial relations draws on concepts from various fields. For instance, pluralism or corporatism may be discussed in industrial relations, but this discussion is based on work by political scientists and political sociologists. In like manner, equity theory or expectancy theory, from the field of psychology, along with concepts of market pay from economics, are utilized by industrial relations experts working in the area of compensation.

Insofar as there is a common body of thought underlying industrial relations as it is taught in the U.S. today, I would identity it as the institutional tradition, broadly defined. Institutionalism, of course, does not have an easy or simple definition.[4] Kaufman (1988, 190) argues that institutionalism:

> is most properly interpreted as meaning an attempt to develop an economic theory that is built around a model of man more congruent with the principles of social psychology, a model of markets that is grounded in the economics of imperfect competition, and a conception of the market process that gives considerable weight to the role of institutions (broadly defined).

I use "institutional" or the "institutional tradition, broadly defined" to refer not only to the original institutionalists—the Wisconsin school of Commons, Perlman, and their students—but also to the post-WWII group of "neoinstitutionalists," even though some of their members abjure that label (Kerr 1988), and furthermore to contemporary "third-generation-institutionalists" who regard neoclassical market theory as seriously incomplete. Scholars of internal labor markets would certainly qualify for that designation, but so too would strategic choice theorists, and many other IR scholars adopting the institutional "normative assumptions" identified by Kochan (1980) that labor is more than a commodity and that there is an inherent conflict of interest between employers and employees.

Despite its importance to the field, the world view of the institutional group underlies some subfields of contemporary industrial relations to a much greater extent than it does other subfields. Institutional ideas are far more important in labor relations, collective bargaining, or the study of labor markets, than in the areas of human resource management or organizational behavior. Institutional theory is important within industrial relations, but it has never achieved the hegemonic position that neoclassical thought has within the discipline of economics.

A second source of diversity in industrial relations is essentially ideological. Differences in values and political orientation lead to marked divergence between theorists with regard to what are the main topics of discussion. Marxist-influenced IR theorists working from theories of the labor process frame their research in divergent ways from management-oriented behavioralists concerned with enhancing the communication process within corporations! The fact that neither group is represented in significant numbers at a typical Industrial Relations Research Association (IRRA) meeting in the U.S. is beside the point. Both groups are still part of the wider academic community contributing ideas to contemporary industrial relations.

The very selection of the central issues open to theoretical dispute is itself a matter of theory, and the different varieties of industrial relations scholars have never agreed on a common list of central IR theory questions, much less on the boundaries of the discipline. John Dunlop once constructed such a list in conjunction with a review of the industrial relations theories of Marx, the Webbs, Commons, Perlman, Hoxie, and Tannenbaum (Dunlop 1948, 164-5). He summarized "theories of the labor movement" (itself only a subset of IR theory) as being related to four questions:

1. How is one to account for the origin or emergence of labor organizations? What conditions are necessary and what circumstances stimulate the precipitation of labor organization? Why have some workers organized and others not?
2. What explains the pattern of growth and development of labor organizations? What factors are responsible for the sequence and form in which organizations have emerged in various countries, industries, crafts, and companies? Since there is great diversity in the patterns of development, any theory of the labor movement must account for these differences.

3. What are the ultimate goals of the labor movement?
What is its relationship to the future of capitalism? What
is its role in the socialist or communist state?
4. Why do individual workers join labor organizations?
What system of social psychology accounts for this behavior of the employee?

These questions are strikingly limited from the viewpoint of
modern industrial relations theory, in part because IR theory is
much more than a theory of the labor movement. My main point,
however, is a different one. Dunlop's questions themselves reflect
the intellectual influence of Selig Perlman in American industrial
relations in the 1940s, as is indicated by Dunlop's judgment that
Perlman is the only theorist to have tackled all these issues! This is
an example of how the very questions of IR theory reflect the central
preoccupations of the theoretical system of which they are a part.

For those of us who are institutionalists in a broad sense, it is
tempting when teaching IR theory to reduce the diversity of the
subject by constructing a course focused around the development
of institutional thought as a middle-ground reaction to both the
neoclassical/managerial celebration of the market system and the
Marxist condemnation of capitalism. Taking this approach, it is
possible to structure some consideration of diverse influences on
the dominant institutional tradition (for instance, human relations
theory) by asking how these intellectual traditions were assimilated
by earlier institutionalists, or how they could be assimilated by
contemporary institutionalists, or why they were or should be
rejected. Alternatively, competing ideas can be examined by contrasting them with a particular aspect of institutional thought. As I
will explain below, I have used this approach in structuring my own
course. Imposing a semblance of unity on IR theory in this way has
the advantage of providing a more intelligible structure for the
student. However, it is important that a central focus on institutional
thought not restrict the subject matter of IR theory too narrowly.[5] I
leave it to the reader to judge whether or not my course meets this
important test.

IR Theory at the University of Wisconsin

At the University of Wisconsin, industrial relations theory is required of all Masters and doctoral students in industrial relations, and the one semester course is also taken by doctoral students in sociology, political science, and economics who are minoring in industrial relations. Doctoral students are further required to pass a preliminary exam in the subject. Jack Barbash developed the theory course partly at the instigation of a group of graduate students and taught it for more than ten years; I inherited it in 1982. Barbash was, of course, a member of the second generation of American institutionalists and he used his own theoretical perspective to structure the course in terms of the functional roles played by the various parts of our industrial relations system. (See Barbash 1984, for the key ideas from his course.) Major topics in the Barbash course included the cost discipline of our economic system, the work society in an organization, unionism and collective bargaining, the role of the state, comparative industrial relations, industrial conflict, and an examination of what constitutes IR theory.

Upon inheriting the Wisconsin IR theory course, I chose to restructure it. My basic approach is historical, in terms of competing theoretical paradigms as they developed over time, rather than in terms of the functional areas of industrial relations, or as has been suggested to me by other instructors, by social science discipline of origin.[6] This has the advantage of creating a central focus on the historical development of the institutional tradition, while allowing for coverage of competing approaches. As before, the course covers IR theory in the U.S. and only uses material from other countries insofar as it is necessary. A current reading list from my IR theory course is presented in the Appendix. After discussing the logic of the current course, I will consider several problems or issues that have arisen with regard to it.

When the class begins, I briefly survey the scope of IR theory and talk about its history (using Kochan's opening chapter in the first edition of his text, *Collective Bargaining and Industrial Relations*). In large part, the course is structured in terms of the historical development of major theories, beginning with Marx. This structure permits me to trace the influence of one theory upon another.

Before pursuing this essential historical strategy, however, I open the course with a discussion of some contemporary trends in industrial relations and its theory. At present, the focus is on the debate regarding whether or not there has been a fundamental transformation of the U.S. industrial relations system in the 1980s, given marked declines in union organization, concession bargaining, and various innovations in work organization and compensation in both the union and nonunion sectors. Logically, such contemporary material would be placed at the end of an IR theory course and for many years that was my practice. However, contemporary material makes a good course opening insofar as entering IR graduate students are eager to discuss these matters. Beginning with the present engenders a positive social process in the course, one which stimulates many students to contribute to discussions, decide that IR theory is of some interest to them, and otherwise become involved in the ideas of our discipline.

Contemporary material creates a much better initial social process than does classical Marxism, the topic with which I once began the course, simply because our IR students are especially diverse in their previous knowledge of Marx; some have had entire courses on Marx or have knowledge of Marxist thought based on political activism, whereas the majority knows virtually nothing, finds the material difficult, and are quite inhibited in class discussions. Adhering to a strictly historical framework sets in motion a dynamic whereby the latter group rarely speak for the rest of the semester.

After examining contemporary controversies, the remainder of the course is ordered by major topic in rough historical order, with discursions to more recent papers when that provides a useful contrasting theory or an illustration of the continuing usefulness of a theoretical construct. We begin with classical Marxism, focusing primarily on the meaning of dialectical materialism, the theory of exploitation and its connection to the labor process, the theory of alienation under capitalism, and the role the working class is presumed to play in the transition from capitalism to socialism. These are the portions of Marx which I find to be most relevant for later IR theory. I follow with a discussion of Marxism-Leninism and social democracy, and then an examination of some key ideas from Sidney and Beatrice Webb. I focus primarily on the Webb's contributions to the study of collective bargaining and discuss the various ways in which they pioneered key aspects of the institutional tradition.

Next we consider the work of the original American institutionalists, John R. Commons and Selig Perlman. I contrast Common's approach to the labor market with the neoclassical economics of his day, and then shift to comparing his approach to labor history with that of Marx. Perlman's theory of the labor movement is my next concern and I ask students to consider how Perlman's ideas differ from those of his mentor. After some discussion of these and other contributions of the Wisconsin School, and that of their contemporary Robert Hoxie, I contrast the approach of the Wisconsin labor historians to the approach of the new labor historians. This is an example of how it is possible to deviate from a strictly historical approach to the subject of IR theory and to use a contemporary theoretical debate to illuminate and enliven older material. In the same spirit, we consider the contemporary relevance of Perlman's concept of "job consciousness."

At this point, the course turns to management theory, evaluating the scientific management movement and the continuing theoretical controversies between the labor process theorists and others over the contribution of Frederick Taylor. The human relations school, with a focus on the work of Elton Mayo is next, followed by several classic works in social psychology, organizational behavior, and industrial sociology—Maslow, McGregor, Blauner, and Gallie. Worker alienation and job satisfaction are a central themes of this section of the reading list. We end the section with a discussion of the impact of contemporary trends in work organization and technology, most prominently the discussion engendered by the flexible specialization theorists. Here I focus primarily on a critical examination of Piore and Sabels' thesis that increasing fragmentation of contemporary product markets, and rapid shifts in consumer tastes, has created an opportunity for companies specializing in high value-added products aided by a highly skilled and committed workforce which can be deployed and redeployed flexibly.

After a midterm at about this point in the course, we consider the work of the second generation of American institutionalists: Kerr, Dunlop, Reynolds, Ross, Lester, Barbash, Harbison, Myers, and others. We begin with a critical examination of the notion of an industrial relations system, discussing both its usefulness and the structural functionalism on which it is predicated. The political theory of this group of scholars—pluralism—is considered after a brief review of liberalism and conservatism in classical political theory.[7] A contrast of pluralism and corporatism is used to clarify the meaning of the pluralist approach to industrial relations. Corporatism, a relatively unfamiliar political theory, is quite difficult to explain to IR graduate students in my experience, and I rely on the work by Grant (1985) and Schmitter (1974, 93-4) who defines corporatism as follows:

> (Corporatism is) a system of interest representation in which the constituent units are organized into a limited number of singular, compulsory, noncompetitive, hierarchically ordered and functionally differentiated categories, recognized or licensed (if not created) by the state and granted a deliberate representational monopoly within their respective categories in exchange for observing certain controls on their selection of leaders and articulation of demands and supports.

As before, my strategy is to illuminate an important part of the institutional tradition (pluralism) by contrasting it with a very different way of viewing unions (corporatism) and by using a current theoretical debate to enliven classic material.

Following an examination of pluralism, other key ideas of the second generation of U.S. institutionalists are examined, including the theory of "multiway partial convergence" developed in *Industrialism and Industrial Man* (Kerr, Dunlop, Harbison, and Myers 1960), and their position on the functional contribution of the right to strike for the resolution of conflict. The neoinstitutional perspective on industrial conflict is compared and contrasted with that of neo-Marxists like Hyman and sociological power resource theorists like Korpi (1980), or Snyder and Tilly (1972).[8]

The course now ends with a discursion into yet another contribution of this group of scholars, extended as it has been by their students, the third generation of American institutionalists—the concept of internal labor markets. Here we briefly compare the institutional approach to labor markets with that of neoclassical economics, as well as elaborating the theoretical controversy between them and some neo-Marxists regarding the origins of internal labor markets. A second focus is on the connection between the institutional approach to labor markets and the evaluation of the impact of unions and collective bargaining on the economy, a line of theory that runs from Lloyd Reynolds (1951) to Richard Freeman and James Medoff (1979). A consideration of the ways public goods theory has been applied to unions by Freeman and Medoff, following Mancour Olson (1965) currently draws the Wisconsin IR theory course to a close.

Dilemmas and Further Issues for IR Theory Courses

A number of dilemmas present themselves to any prospective instructor of an IR theory course. One set arises from the diversity and multidisciplinary origin of our subject. There is the difficulty of differentiating the boundaries of IR itself from the various related management and social science disciplines. It is hard to determine whether a given theory on the impact of technological change on work is IR or sociology! One might take the position that boundary definition is ultimately irrelevant—but even then one still has to decide which sociological theories are sufficiently important to industrial relations to merit coverage in an IR theory course. Furthermore, it is difficult to decide whether a theory important in a subfield, like the theory of bargaining power from the study of collective bargaining, should be taught in a general IR theory course. Both are frankly judgment calls, and they are related to a further issue that arises in the teaching of our subject: the necessity of teaching material that is not truly IR theory, but which is a prerequisite for the intelligent discussion of IR theory.

Graduate students in industrial relations have assorted undergraduate degrees, and hence it is often necessary to cover fundamental ideas from associated social sciences that would ideally be part of every liberal education, but which unfortunately have not been mastered by all beginning industrial relations graduate students. Consider, for instance, the classical liberalism of Locke, the original meaning of the term "conservative," or the meaning of "social democrat." Some but by no means all IR graduate students have a working knowledge of these basic political terms when they enter graduate school. "What was enclosure?" they ask, or "Who was this guy Lenin anyway?" Sociological concepts present similar issues. Durkheim's concept of "anomie" is *terra incognita* to most students. Few have ever heard of "structural functionalism," or thought about it as a way of approaching social science questions, although many recognize the approach implicitly. The point is that the realistic teacher of industrial relations theory is more or less forced to teach a number of things that are not IR theory per se.

Perhaps the greatest dilemma in this regard arises with the basic doctrines of neoclassical economics. Like most industrial relations programs, we require that students take a class in labor economics, but of course, this may or may not be taken before IR theory. At one time, a majority of IR graduate students had a number of undergraduate courses in economics, if not an undergraduate degree in economics, and it was reasonable to assume that students would already understand basic economic concepts, as well as some of the difficulties of applying neoclassical ideas to the labor market. Consequently, the IR theory teacher could assume that most students would be familiar with the neoclassical economic perspective without actually teaching it in the IR theory course. In the last decade, however, there has been a marked shift in the disciplinary background of our students; increasingly, IR programs have been drawing persons with undergraduate degrees in psychology or business rather than economics (Franke 1988). Indeed, in the 1980s, only 11 percent of entering IR students at the University of Illinois had undergraduate majors in economics and the situation is now very similar at the University of Wisconsin. This shift has made the assumption that students have some bedrock knowledge of economics increasingly suspect, placing instructors of IR theory in a dilemma. Much IR theory in the United States was written by institutional labor economists reacting implicitly, if not explicitly, to the shortcomings of the neoclassical economic paradigm, and consequently it is difficult for a person who is not well-versed in neoclassical theory to comprehend the unique contribution of the institutional and neoinstitutional IR theorists. But it is impossible to teach neoclassical economics in an IR theory course without expanding it beyond a one semester framework or without eliminating other important material. One solution might be to make additional classes in economics a prerequisite for IR theory. Another might be to create a two-semester sequence in theory, a solution that would also permit the coverage of more theoretical material from countries other than the United States.

Sometimes it is difficult as a teacher to deal with the great variety of contemporary IR theory; it is difficult to be sufficiently informed of the basic concepts and more recent developments in all the disciplines supporting and/or comprising industrial relations. And that also makes it arduous to recruit or to train new professors of IR theory. At the same time, the very challenge of keeping up with a wide range of ideas makes industrial relations theory an exciting and rewarding field of endeavor.

Another set of issues for IR theory arises from contemporary trends in U.S. industrial relations. The dramatic decline in union-ization, and the consequent reduction within industrial relations programs in the importance of the field of collective bargaining relative to human resource management and organizational behav-ior has potentially serious implications for IR theory. The institu-tionalists on whom I focus my course were intellectuals whose main research interests were in the fields of labor history (particularly the history of organized workers), labor law, public policy with regard to collective bargaining, and institutional labor economics. Their normative framework tended to be supportive of unions insofar as they emphasized that labor is more than a commodity and that there is inherently a conflict of interest between employer and employee. Recent developments in the United States raise the issue of whether or not employee needs can be served by a system in which employees are largely unrepresented by independent labor organizations, or how to best meet employee needs in the absence of unionization.

From the perspective of at least some management and behav-ioral theories, declining unionization is not a problem. With good management, the argument goes, unions are unnecessary. This theoretical position is not well represented in my IR theory reading list. This is only in part a reflection of my own distaste for this perspective. It is also a reflection of the extent to which human resource management and industrial psychology were divorced from the mainstream of industrial relations in earlier years. Indeed, this managerial perspective is still underarticulated within the field of industrial relations, and there are relatively few articles, to my knowledge, in which a theorist with the "unions are unnecessary" viewpoint attempts to grapple with the opposing position of the institutional tradition.[9] More systematic and critical expositions of this perspective from within the field of industrial relations are needed.

Perhaps the increasing location of IR scholars in U.S. business schools will eventually create a body of academics who are well-versed in both academic IR theory and management thought and who are interested in bridging the contemporary gap between the two.[10] We have already seen some evidence of this trend with the "strategic choice" theorists' attempting to integrate the concept of managerial strategy into industrial relations theory, with reinvigorating effects for the institutionalist tradition. When we get additional work in IR theory, from still other scholars who do not accept the normative framework of the institutional group, perhaps more debate will ensue regarding the value of maintaining that framework. The result will be a reinvigoration of the institutionalist tradition and of our IR theory courses, at the same time the ideas in these courses become even more varied.

Concluding Thoughts on IR Theory Courses

IR theory courses reflect both the past and the future of the field of industrial relations. They transmit to a new generation the great ideas of our discipline and of the social science disciplines which gave birth to the field of industrial relations. They also point to the future and must change as industrial relations itself changes. For all the diversity, for all the dilemmas, both goals can be achieved in a one semester course in industrial relations theory.

Notes

1. The American Economics Association schedules its annual meetings together with forty-six organizations, some devoted to subfields within economics (e.g. the Econometric Society) and some representing particular minority viewpoints in contemporary economics. These would include the Union of Radical Political Economics, the Association for Evolutionary Economics, the Association for Social Economics, the Association of Christian Economists, and of course, the Industrial Relations Research Assocation (IRRA). Many dissidents from the neoclassical world view are members of no particular organization, The IRRA contains institutional labor economists, a smaller number of neoclassical labor economists, and noneconomists interested in industrial relations.

2. IR theory plays a larger role in the training of our Ph.D.s than our masters students. Nonetheless, the role of disciplinary theory per se is considerably less for IR than economics doctoral students, partly because IR doctoral students must also master the theory of at least one contributing discipline.

3. Steve Hills has commented that IR scholars often explicitly, sometimes implicitly, dissented from the theory of their discipline of origin. A classic example would be the dissent of the institutional labor economists from the theory of neoclassical economics. Hills also notes how IR scholars objected to the classical management view that there is one best way of organizing production which can be arrived at scientifically. He regards these theoretical differences as indicating that theory is, indeed, a central concern in industrial relations.

4. The Random House Encyclopedia stresses the rejection of neoclassical economics in its definition of institutionalism:

Institutionalism, school of 20th-century American economists . . . who disagreed with the traditional orthodox approach to economics, which relied mainly on abstract reasoning. Institutionalists believe that a more descriptive approach should be employed, with the focus on institutions and their roles. Each economic entity is examined in the context of the institutions that conditioned its development.

5. Steve Hills points out that structuring a course around institutional IR theory tends to make a stepchild out of the psychological approach to the employment relationship. I would concur that this is a potential problem.

6. I have been asked if I regard a focus on functional roles as being nontheoretical and precluding discussion of competing theories. The answer is that I do not. I do wish to divorce the structure of the course, however, from a systems theory emphasis on functional roles.

7. The Random House Encyclopedia offers the following short definition of these terms:

Pluralism, sociopolitical theory advocating the participation of all groups in a society in the decision-making process. A pluralist society is one made up of a number of different interests whose views, theoretically, are ultimately synthesized into one policy. Pluralism is considered a hallmark of a democratic society.

Liberalism, political and social philosophy that stresses protection of individual liberties and civil rights. The liberal doctrines,
which evolved in the late 18th century, were an outgrowth of
John Locke's theories, reflecting his faith in man's rational
nature and urging limits upon governmental power.

Conservatism, political philosophy that favors the preservation
of traditional institutions and practices. The conservative, basi-
cally distrustful of politics, believes that human attitudes and
behavior cannot be improved through legislation. . . . He believes
social change should be gradual and occur within a historical
framework, Created as a reaction to the ideas of the Enlighten-
ment, conservatism relies on habit and experience, not pure
reason, as the basis for social order.

8. The former critique the neoinstitutionalists for their value emphasis
on the resolution of conflict. The power resource theorists sharply differ
with a number of the views of the institutionalists, including the notion
that political and industrial conflict are institutionally separated in advanced industrial society. See Korpi (1980) for a useful contrast of views.
    9. Neoclassical economics provides, of course, a well-articulated
theoretical argument as to why unions reduce social welfare. That theory,
however, is a different intellectual tradition from the management and
behavioral theory underlying human resource management and organizational behavior. It also does not address in large part the arguments of the
institutionalists.
    10. Bruce Kaufman of Georgia State University is currently writing
a book covering the history of both human resource management theory
and the institutional tradition in industrial relations.

Works Cited

Barbash, J. 1984, *The Elements of Industrial Relations,* Madison, WI:
    University of Wisconsin Press.
Dunlop, J. T. 1948, "The Development of Labor Organization: A Theo-
    retical Framework," in R. A. Lester and J. Shister, eds., *Insights into
    Labor Issues,* New York: Macmillan, pp. 163-193.
Franke, W. 1988, "Accommodating to Change: Can IR Learn from It-
    self?," *Proceedings of the Fortieth Annual Meeting of the Industrial
    Relations Research Association,* December 28-30, 1987, Chicago.
    Madison, WI: IRRA, pp. 474-81.

Freeman, Richard B., and James L. Medoff. 1979, "The Two Faces of
    Unionism," *Public Interest,* no. 57, pp. 69-93.
Grant, W. 1985, "Introduction," to W. Grant, ed., *The Political Econ-
    omy of Corporatism,* London: Macmillan, pp. 1-31.
Kaufman, B. 1988, "The Postwar View of Labor Markets and Wage De-
    termination," in *How Labor Markets Work: Reflections on Theory
    and Practice,* by J. Dunlop, C. Kerr, R. Lester, and L. Reynolds,
    ed. B. Kaufman, Lexington, MA: Lexington Books.
Kerr, C. 1988, "The Neoclassical Revisionists in Labor Economics
    (1940-1980)—R.I.P.," in *How Labor Markets Work: Reflections on
    Theory and Practice,* by J. Dunlop, C. Kerr, R. Lester, and L.
    Reynolds, ed. B. Kaufman, Lexington, MA: Lexington Books.
Kerr, C., J. T. Dunlop, F. Harbison, and C. Myers. 1960, *Industrialism
    and Industrial Man,* Cambridge, MA: Harvard University Press.
Kochan, T. A. 1980, "Historical Development of Industrial Relations,"
    Chapt. 1 of *Collective Bargaining and Industrial Relations: From
    Theory to Policy and Practice,* Homewood, IL: Richard Irwin, pp.
    1-23.
Korpi, W. 1980, "Industrial Relations and Industrial Conflict: The Case
    of Sweden," in B. Martin and E. M. Kassalow, eds., *Labor
    Relations in Advanced Industrial Societies: Issues and Problems,*
    Carnegie Endowment for International Peace.
Olson, M., Jr. 1965, *The Logic of Collective Action: Public Goods and
    the Theory of Groups,* Chapt. 3, "The Labor Union and Economic
    Freedom," Cambridge, MA: Harvard Univerity Press.
Reynolds, L. G. 1951, *The Structure of Labor Markets: Wages and
    Labor Mobility in Theory and Practice,* New York: Harper and Bros.,
    pp. 207-225; 248-256.
Schmitter, P. 1974, "Still the Century of Corporatism?," *Review of Poli-
    tics,* vol. 36, no. 1, pp. 85-131.
Snyder, D., and C. Tilly. 1972, "Hardship and Collective Violence in
    France, 1830 to 1960," *American Sociological Review,* vol. 37, no. 5,
    pp. 520-532.
Wheeler, H. 1989, "Is There a Pattern? A Report on a Survey of Gradu-
    ate IR Curricula," *Proceedings of the Firty-First Annual Meeting of
    the Industrial Relations Research Association,* December 28-30,
    1988, New York. Madison, WI: IRRA, pp. 445-451.

Appendix: Reading List from Wisconsin's IR Theory Course

This course surveys major industrial relations theories. While no books have been ordered, the reading list is extensive. Consequently, the readings have been classified as follows:

** two asterisks FIRST PRIORITY. Read these works. Thorough study of some is appropriate.
* one asterisk SECOND PRIORITY. Consult each of these works and be familiar with what it contains. Determine whether you wish to read it. Insofar as possible, I will survey this material in lectures.
no asterisk THIRD PRIORITY. References for students interested in further readings on a given topic.

Evaluation will be based on class participation and two in-class essay exams.

I. Introduction

**Thomas A. Kochan, "Historical Development of Industrial Relations," Chapt. 1 of *Collective Bargaining and Industrial Relations: From Theory to Policy and Practice* (Homewood, IL: Richard Irwin, 1980), pp. 1-23.

II. The Present: A Time of Profound Change?

**George Strauss, "Industrial Relations: Time of Changes," *Industrial Relations*. Vol. 23, No. 1 (Winter 1984), pp. 1-15.
**Thomas A. Kochan, Harry C. Katz, and Robert B. McKersie, *The Transformation of American Industrial Relations* (New York: Basic Books, 1986), Chapt. 1, pp. 3-20.
**John T. Dunlop, "Have the 1980's Changed U.S. Industrial Relations?" *Monthly Labor Review*, Vol. III, No. 5 (May 1988), pp. 29-34.
**Irving Bernstein, "Union Growth and Structural Cycles," in *IRRI Proceedings, 1954*, pp. 202-230, and following. "Discussion," by Daniel Bell, pp. 231-236.

**Richard B. Freeman and James L. Medoff, *What Do Unions Do?* (New York: Basic Books, 1984), pp. 221-245.
**Thomas A. Kochan and Kirsten R. Wever, "American Unions and the Future of Worker Representation," in George Strauss, Daniel G. Gallagher, and Jack Fiorito, eds. *The State of the Unions,* (Madison, WI: IRRA, 1991), pp. 363-386.
**Michael J. Piore, "The Future of Unions," in George Strauss, Daniel G. Gallagher, and Jack Fiorito, eds. *The State of the Unions,* (Madison, WI: IRRA, 1991), pp. 387-410.
* Sanford M. Jacoby, "Union-Management Cooperation in the United States: Lessons from the 1920s," *Industrial and Labor Relations Review,* Vol. 37, No. 1 (October 1983), pp. 18-33.
Paula B. Voos, "Cooperative Labor Relations and the Collective Bargaining Environment," *IRRA Proceedings,* 1985, pp. 287-295.
**James W. Driscoll, "Discussion," *IRRA Proceedings,* 1981, pp. 161-165.
**Sar A. Levitan and Clifford M. Johnson, "Labor and Management: The Illusion of Cooperation," *Harvard Business Review,* Vol. 83, No. 5 (September-October, 1983), pp. 8-16.
* Adrienne Eaton and Paula B. Voos, "Unions and Contemporary Innovations in Work Organization, Compensation, and Employee Participation," in *Unions and Economic Competitiveness,* ed. by L. Mishel and P. Voos, M. E. Sharpe, Armonk, NY, 1992.

III. The European Classics: Marx and the Webbs

**John G. Gurley, "The Materialist Conception of History," excerpted from *Challengers to Capitalism: Marx, Lenin, and Mao* (San Francisco: San Francisco Book Co., 1976) in Richard C. Edwards, Michael Reich, and Thomas E. Weisskopf, eds. *The Capitalist System,* 2nd ed. (Englewood Cliffs, NJ: Prentice-Hall, 1978), pp. 43-49.
**Richard C. Edwards, Michael Reich, and Thomas Weisskopf, *The Capitalist System,* 2nd ed. (Englewood Cliffs, NJ: Prentice-Hall 1978), "Alienation," pp. 265-268.
**Howard Selsam, David Goldway, and Harry Martel, eds. *Dynamics of Social Change: A Reader in Marxist Social Science* (New York: International Publishers, 1970), pp. 319-321 and pp. 329-335. (Optional: pp. 360-366).
Karl Marx and Frederick Engels, *The Communist Manifesto* (New York: International Publishers, 1948).
Karl Marx, *Capital,* Vol. 1, Chapts. VI, VII, XIV, XV (New York: International Publishers, 1967).

**V. I. Lenin, *What Is To Be Done?* (Peking: Foreign Languages Press, 1973), excerpt in Bertram Silverman and Murray Yanowitch, eds. "The Worker" in *Post-Industrial Capitalism: Liberal and Radical Responses* (New York: Free Press, 1974), pp. 44-49.

**Simeon Larson and Bruce Nissen, eds. *Theories of the Labor Movement* (Detroit: Wayne State Univ. Press, 1987), "The Labor Movement as an Agent of Industrial Reform: Introduction," pp. 186-187.

**Sidney and Beatrice Webb, *Industrial Democracy* (London: Longmans, Green, 1920), excerpt in E. Wight Bakke, Clark Kerr, and Anrod, eds., *Unions, Management and the Public,* 3rd ed. (New York: Harcourt, Brace and World, 1967), pp. 39-42.

IV. The U.S. Classics: Commons, Perlman, and Hoxie

*John T. Dunlop, "The Development of Labor Organization: A Theoretical Framework," in R. A. Lester and J. Shister, eds., *Insights into Labor Issues* (New York: Macmillan, 1948), pp. 163-193.

**Jack Barbash, "John R. Commons and the Americanization of the Labor Problem," *Journal of Economic Issues,* Vol. I, No. 3 (Sept. 1967), pp. 161-167.

**John R. Commons, "American Shoemakers, 1648-1895," in *Labor and Administration* (New York: Macmillan, 1913), pp. 210-264. Reprinted in Richard L. Rowan, ed. *Readings in Labor Economics and Labor Relations,* 4th ed. (Homewood, IL: Richard Irwin, 1980), pp. 57-69.

John R. Commons, "Introduction," in Commons, et. al. *History of Labor in the United States,* Vol. I (New York: Macmillan, 1918), pp. 3-21.

**Selig Perlman, *A Theory of the Labor Movement* (New York: Macmillan, 1928), excerpt in Reynolds, Masters, Moser, eds. *Readings in Labor Economics and Labor Relations,* 2nd ed. (Englewood Cliffs, NJ: Prentice Hall, 1978) pp. 256-261.

*Selig Perlman, "Labor and the New Deal in Historical Perspective," in Milton Derber and Edwin Young, eds. *Labor and the New Deal* (Madison: University of Wisconsin Press, 1957), pp. 363-370.

**Adolf Sturmthal, "Comments on Selig Perlman's A Theory of the Labor Movement," *Industrial and Labor Relations Review,* Vol. 4, No. 2 (July, 1951), pp. 483-496.

**David Brody, "The Old Labor History and the New: In Search of an American Working Class," *Labor History,* Vol. 20, No. 1 (Winter, 1979), pp. 111-126.

David Montgomery, "To Study the People: The American Working Class," *Labor History,* Vol. 21, No. 4 (Fall, 1980), pp. 485-512.

Robert F. Hoxie, *Trade Unionism in the United States* (New York:
    D. Appleton Century, 1921), excerpt in Bakke, Kerr, and Anrod,
    eds. *Unions, Management and the Public*, 3rd ed. (New York:
    Harcourt, Brace and World, 1967), pp. 53-55.
**David Brody, "Labor's Crisis in Historical Perspective," in George
    Strauss, Daniel G. Gallagher, and Jack Fiorito, eds. *The State of
    the Unions*, (Madison, WI: IRRA, 1991), pp. 277-311.

V. Management Theory and Industrial Sociology

**Frederick W. Taylor, *Scientific Management* (New York: Harper and
    Row, 1947), pp. 39-73, excerpted in D. S. Pugh, ed. *Organization
    Theory: Selected Readings* (Harmondsworth, Middlesex: Penguin
    Books, 1971), pp. 124-146.
**Harry Braverman, *Labor and Monopoly Capital: The Degradation of
    Work in the Twentieth Century* (New York: Monthly Review, 1974),
    Chapts. 4 and 5.
**Edwin A. Locke, "The Ideas of Frederick W. Taylor: An Evaluation,"
    Academy of Management Review, Vol. 4, No. 1 (1982), pp. 14-24.
*Emile Durkheim, "Social Contract and Anomie," an excerpt from
    Emile Durkheim, *The Division of Labor in Society*, in Clark Kerr
    and Paul D. Staudohar, eds. *Industrial Relations in a New Age:
    Economic, Social and Managerial Perspectives* (San Francisco:
    Jossey-Bass, 1986), pp. 17-18.
**Elton Mayo, *The Social Problems of an Industrial Civilization* (New
    York: Routledge, 1949), excerpted in D. S. Pugh, ed. *Organization
    Theory: Selected Readings* (Hammondsworth, Middlesex: Penguin
    Books, 1971), pp. 215-229.
**Clark Kerr and Lloyd Fisher, "Plant Sociology: The Elite and the
    Aborigines," in Clark Kerr, *Labor and Management in Industrial
    Society* (New York: Anchor, 1964), pp. 43-82.
**J. Steven Ott, ed., "Motivation," in *Classic Readings in Organiza-
    tional Behavior* (Pacific Grove, CA: Brooks/Cole, 1989), pp. 27-35.
**Abraham H. Maslow, "A Theory of Human Motivation," an excerpt
    from an article of the same title, *Psychological Review*, 50 (1943)
    in J. Steven Ott, ed. *Classic Readings in Organizational Behavior*
    (Pacific Grove, CA: Brooks/Cole, 1989), pp. 48-65.
**Douglas McGregor, "The Human Side of Enterprise," an excerpt
    from an article of the same title, *Management Review*, (1957) in J.
    Steven Ott, ed. *Classic Readings in Organizational Behavior* (Pacific
    Grove, CA: Brooks/Cole, 1989), pp. 66-73.
**Robert Blauner, "Alienation and Freedom in Perspective," an excerpt
    from Blauner, *Alienation and Freedom: The Factory Worker and
    His Industry* (Chicago: University of Chicago Press, 1967), in

Bertram Silverman and Murray Yanowitch, eds., *The Worker in
"Post-Industrial" Capitalism* (New York: Free Press, 1974),
pp. 137-147.
**Duncan Gallie, *In Search of the New Working Class: Automation and
Social Integration Within the Capitalist Enterprise* (Cambridge:
Cambridge University Press, 1978), Chapt. 1, pp. 3-38.
John H. Goldthorpe, David Lockwood, Frank Bechhofer, and Jennifer
Platt, *The Affluent Worker in the Class Structure* (Cambridge
University Press, 1969).
**Thomas A. Kochan and Harry C. Katz, *Collective Bargaining and
Industrial Relations: From Theory to Policy and Practice,* 2nd ed.
(Homewood, IL: Richard D. Irwin, 1988). Section on "The
Technological Context," from Chapt. 3, "The Environment of
Collective Bargaining," pp. 92-95.
**Michael J. Piore and Charles F. Sabel, *The Second Industrial Divide:
Possibilities for Prosperity* (New York: Basic Books, 1984, Chapt. 8,
"Corporate Response to the Crisis," pp. 194-220, and Section on
"Flexible Specialization," from Chapt. 10, "Possibilities for
Prosperity," pp. 258-263.
**Stephen Wood, "From Braverman to Cyberman: A Critique of the
Flexible Specialization Thesis," in Wout Buitelarr, ed., *Technology
and Work: Labour Studies in England, Germany and the Netherlands*
(Aldershot, Hants, England: Avebury, 1988), pp. 27-42.

VI. Neoinstitutionalism: Industrial Relations Systems, Pluralism, and the Contrast with Corporatism

**John T. Dunlop, *Industrial Relations Systems* (New York: Holt,
1958), excerpt in Bakke, Kerr, and Anrod, eds. *Unions, Manage-
ment and the Public,* 3rd ed. (New York: Harcourt, Brace and
World, 1967), pp. 3-9.
**Ralf Dahrendorf, *Class and Class Conflict in Industrial Society*
(Stanford: Stanford University Press, 1959), pp. 157-173 and
pp. 213-215.
**H. A. Clegg, "Pluralism in Industrial Relations," *British Journal of
Industrial Relations,* Vol XIII, No. 3 (November 1975), pp. 309-316.
**Clark Kerr, "Unions and Union Leaders of Their Own Choosing," in
Clark Kerr, *Labor and Management in Industrial Society* (New
York: Anchor, 1964), pp. 21-42.
**Seymour Martin Lipset, "The Political Process in Trade Unions: A
Theoretical Statement," in Walter Galenson and Seymour Martin
Lipset, eds. *Labor and Trade Unionism: An Interdisciplinary Reader*
(New York: John Wiley, 1960), pp. 216-242.

**Wyn Grant, "Introduction," to *The Political Economy of Corporat-
   ism,* ed. by Wyn Grant (London: Macmillan, 1985), pp. 1-31.
**Philippe C. Schmitter, "Corporatism (Corporativism)," forthcoming
   in *The Encyclopedia of the Social Sciences,* Figure 1 (p. 6)
   (Handout).
* Frank Tannenbaum, *A Philosophy of Labor* (New York: Alfred
   A. Knopf, 1951), excerpted in Bakke, Kerr, and Anrod, eds.,
   Unions, Management and the Public, 3rd ed. (New York: Harcourt,
   Brace and World, 1967), pp. 57-61.
John Paul II, *On Human Work, Encyclical Laborem Exercens* (Wash-
   ington, DC: U.S. Catholic Conference, 1981). Especially sections
   7, 8, 11, 12, 13, and 20.
Clark Kerr, John T. Dunlop, Frederick Harbison, and Charles Myers,
   Industrialism and Industrial Man (Cambridge: Harvard University
   Press, 1960).
* Clark Kerr, John T. Dunlop, Frederick Harbison and Charles Myers,
   "Industrialism and World Society," in Clark Kerr, *Labor and
   Management in Industrial Society* (New York: Anchor, 1964),
   pp. 345-372.
**John Dunlop, Clark Kerr, Frederick Harbison and Charles Myers,
   Industrialism and Industrial Man Reconsidered, pp. 41-42
   (Handout).
Ronald Dore, *British Factory-Japanese Factory: The Origins of Diver-
   sity in Industrial Relations* (Berkeley: University of California Press,
   1973), Preface and Chapt. 15.
* Jack Barbash, "Do We Really Want Labor on the Ropes?" *Harvard
   Business Review,* Vol. 63, No. 4 (July/August 1985), p. 10 and
   following.

VII. Class Conflict, Industrial Conflict, and Strikes

**Clark Kerr, "Industrial Conflict and Its Mediation," in Clark Kerr,
   Labor and Management in Industrial Society (New York: Anchor,
   1964), pp. 167-200. Originally in *American Journal of Sociology,*
   LX (Nov. 1954), pp. 230-245.
**Clark Kerr and Abraham Siegel, "The Inter-Industry Propensity to
   Strike—An International Comparison," in Arthur Kornhauser, Robert
   Dubin, and Arthur M. Ross, eds. *Industrial Conflict* (New York:
   McGraw-Hill, 1954), pp. 189-212. Also reprinted in Kerr, *Labor
   and Management in Industrial Society,* op. cit.
P. K. Edwards, "A Critique of the Kerr-Siegel Hypothesis of Strikes
   and the Isolated Mass: A Study of the Falsification of Sociological
   Knowledge," *Sociological Review,* Vol. 25 (1979), pp. 551-571.

**Arthur M. Ross, "The Natural History of the Strike," in Arthur
   Kornhauser, Robert Dubin and Arthur M. Ross, eds. *Industrial
   Conflict* (New York: McGraw-Hill, 1954), pp. 23-36.

Arthur M. Ross, "Changing Patterns of Industrial Conflict," *IRRA
   Proceedings*, 1959, pp. 146-169 and "Discussion" by Everett
   Kassalow, pp. 170-173.

* Alan Fox and Allan Flanders, "The Reform of Collective Bargaining:
   from Donovan to Durkheim," *British Journal of Industrial Relations*,
   Vol. 7, No. 2 (July 1969), pp. 151-180.

* John H. Goldthorpe, "Industrial Relations in Great Britain: A Critique of Reformism," *Politics and Society*, Vol. 4, No. 4 (1974), pp.
   419-452.

* Richard Hyman, *Industrial Relations: A Marxist Introduction* (London: Macmillan, 1975), Chapt. 4, pp. 74-88, and Chapt. 7, pp.
   185-203.

David E. Feller, "A General Theory of the Collective Bargaining Agreement," *California Law Review*, Vol. 61, No. 3 (May, 1973), pp.
   663-856.

Katherine Stone, "The Post-War Paradigm in American Labor Law,"
   The Yale Law Review, Vol. 90 (1981), pp. 1509-1581.

*Karl E. Klare, "Judicial Deradicalization of the Wagner Act and the
   Origins of Modern Legal Consciousness, 1937-1941," *Minnesota
   Law Review*, Vol. 62, No. 3 (March, 1978), pp. 265-339.

**Walter Korpi, "Industrial Relations and Industrial Conflict: The Case
   of Sweden," in Benjamin Martin and E. M. Kassalow, eds., *Labor
   Relations in Advanced Industrial Societies: Issues and Problems*
   (Carnegie Endowment for International Peace, 1980).

David Snyder and Charles Tilly, "Hardship and Collective Violence in
   France, 1830 to 1960," *American Sociological Review*, Vol. 37,
   No. 5 (1972), pp. 520-532.

Edward Shorter and Charles Tilly, *Strikes in France: 1830-1968*
   (London: Cambridge University Press, 1974).

VIII. The Labor Market and Industrial Relations

**Henry C. Simons, "Some Reflections on Syndicalism," *Journal of
   Political Economy*, LII (March, 1944), pp. 1-19, excerpted in
   Richard A. Lester, *Labor, Readings on Major Issues* (New York:
   Random House, 1965), pp. 200-209.

**Lloyd G. Reynolds, *The Structure of Labor Markets: Wages and
   Labor Mobility in Theory and Practice* (New York: Harper and Bros.,
   1951), pp. 207-225 and pp. 248-256.

Clark Kerr, "The Balkanization of Labor Markets," in E. Wight Bakke,
et. al. *Labor Mobility and Economic Opportunity* (Cambridge: MIT
Press, 1954), pp. 92-110.

**John T. Dunlop, "Needed: an Interdisciplinary Approach to Labor
Markets and Wage Determination," *Monthly Labor Review,* Vol. 108,
No. 7 (July 1985), pp. 30-32.

**Peter Doeringer and Michael Piore, *Internal Labor Markets and
Manpower Analysis* (Lexington, MA: Heath, 1971), Chapts. 1
and 2.

Richard Edwards, *Contested Terrain: The Transformation of the Workplace in the Twentieth Century* (New York: Basic Books, 1979).

* David M. Gordon, Richard Edwards, Michael Reich, *Segmented
Work, Divided Workers: The Historical Transformation of Labor
in the United States* (London: Cambridge University Press, 1982),
Chapt. 1 and Epilogue.

**Stanford M. Jacoby, "Industrial Labor Mobility in Historical Perspec-
tive," *Industrial Relations,* Vol. 22, No. 2 (Spring, 1983), pp.
261-282.

**Bernard Elbaum, "The Internalization of Labor Markets: Causes and
Consequences," *American Economic Review,* Vol. 73, No. 2 (May,
1983), pp. 260-265.

**Mancur Olson, Jr. *The Logic of Collective Action: Public Goods and
the Theory of Groups,* (Cambridge: Harvard Univ. Press, 1965),
Chapt. 3 "The Labor Union and Economic Freedom."

**Richard B. Freeman and James L. Medoff, "The Two Faces of
Unionism," Public Interest, No. 57 (Fall 1979), pp. 69-93.

Additional references not found in the Appendix

Adams, R. 1992, " "All Aspects of People at Work": Unity and Division in the Study of Labor and Labor Management," this volume.

Barbash, J. 1984, *The Elements of Industrial Relations,* Madison, WI:
University of Wisconsin Press.

Franke, W. 1988, "Accommodating to Change: Can IR Learn from
Itself?," *Proceedings of the Fortieth Annual Meeting of the Industrial
Relations Research Association,* December 28-30, 1987, Chicago
(Madison, WI: IRRA), pp. 474-81.

Kaufman, B. 1988, "The Postwar View of Labor Markets and Wage Determination," in *How Labor Markets Work: Reflections on
Theory and Practice* by John Dunlop, Clark Kerr, Richard Lester,
and Lloyd Reynolds, ed. B. Kaufman (Lexington, MA: Lexington
Books).

Kerr, C. 1988, "The Neoclassical Revisionists in Labor Economics
(1940-1980)—R.I.P.," in *How Labor Markets Work: Reflections on*

Theory and Practice by John Dunlop, Clark Kerr, Richard Lester and Lloyd Reynolds, ed. B. Kaufman (Lexington, MA: Lexington Books).

Random House Encyclopedia, 1990. *Infodesk,* Computer Program, Microlytics, Pittsford, NY.

Schmitter, P. 1974. "Still the Century of Corporatism?," *Review of Politics,* vol. 36, no. 1, pp. 85-131.

Wheeler, H. 1989, "Is There a Pattern? A Report on a Survey of Graduate IR Curricula," *Proceedings of the Forty-First Annual Meeting* of the Industrial Relations Research Association, December 28-30, 1988, New York (Madison, WI: IRRA), pp. 445-51.

A Framework to Organize Theory: The Structure of a Doctoral-Level Seminar on Industrial Relations Theory

Joel Cutcher-Gershenfeld

Introduction

Organizing a doctoral-level seminar in industrial relations theory is a unique undertaking. It requires the creation of a framework to classify and present leading texts from a broad array of disparate literatures. At its best, it is an exercise in meta-theory-building insights into the very nature of theory. Inevitably, it is also an exercise in frustration, since only a limited amount of material can be covered in a given course.

This article serves two purposes. First, for the scholar undertaking to teach an advanced graduate class in industrial relations theory, a model is presented—with sample readings—that may be of value. Second, the way that this course is organized yields potentially useful insights into the nature of industrial relations theory itself. These insights concern core underlying assumptions about common and conflicting interests between labor and management, the way a disciplinary perspective serves as a lens (pro-

viding focus, yet limiting the scope of view), and the application of
theory to current issues relating to transformation and change in
industrial relations.

Background on Course Goals and Structure

This article is based on a doctoral-level course that I teach at
the School of Labor and Industrial Relations at Michigan State
University. Although the course features readings by scholars in
many nations, there is a bias toward the U.S. literature—reflecting
the course's location. The course, which is a modified version of
the industrial relations theory course offered by Professor Thomas
Kochan at the Massachusetts Institute of Technology, has three
broad goals, that are listed in the syllabus as follows:

> 1. To provide a forum for Ph.D. students and other highly
> motivated students to critically examine core theory in industrial
> relations and related disciplines. We will trace the intellectual
> roots of different disciplines and current voices in various liter-
> atures — each as an alternative lens for the study of industrial
> relations.
> 2. To explore methodological issues associated with the transla-
> tion of theory into research on specific topics in Industrial
> Relations.
> 3. To have a positive learning experience.

Of the first two goals, examining of core theory occupies over
three-quarters of the classes. For each topic area, the literature is
generally divided into three groups: classic texts, more recent
commentaries on selected classic texts, and current voices in the
thematic area addressed by the classic texts. Even the edited sets of
readings are extensive. As a result, some are readings marked with
an asterisk (*) indicating that they are required readings, while
others are marked with a plus (+) indicating that they are recommended.

The exploration of methodological issues arising in the trans-
lation of theory into research is a theme that surfaces throughout
the course, but is specifically addressed in the final classes by
focusing on issues of current interest. For example, in the version

of the course discussed here, the final classes center on debates about the transformation of industrial relations and analysis of the economic performance literature on related issues such as worker participation.

Because of the large volume of readings associated with the course, and its being structured as a group-managed seminar, the syllabus comes with a warning:

Advanced Warning

This will be a very demanding course. It will be run in a seminar format, with every class member expected to contribute to our collective efforts to come to grips with classic texts in the field. As well, certain assignments and readings will require an ability to examine methodological choices made in leading research articles. The course has been designed for Ph.D. students— masters students may enroll as well, but a strong interest in theory and background in research methods will be essential.

So, with this structure in mind, here are the readings and their underlying logic.

Assumptions About Employment Relations as the Point of Departure

At the heart of any theory relevant to industrial relations are a set of core assumptions about the interests of employees and employers. The issue was vividly surfaced by Karl Marx, who argued that the interests of employees and employers were funda-mentally irreconcilable in capitalist society. In direct contrast, early organizational theorists argued that it was not only possible, but desirable to align organizational structures and rewards with the underlying mutual interests of employees and employers. A third group, pluralist scholars emphasized the mixed-motive nature of employment relations—seeing conflict between employees and employers as inevitable, but as a product of their roles and functions (not as a result of a deeper conflict between capital and labor). As a result, unions and managers are seen as providing an essential "check and balance" to one other.

The first part of this course on industrial relations theory is organized around these three alternative assumptions. In each case, a set of historical and more current readings is identified. The first readings are from the mixed-motive perspective since these are widely seen as the classic texts in industrial relations. Then, Marxist and other conflict-based readings are presented as a counterpoint. Finally, classic organizational readings are presented as a contrast to both of the first two perspectives. Students are invited to come along for the journey and "try out" alterative assumptions so as to surface their own core views of the employment relationships.

The Mixed-Motive Assumption as Reflected in Pluralist Perspectives:

In 1897 Sidney and Beatrice Webb stated: "The issue turns essentially on whether or not the employers are prepared to forego their dictatorship inside their own workshops and honestly to submit the conditions of employment to an effective joint control, whether by collective bargaining or otherwise" (Webbs 1897). Their analysis and the writings of John R. Commons and Selig Pearlman addressed this core question. (Figure 1 illustrates selected readings by these early theorists, along with relevant commentaries.) This work is important not just for presenting useful theses, but also for carving out the intellectual foundation for industrial relations as a discipline. It has been labeled as "mixed-motive" in that both employers and employees are seen as having legitimate, but distinct interests. The focus is both on the inevitable conflicts and on the capacity, particularly via collective bargaining, to identify common ground as well. The pluralist conception builds from the mixed-motive assumption, since all of these scholars highlight unions as independent work place institutions interacting with employers.

Figure 1 — Pluralist Roots

*Sidney and Beatrice Webb. 1897. *Industrial Democracy*, London:
   Longmans, pp. 805-850.
*John R. Commons. 1935. "Introduction," in Commons, et al., *History
   of Labor in the United States*, Vol. 1. New York: Macmillan (1935);
   and John R. Commons. 1909. "American Shoemakers, 1648-1895"
   in *Quarterly Journal of Economics* (November), as condensed in
   Theories of the Labor Movement, Simeon Larson and Bruce Nissen,
   eds. 1987. Detroit: Wayne State University Press, pp. 134-139.
Commentary:
+Kenneth H. Parsons. 1963. "The Basis of Commons' Progressive
   Approach to Public Policy" in *Labor, Management, and Social
   Policy*. Madison, Wis: The University of Wisconsin Press, pp. 3-22.
*Selig Perlman. 1928. *A Theory of the Labor Movement*. New York:
   MacMillan (1928), as condensed in *Theories of the Labor
   Movement*, Simeon Larson and Bruce Nissen, eds. 1987. Detroit:
   Wayne State University Press, pp. 161-173.
Commentary:
+Charles A. Gulick and Melvin K. Bers. 1953. "Insight and Illusion in
   Perlman's Theory of the Labor Movement" in *Industrial and Labor
   Relations Review*, Vol. 6—as condensed in *Theories of the Labor
   Movement*, Simeon Larson and Bruce Nissen, eds. 1967. Detroit:
   Wayne State University Press, pp. 174-184.

* Required Readings; + Recommended Readings

Building on the pluralist roots are a set of four core theories,
with excerpts and commentaries listed in Figure 2. First, John T.
Dunlop (1958) presents a systems-based framework in which he
argues that the interplay of employer, employee, and government
interests are observable in the rules they generate. Then, we have
an example of a clear social science prediction—that the rising
world industrialization would also bring a convergence in industrial
relations practices (Kerr, Dunlop, Harbison, and Meyers 1960).
Although the divergence in practice during the 1970's spurred great
debate and controversy over the predictive power of the theory, it
has a new currency given the parallels in industrial relations practices that seem to be accompanying the integration of world markets. In contrast to the focus on rules and technology, Richard E.
Walton and Robert B. McKersie (1965) focus on the interaction

Figure 2 — Core Theory Building on Pluralist Roots

*John T. Dunlop. 1958. *Industrial Relations Systems.* New York: Henry Holt, Chapters 1 and 10.
Commentary:
+R. Singh. 1976. "Systems Theory in the Study of Industrial Relations: Time for a Reappraisal?" in *Industrial Relations Journal,* Vol. 7, No. 3, pp. 59-71.
*Clark Kerr, John T. Dunlop, Frederick H. Harbison, and Charles A. Meyers. 1960. *Industrialism and Industrial Man.* Cambridge, Mass.: Harvard University Press, as condensed in *Theories of the Labor Movement,* Simeon Larson and Bruce Nissen, eds. 1967. Detroit: Wayne State University Press, pp. 315-336.
*Richard Walton and Robert McKersie. 1965. *A Behavioral Theory of Labor Negotiations.* New York: McGraw-Hill, Chapter 1.
*Alan Fox. 1974. "Industrialization; Contract; and the Division of Labour: Some Relevant Theorizing," "Industrial Relations and Frames of Reference" and "Patterns of Management-Employee Relations" in *Beyond Contract: Work, Power and Trust Relations.* London: Faber and Faber Limited, pp. 207-313.
Commentary:
+Mark Perlman. "Assaying the Five Theories" in *Labor Union Theories.* pp. 214-241.

* Required Readings; + Recommended Readings

---

process, which they explain by the interplay of integrative, distributive, attitudinal, and intraorganizational subprocesses. The process orientation is further extended by Alan Fox (1974), who traces conflict cycles and other industrial relations dynamics. These four theories all represent attempts to codify and extend theory using modern social science principles.

Underlying the four theories presented in Figure 2 are a common set of pluralist and mixed-motive assumptions. Of the four, Walton and McKersie are most explicit in focusing both on the conflictual and common interests. These assumptions have themselves been the subject of debate in the field—especially in England. Figure 3 lists a set of articles that are illustrative of these debates.

Figure 3 — Debates Over Pluralism

*Hugh Clegg. 1975. "Pluralism in Industrial Relations," *The British Journal of Industrial Relations*, Vol. 13, pp. 309-316.
*Stephen Wood. 1978. "Ideology in Industrial Relations Theory" in *Industrial Relations Journal*, Vol. 9, No. 4, pp. 42-56.
+William K. Roche. 1986. "Systems Analysis and Industrial Relations: Double Paradox in the Development of American and British Industrial Relations Theory" in *Economic and Industrial Democracy*, Vol. 7, pp. 4-28.
+Alessandro Pizzorno. 1981. "Interests and Parties in Pluralism" in *Organizing Interests in Western Europe: Pluralism, Corporatism, and the Transformation of Politics*, Suzanne Berger, ed. Cambridge: Cambridge University Press, pp. 247-284.

* Required Readings; + Recommended Readings

Altogether, the first three sets of readings provide a foundation in what are traditionally seen as core industrial relations theory texts. The particular focus here has been on a common underlying mixed-motive assumption about the interests of employees and employers and a pluralist conception regarding the interplay of these interests. To fully understand the nature of these theories, it is important to understand a key alternative in social science—the conflict-based theories rooted in Marxism.

Conflict Assumptions as Reflected in Marxist Perspectives

At the heart of Marx's dialectical analysis of history lies the assumption that there is a fundamental conflict between capital and labor, which gives rise to exploitation by capital and alienation by labor. As Marx demonstrated, evidence to support the assumption can be found throughout history and, once this assumption is granted, there is a compelling logic that points toward worker ownership of the means of production as the only means for overcoming the exploitation and alleviating the alienation. In the context of industrial relations theory, the early writings of Marx, V.I. Lenin, Rosa Luxemburg, and Antonio Gramsci (all of which are represented in Figure 4) provide a powerful challenge to the

Figure 4 — Marxist Roots

*Karl Marx. 1891. "Wages, Labour and Capital," reprinted in Robert
  C. Tucker, ed. 1978. *The Marx-Engels Reader.* New York: Norton,
  pp. 167-190.
*V.I. Lenin. 1975. "What is to be done?" in *Lenin's Selected Works,*
  Moscow: Progress Publishers, pp. 92-234—as condensed in
  Theories of the Labor Movement, Simeon Larson and Bruce Nissen,
  eds. 1987. Detroit: Wayne State University Press, pp. 48-58.
*Rosa Luxemburg. 1970. "Introduction," "The Opportunist Method,"
  and "Cooperatives, Unions, Democracy" in *Reform or Revolution.*
  New York: Pathfinders, pp. 5-13 and 41-48.
+Antonio Gramsci. 1971. "Problems of History and Culture" and
  "Americanism and Fordism" in *Selections from the Prison
  Notebooks,* Quintin Hoare and Geoffrey Nowell Smith, eds.
  New York: International Publishers, pp. 1-14 and 277-316.
Commentary:
+Shlomo Avineri. 1968. "Hegel's Political Philosophy Reconsidered"
  in *The Social and Political Thought of Karl Mark.* Cambridge,
  England: Cambridge University Press, pp. 8-40.
+Stephen A. Marglin. 1974. "What Do the Bosses Do? The Origins and
  Functions of Hierarchy in Capitalist Production" in *Review of
  Radical Political Economics.* Vol. 6, No. 2, pp. 60-92.

* Required Readings; + Recommended Readings

pluralist, mixed-motive perspective—essentially asking: Are the
pluralists merely apologists for the existing order?

Among current voices that build on a conflict assumption, the
set of readings in Figure 5 highlights the works of Richard Hyman
(1975), Harry Braverman (1974), Richard Edwards (1979) and
Michael Burawoy (1985). While these are all distinct voices and
they are sometimes at odds with one another (as is the case with
Braverman and Burawoy), they all conduct their analysis in a more
recognizably current context, dealing with manifestations of the
capital-labor struggle in their treatment of new technology and the
organization of work.

Figure 5 — Current Conflict Theorists

*Richard Hyman. 1975. "What is Industrial Relations?" in *Industrial Relations: A Marxist Introduction*. London: MacMillan, pp. 9-31.
*Harry Braverman. 1974. "Introduction" and "The Habituation of the Worker to the Capitalist Mode of Production" in *Labor and Monopoly Capital*. New York: Monthly Review Press, pp. 1-41 and 139-152.
+Michael Burawoy. 1985. "Introduction: Bringing the Workers Back In" and "The Changing Face of Factory Regimes Under Advanced Capitalism" in *The Politics of Production*. London: Verso.
*Richard C. Edwards. 1979. *Contested Terrain: The Transformation of the Workplace in the Twentieth Century.*New York: Basic Books, pp. vii-ix, 3-22, 111-183.

* Required Readings; + Recommended Readings

In a doctoral seminar, the earlier Marxist readings raise fundamental questions. For students unfamiliar with a conflict perspective, the later readings extend the questions into a more familiar and hence more challenging domain. By the end of these sessions, the conflicts noted by the pluralists have been reinforced by the Marxists. The journey into alternative perspectives on employment relations has led the class into a world highly skeptical of employers, which sets the stage for readings from a unitarist and consensus perspective.

Unitary, Consensus Assumptions as Reflected in Human Relations and Related Organizational Perspectives

Organizational behavior theorists do not often appear on industrial relations theory reading lists. Yet, a central focus of this literature—especially the early studies—is on the employment relationship. Selected readings from George Homans (1950), Douglas McGregor (1960), and F. T. Roethlishberger (1965) are listed in Figure 6 along with various commentaries. These works are among the early writings that build on a consensus assumption, essentially holding that conflict is dysfunctional and preventable

Figure 6 — Roots of Unitary, Consensus Assumptions

*George Homans. 1950. "Plans and Purposes" and "The Elements of
  Behavior" in *The Human Group*. New York: Harcourt, Brace and
  Company, pp. 1-47.
*Douglas McGregor. 1960. "Part One: The Theoretical Assumptions
  of Management" in *The Human Side of the Enterprise*. New York:
  McGraw-Hill Book Company, Inc., pp. 3-57.
+F. J. Roethlishberger. 1965. "Introduction," "The Road Back to
  Sanity," and "What is Adequate Personnel Management?" and
  "Concerning People Who Theorize about Cooperative Phenomena"
  in *Management and Morale*. Cambridge, Mass: Harvard University
  Press, pp. 3-26, 109-136, and 160-174.

A Marxist Perspective on the Hawthorne Experiments:
+Dana Bramel and Ronald Friend. 1981. "Hawthorne, the Myth of the
  Docile Worker, and Class Bias in Psychology" in *American
  Psychologist,* Vol. 36, No. 8, pp. 867-878; plus letters in response,
  American Psychologist (July 1982), pp. 855-861.

A Decision-Making Perspective on Organizational Identification:
+Herbert A. Simon. 1947. "Decision-Making and Administrative Orga-
  nization" and "Loyalties and Organizational Identification" in
  Administrative Behavior. New York: The Macmillan Company,
  pp. 1-19 and 198-219.
Commentary:
+Harold Koonitz. 1961. "The Management Theory Jungle" in *The
  Academy of Management Journal* (December), reprinted in *Classics
  of Organizational Behavior,* Walter E. Natemeyer, ed. 1978. Oak
  Park, IL: Moore Publishing Company, Inc., 19-31.

* Required Readings; + Recommended Readings

through appropriate managerial practices. The ideal is a unitary
conception of organizations where all members are (in the current
lingo) pulling together as one team.

While the classic organizational behavior theorists make the
basic normative argument in favor of a consensus-based perspective, it is current scholars that fill in the road map for this portion
of the journey. The discussion covers issues ranging from job design
(Hackman and Oldham 1980), to high commitment systems (Wal-

Figure 7 — Current Voices from a Unitary or Consensus-Based Perspective

*J. Richard Hackman and Greg R. Oldham. 1980. "Work Redesign in Organizational and Societal Context" in *Work Redesign*. Reading, Mass.: Addison-Wesley, as reprinted in *Perspectives on Behavior in Organizations*, Second Edition, J. Richard Hackman, Edward E. Lawler III and Lyman W. Porter, eds. 1983. New York: McGraw-Hill Book Company (1983), pp. 586-598.
*Richard E. Walton. 1985. "Toward a Strategy of Eliciting Employee Commitment Based on Policies of Mutuality" in *HRM Trends and Challenges*. Boston: Harvard Business School Press, pp. 35-65.
*William G. Ouchi and Raymond L. Price. 1978. "Hierarchies, Clans, and Theory Z: A New Perspective on Organizational Development" in *Organizational Dynamics*, (Autumn), as reprinted in *Perspectives on Behavior in Organizations*, Second Edition, J. Richard Hackman, Edward E. Lawler III and Lyman W. Porter, eds. 1983. New York: McGraw-Hill Book Company, pp. 564-577.
+Edward E. Lawler III. 1988. "Changing Approaches to Management," "Why Participative Approaches Meet Today's Needs" and "Participation and Organizational Effectiveness" in *High-Involvement Management*. San Francisco: Jossey-Bass Publishers, pp. 12-43.

* Required Readings; + Recommended Readings

---

ton 1985), to clan-based organizational structures (Ouchi and Price 1983), to employee participation and rewards (Lawler 1988)—all of which are represented in Figure 7.

At this point in the course, the journey has become something of a roller coaster ride. It is no surprise that the unitary perspectives serve as a sharp counterpoint to the conflict-based literature, but more telling is the challenge to the pluralist, mixed-motive literature. Now, the pluralists are in effect charged with being sentimental apologists for trade unions and collective bargaining—a charge that has increased force given the broad diffusion of nonunion human resource management systems in the 1980's.

Ultimately, all three broad perspectives each reveal a coherent logic that builds from the core assumptions about employee-employer relations. For the student (and even the professor), our own assumptions invariably come under scrutiny as we examine the work of others. We also become somewhat accustomed to viewing employment relations from alternative perspectives. The next part of the course extends the notion of alternative perspectives by examining employment relations from three distinct disciplinary lenses.

Alternative Disciplinary Lenses

Like other interdisciplinary fields, industrial relations is enriched and complicated by the many vantage points from which people study the employment relationship. The focus here is on three disciplinary perspectives—economics, sociology, and history. While these are not the only disciplines relevant to industrial relations theory (consider, for example, psychology, political science, organizational behavior, and cultural anthropology), they are sufficient to establish the double-edged quality of any disciplinary perspective. Disciplinary lenses are double-edged in that they provide a focus and frame of reference, but also constrain what can be seen.

Individualistic and Institutional Assumptions as Reflected in Neoclassical Economic Perspectives

Early industrial relations scholars drew heavily on economics. Indeed, at one time "the labor problem" was seen as the most pressing issue facing the field of economics. Of course, the field of industrial relations continues to be influenced by the work of labor economists and by econometric methods—though advances in econometric methods make parts of the literature inaccessible to those operating outside the discipline.

The first set of readings selected for this portion of the course, which are listed in Figure 8, highlight the work of early theorists, including Adam Smith (1776), J. R. Hicks (1932) and Charles Lindblom (1949), as well as some more current classics by John Dunlop (1950), Mancur Olson (1971), and Milton Friedman (1963). (Note that many of these individuals should properly be

Figure 8 — Roots of Neoclassical Economic Perspectives

*Adam Smith. 1776; 1963. Chapters 1, 2, and 3 on the Division of
    Labour, in *An Inquiry into the Nature and Causes of the Wealth of
    Nations.* Homewood, Ill.: Richard D. Irwin, pp. 4-17.
*J.R. Hicks. 1932; 1973. "The Theory of Industrial Disputes" in *The
    Theory of Wages.* New York: Macmillan, pp. 136-158.
*Charles Lindblom. 1949. "Worker, Union, and Price System" and
    "Industrial Democracy and the Price System" in *Unions and
    Capitalism.* New Haven, Conn.: Yale University Press, pp. 1-21 and
    215-227.
*John T. Dunlop. 1950. "Economic Model of a Trade Union" in *Wage
    Determination Under Trade Unions.* New York: Augustus M. Kelly,
    Inc., pp. 28-44.
*Mancur Olson. 1971. "A Theory of Groups and Organizations" and
    "The Labor Union and Economic Freedom" in *The Logic of
    Collective Action.* Cambridge, Mass.: Harvard University Press,
    pp. 5-52 and 66-97.
+Milton Friedman, with Rose D. Friedman. 1963. "Monopoly and the
    Social Responsibility of Business and Labor" in *Capitalism and
    Freedom.* Chicago: University of Chicago Press, pp. 119-136.
Commentaries:
+E.H. Phelps Brown. 1963. "The Economist's Study of Labor" in *The
    Economics of Labor.* New Haven, Conn.: Yale University Press
    (1963), as reprinted in *Economics of Labor in Industrial Society,*
    Clark Kerr and Paul D. Staudohar, eds. 1986. San Francisco:
    Jossey-Bass Publishers, pp. 384-387.
+Ronald G. Ehrenberg and Robert S. Smith. 1982. "Introduction" in
    Modern Labor Economics: Theory and Public Policy. Glenview,
    Ill.: Scott, Foresman and Company, pp. 1-11.

* Required Readings; + Recommended Readings

classified as political economists.) During this portion of the journey, we bear witness to a debate within the economics profession—
whereby employment relations and institutional patterns are
distinguished from pure market interactions, yet demonstrated to
be still tractable within an economic framework.

In a second set of more current economics readings, the focus
is outward—on how the tools of economics can inform broader

Figure 9 — Contemporary Voices in Economics

*Barry Bluestone and Bennett Harrison. 1982. "Capital vs. Commu-
nity" in *The Deindustrialization of America: Plant Closings,
Community Abandonment, and the Dismantling of Basic Industry.*
New York: Basic Books.
*Richard B. Freeman and James L. Medoff. 1984. "A New Portrait of
U.S. Unionism" and "Conclusion and Implications" in *What Do
Unions Do?* New York: Basic Books (1984), pp. 3-25 and 246-251.
*Paul Osterman. 1984. *Internal Labor Markets.* Cambridge, Mass:
MIT Press (1984), pp. 1-22.
Commentaries:
*Sanford M. Jacoby. 1988. "What Can Modern Labor Economics
Learn from the Industrial Relations Tradition?" *Proceedings, 1988
meetings of the Industrial Relations Research Association.* Madison,
Wisc.: IRRA.
+Martin Segal. 1986. "Post-Institutionalism in Labor Economics: The
Forties and Fifties Revisited" in *Industrial and Labor Relations
Review,* Vol. 39, No. 3, pp. 388-403.

* Required Readings; + Recommended Readings

---

discourse in social science on employment relations issues. These
readings, which are listed in Figure 9, feature Bluestone and Harrison (1982) on deindustrialization, Freeman and Medoff (1984) on
unions, and Osterman (1984) on internal labor markets.

While many of the readings in the first part of the course
(emphasizing assumptions) were written by economists—especially in the mixed-motive and conflict based literatures—the two
sets of readings in this section of the course make explicit the
disciplinary frame of reference provided by economics. We see the
value of tracing the dynamics and limitations of labor markets, as
well as the precision afforded through the application of econometric methods. However, no sooner do we become accustomed to
viewing the world through this lens, than it becomes time to shift
disciplines.

*Assumptions About Class and Class Conflict in the Sociological
Literature*

Sociologists have always been concerned about social relations
at work, and that discipline is an especially dominant influence
among Western European industrial relations scholars. Still, much
of the scholarship on employment relations in sociology has un-
folded outside of the main industrial relations journals or the
proceedings of the Industrial Relations Research Association (see
Roy Adams' paper on "All Aspects of People at Work" in this
volume). To enter the field, we begin with selections from the work
of four core theorists—Max Weber, Robert Michels, Ralf
Dahrendorf, and Robert K. Merton—which are listed in Figure 10.
These scholars paint a distinctive portrait of workplaces by high-
lighting class, conflict, bureaucracy, social structure, oligarchy, and
other core concepts.

Figure 10 — Sociological Roots

*Max Weber. 1982. "Selections from *Economy and Society,* Vols. 1 and
    2; and "General Economic History" in *Classes, Power, and Conflict,*
    Anthony Giddens and David Held, eds. Berkeley: University of
    California Press, pp. 60-86.
*Robert Michels. 1962. "Introduction, by Seymour Martin Lipset" and
    "Introduction — Chapters 1 and 2" , "The Conservative Basis of
    Organization," "Democracy and the Iron Law of Oligarchy," and
    "Final Considerations" in *Political Parties: A Sociological Study
    of the Oligarchical Tendencies of Modern Democracy.* New York:
    The Free Press, pp. 15-60 and 333-372.
*Ralf Dahrendorf. 1959. "Social Structure, Group Interests, and
    Conflict Groups," "Conflict Groups, Group Conflicts, and Social
    Change" and "Classes in Post-Capitalist Society I: Industrial
    Conflict" in *Class and Class Conflict in Industrial Society.* Stanford,
    Calif.: Stanford University Press, pp. 157-279.
*Robert K. Merton. 1957. "Introduction" and "Sociological Theory" in
    Social Theory and Social Structure. London: The Macmillan
    Company, pp. 3-117.

* Required Readings; + Recommended Readings

Figure 11 — Current Voices in Sociology

+Alan Fox. 1971. "The Social Organization of Industrial Work" in *A Sociology of Work in Industry.* London: The Macmillan Company, pp. 26-69.
*Marc Maurice, Francois Sellier and Jean-Jacques Silvestre. 1986. "Introduction," "Industrial Skills and Worker Mobility," "Work Systems, Spans of Qualification, and Hierarchy," and "The Industrial Dynamics of Conflict and Negotiation" in *The Social Foundations of Industrial Power: A Comparison of France and Germany,* Arthur Golhammer, trans. Cambridge, Mass.: The MIT Press.
+Anthony Giddens. 1982. "Class Structuration and Class Consciousness" in *Classes, Power, and Conflict,* Anthony Giddens and David Held, eds. Berkeley: University of California Press, pp. 157-174.
+William Foote Whyte and Joseph R. Blasi. 1982. "Worker Ownership, Participation, and Control: Toward a Theoretical Model" in *Policy Sciences,* Vol. 14, pp. 137-163.

* Required Readings; + Recommended Readings

Building from these classics, we turn to current scholars who employ the tools of sociology to examine more current workplace patterns. Figure 11 lists four distinct sociological studies that demonstrate the continuing value of examining social structures—especially those that derive from work organization, social structure, and class divisions in society

Although this treatment of sociologists has been all too brief, it has served to highlight a framework and set of tools that are very different than we found among the economists. The concepts of class and social structure have called for a greater reliance on qualitative methods and brought a more critical perspective to the discussion of employment relations.

Assumptions About Workers and Unions in the New Labor History

We are all, to some degree, labor historians. Many of the readings in every section of this course are based on historical

Figure 12 — The New Labor History

*Herbert G. Gutman. 1976. "Work, Culture, and Society in Industrializing America, 1815-1919" in *Work, Culture and Society in Industrializing America*. New York: Vintage, pp. 3-78.
*David Brody. 1973. "The Old Labor History and the New: In Search of the American Working Class" in *American Historical Review*, Vol. 78, as reprinted in *The Labor History Reader*, Daniel J. Leab, ed. 1985. Urbana, Ill.: University of Illinois Press, pp. 1-27.
*David Brody. 1989. "Labor History, Industrial Relations, and the Crisis of American Labor" in *Industrial and Labor Relations Review*, Vol. 43, No. 1, pp.7-18.
*Fink, Leon. 1991. "AHR Forum: 'Intellectuals' Versus 'Workers:' Academic Requirements and the Creation of Labor History," in *American Historical Review*, pp. 395-421 and 429-431.
*Fitzpatrick, Ellen. 1991. "AHR Forum: Rethinking the Intellectual Origins of American Labor History" in *American Historical Review*, pp. 422-428.

* Required Readings; + Recommended Readings

arguments. Thus, it is helpful to examine current debates among labor historians. The focus in the readings listed in Figure 12 is not on tracing the roots of labor history or identifying classic texts. Some of this work has already been covered, for example through the earlier examination of the work of Commons and Perlman. Because of the inevitable limits of time and space, we go directly to current debates around what is termed the "new labor history." These debates are important because they directly address the way a disciplinary perspective can limit the field of study.

The new labor historians urge a broadening of the disciplinary lens—to look beyond the history of institutions and trace the history of workers. This has brought into the analysis issues of citizenship, culture, family, gender, race, and other matters that received only passing mention in older labor history texts. In addition, the last two readings by Leon Fink (1991) and Ellen Fitzpatrick (1991) highlight an emerging dialogue in the profession around a renewed appreciation of the "old" labor historians and previously overlooked early social historians. Although not represented among these readings, the past decade has also seen the rise of a neoinstitutionalism that returns to the historical study of unions, but focusing on the social dimensions highlighted by the "new" labor history. The rise of the new labor history and the subsequent debates have been central to a larger unfolding dialogue in the field of history on issues of community, gender, race, work, and the very nature of the field of history, but these labor historians have had only limited success in extending the dialogue to the mainstream of the industrial relations field.

In many ways, the continuing debate within the discipline of labor history is symbolic of our entire journey across three disciplines. In each case, we have attempted to view the world through a particular lens, discovering what comes into sharp focus and what is excluded. The broader challenge that we each face as scholars is in choosing and justifying what we think should be in focus.

Current Debates About the Stability and Transformation of Industrial Relations

The entire journey across alternative assumptions about collective interests and disciplinary perspectives has laid the foundation for examining a key set of current debates in the field. These debates center on the degree to which fundamental shifts have taken place in employment relations. Scholars have entered this discussion from conflict, mixed-motive and consensus based assumptions. They have also come to the topic employing disciplinary lenses including economics, sociology, history, and organizational behavior.

We begin the discussion with two readings on what has come to be termed the "New Deal" system of U.S. industrial relations. Listed in Figure 13 is both an article by Christopher Tomlins (1985) celebrating the stability of the system (from a pluralist perspective) and an article by Katherine Van Wezel Stone (1981) identifying flaws in the system (from a conflict perspective).

Figure 13 — The Stability of "New Deal" Industrial Relations

*Christopher L. Tomlins. 1985. "The New Deal, Collective Bargaining, and the Triumph of Industrial Pluralism," in *Industrial and Labor Relations Review*, Vol. 39, No. 1, pp. 19-34.

A Critical Theory Perspective:
*Katherine Van Wezel Stone. 1981. "The Post-War Paradigm in American Labor Law," in *The Yale Law Journal*, Vol. 90, No. 7, 1511-1580.

* Required Readings; + Recommended Readings

Figure 14 — The Transformation of American Industrial Relations

*Thomas A. Kochan, Harry C. Katz., and Robert B. McKersie. 1986. "A Strategic Choice Perspective on Industrial Relations" and "Strategic Choices Shaping the Future" in *The Transformation of American Industrial Relations*. New York: Basic Books, pp. 3-46 and 226-253.
Commentary:
+"Review Symposium: The Transformation of American Industrial Relations," John F. Burton, Jr., ed. 1988. *Industrial and Labor Relations Review*, Vol. 41, No. 3, pp. 439-455.

Counterpoint to the Transformation Thesis:
*John T. Dunlop. 1988. "Have the 1980's Changed U.S. Industrial Relations?" in *Monthly Labor Review*, May, pp. 29-34.

Counterpoint to the counterpoint (back to fundamental change):
*Audrey Freedman. 1988. "How the 1980's Have Changed Industrial Relations" in *Monthly Labor Review*, May, pp. 35-38.

* Required Readings; + Recommended Readings

The focus then turns to the work of Thomas Kochan, Harry Katz, and Robert McKersie (1986), who offer a historical argument based on the ascendancy first of the "New Deal" system and then of the nonunion human resource management system. Interactions across three levels of industrial relations activity provides the mechanism for explaining the shift (which integrates industrial relations, sociological, organizational, and economic analyses). Figure 14 lists selected readings from this book and from various commentaries on it.

The analysis offered by Michael Piore and Charles Sabel (1984), which is one of the readings featured in Figure 15, is noteworthy for spanning disciplines as they trace fundamental shifts in markets and technology. The authors argue that the "first industrial divide" was the shift from craft to mass production, while the "second industrial divide" involves a current shift from mass production toward what they term "flexible specialization" oriented around global, fragmented markets. The analysis is bold in its cross-national scope and unique in its integration of economics, political science, sociology and history. The issue of fundamental change is examined in other readings by Charles Heckscher (1988), Seymour Martin Lipset (1986), and Bernard H. Moss (1988) with varying emphasis on culture, history, organizational dynamics, and work organization/production systems.

In traveling among these readings on fundamental change we see that no one discipline or perspective is sufficient to define and explain current developments in industrial relations. Further, the many underlying assumptions and disciplinary perspectives offer familiar landmarks, useful roadmaps, and valuable lenses for the journey. In many ways, the discussion serves as a capstone to the course. However, this inquiry into industrial relations theory is not complete without consideration of specific methodological issues that arise in the testing of theory.

One key issue that arises out of the industrial relations literature on transformation and change involves an examination of economic performance implications. Central to the transformation argument is the increased importance of employer-driven initiatives, which surfaces questions about the economic gains associated with one set of new initiatives—those focused on employee participation. The readings in Figure 16 trace a decade's scholarship on this

Figure 15 — Fundamental Changes in Technology,

Markets, Unions and Law

*Michael Piore and Charles Sabel. 1984. "Introduction," "Mass Pro-
  duction as Destiny and Blind Decision," and "Possibilities for
  Prosperity: International Keynesianism and Flexible Specialization"
  in *The Second Industrial Divide: Possibilities for Prosperity* New
  York: Basic Books, pp. 3-48, 251-280.

Counterpoint:
+Richard Hyman. 1988. "Flexible Specialization: Miracle or Myth? in
  New Technology and Industrial Relations, Richard Hyman and
  Wolfgang Streeck, eds. London: Basil Blackwell, pp. 48-60.
*Charles C. Heckscher. 1988. "Three Elements of Representation" and
  "Completing the System" in *The New Unionism: Employee
  Involvement in the Changing Corporation.* New York: Basic Books,
  pp. 155-231.
*Seymour Martin Lipset. 1986. "North American Labor Movements:
  A Comparative Perspective" in *Unions in Transition: Entering the
  Second Century.* San Francisco: ICS Press, pp. 421-452.
+Bernard H. Moss. 1988. "Industrial Law Reform in an Era of Retreat:
  The Auroux Laws in France" in *Work, Employment and Society,*
  Vol. 2, No. 3, pp. 317-334.

* Required Readings; + Recommended Readings

question. Since the question is a relatively narrow one, we see the
relevance of different levels of analysis, variation in the quality of
data, and alternative theoretical models.

Reviewing this literature reveals a shift from relatively ambiguous connection between participation and economic performance
to a fairly precise linkage. Critical to making the linkage, however,
is not just improvements in the level of analysis and the quality of
the data. In my own contribution to this literature (Cutcher-
Gershenfeld 1991), I argue that the link to economic performance
can only be observed through the concurrent analysis of patterns of
cooperation and conflict resolution. It is a line of analysis that
explicitly builds on the mixed-motive assumption.

Figure 16 — Economic Performance Issues

*Richard D. Rosenberg and Eliezer Rosenstein. 1980. "Participation
   and Productivity: An Empirical Study" in *Industrial and Labor
   Relations Review*, Vol. 33, April, pp. 355-367.
+Michael Shuster. 1983. "The Impact of Union-Management Coopera-
   tion on Productivity and Employment" in *Industrial and Labor
   Relations Review*, Vol. 36, April, pp. 415-430.
+Harry C. Katz, Thomas A. Kochan, and Kenneth Gobeille. 1983.
   "Industrial Relations Performance, Economic Performance, and
   Quality of Working Life Efforts" in *Industrial and Labor Relations
   Review*, Vol. 37, pp. 3-17.
+Harry C. Katz, Thomas A. Kochan, and Mark Weber. 1985. "Assess-
   ing the Effects of Industrial Relations and Quality of Working Life
   on Organizational Performance" in *Academy of Management
   Journal*, Vol. 28, pp. 509-27.
*Walter J. Gershenfeld. 1987. "Employee Participation in Firm Deci-
   sions" in *Human Resources and the Performance of the Firm*,
   Morris M. Kleiner, Richard N. Block, Myron Roomkin, and Sidney
   Salsburg, eds. Madison, Wisc.: Industrial Relations Research
   Association, pp. 123-158.
*Harry C. Katz, Thomas A. Kochan, and Jeffrey Keefe. 1988. "Indus-
   trial Relations and Productivity in the U.S. Automobile Industry" in
   Brookings Papers on Economic Activity, Vol. 3, pp. 685-715.
+John F. Krafcik. 1988. "The Triumph of the Lean Production System"
   in *Sloan Management Review*, Vol. 30, pp. 41-52.
*John Paul MacDuffie and Thomas A. Kochan. 1989. "Human Re-
   sources, Technology, and Economic Performance: Evidence from
   the Automobile Industry" in *Proceedings of the Forty-First Annual
   Meeting*, Barbara Dennis, ed. Madison, Wisc.: IRRA, pp. 159-171.
+John Thomas Delaney, Casey Ichniowski and David Lewin. 1989.
   "Employee Involvement Programs and Firm Performance" in
   Proceedings of the Forty-First Annual Meeting, Barbara Dennis, ed.
   Madison, Wisc.: IRRA, pp. 148-158.
*Joel Cutcher-Gershenfeld. 1991. "The Impact on Economic Perfor-
   mance of a Transformation in Workplace Relations," in *Industrial
   and Labor Relations Review*, Vol. 44, No. 2, pp. 241-260.

* Required Readings; + Recommended Readings

Conclusion

This article has provided narrative during a journey through an advanced graduate course on industrial relations theory. Future versions of the course will inevitably feature revisions in the mix of readings. Still, these selections may be helpful to others organizing similar courses. Perhaps more importantly, a particular logic has been presented for organizing such a course.

The three main sections of the course each surfaced a key theme. The first sets of readings highlighted core assumptions about the employment relationship—contrasting mixed-motive, conflict, and consensus assumptions. We saw that core assumptions about collective interests set the stage for the construction of coherent theoretical arguments. The second sets of readings highlighted alternative disciplinary perspectives—featuring economics, sociology, and history. We saw that a disciplinary lens is double-edged —both sharpening and limiting out focus. The final sets of readings served to integrate theory in a discussion of transformation and change in industrial relations, as well as to allow consideration of key methodological issues.

The journey has been akin to a roller coaster ride. We have had the gradual increase in enthusiasm as we read classic texts within a given perspective, followed by a rapid mix of impressions based on the work of current scholars, only to be shaken by a sudden sharp turn into an alternative perspective. When the ride is complete, we are a bit shaken. But, given the many sights visible when we are at the peak of a particular area and the tempering quality of sharp turns, we should now be better able to enjoy the rest of the carnival.

The Founders of Industrial Relations as a Field of Study: An American Perspective

Jack Barbash

This article is about the men and one woman whom I think of as the founders of the American (and in a more restricted sense, the Western) intellectual tradition of industrial relations. I think of them as founders because their works set the basic terms of industrial relations as a field of study and shaped the academic treatment of the labor problem and industrial relations. The article tries to get at the defining essence of each of the founders, directing readers who want more to works cited in the bibliography.

I make no special claim for the validity of the selection except that it seems to have worked out in several decades of teaching and writing about industrial relation theory.

Introductory

Industrial relations in understood here as the resolution of tension and conflict among the contending interests in the employment relationship, namely, management efficiency, employee security and maintenance of economic stability and social peace by the state. The context is the industrialized employment relationship of Western capitalism because this is industrial relations' native habitat. (For a fuller statement, see Barbash 1984.)

Industrial relations is both theory and practice. Theory is ideas, values, concepts, and represents the primary focus here. Practice is behavior on the shop floor, union hall, boardroom and government agency and provides the basis for theory.

The tension and conflict generated by the application of management efficiency to the labor input is mainly resolved by the methods of equity. Equity in the industrial relations context is a kind of "civil rights in industry" (Slichter 1941, 1) incorporated variously in the collective agreement, law, management policy, and common practice (Barbash 1989).

Karl Marx (1818-1883)

Marx was the first great expositor of modern capitalism's labor problem. (See Tucker 1978, Lichtheim 1961, Marx 1912, McClellan 1975.) He was not the first to analyse capitalism's victimization of labor. Before Marx the Utopians were also highly critical of capitalist exploitation. Their remedy for capitalism's ills was withdrawal into islands of self-help cooperation. By contrast, Marx's "scientific socialism" let historic necessity work its way toward capitalism's full development and ultimate collapse, a dialectic process which would be reenforced by a working class that was increasingly conscious of its exploitation and alienation.

Marx is a founder of industrial relations intellectual tradition because he was the first to see capitalism whole and identify its constituent elements: specifically, the clash of the classes, i.e., capitalists and the state as their ally versus the workers and the party as the vanguard of the working class; the historic necessity of a proletarian revolution driven by the exploitation and alienation of the capitalist labor process; and capitalism's ultimate collapse and its replacement by socialism. Equity for the working class is finally accomplished by socialism.

Western industrial relations is anti-Marxist in the sense that it holds out the likelihood of amelioration of exploitation and alienation under capitalism. Marxist theory has refused to accept the legitimacy and efficacy of an independent management function to economise on labor resources. This has proved to be one of the flaws that brought down Soviet-style socialism. Nor was Marxism finally willing to come to theoretical terms with a welfare state

under capitalism which could moderate immiseration, and a pluralistic democracy which was not "a committee for managing the
common affairs of the whole bourgeoisie" (Marx 1959, 9). All of
these were devices by which capitalism, in reality, changed its ways
to counter the Marxist scenario.

The extenuating circumstance in Marx's miscalculation was
that capitalism had not yet in his time shown the adaptability which
it was able to demonstrate later. When Marx and Engels are report-
ing on the labor problem in their own time they come pretty close
to the reality. But they didn't appreciate, as Engels did later, that
what they were witnessing was not capitalism's death throes but its
growing pains.

Max Weber (1864-1920)

Alone in this company Max Weber was not specifically a labor
reformer, but his conceptualisation of capitalism is necessary for
an understanding of the labor problem. (See Weber 1958, 1961;
Bendix 1962.) Weber came to capitalism as a social scientist not as
revolutionist. Because Weber did not accept Marx's closed system,
he saw what Marx could not see without abandoning his system.
To begin with, Weber saw capitalism as a more complex and less
deterministic process. Management which "seeks profit rationally
and systematically" (Weber 1958, 76) constitutes a unique and
legitimate function; indispensable, as it turned out, both to capitalist
and socialist economic systems alike.

Weber's bureaucracy becomes the instrument of rationality to
enforce management authority and the division of labor in the
complex, large-scale organisation. Bureaucracy as concept is a
forerunner of the "managerial revolution" (Burnham 1941) and the
"technostructure" (Galbraith 1972) which transformed capitalism's
power base in the sense of what matters is who controls, not who
owns the means of production. Bureaucracy is also expressed in the
"new class" (Djilas 1957) which usurped power from the working
class under Soviet-style socialism.

Bureaucracy, more realistically than class, gets at the dynamic
power elements in the making of capitalist and socialist industrialism. In general, Weber's multicausal analysis is also superior to

Marx's economic determinism in probing the complexity of the driving forces in industrial relations.

Frederick Taylor (1856-1915)

Frederick Taylor's "Scientific Management" amounts to the systematic application of Weber's management rationality to the labor input. (See Taylor 1947, Nelson 1980.) To critics, Taylorism represented the "final disintegration of workmen's skills" (Commons 1919, 15) and the ultimate reduction of human labor into a fungible commodity. Taylor himself justified scientific management as a species of equity, an "equitable code of laws," scientifically determined, to overcome the "arbitrary judgment" of conventional management and trade unionism (Taylor 1947, 189).

Taylorism foreshadowed the systematic rationalization, not only for work and pay, but of all aspects of the labor input from recruitment to retirement. The systematic organization of work which Taylorism fostered may have been as significant as hard technology in advancing industrial development and evoking protest, hence bringing industrial relations into being to deal with protest.

Taylor, like Marx, provoked countermovements reflected here in Mayo, Commons, and Hoxie below and in trade unionism as a protective institution. Trade unionism and collective bargaining, in turn, converted Taylorism's unilateral "one best way" into bilateral negotiation.

Elton Mayo (1880-1949)

Mayo's human relations straddles the industrial relations process. (See Roethlisberger 1947; Trahair 1984; Mayo 1945, 1960.) As a management instrument, human relations buys out employee resistance to management efficiency. From the employee side, Mayo and the research which he stimulated created the construct of an informal protective work society which seemed to defend labor resistance to efficiency.

Mayo's human relations and the Mayo-inspired Western Electric experiments (Roethlisberger and Dickson 1947) sought to refute Taylor and the economists' "rabble hypothesis" (Mayo 1945, 40) that "the workman . . . [was] a mere item in the cost of production rather than . . . a citizen fulfilling a social function" (Mayo 1970, 35). Mayo comes close to alienation theory in embracing Durkheim's "anomie" to describe the worker's "social isolation" in the workplace.

Unions to Mayo were an unnecessary breeding ground for conflict. Professionalized managerial human relations, as in the Western Electric Hawthorne experiments, was deemed sufficient to protect human values in the production process.

The researches of the Mayoists can be read to mean that labor problems, far from aberration, are inherent in the industrial mode of employee utilization, unions or no. As Frank Tannenbaum put it: "The same process that had gathered these laborers together had forged a 'society' in which a sense of identity became inevitable" (1951, 59). The informal society also engages in a species of bargaining, albeit "cryptobargaining," relying on restriction of output and other modes of civil disobedience on the shop floor as the sanction which makes management listen.

Human relations and its subsequent variations may also be interpreted, perversely perhaps, as justifying the union function—if not unionism as an institution. Human relations becomes a kind of union-substitution strategy in which management in its own self-interest does just about everything that a union does but without the risks of an active "permanent opposition" (Clegg 1972, 76). Indeed, a member in a good standing of the human relations school has said, "If unions didn't exist we should have to invent them" (Homan 1954, 57).

The Webbs (Beatrice: 1858-1943; Sidney: 1859-1947)

Beatrice and Sidney Webb, although committed socialists, had the insight to see that socialist no less than capitalist management efficiency required the protective presence of trade unions to keep management from overreaching itself as, indeed, it has. Workers must have a right "even under the most complete collectivism" to take positions against management policies and to enforce them if necessary by striking (Webb 1897, 824). "Trade unionism [therefore] is not merely an incident of the present phase of capitalist industry. [It] has a permanent function to fulfill in the democratic state" (Webb 1897, 823). In the twilight of their lives they seemed, however, to waver on this point as it applied to the Soviet Union (Webb 1937, 1215).

The Webbs are responsible for the enduring typologies of trade union methods and expedients. The trade union methods are mutual insurance, collective bargaining (a term which they invented), legal enactment and arbitration. The expedients include the "device of the common rule," "the restriction of numbers" and the "standard rate" (Webb 1896, 145-323). The trade union as a "continuous association of wage earners for the purposes of monitoring or improving the conditions of their working lives" (Webb 1896, 1) remains the classic definition.

"It is almost true," Leonard Woolf said, "that [the Webbs] not only discovered but invented [trade unions]." Before the Webbs "neither governments, nor civil servants, nor politicians, nor trade unionists themselves [knew] what the form of the trade union movement was, what it had achieved, and what its functions had been and might be" (1949, 254).

John R. Commons (1862-1945) and Company

Commons comes close to being the pivotal figure in this company because he endowed all of the "actors"—unions, employees, management, and the state—in the industrial relations process with legitimacy and functionality and formulated the essential logic of industrial relations. Systematic theory was not Commons' strong suit, although he tried hard to build "a whole system of political economy on the foundations of labor" (Commons 1964, 131). (See also Barbash 1991, 21-36.) It is nonetheless possible to derive a coherent theoretical standpoint from Commons' output that is consistent with the underlying spirit of his practical and theoretical works.

One of Commons' difficulties with high-theory was that he wasn't really interested in theory for its own sake. As a problem-solving activist he used theory as a guide to practice and policy, thereby reflecting the ambivalence of industrial relations generally toward high-theory.

Commons' analysis takes as its starting premise the "peculiar" nature of labor as a human commodity and builds his scheme on it. This is also the point at which institutional labor economics and later, industrial relations, part company with economics. Classical and neoclassical economics also recognised the peculiar nature of labor as a commodity but did little with it analytically, whereas industrial relations constructs its whole logic on it. Labor's "soul" and human beings with "wills of their own" (Commons 1950, 155) do not easily bend to management cost discipline and the engineer's theory of labor as machinery.

The worker as a "propertyless seller of himself" lacking bargaining power of the "propertied buyer" of labor is unable to bargain on a plane of equality (Commons and Andrews 1936, 1). Bargaining inequality is resolved not by eliminating capitalism but by reforming it by equity remedies enforced through 1) a democratic pluralist state, 2) bargaining between trade unions and employers and 3) the enlightened employer acting in his own self-interest. Bargaining is responsive to labor's human form by giving it voice in how it is to be employed. Commons' "new equity . . . protect[ed] the job as the older equity protected the business" (Commons 1959, 307).

Common's "American exceptionalism" (not his phrase though) differentiated the American labor experience from the radical working-class struggles of Europe as a way of making equity compatible with American individualism. Far from being imported by foreign agitators, the American labor problem grew out of native American soil and the inner processes of the work society. Popular political institutions evolved in such a way to make it possible to achieve equity by "reasonable value" and "due process" under capitalism (Commons 1959, 145).

Industrial relations, for Commons, is, to be sure, a product of a clash of interests among the classes and he recognized there are times when employees assert conflict of interest as much against other groups of employees as against management. But, unlike Marx, these clashes can be mediated by equity under capitalism to the advantage of all. State intervention in the labor problem need not proceed along the European path of the centralized state, but can be decentralized by federalism, professionalized rather than politicized administration, and by involvement of unions and management in the public policymaking process.

Labor's "goodwill" is capable of improving efficiency. "Intangible goodwill of labor may be as profitable as the scientific management of labor" (Commons 1919, 18).

Much of Commons' framework was fleshed out by his students. Selig Perlman (1888-1958) spelled out the Wisconsin model of job-conscious unionism. (See Perlman 1958, Taft 1976.) Perlman, like his mentor, rejected socialism as the necessary historical mission of the working class and the trade union movement and, indeed, saw socialism as a threat to the middle-class acceptance of unionism. Closer to the manual workers' interest were "shop rights . . . which reach the workman directly and with certainty . . . and never get lost en route, like the 'broader' liberty promised by socialism" (Perlman 1949, 275). Workers care more about "strik[ing] the best wage bargain possible" than they care about who owns the means of production (Perlman 1922, 266-67).

Sumner H. Slichter (1892-1959), another Commons student, began with the duality inherent in labor as a commodity. More incisively than anybody else, the young Slichter formulated the major—not always stated—premise of industrial relations that the labor problem "exists because man is not only the end but also a means of production" causing "a clash between life and work" (Slichter 1928, 287). Slichter foresaw "specialized personnel administration" as "the most significant development in industrial relations in several decades" (Dorfman 1959, 539-40).

Slichter's detailed investigation of collective bargaining led him to "industrial jurisprudence," "civil rights in industry" and "management by rule rather than by arbitrary decision" (Slichter 1941, 2). It is Slichter, finally, who took note of the high point of equity in the "laboristic state," "the gradual shift from a capitalistic community . . . to a community in which employees rather than businessmen are the strongest single influence" (Slichter 1961, 255).

Robert F. Hoxie (1868-1916)

Robert F. Hoxie came to the labor problem by an intellectual route somewhat different from the Commons group. (See Perlman 1958, 128-42.)

Hoxie, too, sought to put the study of labor on a new basis. However, his present standing in the industrial relations tradition rests on his formulation of functional union types; namely, business, uplift, revolutionary, predatory and dependent unionism. Comparable to Perlman's job-conscious unionism, Hoxie's business unionism is "mainly . . . a bargaining institution," trade conscious rather than class conscious, oriented to craft and industry "rather than to the working class as a whole" and exclusive rather than inclusive as to membership. Business unionism wants "more here and now" in the form of higher wages, shorter hours and better working conditions. It is "conservative and" accepts capitalism and the wage system (Hoxie 1923, 45).

As an investigator for the United States Commission on Industrial Relations, Hoxie synthesized the classic union case against scientific management. Scientific management "looks upon the worker as a mere instrument of production and reduces him to a semiautomatic attachment to the machine or tool"; it was "undemocratic" and a reversion to industrial autocracy. Far from encouraging peace and cooperation, as Taylor claimed, scientific management caused "mutual suspicion and controversy" (Hoxie 1915, 15-19).

Common Attributes

Most of the founders, even Marx, came to the labor problem as a result of moral conviction and a conviction, too, that social science could be put in the service of moral ends. Most of the founders brought the problem-solving temperament of reformers to their research. They were not only thinkers but highly committed doers, perceiving their research as part of a larger social agenda.

Beveridge said about the Webbs that they thought of themselves as putting "social science on a new basis" (Beveridge 1949, 41). So did almost all of the others. Marx was encouraged to believe that his "scientific socialism" had unlocked "the laws of history" (Marx 1912, 23). Weber argued for a scientific "value-free" sociology (Roth and Berger 1966), Commons' notion of "reasonable value" stressed "due process of thinking"—the method of arriving at a result rather than the result itself (Commons 1959, 351). Taylor thought he was replacing arbitrary power with, literally, scientific management. Mayo wanted to rid the "human and sociopolitical sphere" of haphazard guess and "opportunist fumbling" (Mayo 1960, 132). Hoxie's genetic standpoint . . . "aimed at a reasoned explanation of trade unionism in terms of the efficient causes which have made the movement what it is, and is becoming" (Downey 1923, xvii).

The founders were not only important in their own right, they also spawned extraordinarily influential movements. Marx became Marxism, Commons "was the intellectual origin of the New Deal" (Boulding 1956, 7) and "more than any other economist he was responsible for the conversion into public policy of reform proposals designed to alleviate defects in the industrial system" (Dorfman 1959, 377). Elton Mayo was the progenitor of the most important personnel management movements of our times including human relations and human resources management. The Webbs were "the greatest internal influence in British history for the first half of the twentieth century" (Boulding 1956, 3).

Some intellectual movements, it turns out, are as important for the opposition they stir up as they are in their own right. Commons and the Wisconsin School "Americanized" the labor problem to save it from guilt by Marxist association. (See Barbash 1967.) Weber offered a multicausal explanation of history—Protestantism, charisma, bureaucracy—against Marx's determinism, economism, and scientism (Roth and Berger 1966). Mayo's human relations sought to rebut Taylor's scientism and economic hyperrationality applied to human beings. Mayo, Taylor, and Commons took on the dominant market economics for its overarching economism and its insensitivity to human needs.

The Western Industrial Relations "Model"

The history of industrial relations as an intellectual field begins with Marx because he was the first to comprehend the labor process as a product of capitalism, raise the enduring questions about capitalism's equity, and scare capitalist management into industrial relations. Western industrial relations has led to a refutation of Marxism by demonstrating the feasibility of labor reform under capitalism, albeit democratic, welfare state, or reform capitalism.

Max Weber's rationality and bureaucracy, Taylor's application of the rationality principle through scientific management, and Mayo's human relations characterize capitalist management's administration of the labor system. But rationality and scientific management, left to their own devices, lead to Marx's alienation and exploitation of human labor; and by another route to Mayo's and Durkheim's anomie unless mediated internally by Mayo's management human relations.

Equity by way of "business unionism," industrial jurisprudence, collective bargaining, and legal enactment of Commons, Perlman, Slichter, Hoxie, and the Webbs make efficiency more or less compatible with security. We learn from these founders, too, that employees and unions don't only confront the employer but each other as well.

The founders undertook analysis of the employment relationship and its problem under capitalism. But it turns out that the management-efficiency/union-employee-security and legal enactment are likely to be relevant as well to industrial socialism's labor problems.

This discussion of the founders has had the collateral purpose of stressing industrial relations' strong ties with the larger realm of ideas. In addition to being a vocation and a profession industrial relations is a field of study that takes on many of the aspects of a liberal education. (See Douglas, Hitchcock, and Atkins 1925; Bakke, Jerr, and Anrod 1967; Kerr and Staudohar 1986; as examples of industrial relations reading collections which demonstrate such a standpoint.)

Works Cited

Bakke, E. W., C. Kerr, and C. Anrod. 1967, *Unions, Management and the Public*, New York: Harcourt, Brace and World.

Barbash, J. 1967, "John R. Commons and the Americanization of the Labor Problem," *Journal of Economic Issues*, vol.1, no. 3, pp. 161-67.

_____. 1984, *The Elements of Industrial Relations*, Madison, WI: University of Wisconsin Press.

_____. 1989, "Equity as Function: Its Rise and Attrition," in *Theories and Concepts in Comparative Industrial Relations*, eds. J. Barbash and K. Barbash, Columbia, SC: University of South

Carolina Press.

_____. 1991, "John R. Commons and the Western Industrial Relations Tradition," in *Comparative Industrial Relations*, ed. R. Adams, London: Harper Collins Academic.

Bendix, R. 1962, *Max Weber*, New York: Anchor Books.

Beveridge, Lord W. 1949, "The London School of Economics and the University of London," in *The Webbs and Their Work*, ed. M. Cole, London: Frederick Muller, Ltd.

Boulding, K. 1956, "A New Look at Institutionalism," *American Economic Review*, Papers and Proceedings, pp. 1-27.

Burnham, J. 1941, *The Managerial Revolution*, New York: John Day Co.

Clegg, H. A. 1972, "Trade Unions as an Opposition Which Can Never Become a Government," in *Trade Unions*, ed. W. E. J. McCarthy, London: Penguin.

Commons, J. R. 1919, *Industrial Goodwill*, New York: McGraw-Hill.

_____. 1950, *The Economics of Collective Action*, New York: Macmillan.

_____. 1959[1924], *The Legal Foundations of Capitalism*, Madison, WI: University of Wisconsin Press.

_____. 1964[1934], *Myself*, Madison, WI: University of Wisconsin Press.

Commons, J. R., and J. B. Andrews. 1936[1916], *Principles of Labor Legislation*, 4th ed., New York: Harper & Brothers.

Djilas, M. 1957, *The New Class*, New York: Frederick H. Praeger.

Dorfman, J. 1959, *The Economic Mind in America, 1918-1933*, New York: Viking Press.

Douglas, P. H., C. N. Hitchcock, and W. W. Atkins. 1925, *The Worker in Modern Economic Society*, Chicago: University of Chicago Press.

Downey, E. H. 1923[1927], "Introduction," in *Trade Unionism in the United States*, R. F. Hoxie, 2nd ed., New York: Appleton.

Galbraith, J. K. 1972, *The New Industrial State*, 2nd ed., rev., New York: New American Library.

Homan, G. C. 1954, "Industrial Harmony as a Goal," in *Industrial Conflict*, ed. A. Kornhauser, R. Dubin, and A. M. Ross, New York: McGraw-Hill.

Hoxie, R. F. 1915, *Scientific Management and Labor*, New York: D. Appleton & Co.

_____. 1923[1917], *Trade Unionism in the United States*, 2nd ed., New York: D. Appleton & Co.

Kerr, C., and P. Staudohar. 1986, *Industrial Relations in a Changing Age*, San Francisco: Josey-Bass.

Lichtheim, G. 1961, *Marxism, An Historical and Critical Study,* New York: Praeger.

Marx, K. 1912[1857], *Capital,* vol. 1, Chicago: Chas. H. Kerr.

Marx, K., and F. Engels. 1959, "The Manifesto of the Communist Party," in *Marx and Engels: Basic Writings on Politics and Philosophy,* ed. L. F. Feuer, New York: Doubleday Anchor.

Mayo, E. 1945, *The Social Problems of an Industrial Civilization,* Cambridge, MA: Harvard University Press.

_____. 1960[1933], *The Human Problems of an Industrial Civilization,* New York: Viking Press.

_____. 1970, "Social Growth and Social Disintegration" [1919] in *Readings in Management,* ed. E. Dale, New York: McGraw-Hill.

McClellan, D. 1975, *Karl Marx, His Life and Thought,* New York: Viking Press.

Nelson, D. 1980, *Frederick W. Taylor and the Rise of Scientific Management,* Madison, WI: University of Wisconsin Press.

Perlman, M. 1958, *Labor Union Theories in America,* Evanston, IL: Row Peterson & Co.

Perlman, S. 1922, *A History of Trade Unionism in the United States,* New York: Macmillian.

_____. 1949[1928], *A Theory of the Labor Movement,* New York: Augustus Kelley.

Roethlisberger, F. J., and W. J. Dickson. 1947, *Management and the Worker,* Cambridge, MA: Harvard University Press.

Roth, G., and B. M. Berger. 1966, "Max Weber and the Organized Society," *The New York Times Book Review,* April 5.

Slichter, S. H. 1928, "What Is the Labor Problem," in *American Labor Dynamics,* ed. J. B. S. Hardman, New York: Harcourt Brace.

_____. 1941, *Union Policies and Industrial Management,* Washington, D C: Brookings Institution.

_____. 1961, "Are We Becoming a 'Laboristic' State?" in *Potentials of the American Economy,* ed. J. T. Dunlop, Cambridge, MA: Harvard University Press.

Taft, P. 1976, "Reflections on Selig Perlman as a Teacher and Writer," *Industrial & Labor Relations Review,* vol.29, no.2, pp. 249-57.

Tannenbaum, F. 1951, *A Philosophy of Labor,* New York: Knopf.

Taylor, F. W. 1947[1911], *Scientific Management,* New York: Harper.

Trahair, R. C. S. 1984, *The Humanist Temper,* New Brunswick, N.J.: Transaction Books.

Tucker, R. C. 1978, *The Marx-Engels Reader,* 2nd ed., New York: W. W. Norton.

Webb, B., and S. Webb. 1896, *The History of Trade Unionism,* London: Longmans, Green.

_____. 1897, *Industrial Democracy*, vol.2, London: Longmans, Green.

_____. 1937, *Soviet Communism*, 2nd ed., London: Longmans, Green.

Weber, M. 1958[1904-05], *The Protestant Ethic and the Spirit of Capitalism*, New York: Chas. Scribner's Sons.

_____. 1961[1927], *General Economic History*, New York: Collier Books.

Woolf, L. 1949, "Political Thought and the Webbs," in *The Webbs and Their Work*, ed. M. Cole, London: Frederick Muller, Ltd.

Is Euro-American Union Theory Universally Applicable?: An Australasian Perspective

Kevin Hince

Both Australia and New Zealand were part of the British colonial empire and the earliest unions were an offshoot of British unionism. Australia comprised six colonies, which became independent in a federation in 1901. New Zealand debated, for a short time, whether to join the federal state at that time, but ultimately opted for Dominion status (in 1908) and full independence (at a later date). The term Australasian was in common usage in the 19th century to encompass discussion of the six Australian colonies and New Zealand. Into the 20th century it has been used to embrace the two separate countries within a common phrase.

Howard (1977) was the first and to date only significant attempt to explain the origins, development, and role of Australian unions in the context of union theory. He argued that Australian trade unions of the 20th century can be regarded as institutions which were created by a bureaucratic mechanism (the arbitration system)

Thanks to Bill Howard, Gerry Griffin, Pat Walsh, and Lorraine for extremely helpful comments on earlier drafts. Thanks also to Roy Adams for several valuable suggestions. In particular the synthesis in the final sections of the chapter owes much to his insight. Responsibility remains mine. Writing was facilitated by research funds made available by the Faculty of Commerce and Administration, Victoria University of Wellington.

to enhance the functioning of that mechanism. Further, the mechanism called unions into existence, or at least sought to encourage them, and, as a consequence, the growth in union membership in the first two decades of the system is unmatched (in relative terms) elsewhere in the capitalist world. Howard continued the argument asserting that a trade union movement that had grown to the relative size of the Australian labor movement (approximately 50 percent penetration by 1921), and had achieved its growth by struggle and power, would have insisted on determining its own destiny. Instead the Australian labor movement needs to be seen as a labor movement in form and intention rather than in tactics and achievement.

Griffin and Scarcebrook (1990) tested one aspect of the Howard hypotheses, namely the role of the state-functionary, the Registrar. Their empirical analysis identifies a less central role for the Registrar than Howard's "casual empiricism" supports, but they conclude that " . . . registered organizations already within the system use the mechanism of the Act to jealously guard their position." That is, the data does support the broad position enunciated by Howard that Australian trade unions "rely on, and extensively use, *state-provided legal mechanisms to protect their membership coverage rather than on membership preferences and organising drives*" (my emphasis).

While Howard was prepared to concede that Australian unions of the late 19th century may have been a response to conventional stimuli, those of the 20th century were not. Trade unions in this later period were created by the state and were dependent on the state. Moreover, unions that had emerged prior to the arbitration statutes were subjected to political and legislative pressure to adapt both function and behavior. It is the case, Howard (1977 and 1983) argued, of a union movement brought into being and shaped to provide comfort, security, and peace of mind—not to unionists alone, but to society. It followed, therefore, that European and American theories of the labor movement are inadequate to explain the origin, growth, and role of Australian unions of the 20th century, and that predictions about union behavior derived from international experience may be based on irrelevant premises.

The purpose of this chapter is to test the central theoretical explanations of Howard as they may apply in the case of New Zealand trade unionism, and thus to extend the questioning of the relevance of Euro-American theories of the labor movement to

encompass both Australian and New Zealand. The immediate prov-
ocation for this test is the essential similarity of the legislative
provisions developed in each country, at approximately the same
time, the Industrial Conciliation and Arbitration Act 1894 (IC and
A Act) in New Zealand, and the Commonwealth Conciliation and
Arbitration Act 1904 (CC and A Act) in Australia. The vehicle for
the test is the specific case of the Wellington Shop Assistants Union,
set within the general 20th century historical context of union
development within New Zealand. In a way the essay is intended
as a tentative step in the development of an Australasian theory of
unionism and a contribution towards a more general theory.

Euro-American Theories of the Union Movement

European theories of the labor movement highlight competition in the labor market and the class struggle between capital and
labor, as central forces in explaining the origin, development and
purpose of unions. The Webbs (Sidney and Beatrice Webb 1926)
saw the competitive market forces of capitalism place pressure on
the return available from production and, in turn, on the worker.
Competition between workers assisted downward pressure on
wages and conditions of employment. The union, the collective,
argued the Webbs, could not eliminate "classes" but would minimize the worst effects of competition within and between "classes"
by joint regulation. Marxist theory ascribed to the union a short-
run economic function of limiting competition in the labor market.
But the trade union would, in the long run, become the center of a
revolutionary movement to change the nature of society. Polanyi,
another European theorist, also saw competitive forces in the labor
market as a central explanatory variable. He focussed on the concept of a social protection movement as a spontaneous effort by
people to protect their social relationships by creating barriers to
control the effect of the competitive market. Trade unions were a
product of this social protection movement, bringing workers together with the common cause of acting jointly to set common terms
and erect common defenses instead of allowing themselves to be
bought and dismissed as individuals (Polanyi 1944, Chamberlain
1965).

American union theorists sought to explain unionism within a
capitalist production system, but rejected the class-based model.
But competition was still a critical force. Commons (1968), in his
"American Shoemakers" essay presented a theoretical study of the
emergence and development of unions in an expanding economic
context and frontier society. He argued that as competition in the
product market accelerated, pressure on the worker intensified, and
the union emerged and developed as a sectional interest to pursue
protection of the worker (embracing philosophies of restricting
competition, protectionism, the union label, and opposition to migration and the employment of women and children). However, this
is a "business model" of unionism which comes to terms with a
capitalist society and seeks accommodation within that system. As
Barbash (1989) notes:

> Adversarialism is central to Commons and Marx. But Marx's
> unremitting class struggle under capitalism runs counter to
> Commons' mediation of class conflict through equity.
>
> Commons identifies an essential common ground between man-
> agement and employees which Marx rejects.

To Commons the pattern of union development is determined by
market fluctuations.

Both Perlman (1928) and Marx share a common starting point,
namely similar perspectives in respect to conflict within the capitalist system, and both embrace the notion of trade union consciousness as a developmental force. For Perlman, however, that
consciousness is a product of, and focussed more specifically on,
the individual position of the need for control against the "scarcity"
of job opportunities. The group is the vehicle through which control
of entry, a network of job rules, and a concept of property rights
within the job, can be achieved. If left alone, Perlman argued,
workers would exhibit job consciousness rather than political consciousness; political action as endorsed by Marx was a result of
external influences.

Tannenbaum was one American theorist who came close to
embracing the class basis common to European theorists. An ultimate goal of organization was the displacement of the capitalist
system by a participative democratic model. Competition was a

basic feature, in Tannenbaum's argument, developing within the technology of machine-based production and threatening the security of the individual worker. Unionism is a defense against such competition. (Dunlop 1968).

A variety of causal forces are identified to explain the emergence and development of trade unions. Common ground exists, as do differences of substance and emphasis. However, in none of the European and American theories of the labor movement is there an explicit basic, central, or even ancillary role for the state. It is this omission which limits the universality of the Euro-American labor union theories.

A Common Heritage

Howard considers that conventional stimuli, class, competition, revolutionary zeal, job protection, and the needs of workers are appropriate to explain unionism in the late 19th century in Australia. British migration was a common historic source of early unionism in both Australia and New Zealand. Craft societies emerged, based on the British model in each case, and quickly focussed on job control, and direct bargaining. Industry unions, of unskilled and semiskilled, emerged later in shearing, stevedoring, seamen, mining, and transport. Competition, especially as boom turned to depression, was a threat to be tackled by collectivism. Similar developments occurred in both Australia and New Zealand, and, in fact, were reinforced by extensive trans-Tasman migration of labor in each direction. Howard (1977) synthesized the Australian experience indicating that initially the labor movement developed as a "conventional job centred organization, spreading with the market." The "new" unionism of the 1870s was class oriented and some unions embraced the revolutionary struggle and extended their philosophy to that of the "one big union." However, as Howard notes in the first major class-based confrontation (of the 1890s) with employers, the unions lost, were all but wiped out, and retired at once from the industrial field. The confrontations of the 1890s spread across the Tasman and involved the industrial unions of seamen, stevedores, and miners, challenging employers and the state.

In Australia, the issue of state control of industrial conflict was debated at the constitutional conferences during the 1890s. Some colonies experimented with arbitration legislation during the period. In New Zealand, the reaction of the state was faster. In 1894 the Industrial Conciliation and Arbitration Act became law, providing *inter alia* for the registration of trade unions (in fact, the original statute was subtitled, in part "An Act to encourage the formation of industrial unions . . . ") and the resolution of industrial disputes by compulsory arbitration within a Court of Arbitration framework. The IC and A Act of 1894 was, at least in part, a reflection of "a movement for state regulation of industrial relations by a community determined it should not again be subjected to the discomforts of widespread industrial warfare" (Woods 1963). The parallel statute in Australia emerged ten years later as the Commonwealth Conciliation and Arbitration Act of 1904. One object of that Act was, and still is, "to encourage the organization of representative bodies of employers and employees and their registration under this Act" (S. 2).

Howard (1977) sees the New Zealand example as the dominant influence on the Australian statute. His direct linking oversimplifies the bilateral debate of the late 1880s and early 1890s, the interchange of ideas, philosophies, and proposed plans of action, between the colonies of the Australian mainland and New Zealand (see, for example, McIntryre and Mitchell 1989; Pember-Reeves 1968). Cross-fertilization produced the similarity of legislative approach. But the outcomes that Howard ascribed for the Australian situation are equally appropriate to the New Zealand case. The legislation overcame two problems of contemporary labor, not just in Australia, but in both countries. First, compulsory arbitration negated the problem of how weak unions would force recognition from strong employers (a third party would determine whether a union was legitimate party to a dispute and would prescribe the outcome of that dispute without regard to relative strength). Second, nonunion labor became increasingly less attractive to employers as awards emerging from the arbitration machinery were statutorily applicable to union and nonunion employees.

Also, such awards in both countries soon began to prescribe various elements of preference for unionists in employment, further enhancing the position of unions. In addition, the registration of rules provided legally enforceable demarcation of membership territory for the unions. The new regime in both countries was viewed as the substitution of the rule of law and order for the use of strike action. Consequently, the legislation in each country supported enforcement by a state agency, the Arbitration Court, with penalties that could be imposed in respect to unlawful acts, including specified strikes, and a policy of direct government intervention to regulate and control strike action, as and when deemed necessary.

It can also be noted that the common heritage also extended to a development and perpetuation of a common mythology of unionism based on struggle, class division, and oppression by the capitalist and the state. After the 1890s, in each country some unions continued to embrace the class struggle and opposition to the capitalist ideology, but the mythology really becomes more and more just that.

The Specific Case: The Wellington Shop Assistants Union

The Wellington Amalgamated Society of Shop Assistants Union was formed in 1936 as an amalgamation of four unions, the Wellington Operative Butchers (formed 1898-1899), the Grocery Employees Union (1899), the Napier Shop Assistants (1908-10) and the Wellington Softgoods Employees (1912).

A union of butchers was first formed in Wellington in 1890, but soon ceased to function. Another attempt was made in 1898 (the union was officially registered on 1 November 1898), and at that time a log of claims was served on the Master Butchers Association, under the provisions of the recently passed IC and A Act. One meeting was held with the employers to discuss the log, and although a decision to file the dispute with the "Court" was taken, no further progress was made. Meetings in early 1899 lapsed for want of a quorum, and one agenda showed a "notice of motion" to reduce the number for a quorum. A quorum was fifteen members, one less, in fact, than the number of members on the committee established to draft the union rules and log. Despite the legislative props of the IC and A Act, the union ceased to function. Later that year, on 3 October, a meeting of butchers endorsed the motion "that the Wellington Operative Butchers Union be reconstructed" (Hince, Peace, and Biggs 1990). This time the log did go before the

Conciliation Board for negotiation and to the Arbitration Court to resolve the failure to agree.

The first award covering members of the Wellington Operative Butchers Union was handed down in July 1900, covering, *inter alia,* minimum wage rate for adults and juniors, maximum hours of work, and a restriction on the number of boys who could be employed (one to every three men). Each of the other constituent unions of the 1936 amalgamation received award coverage in the same way, soon after formation and registration. However, it must be emphasized that the Butchers Union received award coverage despite a frequent inability to achieve a quorum of members at meetings held to plan or endorse action. In the case of the Softgoods Union, financial membership was only one hundred and fourteen members at the time of formation, 22 March 1912, but an award was obtained by the middle of that year.

Compliance with the procedural rules of the IC and A Act for the resolution of disputes and acceptance of the constraints on the use of strike action (and penalties for breach) was the principle *quid pro quo* conceded by the registered unions. It was also necessary to accept external control of many aspects of the internal affairs of the organization (generally, but not exclusively, pertaining to the mode of operation and financial accountability). The cliche, that registration accords both rights and obligations, became part of the liturgy of the arbitration state. It was also part of the award system that an inspectorate of a state agency, (the Department of Labor) and the general Court system, were central to the enforcement of the minimum terms and conditions of employment encompassed by these awards. As Walsh (1991) notes, these unions " . . . tended to be highly centralized, with very limited opportunity for membership participation, and weakly organized at lower levels with almost no effective workplace presence." Under arbitration the need for, and role of, union power and on-the-job action was avoided, or where it had existed it was eroded.

The effects of statutory change on the formation and growth of unions in New Zealand was dramatic, paralleling the similar pattern discerned in Australia by Howard (1977). It is estimated that in 1894 there were 8,000 members in 70 unions (Roth 1973). By 1896 there were 75 unions registered under the IC and A Act; by mid-1900 the number was 133. Union membership was estimated at 14,480 in 1896. By 1907, 290 unions with 45,614 members were registered.

The dramatic growth in the number of individual unions need be specifically noted. Such unions were typically small in size, regional and occupational in jurisdiction, limited in resources, and restricted in the scope of their activities. (Walsh 1991).

The next spurt of growth occurred in 1936 after the first Labor government amended the IC and A Act to prescribe that every award and agreement registered under the Act should provide for union membership as a condition of employment for all employees over 18 years of age. The number of shop employees in unions throughout the country had increased markedly. By 1935, there were 25 shop assistants unions of one kind or another registered under the IC and A Act. Together they had a combined membership of 3,778. Two years on aggregate membership of registered shop assistants unions had reached 17,351. The Wellington Shop Assistants Union shared in this growth. The aggregate picture shown in Table 1 indicates the same dramatic change:

Table 1

Year	No. of unions	Members
1935	410	80,829
1936	489	185,527
1937	499	233,986

Source: Roth (1973) from Department of Labor data.

Growth as a result of legislative act by the state is one thing; the nature of the expanded organization is another. The assessment of Walsh is referred to above. Woods (1963) asserts further that the compulsory unionism provision was one where a minority of unions and unionists held the view that such a provision "saps the initiative and real strength and solidarity of a trade union by the inclusion of lukewarm, apathetic, and even unsympathetic members." The 1936 amendments also prescribed a limit on the level of union subscriptions—a limit which could only be changed by further legislation or by a "decision of meeting of the union of which every member had received seven days' notice in writing . . . " (Woods 1963). In the case of the Wellington Shop Assistants Union, these fees, set legislatively, first at 1s. per week in 1936 and soon after at 2s. per week, were not increased again until 1966. Further provisions of the 1936 Act empowered the inclusion of a "right of entry clause" in an award, and rights of union officials to meet with members at the workplace.

Woods' reaction to the New Zealand provisions reflects the views of Howard formed from Australian experience:

> These various provisions relating to trade unions considerably increased their status and privileges under the Industrial Concil-iation and Arbitration Act. They also increased the reliance of trade unions on the Act. They were made more dependant on the Court than ever before . . .
>
> . . . it would be reasonable to expect the quality of trade union leadership to deteriorate. A union assured of its membership and its revenue by legislation could be expected to show two symp-toms of degeneration—a falling off in the fighting initiative of executives who no longer had to convince workers of the advan-tages of membership or to maintain an adequate personal rela-tionship with the individual members to retain that membership; and a tendency to shift union discussions from the practical situation in the industry to the more remote topics of political platforms (Woods 1963).

For the Wellington Shop Assistants Union, the major day-to-day tasks were maintaining the appropriate award coverage for existing members and helping to extend award coverage to other shop assistants. In the former situation the requirement was met by serving, from time to time, a log of claims to enhance the existing terms and conditions and by supporting that claim through the formal channels of a Conciliation Board and, if necessary, the Arbitration Court. In the latter situation the process involved serv-ing a log seeking coverage of the additional group of workers. An award would be made by the Court and, given the compulsory unionism provisions in awards of the period, union membership would increase accordingly.

When significant blockages developed or failures occurred, the Wellington Shop Assistants Union, in line with the general reaction noted by Woods (1963), turned to political leverage (rather than industrial action). One such instance followed the refusal of the Arbitration Court to extend to shop assistants the forty-hour working week, granted in 1937 to employees in manufacturing. Legislative change had enabled the Court to make reductions in the standard hours of work in the light of the circumstances of the trade and industry. The Court held that such a reduction was not practicable for the retail industry. The union commenced a campaign of political lobbying. Although the union was affiliated to the New Zealand Labor Party (the party of government at that time), the lobbying was unsuccessful. The reaction of disappointment was to withdraw party affiliation.

During the 1960s, union resistance to extended trading hours largely involved administratively opposing and delaying the spread of exceptions to the general provisions of the legislation. The Shops and Offices Act, as amended in 1955, continued the power of the Arbitration Court to fix the opening and closing hours of shops in awards, but it also created a class of "exempted goods" that could be sold at any time. The union continued to oppose extensions to the list, report offenders to the Department of Labor, and monitor the enforcement.

While an initial intent of the arbitration statutes in both Australia and New Zealand was to encourage bargaining, that reality was never achieved. There has always been bargaining within the arbitration framework, but both the process and the outcomes have been dominated by mandatory state-provided third-party assistance (conciliation), the ultimate availability of compulsory arbitration in all disputes (including interest disputes), and severe legal punitive constraints on strike action. In fact, the Australasian experience, dating back to the 1890s and early 1900s, is the earliest and longest test of the view that emerged much later in North America of the inhibiting, stultifying effect of compulsory arbitration on "real" bargaining in interest disputes.

From time to time bargaining outside of the third-party intervention system (termed over-award bargaining in Australia, second-tier bargaining in New Zealand) did occur, but it has been infrequent, appearing particularly in periods of tight labor markets, and then in specific areas of the market (skills, remote location, for example). Further, such bargaining has been incremental, or additive to the base award, and marginal, in the aggregative sense, to the impact of the centralized third-party system.

The Wellington Shop Assistants Union did not conduct its first strike action until 1972, when a series of stopwork meetings were held to discuss a lack of progress in award negotiations. In 1977, a strike of all members, one-day for some, two-day for others, occurred against a backdrop of government moves to extend shop trading hours. In the 1970s and 1980s, several cases of localized strike action occurred, but in no way does the overall pattern distort the view that the union had continued to develop as an "arbitration" union par excellence. And in this way it was typical of the pattern of the mainstream of New Zealand trade unionism of the 20th century.

The essential nature of so-called "arbitration" unions is determined by the conditions of registration, the provision of preference or compulsory unionism, and the legislative provisions compelling the parties to settle differences, ultimately, by arbitration. In the case of the shop employees' unions, the generally conservative, trade status, and career conscious nature of most members was added to these external forces.

Four major characteristics of an "arbitration" union derived from these forces. The first was meticulous management. Careful attention was paid at all times to detailed organization, financial prudence, and accountability. Meetings were called by proper notice, minutes kept, and reports prepared. Members' funds were accounted for with regular audited reports and were carefully husbanded. A second characteristic of the "arbitration" union was that running the union was left to a very small group of enthusiasts. For these members union business involved a continual round of executive, monthly, quarterly, annual, and special meetings. The third characteristic was that the maintenance, interpretation, and enforcement of the award was the fundamental and central task of the union. This activity represented the major service for its membership, and officials took immense pride in the detail involved, overcoming the difficulties encountered, and even in the time spent on it all. The fourth characteristic, that of lobbying and persuasion (that is, working through established political processes), was seen as an ancillary means of furthering members' needs. The Wellington Shop Assistants Union, and other "arbitration" unions, adopted each of these characteristics, rather than those of the strike, and participation in the heart of the class struggle. Leadership was in the hands of officials who were solid and accountable administrators, well versed in industrial law and the practices of conciliation and arbitration.

Unionism, as an institution, prospered under these conditions, and the needs of the state for regulation and control of industrial affairs were satisfied. By 1951, the number of registered unions (415) reached a peak. Membership at that time was 272,843, and the average size of unions was 657 members. In general, aggregate membership expanded with the growth of employment. Prior to 1936, unions could only register under the IC and A Act for coverage of a category of employees in a single industrial district. New Zealand was divided administratively into eight industrial districts. Hence, a state-based rationale existed for union proliferation and limited industrial strength. A reversal of this policy, with a legislative change in 1936 permitting multidistrict unions, began a process of consolidation, concentration of membership, and growth in the average size of unions. By 1953 despite an average union size of 704 members, 74 percent of union members were in unions with 1,000 members or more, and 36 percent in unions with 5,000 members or more. Again, the centrality of the influence of action by the state in shaping the industrial labor movement is illustrated.

Exceptions that Prove the Rule

It has been conceded that the unions of the 19th century, in both Australia and New Zealand, accorded more to the presumptions of the Euro-American theorists. Craft unions behaved as Perlman and Commons described and predicted, focussing on job scarcity, responding to pressures of the market, seeking to control the job, and utilizing collective action to pursue members needs. "New" unionism emerging in the 1870s and centered on the industrial and occupational unionism of miners, seafarers, shearers, wharf laborers and transport workers, was class-based, a product of a capitalist/worker clash of needs, and pursued collective action (the union contract) with a radical militant ideology. Organization and action was a direct challenge to the state. The unionization of these groups of workers, their collective demands, and the associated strikes of the 1890s, in both Australia and New Zealand, provoked a similar legislative response in each country (the respective Conciliation and Arbitration Acts).

In New Zealand, during the early years of the 20th century, some unions continued to seek progress by militant action and maintained a degree of independence from the state-imposed machinery. The first overt defiance of the arbitration system by a registered union was a short strike by Auckland tramwaymen in 1906. In 1908, a three-month strike of coal miners at Blackball, on the West Coast of the South Island, was a more substantial challenge. In both cases militancy brought clea · success. In Auckland, reinstatement of two conductors dismissed for refusing to obey a management directive to train learners was achieved. At Blackball both the substantive issue, an increase in crib (lunch) time, and reinstatement of dismissed strike leaders, were achieved. The demonstration effect was dramatic.

The New Zealand Federation of Miners (soon renamed the New Zealand Federation of Labor) was formed. The Federation adopted the preamble of the International Workers of the World (IWW) in its constitution (it came to be known by the term Red-Fed), declined to register under the IC and A Act, and began a process of seeking agreements from employers outside the Court. West Coast workers, shearers and wharf laborers joined the miners in the Federation. By 1912-13, some 15,000 unionists, approximately one-fifth of all union members, were part of, or supported, the notion of the Federation and were rallying behind an organization that openly proclaimed the class struggle and the overthrow of the capitalist system. (Roth 1973, Olssen 1988). Strikes by miners at Waihi and Reefton in 1912 and by waterside workers in Wellington in 1913, the latter to become the basis for a call for a general strike, challenged the state and provoked a progressive acceleration in the level of response by the state. At a peak, the 1913 strike action involved 16,000 unionists including 2,000 seamen, 5,000 wharf laborers and 4,000 miners (Roth 1973).

The reactions of government in 1912 and 1913 included widespread use of volunteers to undertake work and of police and special volunteers to protect the "scab" labor. The "exclusive coverage" provisions of the Arbitration Act were used to register new unions as a legal alternative to some of the striking unions that had cancelled registration under the Act. Action taken in the Supreme Court produced *inter alia* a ruling that unions registered under the

the IC and A Act could not use funds in support of the strike. In fact, many "arbitration" unions, including the Wellington Butchers, had refused financial aid, but the ruling did mean a traditional way of expressing solidarity was denied.

Further, the government passed the Labor Disputes Investigation Act, removing the immunity from penalties for certain strike action by unions not registered under the IC and A Act. In addition, disputes involving such nonregistered unions could be notified to the Minister of Labor and a compulsory conference established before a Labor Disputes Committee (effectively an ad-hoc Arbitration Court). A mandatory secret ballot prior to strike action then became a further bureaucratic inhibition to militancy. The 1913 strike collapsed, and the Red-Fed disintegrated, with some segments becoming associated with the more dominant "arbitration" union movement in the development of an alternative trade union center, and the establishment of a political grouping, a Labor Party. A rump of militant, class-based, industrial struggle-oriented unionism did remain, centered around the waterfront, freezing workers, seamen and miners. A continuing tension did exist between the "militant" minority and the "arbitrationist" majority as to which sector was the prime driving force for union development. The militants argued that it was gains in the industrial arena that were translated into the arbitrationist awards.

However, a further, and arguably the last, major, militant expression of this ideology occurred in 1951. Once more the Wellington waterfront was the setting. The stoppage, a strike or lockout according to the perspective, commenced on 9 February 1951 and continued for 151 days. A number of specific state-sponsored measures were taken. Unions, including the Waterside Workers Union, involved in strike action were deregistered, and alternative unions formed and registered. Emergency regulations were promulgated under which the strike was declared unlawful, funds of striking unions were frozen, precluding financial support for the strikers, and awards were suspended. The regulations permitted, and use was made of, the armed forces to work the waterfront.

Internal division within the labor movement alerted government to the situation whereby a significant majority of unions viewed the strike as a threat to the arbitration system. Such unions, while perhaps not agreeing with specific actions of government, implicitly endorsed the intended result of the actions. Woods (1963) summarized the position, asserting that

> ... the strike was defeated mainly by the firm opposition of trade unionism to undermine the traditional law-abiding procedures of conciliation and arbitration and to impose a pattern of organization and order which New Zealand trade unionism and the New Zealand community did not like.

Not only was the origin, and pattern of growth, of New Zealand trade unions due to the needs and mechanisms of the arbitral system, but a central goal of unionism became the perpetuation of that system. In both 1913 and 1951, that part of the union movement which had sought to determine its own destiny (see Howard 1977) was brushed aside by a combination of the power of the state and the dominant strand of "arbitration" unions.

More Recent Evidence: New Zealand

Recent events in New Zealand have reaffirmed the validity of the contentions of Howard vis-a-vis the role of the state in shaping unions and have also provided a potential basis for a longitudinal test of elements of his approach. In 1983, government abolished compulsory unionism, while a change of government in 1984 saw this position reversed. The state was continuing to seek to shape unionism. The Labor Relations Act 1987 continued this thrust. It contained, *inter alia,* a provision raising the minimum size for registered unions to 1,000 members (from a range of 10 to 40 members depending on geographic coverage of the union). The results were dramatic, and Table 2 illustrates the speed and extent of the state-sponsored reshaping of trade unionism.

The full impact of this intervention has not had time to develop, for even more recent events have led to the abandonment, after almost one hundred years, of the centrality of the relationship of trade unions and the state in the industrial relations system of New Zealand.

Table 2. Number and Size of Union — New Zealand

Year	1000	1000+	Total
Dec. 1986 (No.)	147	76	223[1]
(%)	65.9	34.1	100
April 1988 (No.)	135	97	232
(%)	58.2	41.8	100
April 1989 (No.)	69	99	168
(%)	41.1	58.9	100
Sept. 1989 (No.)	19	93	112
(%)	17.0	83.0	100

[1] Excludes 31 public sector unions brought under the Labor Relations Act on 1 April 1988.

Source: Fuller (1989).

The Employment Contracts Act of 1991 again abandoned compulsory unionism. It also abandoned the concept of registration of unions. In fact, the statute does not include a single reference to the notion of trade unions or trade unionism. All sections of earlier legislation dealing with union rules, membership, financial accountability, and elections within unions have been repealed. All exclusive rights previously accorded to unions, including the rights to represent workers in collective negotiations and in processing grievances, have been explicitly withdrawn. While unions are free to play a role in industrial relations under the Employment Contracts Act, they no longer have automatic and exclusive rights in the workplace. The statute uses the term "employee organization," but such organizations are accorded neither registered status, nor any of the historic rights that pertained to trade unions. It is provided that unions are to be incorporated under a 1908 statute that provides for incorporation and regulation of societies which are not established for pursuing economic gain. In this way, the rights of unions to enter contracts, recover debts, and to finance operations, are protected. But wider and more substantial rights and controls built up under the IC and A Act 1894, and its successors, have been abandoned. Compulsory arbitration of interest disputes has been finally abandoned, and the "award" system dismantled. The statute emphasises individual employment contracts, reversing the previous assumption of the centrality of the collective contract.

Further social and legislative change may emerge. For the moment, however, neither the perception that the state and a state-sponsored dispute-settling system are central to industrial relationships, nor the view that registered unions are a necessary requirement, are part of the New Zealand scene. If the regime of the Employment Contracts Act continues, then a longitudinal test of our "Australasian" model will be possible. New Zealand unions of the late 20th and early 21st centuries operating within market capitalism, reacting to competition, and accommodating to the market, may by then accord more and more to the Commons and Perlman models.

Conclusion: Some General Principles and Further Work

Several general principles of potential value to the development of labor union theory emerge from the Australasian experience. These are as follows.

1. Contrary to theory developed in Europe and North America, trade unions, even in capitalist countries, are not universally a reaction to the insecurity created for working people by competitive markets. Under certain circumstances unions may be creatures of government policy and legislation.

2. Governments in capitalist countries are capable of taking action which will shape not only union behavior but also union character. To a significant extent, "arbitration unions" in Australasia were arms of the state rather than independent representatives of worker interests. In this sense the Australasian case supports the syndicalist notion that all government action is to be mistrusted and that unions must depend only on their own means or suffer

negative consequences with respect to their mission as agents of worker interests.

3. If government action, and not arbitration legislation per se, is the effective variable there is a prima facie case for a broader reevaluation of the role of the state in explaining "unionism." The impact of legislative change on unionism in the recent years of the Thatcher government in the United Kingdom warrants examination in this respect. In the United States, for example, unions have learned to function effectively under the Wagner Act, but are apparently incapable of acting effectively outside of its confines. It is not necessary for unions to be certified in the United States to bargain collectively and to go on strike, but unions almost never make use of that right because they have become addicted to the procedures elicited by legislation.

4. Between about 1900 and 1940, almost all of the then industrialized countries passed legislation designed to control industrial conflicts—the methods used varied considerably. Detailed comparative research would most likely show that such legislation had significant effects on union behavior in each country, although probably not as dramatic as in the Australasian case.

Questions of whether unions are intrinsically weak or whether they have served their members well are valid questions, but are not those addressed by Howard. He seeks a theoretical basis for explaining the origin, growth, and purpose of trade unions. He asserts that elsewhere (than Australia) the social consensus that has legitimized unions had typically been reached between already powerful unions which could no longer be denied, employers, and governments. In the Australian case, society passed to government the task of creating an industrial relations mechanism which would provide a measure of peace and which would shield the whole society from the distasteful effects of industrial struggles. (Howard 1977.)

The New Zealand case accords to that outlined by Howard. The specific instance of the Wellington Shop Assistants Union, the general example of "arbitration unions," and the role of the state and the "arbitration" unions in containing radicalism, each independently and collectively support this view. Thus, in both the New Zealand and Australian cases, a theory of trade unionism needs to incorporate an identifiable determinism for the state and specified agencies of the state, for in each country their role has been pervasive and dominant. A universal or general theory of unionism must recognize the impact of the state. While the Australasian model provides the strongest evidence, and the more direct links, it is neverthelss likely that wider historical and comparative research would establish a more general basis for recognizing the role of the state in a general theory of unionism.

Works Cited

Barbash, J. 1989, "John R Commons and the Western Industrial Relations Tradition," in *Recent Trends in Industrial Relations Studies and Theory*, Volume V, Proceedings of the 8th World Congress, International Industrial Relations Association, pp. 139-52.

Chamberlain, N. W. 1965, *The Labor Sector*, New York: McGraw-Hill.

Commons, J. R. 1968, "American Shoemakers, 1648-1895," in *Readings in Labor Economics and Labor Relations*, eds. R. L. Rowan and H. R. Northrup, Homewood, IL: Richard D. Irwin. Originally published in *The Quarterly Journal of Economics*, vol. 24.

Dunlop, J. 1968, "The Development of Labor Organization: A Theoretical Framework," in *Readings in Labor Economics and Labor Relations*, eds. R. L. Rowan and H. R. Northrup, Homewood, IL: Richard D. Irwin. Originally published in *Insights into Labor Issues*, eds. R. A. Lister and J. Shister, New York: Macmillan, 1948.

Fuller, C. 1989, "The Functioning of the Labor Relations Act 1987 Unions," in *Evaluating the Labor Relations Act 1987*, ed R. Harbridge, Wellington, New Zealand: Industrial Relations Center.

Gardner, M. 1989, "Union strategy: A Gap in Union Theory," in *Australian Unions: An Industrial Relations Perspective*, 2nd ed., eds. B. Ford and D. Plowman, Melbourne: Macmillan.

Griffin, G., and V. Scarcebrook. 1990, "The Dependency Theory of Trade Unionism and the Role of the Industrial Registrar," *Australian Bulletin of Labor Studies*, vol. 16, no. 1, pp. 21-31.

Hince, K. W., K. Taylor, J. Peace, and M. Biggs. 1990, *Opening Hours: History of the Wellington Shop Employees Union*, Wellington, New Zealand: Industrial Relations Center.

Holt, J. 1986, *Compulsory Arbitration in New Zealand the First Forty Years*, Auckland: Auckland University Press.

Howard, W. A. 1977, "Australian Trade Unions in the Context of Union Theory," *Journal of Industrial Relations*, vol. 19, no. 3, pp. 255-73.

_____. 1983, "Trade Unions and the Arbitration System," in *State and Economy in Australia*, ed. B. W. Head, Oxford: Oxford University Press.

Macintyre, S., and R. Mitchell, eds. 1989, *Foundations of Arbitration: The Origins and Effects of State Compulsory Arbitration*, Melbourne: Oxford University Press.

Olssen, E. 1988, *The Red Feds*, Auckland: Oxford University Press.

Pember-Reeves, W. 1968, *State Experiments in Australia and New Zealand*, Volume 2, Melbourne: Macmillan. Originally published 1902.

Perlman, S. 1928, *Theory of the Labor Movement*, New York: Macmillan.

Polanyi, K. 1944, *The Great Transformation*, New York: Holt, Rinehart and Winston.

Roth, H. 1973, *Trade Unions in New Zealand*, Wellington: Reed Education.

Tannenbaum, F. 1921, *The Labor Movement, Its Conservative Functions and Social Consequences*, New York: G. P. Putnam's Sons.

Walsh, P. 1991, *Trade Unions in New Zealand and Economic Restructuring*, Working Paper No 17, Sydney: ACIRRT.

Webb, S. , and B. Webb. 1926[1897], *Industrial Democracy*, London: Longman Green.

Woods, N. S. 1963, *Industrial Conciliation and Arbitration in New Zealand*, Wellington: Government Printer.

Industrial Relations:Theorizing for a Global Perspective

Michael Poole

The far reaching political and economic transformations of the modern era are characterized by an accelerating pace of movement with market systems becoming increasingly ascendant. It scarcely needs emphasizing that these eventualities were not typically countenanced by industrial relations analysts ten or twenty years ago when corporatism and socialism were generally considered to be far more likely outcomes. Yet few would wish to propound the view that the current situation is inevitable, let alone the outcome of a deterministic "iron law" of history. Clearly, then, any attempt to formulate global theories of industrial relations in a rapidly changing international order is likely to prove daunting and problematic. Hence, in this contribution, some of the building blocks of general conceptual models are established, rather than an attempt being made to establish predictive theories of the future shape and dynamic operation of the world's industrial relations systems.

This chapter commences with a revisitation of the thesis that there is a broad trend to convergence in industrial relations sytems. The argument is that there are new forces for convergence evident in the internationalization process, but there remain no less compelling reasons for assuming that variety and diversity will characterize industrial relations in the future. The main models for

The author wishes to thank Roy Adams and Jack Barbash for valuable comments on an earlier draft of this chapter.

understanding diversity are then presented. A spatial model involves isolating the importance of strategic choice and identifies differences in the wider environment of industrial relations, as well as in power relations and institutional processes.

A temporal model is then specified in which the focus in on the process of institutionalization and their propensity to operate to some extent independently of wider environmental conditions.

Convergence Revisited

The first attempt to formulate a general theory of international industrial relations is usually traced to Clark Kerr and his colleagues' (1960) seminal work, *Industrialism and Industrial Man,* though in subsequent discussions, its central arguments have been frequently misinterpreted. To be sure, Kerr et al. envisaged a convergence to a *greater* degree of uniformity in the world's industrial relations systems in the future. Moreover, the central logic of industrialism or "common denominator" was seen to stem from the homogenizing forces of new technology. And a wide variety of sources of uniformity were identified that included history and homogeneity, technology and society, the push of progress, education and equality, government and enterprise, and the "compulsion of comparisons." But various potent "threads of diversity" were also isolated that included the persistence of strategies, the imprint of culture, the hour clock of evolution, the culture of industry and "people and performance." And the upshot was that

... pluralistic industrialism will never reach a final equilibrium. The contest between the forces for uniformity and for diversity will give it life and movement and change. This is a contest which will never reach an ultimate solution. Manager and managed also will struggle all up and down the line of hierarchies all around the world; quiet but often desperate little battles will be fought all over the social landscape.

The uniformity that draws on technology, and the diversity that draws on individuality; the authority that stems from the managers, and the rebellion, however muted, that stems from the managed these are destined to be the everlasting threads of the future. They will continue in force when class war, and the contest over private versus public initiative, and the battle between the monistic and atomistic ideologies all have been left far behind in the sedimentary layers of history. (277)

This position was further developed by Kerr (1983) in the *Future of Industrial Societies* where the idea of a relatively wide range of possible industrial relations patterns within pluralistic industrialization was reaffirmed and extended. Indeed, although various elements of "current comparability" and "increasing similarity" were noted an extensive range of areas of "continuing substantial dissimilarity" between the world's economic and industrial relations systems was also observed. This applied not least in the areas of ideology and patterns of belief.

The tools of production may be the same in industrial societies but religions remain different, national and ethnic divisions continue largely intact, ideas about the highest goals of society retain their contrasts, and even national personality and cultural traits endure. Currently, in fact, there seems to be a revolt in several parts of the world against homogenization of peoples and in favor of the preservation of their group identities . . .

Tradition is likely to persist particularly where there is no one clearly better way (for example, religious beliefs), where strong institutions are established to support it (such as the nation-state and the church), and where the innate human desire for a characteristic identity is not too costly to material results. Tradition also incorporates the wisdom of the past; helps people make choices among alternative patterns of behaviors; and serves as starting point for discussion of the benefits of change.

In the early 1990s, there may well have been a new pattern of convergence in industrial relations systems. There is thus a significant dependence on markets and free enterprise, coupled with trade unions and and employers relatively free from government intervention, and extensive collective bargaining and tripartite consultation. This is occurring not only in the former communist nations but also in the dynamic Asian economies and in Africa and South

America. There remains substatial differences between the democratic market countries, but globally there have been some far reaching convergent trends in industrial relations systems.

But new technology is clearly not the only (or even the main) force behind this movement. Indeed, at least four main forces for similarity in industrial relations are currently identifiable:

1. Markets and global competition;
2. The internationalization of knowledge;
3. The internationalization of production; and
4. New technology.

More specifically, markets appear have advantages over planned systems (at least in peacetime) for satisfying consumer wants. This situation is reinforced by global competition which ensures strategic advantages for particular nations and organizations in supplying consumer requirements. Of course, whether or not this situation will continue is debatable; for example, it is conceivable that environmental exigencies could lead to the need to suppress consumer wants in a way which only planned systems could effectively accomplish. But currently ascendant consumer and market-driven objectives are reflected in the stress on flexibility in the employment relationship and *not least, in a downgrading of the historical importance accorded to the worker within industrial relations analysis and debate.*

A further force underpinning the modern convergence is the vital role of knowledge that occurs at two different levels. The first is in the "compulsion of comparisons" alluded to by Kerr and his colleagues (269).

Man everywhere wants progress and participation, The two are to some extent substitutes for each other, and often progress will be accepted for a time in lieu of participation; but in the end industrial man wants both and will keep pressing for both. Progress means a higher standard of education, better health, more consumer goods and services; participation means choice of jobs, choice of consumer goods, a chance to influence those who guide society itself. These same pressures develop regardless of culture and ideology.

The pressures for progress and participation are enhanced by the world-wide character of industrialization, by international trade, by travel, and by the exchange of ideas. We may never reach Sir William Beveridge's utopia where each man could pick and choose around the world the society he would like to live in; but already people are making comparisons, and these comparisons are having their impact. Generally the impact will be to bring greater uniformity in the nature of the societal product which people widely judge to be the best. People may not be willing to settle for much less in their own system than the standards and performance of competing systems.

The second area is in actual organizations where knowledge of different principles and parties has spread across global frontiers. The increasing emulation of Japanese patterns of employment and employee relations (e.g., single union agreements) is one obvious example of this development.

Convergence in the modern era also stems from international-ization which as Hendry (1991, 415-16) has argued rests on three developments.

1. The increasing internationalization of business, which brings organizations into contact with different national cultures and promotes the spread of management practices across national boundaries;

2. Underlying economic and technological trends, arising in part from the activity of multinational firms but mediated also by international institutions, which may produce sim-ilar patterns of adjustment in the organization and manage-ment of employment at the national, sectoral, and firm level; and

3. The processes whereby businesses become progres-sively international. In particular, the activities of multina-tional enterprises, joint partnerships, and supranational institutions (e.g., the European Community) have all been contributing to greater similarity in industrial relations institutions and processes across national frontiers. Exam-

ples include companies such as IBM and MacDonalds which have relatively uniform industrial relations practices worldwide.

Finally, there is the impact of new technology. Its effects are by no means deterministic, but its current importance is probably no less than at the time when Kerr and his colleagues viewed this as central to the logic of industrialism. The microelectronics revolution is a worldwide influence and, although in industrial relations, it is still feasible for major differences to occur, it is still reasonable to regard new technology as a potent force for similarity. (For a sociological analysis of convergence and technology, see Form 1979).

There are, then, several modern forces for convergence in industrial relations systems. But, the forces for dissimilarity are no less insistent. These include cultural values and ideologies, political and economic conditions, the institutional framework for industrial relations, the power of the actors, and various temporal movements. In particular, new nations may evolve along different trajectories of development from the West and hence emerge with different industrial relations systems (for instance, in respect to the role of the state and legislature and types of trade union). And this may partly override some other homongenizing forces. For instance, international standards and an "ideal model" established by the International Labor Organization (ILO) have had a substantial impact on industrial relations in many developing countries. The World Bank and International Monetary Fund (IMF) also encourage developments in this direction with the result that few nations now specifically outlaw trade unions and collective bargaining.

Diversity in Industrial Relations Systems

How, then, do we explain diversity in industrial relations systems? The most obvious starting point is an action perspective and an emphasis on the importance of choice. In most industrial relations systems, the three main "actors" (employers and managers, labor, and the state) thus have some measure of determination over institutional arrangements; and this builds a high degree of potential diversity into industrial relations systems given the differences in

Figure 1. Strategic choices of the actors

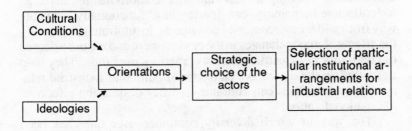

objectives and power balances which are in practice feasible. Moreover, strategic choices have a potential significance as a potent force for stability *and* change (see Kochan, Katz, and McKersie 1986).

But if we are to build a satisfactory spatial model of diversity and similarity in industrial relations systems, the forces which help to shape strategic choices also require identification. After all, the choices of the actors are focussed by orientations which are, in turn, affected by cultural conditions and ideologies. (See Figure 1.)

It is also vital to note the importance of the distribution of power in the shaping of actual industrial relations outcomes. Whether or not given actors are able to achieve their objectives depends on a process of interaction and struggle and the marshalling of different power resources. These, in turn, are linked with, but not determined

Figure 2. Action, power, and structure

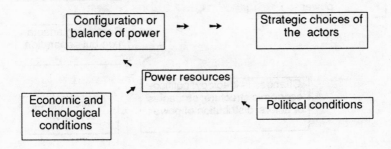

by, wider political, economic, and technological conditions. (See Figure 2.)

A temporal model focuses particularly on processes of institutionalization. This implies that industrial relations institutions (e.g., for collective bargaining) can develop in a "functionally" separate way from wider environmental conditions. Institutions thus modify the effects of major changes in the environment and ensure a degree of continuity in industrial relations practices over time. They help us to explain the distinctive character of particular industrial relations systems which can continue to differ despite the effects of internationalization.

The way in which diversity continues over time has been developed in *Industrial Relations* (Poole 1986, 202-3). The basic model is set out in Figure 3 where the "functional" separation and autonomy for institutions is shown.

At the point when industrial relations institutions become established (or a major development departs from existing arrange-

Figure 3. "Functional" separation

The "functional" separation of institutions from environmental conditions: the maintenance of diversity between industrial relations systems

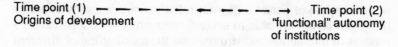

Time point (1) — — — — — — — — → Time point (2)
Origins of development   "functional" autonomy
                                                              of institutions

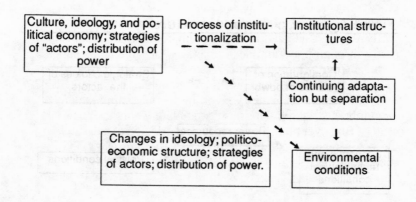

Figure 4. Convergence and divergence

Recent patterns of convergence and divergence in actual industrial relations outcomes

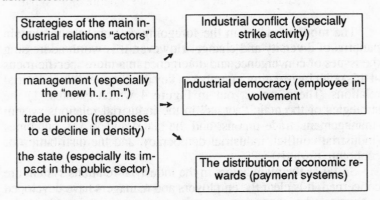

ments), the pattern is the outcome of distinctive strategies of the "actors"—in specific cultural, ideological, and politicoeconomic conditions and with a given distribution of power. *But once institutional structures take root they can continue without major change for prolonged periods, despite marked alterations in, say, political and economic conditions.* This is partly because of efforts of those in dominant roles in the institutions concerned who have a clear interest in "organizational survival" (see Flanders 1970), but also because of processes of socialization (at induction and in committee proceedings and so on) which ensure that new recruits continue to sustain the established machinery. To be sure, institutions do change partly through adaptation to new environmental circumstances, partly through a gradual decline as new arrangements supersede them, and partly through radical transformation in "crisis" periods. In this respect, the importance of the social and economic dislocations consequent upon the two world wars on institutional *development* in industrial relations has been recently emphasized by Price (1991). But, over time, they can develop a degree of autonomy from the environmental conditions in which they are situated and, as such, comprise a valuable explanation for the persistence of national differences. Thus, the institutions of collective bargaining in

the United Kingdom appear to have largely survived the Thatcher
years (MacInnes 1987, Mansfield and Poole 1991).

Continuing Diversity?

The models set out in the foregoing section help to explain
patterns of diversity and change. However, it is worth addressing
the issues of convergence and divergence in a more specific focus
at this point by isolating a number of key developments in industrial
relations. These are set out in Figure 4 which isolates: 1) the
strategies of the main "actors" in the industrial relations system
(management, trade unions, and the state) and 2) key outcomes
(industrial conflict, industrial democracy, and the distribution of
economic rewards).

So far as the main actors in the industrial relations system are
concerned, it is clear the employers and managers have developed
sophisticated human resource management strategies (these are
referred to as the "new" human resources management (HRM) in
North America) and these efforts are likely to continue in the future.
An important reason is that employees of companies are increasingly viewed as the key to competitive success. Indeed, with respect
to Europe, as Krulis-Randa (1990, 138) has observed

> the development of a single European market without political
> integration will intensify internal competition amongst member
> countries. Moreover, because as Porter . . . has proposed the most
> important factors of national competitiveness are skilled human
> resources and the scientific base, it is essential for companies to
> generate strategic human resource management approaches
> rather than to persist with professional personnel management if
> they are to survive and prosper in the emerging European envi-
> ronment of the 1990s. The forces which underpin successful
> competitive strategy will thus not only lead to an increasing focus
> on the firm's human resources, but will intensify the transforma-
> tion of personnel management into human resource management
> after 1992. Moreover, the conclusion must be that the most
> advanced companies and countries in Europe in the 1990s will
> display earliest to the fullest the symptoms of this radical trans-
> formation, which will be manifested most obviously in the

centrality of human resource management for the corporate
strategies of the firms themselves.

But although managers in their human resource strategies are
likely to emphasize the importance of motivation, employee involvement, variable pay systems, systematic "human resource
flow" policies, and high commitment work systems, the *ways* in
which these objectives are recognized are likely to vary and to vary
considerably (Beer et al 1984, Brewster and Tyson 1991). For
instance, on employee involvement, the extent to which trade
unions are involved and the degree of influence of representative
forms such as works councils are likely to reflect both the differences in power of particular trade union movements and their
organizational strength in the firm as well as wider legislative
changes which are likely to vary by country (or groups of countries).
On the other hand, there is an increasing consensus that the "new
HRM" is unlikely to be sustained unless institutions capable of
effectively respresenting the interests of employees at the level of
the enterprise become widespread (see Adams 1988, 1991a).

With respect to trade unions, in most countries the influence of
unions (measured by trade union density) declined in the 1980s.
There have been exceptions (such as Scandinavia and South Korea)
but the overall pattern has been one of significant membership loss,
a situation which is often attributed to the fulfilment of many labor
objectives, as well as to managerial strategies, unfavorable legislation, and economic and industrial change (Baglioni and Crouch
1991). But there do seem to be marked differences in trade union
responses to this situation which are by no means convergent.
Indeed, they vary from a high degree of co-operation with employer
objectives (e.g., the acceptance of single union deals, "no strike"
clauses and so on) to continued implacable opposition (see Price
1991).

There also appear to be different responses by governments and
in the role of the state more generally. A decline in the role of the
state in economic planning is evident in the recent events in the
Soviet Union and Eastern Europe and in the moves to deregulation
and privatization in most countries. But although in industrial
relations there are convergent tendencies, (including some recent
reregulation) diversity continues in the state role as well. For
instance, although in Europe there are moves to harmonization and

labor laws have an increasing degree of affinity in a number of countries (e.g., UK, Ireland), industrial relations in the public (i.e. state) sector in particular has changed quite markedly in some countries (e.g., the UK) but very little in others (e.g., Germany, Holland).

Diversity, as well as some increasing similarities, can be identified in three further key areas of industrial relations: industrial conflict, industrial democracy, and the distribution of economic rewards (see Adams 1991b). Arguably, so far as industrial disputes measured by strike activity are concerned, a reduction in the incidence of conflict did take place (largely for economic reasons) in many industrialized countries in the 1980s. But this tells us little about other aspects of conflict (e.g., absenteeism and labor turnover) as well as other types of protest (e.g., withdrawal of goodwill by workers in Japanese enterprises) which has continued to characterize different industrial relations systems. In many countries there has been greater interest in employee involvement, but the types developed have differed considerably. From the early 1970s until today, "employee involvement" has experienced a variety of phases of development. In the 1970s, it was designed to meet employee demands for more participation and satisfaction. The early 1980s recessions witnessed a general contraction. But the mid-1980s onwards saw a further advance designed to coopt employee knowledge with a view to higher productivity and competitiveness. However, the rates of expansion of employee financial participation in particular have certainly differed globally (being marked in the US and UK, but circumscribed in Germany). (See Poole 1989, Poole and Jenkins 1990.) Moreover, while pay systems in most nations have increasingly encompassed flexibility, performance-related pay (and skill-based pay in the US) and so on, in some countries (e.g., Japan) seniority-based payment systems have continued. Again, then, while some emergent trends which cut across national frontiers have been in evidence, there has been no *uniformity* in implementation and experience despite *some* greater uniformity in human resource management practices worldwide.

Conclusions

For a number of years, the case for the tendency for an increasing diversity in industrial relations systems has seemed to be persuasive. There are, in any event, a number of cylical rather than secular trends evident historically. But there are also different trajectories of development with the "new" nations not passing through similar evolutionary stages as the West. As I have argued elsewhere (Poole 1986, 207).

> On the contrary, there appear to be appreciable "late development" effects, a much faster speed of industrial and technological development that telescopes evolutionary processes, and a varied pace and mode of adaptation in advanced societies as well. And the upshot is that already highly complex patterns at any given moment in time are likely to be compounded in the future by multiform processes of change which are likely to produce diverse, dissimilar, and divergent types of industrial relations experience.

> In sum, then, intricate forces of uneven consequence for industrial relations phenomena have been discovered. Of course, there remain the common elements of the identification of the three main groups of "actors" in the industrial relations system, the focus on conflict and the resolution of disputes, the shared and the diverse interests and the location of industrial relations activities in both production and distribution spheres. But at the heart of comparative analysis remains the basic tension between the forces of creativity and control, the varied strategies, values and convictions of the "actors" themselves and differences in culture and ideology, in politico-economic conditions, in industrial relations institutions and in power. In combination, these produce a multitude of outcomes which, in the long term are only limited by the imagination of those concerned with the shaping of a series of choices of vital consequence for the future of our species.

This is a position which I should still like to reaffirm. The major recent transformations in political and economic systems have occasioned a greater degree of convergence than was once envisaged. But the forces for diversity are no less insistent and are likely to ensure that, even when faced with similar problems, different "actors" will find very diverse solutions and hence produce the varying industrial relations systems which still characterize global experience and are likely to do so well into the 21st century.

Works Cited

Adams, R. J. 1988, "The role of management in a political conception of industrial relations at the level of the enterprise," in G. Dlugos et al., eds., *Management under Differing Labor Market and Employment Systems,* Berlin: de Gruyter.
_____. 1991a, "Industrial Relations in an era of lean production," Working Paper No. 361, McMaster University, Canada.
_____. 1991b, ed., *Comparative Industrial Relations: Contemporary Research and Theory,* London: Harper Collins Academic.
Baglioni, G., and C. Crouch, eds. 1991, *European Industrial Relations,* London: Sage Publications.
Beer, M., B. Spector, P. R. Lawrence, D. Q. Mills, and R. E. Walton. 1984, *Managing Human Assets,* New York: Free Press
Brewster, C., and S. Tyson, eds. 1991, *International Comparisons in Human Resource Management,* London: Pitman.
Flanders, A. 1970, *Management and Unions,* London: Faber and Faber
Form, W. M. 1979, "Comparative Industrial Sociology and the Convergence Hypothesis," *Annual Review of Sociology,* vol.5.
Hendry, C. 1991, "International Comparisons in Human Resource Management," *International Journal of Human Resource Management,* vol. 2, no. 3, pp. 415-440.
Kerr, C. 1983, *The Future of Industrial Societies,* Cambridge, MA: Harvard University Press.
Kerr, C., J. T. Dunlop, F. Harbison, and C. A. Myers. 1960, *Industrialism and Industrial Man,* Cambridge MA: Harvard University Press.
Kochan, T. A., H. C. Katz, and R. B. McKersie. 1986, *The Transformation of American Industrial Relations,* New York: Basic Books.
Krulis-Randa, J. 1990, "Strategic Human Resource Management (SHRM) in Europe after 1992," *International Journal of Human Resource Management,* vol. 1, no. 2, pp. 131-140.
MacInnes, J. 1987, *Thatcherism at work,* Milton Keynes: Open University Press.
Mansfield, R., and M. J. F. Poole. 1991, *British Management in the Thatcher Years,* London: British Institute of Management.

Poole, M. J. F. 1986, *Industrial Relations: Origins and Patterns of National Diversity*, London: Routledge.

_____. 1989, *The Origins of Economic Democracy*, London: Routledge.

Poole, M. J. F., and G. Jenkins. 1990, *The Impact of Economic Democracy*, London: Routledge.

Price, R. 1991, "The Comparative Analysis of Union Growth," in R. Adams, ed., *Comparative Industrial Relations*, London: Harper-Collins.

"All Aspects of People at Work": Unity and Division in the Study of Labor and Labor Management

Roy J. Adams

Introduction

Whether a blessing or a curse, a source of dignity or degradation, work has been the fate of humankind throughout its history. In agricultural societies, waking hours are almost synonymous with working hours. Even in the richest and most technologically advanced countries adults spend, on average, one third of their life at work. Since it is such a dominating activity, understanding the behavior of people at work is crucial if a broader understanding of humankind is to be achieved. Although intellectuals have concerned themselves with work for over two millennia (Tilgher 1930), it has been the subject of systematic and sustained inquiry for only about 100 years (McNulty 1980, 127). At first, research into work and workers was dominated by economists, but over the past century scholars from all of the behavioral and social sciences have looked into some aspects of labor and labor management.

By the 1940s, economists, sociologists, anthropologists, psychologists, historians, legal scholars, and management researchers were all active in the general field. A need began to be felt by some to bring together these disparate efforts in a common forum. The initiative was taken, in the United States, by a group of disgruntled economists who perceived more in common with other labor researchers than they had with other economists. Thus, in 1946, the Industrial Relations Research Association was founded with the primary goal of the bringing together "people from all academic disciplines concerned with labor problems, labor-management relations, and social security, and research workers and professional practitioners in these fields" (McPherson and Derber 1948, 4). There was a need, many felt, for a more integrated approach because the various disciplines "tear the subject apart by concentrating attention on some of its aspects to the exclusion or comparative neglect of others" (Flanders, quoted in Barrett et al. 1975). The new field of industrial relations was conceived of as the institutional vehicle through which a unified understanding of all aspects of people at work would be achieved.

The object of this chapter[1] is to review the evolution of academic scholarship on "all aspects of people at work"[2] and particularly the effort to unify labor research under the banner of industrial relations. Instead of movement towards a more coherent approach to understanding the behavior of working people what one finds is continuing if not increasing diversity. Industrial relations has not been successful in unifying inquiry into labor and labor management. Instead of achieving recognition as the central institutional vehicle for bringing together those who probe into some or "all aspects of people at work," industrial relations has been challenged by the emergence of other interdisciplinary fields the most notable of which are human resources management (personnel) and organizational behavior. Because of continued fragmentation of inquiry and faulty communication across institutional barriers, we are probably no closer today than we were 50 years ago to a coherent and unified understanding of people at work.

Early Work on Labor

Although labor has been of interest to intellectuals throughout written history, it was first systematically studied by the early economists who regarded it as the source of all value. These classical economists conceived of labor as a commodity like any other, subject to the universal forces of supply and demand. They were especially concerned to discover the laws which would determine its price (McNulty 1980). Normatively they were interested (as economists) in economizing; in other words in the conditions under which markets would function most efficiently. Early theories suggested that wages would tend to provide no more than a subsistence income and efforts by workers to improve their lot would be as futile as a sand castle against the tide.

Socialist and utopian writers reacted against this "dismal" proposition. Most combined an analysis of social relations with normative propositions for improving the condition of labor. Utopian writers and activists such as St. Simon, Fourier, Owen, Blanqui, Proudhon, Louis Blanc, Bakunin, Sorel, Cole, Lassalle, Bernstein, and Gramsci, all produced programs which called for active human intervention into the political economy in order to ameliorate the condition of labor (Ader 1966).

Foremost among these activists was Karl Marx and his colleague Frederick Engels. In a series of writings, Marx and Engels criticized "bourgeois" economics bitterly, offered an alternative theory of the operation of economic systems and suggested a programme of action to overcome the human misery evident in the world of their time. Marxist theory had (and continues to have) an enormous impact on intellectuals interested in understanding, explaining, and doing something about labor problems.

Developments in the United States

Institutional Labor Economics

By the late 19th century, American "institutional labor economists" began to react against the high level of abstraction of conventional economics and its dolorous implications for the fate of the common person. They also rejected radical solutions to "the labor problem." Instead they focused on particular issues and sought to discover practical solutions to perceived inadequacies with the economic system.

In the last decade of the twentieth century there was an upsurge of labor unrest in the United States. As a result labor issues became salient in the public mind. In consequence, early in the twentieth century courses in "labor problems" began to appear on curricula of universities across America (McNulty 1980, 148-50). The publication of a best-selling textbook in 1905 helped to solidify this development (Adams and Sumner 1905).

Although they were institutionally placed in departments of economics and were referred to as labor economists, in fact the early labor scholars were interdisciplinarians. They were especially interested in labor history and in the legal aspects of employment relations. One of the most prominent of these scholars was John R. Commons, who produced books with titles like *Social Reform and the Church, The History of Labor in the United States,* and *The Legal Foundations of Capitalism.* Robert Hoxie, another prominent labor economist, produced a treatise on varieties of trade unionism (1917) that was more sociological than economic in character.

In the textbooks used in courses on labor problems, reference to abstract economic theory was all but nonexistent. One of the major centers of labor research in this period was the University of Wisconsin, where John R. Commons and his many students combined research with real-world engagement as drafters of legislation, mediators, arbitrators, etc., to create the "Wisconsin School" (Barbash 1991).

The counterparts to these eclectic researcher-activists in Great Britain were Sidney and Beatrice Webb (1897, 1920), who wrote the first great book on trade unions and spent a lifetime as social reformers. The Webbs in Britain and the Wisconsin group in the United States were responsible for the initial introduction of many of the schemes which now make up the ubiquitous "welfare state" (Kerr 1988, Schatz forthcoming).

The Beginnings of Research on Labor Management

The institutional labor economists saw the world from the point of view of the working person and society as a whole. At the end of the 19th century another group of thinkers began to focus on labor from the perspective of the business manager (Wren 1987). Among key initial contributors were Henri Fayol, Mary Parker Follett, and later Chester Barnard. The objective of these scholars was to identify ways in which the productive organization could be managed in the most effective manner. One branch of this group focused specifically on personnel or labor management.

Frederick Taylor, a brilliant and reflective business executive and consultant, proposed breaking skills down into small parts and systematically reconstructing them in the "one best way." He combined proposals for the scientific study of the way work was done with others on job design, employee recruitment, selection, motivation, and supervision. His philosophy and strategy for labor management became known as "Taylorism." Gradually many of his proposals diffused throughout industry and became the prevalent managerial practice, especially in large scale manufacturing.

The focus on human behavior at work also attracted the interest of many psychologists and industrial psychology came into being as a distinct specialty which took as its function the assisting of managers of large organizations to optimize the use of human resources. The first textbook on the subject was written by Hugo Munsterberg in 1913. The *Journal of Applied Psychology* (which was to become the leading industrial psychology journal) began publishing in 1917 and the field expanded significantly in the period of the First World War as governments utilized the skills of psychologists to recruit, select and place personnel for the war effort (Rose 1988).

In the 1930s, researchers from Harvard University, of which Elton Mayo became the most famous, challenged the Taylorist idea that money was the primary motivator of workers. The Harvard group popularized the idea that worker behavior had complex social and psychological determinants, of which money was only one and often not the most important one. In particular these researchers demonstrated that enterprise policy and supervisory behavior towards workers could make a great deal of difference in how well the workers performed tasks assigned to them. The discovery of human beings stimulated by complex motivations and needs at work spawned the "human relations" movement. The problems framed by the human relationists were to become dominant concerns not only of psychologists but also of sociologists and anthropologists. The rise of human relations also forced the institutional labor economists to consider its implications for their work on labor problems, collective bargaining, and government policies toward labor (e.g., Kerr and Fisher 1964).

Towards Unity—The Founding of the Industrial Relations Research Association (IRRA)

In the 1930s, in the midst of the 20th century's Great Depression, the American labor movement began a period of spectacular growth. As labor's power and influence grew, employment relations drew the attention of a new generation of economists who would generally be lumped together with adherents of the Wisconsin School into the institutionalist category. Clark Kerr, a prominent member of the group, would later insist that this classification was faulty (Kerr 1988). He would call the group the neoclassical realists.

They shared with the Wisconsin School a disdain for abstract armchair theorizing and made a point of observing real-world economic behavior in order to wring from it useful generalizations. Like the institutionalists they drew heavily on the contributions of sociologists, historians, law scholars, and interdisciplinary labor researchers to make sense of the condition of labor. But unlike those associated with the Wisconsin school who "showed no interest in markets," the neoclassical realists "recognized the great role of market forces" (Kerr 1988, 14). "Rather than neoinstitutionalists," Kerr argued, "it would be more accurate to identify the members of this core group as realistic neoclassicists, for their grounding was in neoclassical economics, which they wanted to revise . . ." (p. 14). Prominent members of this group were, in addition to Kerr, John T. Dunlop, Frederick Harbison, Charles Myers, Richard Lester, and Lloyd Reynolds.

By the 1940s, the term *industrial relations* (IR) had been in use for over half a century. It came into general use for the first time as a consequence of the publication of the report of the U.S. Congressional Commission on Industrial Relations in 1915 (Morris 1987). In 1922 an "industrial relations section" was set up in the department of economics at Princeton University with a grant from J. D. Rockefeller (Lester 1986). Additional institutes appeared in the 1920s and 1930s, but a very large expansion occurred in the 1940s. Between 1945 and 1950, some 12 new IR institutes were set up across North America (Lester 1986).[3] The 1940s also saw the establishment of two academic journals with the term in their titles: *Industrial Relations Quarterly Review,* published by Laval University in Quebec, and *Industrial and Labor Relations Review*, published at Cornell University.

This expansion was a response to the growth of the labor movement and the resultant public concern with labor problems, collective bargaining, and labor management. Expansion was also fueled by the intellectual impact of the "human relations school" and by the increasing professionalization of the personnel field and the resultant demand by industry for appropriately trained people. The institutes and schools, especially the ones set up in the 1940s, saw their task as being in part practical to train practitioners for work in industry, government, and trade unions; but also academic to produce scholars knowledgeable about the research and thought on labor and labor management of all branches of social science with a view towards the eventual integration of this knowledge into a comprehensive and holistic framework.[4]

In 1946, at the initiative of several institutional labor economists, steps were taken to set up an association designed to provide an institutional mechanism whereby labor researchers from all disciplines could come together to discuss their common interests. In recognition of the growing use of the term industrial relations, they chose as the name of the organization: Industrial Relations Research Association. A review of the original documents makes it clear that the founders thought of industrial relations as a broad term capable of comprehending the entire labor field. Among the key objectives of the organization was "the encouragement of research in all aspects of the field of labor, social, political, legal, economic, and psychological relations, personnel administration, social security, and labor legislation" (Derber, Preface to first annual IRRA proceedings).

Although recognizing the contributions of each discipline towards the advancement of knowledge about labor, Edwin Witte, in his address as the first president of the association, argued that "it is highly desirable that there should be cross-fertilization between these workers in their differing approaches and points of view and that all people who undertake research in industrial relations should have ready access to what has been done by others. Improvement of the situation in these respects is one of the major objectives of the Industrial Relations Research Association" (p. 20).

To carry out this mandate, the executive of the association made strong efforts to attract scholars from a wide range of academic disciplines. At the inaugural meeting, for example, there was a session which discussed the contributions of psychology, political science, sociology, and law to industrial relations research.

The Rise of ISLLM

Initially all of the IRRA participants were identified with an established social science discipline. However, by the 1980s many association members identified their academic occupation as neither psychology nor economics nor sociology nor any of the other established disciplines. They were graduates of programs which provided for the interdisciplinary study of labor and labor management, or ISLLM, for short. A new breed of scholar had come into being. To see how this happened it is necessary to review the institutional development of labor research from the 1940s.

The industrial relations institutes and schools which proliferated in the 1940s, as well as the growing business schools, provided opportunities for young scholars interested in labor and labor management to study the subject from many different perspectives. Drawing on the work of economists, psychologists, sociologists, historians, and legal theorists as necessary, they began to form a new identity.

Trained in multidisciplinary programs these scholars initially lacked any distinct approach to labor issues. Many utilized the conceptual apparatus of economics, institutional economics especially, others that of psychology, sociology, or management. John Dunlop's formulation in 1958 of the industrial relations systems framework was an attempt to provide the field with a distinctive intellectual outlook and focus.

Dunlop urged industrial relationists to conceive of relations between labor, management, and government as a subsystem of society whose function it was to produce the conditions and regulations under which work was performed. It seems reasonably clear that Dunlop intended the IR systems scheme to provide a framework capable of uniting knowledge about people at work. However, in the book in which the scheme first appeared, he made no attempt to review the broad body of labor research existing at that time nor to demonstrate how his scheme could be used to accomplish that end. As a result its ability to achieve assimilation successfully was debated vigorously (see, e.g., Adams 1977).

In the 1970s and 1980s, the IR systems framework was utilized widely to organize courses and textbooks and to a lesser extent as a tool for carrying out original research. While paying lip service to the proposition that industrial relations was concerned with the broad study of employment relations, in fact the books and the courses which made use of the framework usually focused more narrowly on union-management relations. There were some attempts to knit together in a single text the research from personnel and labor relations (e.g., Kochan and Barrocci 1985).

The IR systems framework had little or no impact on those who taught and did research exclusively on the general problems of labor management (e.g., how to motivate individual workers, how to elicit overall high morale and creativity). In fact, instead of industrial relations, students of these subjects began to refer to their specialty as organizational behavior. Those who concerned themselves more specifically with functional problems such as recruitment and selection of workers also rejected the IR systems framework and many also rejected the appellation of industrial relations. Instead they referred to their specialty as personnel administration or human resources management. Although there was considerable overlap between the three interdisciplinary specialties, each developed its own separate literature and institutional identity. By the late 1980s, although some industrial relationists continued to declare that IR subsumed all aspects of labor and labor-management relations, in reality it had become only one of an interrelated group of interdisciplinary fields. Instead of knitting the field together, Bruce Kaufman was arguing by the early 1990s, the IR systems framework had the effect of driving a wedge between those who continued to follow the institutional economics tradition and those who focused on labor management (a.k.a. personnel or human resources management). [5]

Some students of ISLLM were able to find appointments in industrial relations institutes and schools, but most were employed by the rapidly expanding business schools. Often the separate but interrelated specialties of union-management relations, personnel administration, and organizational behavior combined into a single business school department.

Instead of Multidisciplinary, The IRRA Becomes Interdisciplinary

For those interdisciplinarians who focused on union-management relations, the IRRA became their principal academic association. In the early years they found much in common with the institutional labor economists, at whose initiative the IRRA had come into being, since union-management relations was also a long-time central interest of the institutionalists.

Many personnel management experts and organizational behaviorists also attended the meetings of the IRRA, but they had a difficult time finding common ground with the institutional economists. As a result even more of them made their professional home in the Personnel/Human Resources Division of the Academy of Management. By the late 1980s, that division annually held about as many sessions as the IRRA (Strauss 1989, Cappelli 1991) and a much larger number of scholars who identified their field as human resources management (HRM) or organizational behavior (OB) belonged to the Academy instead of the IRRA.

Scholars from social science disciplines other than institutional labor economics did not respond in large numbers to the multidisciplinary appeal of the IRRA founders. By the 1980s, there were so few members who identified themselves as psychologists, sociologists, or political scientists that the association stopped classifying them separately and instead placed them all in an "other" category. Instead of a meeting ground for labor scholars from many different fields, the IRRA had become more of an association for interdisciplinarians. As of 1990, 452 members of the IRRA identified their academic occupation as industrial relations and 234 as organizational behavior, personnel, or human resource management. Another 120 said business administration. Economists continued to make up the largest group of traditional disciplinarians. The evolution of the occupational composition of the IRRA is given in Table 1.

Table 1. Self-Identified Occupation of Academic Members in the IRRA

	1949	1960	1972	1984	1990
Economics	335	273	410	298	334
Industrial Relations	na	194	367	469	452
Law	34	14	45	89	67
Political Science	19	13	14	11	na
Psychology	36	14	25	8	na
Sociology	31	15	52	27	na
Other/Don't Know	79	73	99	107	154
Business Administration	na	na	215	116	120
Organizational/ Behavior/ Personnel	na	na	na	117	88
Student	na	na	142	299	330
Administration	na	na	152	104	131
Human Resources	na	na	na	na	146
Total	534	596	1521	1645	1822
Less Students			1369	1346	1492

Sources: Membership directories for various years. For 1949, economics and commerce were listed as one category.

With the failure of the IRRA to attract significant numbers of traditional disciplinarians, the term industrial relations, which the founders of the IRRA and of the various institutes had tried to define as the study of the broad expanse of labor issues, came to be regarded more commonly as the study of unions and collective bargaining and the labor market problems of specific groups such as women and other minorities (Strauss and Feuille 1978). Even in 1980, however, in a widely heralded textbook which focused largely on unions and collective bargaining, Kochan would echo the initial ambition of the field by defining industrial relations as the study of all aspects of people at work (p. 1).[6]

Precisely why the IRRA managed to attract so few social scientists interested in labor issues is yet to be explained. From time to time the leaders of the IRRA did make explicit efforts to include sessions of interest to social scientists other than economists. Most presidents of the IRRA were, however, trained as economists and most issues discussed at IRRA meetings were those associated with the traditional concerns of institutional labor economics. In his draft book on the history of industrial relations in the United States, Bruce Kaufman (1993) argues that Dunlop's IR systems framework focused attention on the institutional aspects of union-management relations to the exclusion of concern with labor management issues. Clearly, most of the sessions at the annual meetings of the IRRA were concerned with union-management relations and various labor market problems. No doubt many psychologists and sociologists who came to one or another meeting felt that they had shown up at the wrong party (Whyte 1987).

Despite an erosion of the power and influence of organized labor in the 1960s and 1970s, the field of industrial relations as the study of unions, collective bargaining and labor market problems continued to prosper in the United States. Following the lead of neoclassical labor economics a new breed of industrial relationist began to utilize quantitative methods and model building more aggressively. There was a shift away from inductive theory building to deductive theory testing and a concomitant shift in focus away from institutions such as trade unions to individuals (Cappelli 1985).

As industrial relations began to relax into its identity as the study of unions, collective bargaining, and assorted labor market problems, the search for a theme or framework to unify labor research subsided. In a review of industrial relations research during the 1970s, Kochan, Mitchell, and Dyer noted that during that decade "there appeared little of the soul-searching over the scope of industrial relations as an academic discipline that occurred in the 1960s . . . " (1982, 370). "Instead," they found, "either the work was atheoretical or its theoretical focus shifted back to the basic disciplines closest to the problem areas covered." A committee of the IRRA, assigned the task of reviewing the mandate of the IRRA, recommended that it change its purpose from the assimilation of all researchers interested in the study of labor to all researchers interested in the study of industrial relations (Lester 1977). One of the few "soul searching" articles to appear during the decade declared that efforts to make comprehensive sense of "all aspects of the employment relationship" were foolish. "Pulling this conglomeration together under a single head," the authors insisted, "would be intellectually meaningless" (Strauss and Feuille 1978, 275).

Collective bargaining in the 1960s and 1970s spread into the public sector and continued to be an important force in many parts of the private sector. As a result, courses in unions and collective bargaining were in demand and expanding business schools continued to recruit graduates with expertise in union-management relations. This situation changed significantly in the 1980s.

Abandoned by government and assaulted by employers, collective bargaining dwindled. Students and business school administrators came to see it as being relatively insignificant. Courses in personnel management and organizational behavior expanded at the expense of courses in labor relations and collective bargaining. Because of the success of Japanese business and the imputed relationship between that success and the personnel policies used by Japanese firms, courses which taught the "new HRM"(that is the labor management tactics with which the Japanese were so successful) were in much demand. So were courses which prepared students to deal with the implications of expanding human rights and occupational health and safety legislation.

Those who considered the study of unions and collective bargaining to be the core of academic IR worried for the future of the field (Strauss 1989). Because of the demand for HRM professionals, however, the major industrial relations institutes and schools, continued to flourish. Some changed their names to Institutes of Human Resources Management (the preferred name in the 1980s for the focus which previously was known as personnel management) or Industrial Relations and Human Resources Management.[7] The informal Industrial Relations Center Directors group within the IRRA adopted a formal constitution and renamed itself the Association of Industrial Relations and Human Resources Programs (Strauss 1989).

United States Developments in Economics, Sociology, Law, and History

Labor Economics Becomes Neoclassical

From about the 1960s, the center of gravity of labor economics shifted towards general neoclassical economics (McNulty 1980, Kerr 1988). Largely as a result of the efforts of H. Gregg Lewis and others of the "Chicago School," there was a "redirection of labor economics toward analytical and quantitative work" (McNulty, 192). The new generation of labor economists built sophisticated abstract models and tested them against large data sets. Qualitative institutional analysis began to be thought of as methodologically inferior and those who were unwilling or unable to embrace the new methods no doubt began to feel uncomfortable at the annual meetings of the American Economics Association. Many of them continued to find a friendly reception at the IRRA. In fact the existence of the IRRA may very well have contributed to the demise of realist labor research and teaching within the discipline of economics. As labor economics moved closer to conventional economics, academic departments recruited people with neoclassical skills and propensities. Young scholars interested in realistic labor research, who in an earlier age may have studied institutional labor economics, in the 1970s and 80s found their way increasingly to programs which offered interdisciplinary labor degrees.

More Schisms within Labor Economics

In the 1970s and 1980s, neoclassical labor economists were challenged from within both by a resurgent Marxist group and by a group which came to be known as neoinstitutionalists. The latter, instead of focusing on traditional supply and demand issues took as their challenge finding ways to minimize the cost of transactions between labor and management. They sought to identify the form of labor-management relationship which would produce the most efficient organization in terms of transaction costs (Williamson 1985).[8]

This line of research produced an entirely new vocabulary and a new image of the nature of the labor-management relationship. One of its central propositions was that labor and management conclude "implicit contracts" but that both sides are prone to "shirk" their duties under the contract. As a result a need arises for devices to "monitor" the shirkers. One of the economists key problems, given the above assumptions, is to specify the conditions under which monitoring costs are minimized.

By the 1990s, some dialogue had begun between these neoinstitutional economists and organizational behaviorists and between the neo's and radical labor researchers (see, e.g., Griesinger 1990, Edwards 1990). Hardly any of the neoinstitutionalists found their way to the IRRA. During the 1980s, only a few sessions of the IRRA marginally touched on the issues raised by this new group of economists.

Industrial Sociology Comes and Goes

In the 1940s and 1950s, sociologists, stimulated by the work of Mayo and his colleagues at the Hawthorne Works of Western Electric, focused largely on work groups within industrial enterprises (Simpson 1989). Exemplary of the sociological approach of the period were studies carried out by Gouldner (1954) on the impact of managerial labor policies on worker attitudes and behavior and by Donald Roy (1952) on the effect of work group norms on labor productivity. Anthropologists, such as Warner and Low, whose study of *The Social System of The Modern Factory* was widely read, were also active and the journal *Applied Anthropology* (later changed to *Human Organization*) carried much of their labor research. This work became essential reading for interdisciplinary students of labor and labor management during this period (see, e.g., Strauss forthcoming).

In the 1960s, "the field of industrial sociology bifurcated into work and occupations versus organizations which developed largely separate literatures although they remain in a single American Sociological Association membership section" (Simpson 1989, 567). In both areas research became more abstract and quantitative. Data collection and rigorous statistical analysis of large data sets replaced participant observation and case studies as

preferred research techniques. In terms of methods and problems
addressed industrial sociology moved in the direction of neoclassical labor economics. In Britain there was considerable dialogue
between industrial sociology and industrial relations, but in the
United States very little cross-fertilization took place.

Labor History

Much of the early labor history in the United States was done,
not by historians, but rather by institutional labor economists with
those of the Wisconsin School particularly notable. During its
heyday in the 1940s, 1950s, and 1960s in the United States, many
historians associated themselves with industrial relations. In the
1970s, however, historians began to expand their horizons to study
total working class experience throughout industrial times (Grossman and Moye 1982, Morton 1988, Strauss 1989) while industrial
relationists narrowed their focus to contemporary events. As a result
there was something of a schism between history and industrial
relations.[9]

Labor Law

During the U.S. "golden era" of the 1940s, 1950s, and 1960s,
labor became a specialty within American law schools and because
of extensive legal regulation of union recognition and collective
bargaining, close links developed between labor law and industrial
relations. Indeed for many years papers presented at the spring
meeting of the Industrial Relations Research Association have been
published in the *Labor Law Journal*. Along with many institutional
economists the preponderance of postwar labor lawyers in the
United States adopted a pluralist approach to employment relations.
In essence pluralism held that both labor and management had
legitimate interests in employment relations and that neither set of
interests should be subordinated to the other. Instead disputes
should be worked out through the process of collective bargaining
which was characterized as a form of industrial democracy (Godard
1993).

This normative position, which was dominant in the 50s, 60s, and 70s, was challenged seriously in the 1980s. Critical labor law theorists such as Katherine Stone (1981) and Karl Klare (1978) argued that the reality was not one of industrial democracy but rather of management dominance. Their outlook was closer to the ideological position of political economy than to the dominant pluralism.

Since "mainstream" industrial relations continued to focus on unions and collective bargaining and because union-management relations were so juridified in the United States, law scholars and industrial relationists continue to talk to each other, although the voice of the critical legal scholars is much weaker than that of the pluralists. After economists, law scholars are the largest group of IRRA members who are identified with one of the traditional disciplines, even though law professors made up only about 5% of academic members in 1990.

As legal regulation of human rights, health and safety, pensions, and stock ownership increased during the 70s and 80s, industrial/organizational psychologists, organizational behaviorists, and personnel researchers became more interested in legal issues which led to increasing dialogue between them and law scholars in the United States (Norton and Gustafson 1982). The great recession of the early 1980s resulted in much restructuring and downsizing. For the first time executives were dismissed in large numbers without cause. They responded by seeking the aid of lawyers who found ways to sue employers even though employment in the US was supposed to be at will. As a result the individual contract of employment became the subject of a good deal of legal and personnel research. Books began to appear on personnel law and legal issues found their way into textbooks on personnel and human resource management.

Development of Industrial Relations as a Field Outside of the United States

Until quite recently, industrial relations as a field of inquiry into labor and labor management was primarily an anglophone phenomenon. From its initial appearance in the United States, it spread to

Canada, Britain, Australasia, and to other English-speaking countries such as India, Israel, the Philippines, Nigeria, and South Africa
(Adams 1991). The formation of the International Industrial Relations Association in 1967 at the initiative of industrial relations
associations in the United States and Britain, the Japan Institute of
Labor and the International Institute of Labor Studies in Geneva
provided an impetus for worldwide growth of the field. As of 1992,
the IIRA had individual members in 85 countries and affiliated
associations in 33 countries (IIRA membership directory, 1992). To
review developments in all of these countries would be an interesting task but one that is for some other time. In this section, I will
restrict myself to Canada, Britain, and Australasia.

Industrial relations as a field of inquiry got started in Canada,
the United Kingdom, Australia, and New Zealand somewhat later
than it did in the United States. Several "chairs" in industrial
relations were created in Britain in the 1930s (Roberts 1977) and a
textbook also appeared in that decade (Morris 1987). The field
expanded slowly and deliberately after World War II. An industrial
relations association was set up in the 1950s (Berridge and Goodman 1988) and the *British Journal of Industrial Relations* began to
be published in the early 1960s. But the field did not commence a
"golden age" until the mid-1960s when, as had happened previously in the United States, there was a large increase in government involvement in labor-management relations and a large
increase in the size and power of the labor movement. The appoint-
ment by the government of a national commission (Donovan Commission 1968) to study relations between unions and employers and
to make policy recommendations contributed to giving industrial
relations a high profile (Winchester 1991).

That era ended with the start of the 1980s again consistent with
the decline of the labor movement this time under the exclusionist
policies of Margaret Thatcher. As in the United States, business
schools (which expanded enormously from the mid-1970s) provided a home for scholars trained as experts in labor relations and
labor management (Berridge and Goodman 1988). Consistent with
the United States, human resources management expanded in the
United Kingdom in the 1980s even though the labor movement and
collective bargaining continued as important institutions.

The British were more equivocal than the Americans about the
desirability of achieving unity in the pursuit of knowledge about

labor issues. The *British Journal of Industrial Relations* which began publishing in 1964 took labor in the broadest sense as its universe of concern but, in fact, most contributors chose to write about unions, collective bargaining, and institutional labor market issues.[10] From its inception the British Universities Industrial Relations Association (BUIRA), which was initially dominated by economists like the IRRA, accepted into membership academics from all disciplines but it did not actively recruit them. Instead "the process of recruitment of new members was largely through personal contact with existing members" (Berridge and Goodman 1988, 158). Papers presented over the years clustered around a core concern with union-management relations (Berridge and Goodman 1988). Of 165 papers presented between 1950-1985 only 5 had to do with industrial sociology and 13 with labor law. Berridge and Goodman did not classify any as being concerned with industrial psychology or organizational behavior or personnel management. Twenty-eight addressed wages and labor markets (Berridge and Goodman 1988, 169).

In the mid 1980s, of 307 members of BUIRA, only 40 listed their academic departmental attachment as social studies, which included sociology. The number of psychologists and political scientists was not mentioned but there was an "other" category which contained 41 members. The association had 36 economists and almost 40% of the members were attached to business schools (Berridge and Goodman 1988). Some of those attached to the business schools were initially trained in one of the traditional disciplines. However, apparently few psychologists or sociologists attached to departments of psychology or sociology saw any advantage in interdisciplinary dialogue, under the umbrella of industrial relations, with a view towards a more comprehensive understanding of the labor universe.

According to a recent analysis by Winchester (1991), the field bifurcated in the 1980s. Under the antiunion, anticollectivist policies of Margaret Thatcher, the pluralist consensus of the previous decades collapsed. Human resources management research and teaching expanded rapidly. At the same time research from a "radical" perspective also grew, much of it centered on the nature of the labor process. While traditional pluralist research continued, most of the excitement was generated by the more extreme options.

In Canada, an industrial relations section was first set up in the School of Commerce and Administration at Queen's University in 1937 (Kelly 1987). As in the United States, labor relations were tumultuous in the 1930s and 1940s so that public concern with industrial relations was high. Laval University, in Quebec, set up a Department of Industrial Relations in the 1940s and it began to publish the first journal anywhere with industrial relations in its title in 1945—*Industrial Relations Quarterly Review.* An association, which like the IRRA welcomed both academics and practitioners, was established in the early 1960s.

As in the United States and Britain, the academic fortune of the field was tied to labor-management and political developments. During the 1970s, there was a significant expansion of industrial relations teaching and research concomitant with the growing size and power of the labor movement and subsequent to a high profile national inquiry into labor-management relations (Woods, Crispo and Dion 1968). Unlike the United Kingdom, the federal Conservative Party government which held power in Canada for much of the 1980s was not as adamantly antilabor as was Margaret Thatcher. As a result the union movement maintained much of its strength, labor issues continued to be a public concern and the field of IR continued to expand as new graduate programs were established in several universities. [11]

Unity in the pursuit of knowledge about labor issues was a recurring theme in the Canadian industrial relations literature (see, e.g., Adams 1977, Hebert, Jain, and Meltz 1988, and Boivin 1989), but the field in Canada was no more successful than its counterparts in Britain and the United States in providing an institutional framework for bringing together the broad range of labor researchers. As in the United States and Britain, the labor field was initially dominated by economists. However, by the time the Canadian Industrial Relations Association (CIRA) was founded in the 1960s (it was originally known as the Canadian Industrial Relations Research Institute), the interdisciplinary labor specialties were already coming into being. The meetings of the Canadian Industrial Relations Association focused largely on unions and collective bargaining and miscellaneous labor market problems and were attended predominantly by scholars attached to business schools and industrial relations institutes.[12] Traditional disciplinarians make up a very small proportion of the academic members of CIRA. In contrast to the United States based IRRA, few members of the Canadian Industrial Relations Association list their primary field as economics despite the initial development of labor research within economics departments.

An industrial relations "golden age" was initiated in Australia in the 1980s (Jenkins et al. 1991). At the beginning of the decade the Association of Industrial Relations Academics of Australia and New Zealand was formed (Hince 1991). In the same period a noted labor leader, Bob Hawke, became prime minister and introduced a number of innovative approaches to labor-management-government relations which enhanced the luster of industrial relations teaching and research. As a result, teaching and research expanded significantly during the decade (Lansbury 1991).

The field had developed slowly after World War II, primarily within departments of economics (Laffer 1974). By the 1970s, however, several interdisciplinary programs had been established which provided graduate work leading to postgraduate degrees and business schools had expanded their industrial relations offerings. The Australian *Journal of Industrial Relations* began publishing academic research in 1959 and the 1980s and 1990s saw the addition of several new outlets for industrial relations research and theory.[13]

In New Zealand the field was practically nonexistent until the 1970s when an Industrial Relations Centre was established at Victoria University (Hince 1991). During the next two decades industrial relations teaching expanded to most universities. The *New Zealand Journal of Industrial Relations* made its appearance in 1976 and, as noted, a combined Australian-New Zealand association of industrial relations academics was established in 1983. As in Canada, Britain, and the United States, the Australians and New Zealanders define the field broadly but in fact focus largely on the union-management relations/labor market issues core.[14]

Other Approaches to the Study of Labor and Labor Management

Labor and management are studied by traditional disciplinarians (e.g., economists, psychologists, sociologists, etc.) and by the

major interdisciplinary groups discussed to this point: industrial
relationists, organizational behaviorists and specialists in human
resource management/personnel. That does not exhaust the list,
however. There are in addition many other academics principally
concerned with labor issues who associate together into identifiable
groups. In this section several of these groups will be identified and
their principal characteristics briefly discussed.

American Labor Studies

In the 1960s in the United States, a new distinctive group of
scholars concerned with labor issues appeared. From the early part
of the 20th century, universities had provided a home for labor
educators whose primary function was to provide practical courses
to trade unionists. In the 1960s, however, several universities began
to offer degree programs in labor studies and labor educators
became part of the regular academic staff. Labor studies degree
programs also appeared in Canada in the 1970s and expanded in
the 1980s. In the United States in the 1980s, however, they declined
in tandem with the decline of the labor movement (Parsons 1990).

A seminal article by Dwyer et al. (1976) argued that labor
studies differed from industrial relations in that it was interested in
the achievement of social justice whereas industrial relations was
interested primarily in helping managers make profits. Many industrial relationists, however, did not agree with that assessment. Noah
Meltz (1989), for example, reflecting on the development of the
field argues that what distinguishes IR from other disciplines, and
from economics especially, is that economists view equity and
efficiency as "competing objectives, whereas a central concept of
industrial relations is that they are primarily complementary objectives" (p. 112). Following Jack Barbash, Meltz considers equity to
subsume a concern for social justice.

Indeed, from a right-wing perspective, industrial relations has
always appeared to be somewhat radical because of its apparent
insistence on the legitimacy of labor's concerns. In his reflections
on the development of the field of industrial relations William Foote
Whyte recalls how, when the New York State School of Industrial
and Labor Relations was set up at Cornell University in 1945, it
was referred to as "the cardboard Kremlin." Cardboard referred to

the temporary nature of its quarters while "Kremlin" was meant to be a negative comment on "the school's general commitment to the institution of collective bargaining" (Whyte 1987, 493). On the other hand, the conservative nature of the field is indicated by the recent comment made by a long-time member of the IRRA that in his recollection, "no radical critic has ever presented an IRRA paper" (Strauss 1989, 253).

Despite the apparent rivalry between labor studies and industrial relations, in fact, many scholars attached to labor studies programs show up at the annual meetings of the IRRA and many scholars attached to industrial relations institutes publish articles in *Labor Studies Journal,* the primary communication tool of this group.

"Human Resource Management" (a/k/a the new industrial relations; a/k/a strategic human resource management)

Although the term HRM had been around for a long time, it began to be used in the 1980s (particularly in Britain) to refer to a particular managerial strategy and a derivative teaching and research focus that seemed to be largely the application of Japanese employment relations to the West. David Guest (1987) argued that HRM was something totally different from traditional personnel management and British scholars began to refer to HRM and personnel as distinctively different phenomena. (See also Winchester 1991.) In North America, however, HRM was generally thought of as a new name for personnel management useful to indicate a changed emphasis, perhaps, but not an entirely new phenomena. (See, e.g., Strauss 1989, Beer et al. 1985.) Instead the introduction by American management of labor strategies similar to those common in Japan were more typically classified under the rubric of new industrial relations. (Kochan and Barocci 1985.)

Instead of human resource management the application of the concept of "strategic choice" and particularly strategic choices made by corporations with respect to employment relations became a major growth industry. Research on corporate labor policy (including the adoption of techniques associated with the Japanese) as a means whereby organizations might achieve strategic advantage over competitors was taken up by organizational behaviorists, personnel management experts, and by industrial relationists who specialized in those areas. Within industrial relations, research work carried out at Massachusetts Institute of Technology was seminal (see, e.g., Kochan, McKersie, and Cappelli 1984). By the late 1980s, this new conceptualization had begun to influence research in Canada, Britain, and Australasia. (See Winchester 1991, Jenkins et al. 1991.)

Political Economy

By the 1970s, the institutionalism of the Wisconsin School and of the neoclassical realists had ceased to be in vogue within the discipline of economics. Those interested in labor issues tended to apply highly sophisticated statistical technology to large data sets and utilized an obscure technical vocabulary. Little of their research appeared to have "practical application" (Strauss 1989, 248). As real-world events developed in unexpected ways in the turbulent 1970s, many students of economic life began to doubt the utility of this approach to economic analysis of labor issues.

To get control of inflation and high levels of industrial conflict, governments began actively to seek the cooperation of labor and management in arriving at economic policy. Wage and price controls, anathema to free marketeers, were frequently utilized. This turmoil led to new interest in economic relationships on the part of political scientists and sociologists. The very old term "political economy" began to be used in a new way to refer to analysis of economic relationships which took account of policy intervention by human agents.[15] Out of these developments appeared some identifiably new approaches to the study of labor and management.

Neither economic nor sociological nor psychological theory had much to say about the implications of governmental pursuit of tripartite consensus as a means of achieving economic stability. Political scientists saw it as a form of governance which they referred to as corporatism or neocorporatism to distinguish it from the form of government utilized by the fascist regimes of Europe between 1920 and 1945. In a now classic article, Phillipe Schmitter (1974) defined neocorporatism as a form of government in which the state attempted to govern by incorporating peak organizations of labor and management (and sometimes other influential groups) into the policy-making process. Writing on neocorporatism became a major academic growth industry in the 1970s. It drew the attention of not only political scientists but also of sociologists and industrial relationists who tended to refer to the phenomena as tripartism.

Another approach to develop out of the new sociopolitical concern with economic relationships was the French Regulation School (Noel 1987). These scholars focused on issues such as inflation, wage formation, the international division of labor, the role of the state in the economy, and the causes and consequences of economic crises. They were particularly interested in discovering why, under capitalism, there are intermittent periods of stability when labor seems to accept its fate within a system organized contrary to its interests followed by periods of crisis. They are known as the French Regulation School because they argue that stability is often achieved under capitalism as the result of rules and regulations and routines which tend to dampen revolutionary fervor. There is much overlap between the approach of the French Regulationists and IR systems analysis, which has yet to be explored by theorists.

The French Regulation approach has won wide attention throughout Europe but it has not made much headway in the United States. The absence of any discussion of this approach or of research stemming from it at meetings of the IRRA and CIRA, as well as the absence of references in the French Regulation literature to relevant industrial relations research, suggests that communication between these two islands of labor research is nonexistent.

Labor Process

Historically, the term *political economy* had a very broad usage. In the 1980s, however, many people began to use it to refer to a group of radical academics "more concerned to critically evaluate managerially defined problems than offer solutions to them" (Winchester 1991, 55). Notable among this group were those who focused on "the labor process." Harry Braverman's *Labor and Monopoly Capital,* published in 1974, began the stream of research and thought which expanded enormously in the 1980s. Drawing on Marx, Braverman argued that management's primary function in capitalist society was to convert potential labor power to real labor power and in the process to build value into the products and services produced. This transformation was referred to as the labor process and those who studied it focused their attention on labor-management relations at the point of production. Prior to the 1970s, the workplace had not been a prime focus of Marxist analysis, but during the 1980s workplace-based research from a radical perspective increased dramatically (reviewed by Bray and Littler 1988).

Just as IR began as a multidisciplinary approach, labor process research attracted contributions from several disciplines: sociologists particularly, but also economists, psychologists, and even management scholars. Labor process research and teaching became popular in the 1970s and 1980s in Canada, United Kingdom, Australia, and, to a lesser extent, it seems, in the United States and New Zealand.

Braverman's book also helped to stimulate research on labor market segmentation (the extent to which industrial or occupational markets are sealed off from each other and the implications of such segmentation) and on the effects of technology on employment relations. These issues were taken up by economists and sociologists and industrial relationists but the most vigorous dialogue, in the United States at least, seemed to take place within and between economics and sociology rather than within industrial relations. In Britain, and to a lesser extent in Canada and Australia perhaps, industrial relationists seemed to be more thoroughly involved in this debate.

The Structuring of the Labor Force in the Course of Economic Development

In the 1950s and 1960s, the attention of many scholars interested in employment relations was drawn to the developing countries, many of which were just becoming independent. Relations between trade unions and independence movements and later newly formed governments were of particular interest as was the recruiting, training, and motivating of an industrial labor force as a consequence of the process of economic development. These issues gave rise to a very large project funded by the Ford Foundation.

Four American neoclassical realist economists (Kerr, Harbison, Dunlop, and Myers) who were also very prominent in the Industrial Relations Research Association undertook the study which resulted in the classic book *Industrialism and Industrial Man*. Out of it came the "convergence hypothesis," the proposition that as they advanced economically, societies would become more alike in many other ways. That proposition had an enormous influence on social science research, coming to be the predominate concern of comparative industrial sociology (Form 1979), but it was not to have much influence on industrial relations.

Kerr et al., invited labor economists and industrial relationists to focus their research on the "structuring of the labor force in the course of economic development." Very few accepted that invitation. Following the institutional tradition, short-range, practical problems rather than global visions continued to engage their attention.

The New International Labor Studies

In the 1970s and 1980s, most Western labor scholars lost interest in the third world. As the developed countries entered a period of high inflation and high labor conflict, there were sufficient problems at home to fire the imagination (Fashoyin 1991). In the late 70s, a group of scholars who identified their approach as New International Labor Studies (NILS) began again to focus on the developing world (Munck 1988, Boyd et al. 1987). This group, which was based largely in Canada and Europe, was composed of an assorted group of sociologists, economists, anthropologists, and historians, all of whom were united in a concern to understand and to ameliorate the condition of labor in the third world. For the most part they utilized Marxist concepts to engage their universe of interest. As did the United States labor studies scholars, the NILS group took pains to dissociate itself from industrial relations.

As perceived by a leading spokesman of the group "The world imagined by industrial relations specialists is a formal, carefully constructed, but often ahistorical world" in which,

> is found a tight bargaining environment where collective agreements, grievance handling, arbitration and conciliation proce-

dures, contracts and negotiations take place. It is a world where "labor" normally means a middle-aged, male, trade-union bureaucrat in the capitalist West negotiating with his management counterpart. It is also a world where the principal organs of the working class, the trade unions, are accepted parts of the industrial landscape, institutionally protected but legally regulated and constrained (Cohen 1987, 4).

Cohen does not see this conceptual scheme as being an efficacious one for carrying out relevant research on third world labor problems. Whether the image is correct or not, that such a statement could be made by a credible academic is a very relevant comment on the extent to which industrial relations has come to be one approach among many rather than the meeting ground for all of those interested in labor research, which the founders of the IRRA had hoped it would become.

The Social Relations of Production

In the 1960s, when the International Labor Office set up the International Institute of Labor Studies (IILS), one of its purposes was to look at worldwide labor developments over the long run. One of its first projects focused on the "Futurology of Industrial Relations." To carry out a worldwide forecast of the future of labor the research group created a scheme capable of classifying exhaustively systems of employment relations in all of the countries of the world (Cox 1971). For example, whereas mainstream industrial relations generally ignored agriculture, the IILS framework drew attention to several types of agricultural employment relationships and to the interplay between agricultural systems and industrial systems.

The scheme was not utilized widely by researchers in the 60s and 70s (but see Thompson 1973). However, its major formulator, Robert Cox, continued to work with it and finally published a book utilizing the scheme (Cox 1987). A close collaborator, Jeffrey Harrod, also utilized the scheme to publish another book at about the same time (Harrod 1987). They referred to their method of analyzing labor issues as the "Social Relations of Production" approach. It remains to be seen whether these efforts will stimulate additional research from this perspective. It appears to be ideologically and methodologically compatible with the New International Labor Studies.

Review

When industrial relations became institutionalized as a distinct field of academic endeavor after World War II, many of its adherents hoped that it would become an interdisciplinary crossroad where all of the fields and subfields conducting research into labor issues and problems could come together. In addition, many hoped that the institutes and schools of industrial relations, by offering courses in a variety of areas and by requiring students of industrial relations to take courses from a variety of disciplines, would foster an integration of labor research and theory. That has not happened to any significant extent. Instead industrial relations has come to be regarded primarily as the study of unions and collective bargaining and assorted labor market problems.

One clear objective of the Industrial Relations Research Association was to bring about an integration of two existing multidisciplinary traditions: institutional labor economics and the newer human relations. The marriage was not successfully consummated. Instead human relations gave birth to two institutionally discrete new fields: personnel or human resources management and organizational behavior. The three interdisciplinary fields (industrial relations, organizational behavior, and human resources management) are closely related and tend to cluster together within industrial relations/human resources management schools and institutes or as single departments in schools of business. But members of these fields regard them as separate entities rather than as a single field with separate branches. Each specialty has generated a distinct literature.

Essentially, industrial relations as it exists today is the direct descendent of institutional labor economics and its broad concern for labor problems. Before World War II, labor problems were institutionally placed within departments of economics, although the focus was always interdisciplinary and never paid much regard to conventional economic theory. From the 1940s, the broad study of union-management relations which constituted a major part of the pre-World War II labor studies curriculum migrated from economics departments to industrial relations institutes and business schools.

A large part of what used to be called generally labor economics is now called industrial relations. What is now called labor economics is something quite different from what that term was used to identify before World War II. In the 1960s, the study of labor within economics departments veered sharply towards conventional economics, made consistent use of conventional economic theory, and rejected the traditional emphasis of labor economics on realism and interdisciplinary cross-fertilization. The analysis of such traditional "labor problems" as unemployment, wage determination, and hours of work was taken over to a large extent by the neoclassicals. Some economists continued to follow the older tradition. Those who did found more in common with the eclectic industrial relationists than with the newer breed of neoclassical labor economists.

The three core fields which make up the interdisciplinary study of labor and labor management (ISLLM) continue to have ties with the older disciplines. There are close ties between industrial/organizational psychology and organizational behavior and human resource management and between organizational behavior and industrial sociology, especially the branch which is now identified as the sociology of organizations. Because of the growth of legislation regulating employment, there has been growing interaction between law scholars and human resource management experts and industrial organizational psychologists.

There continues to be a strong link between labor law and industrial relations, but the links between industrial relations and neoclassical and neoinstitutional labor economics are currently very weak. The resurgent field of political economy which may be said to embrace the French Regulationists, the labor process researchers, and others has had little impact on United States industrial relations, but some of it has significantly influenced industrial relations research and thought in Britain, Australia, and Canada.

The extent to which industrial relations has become the study of unions, collective bargaining, and miscellaneous labor market phenomena is indicated by the almost complete separation of industrial relations and labor history. When labor history was the study of the development of working-class institutions there was a close IR-labor history bind, especially in the United States. As labor history has focused more widely on the broader experience of the working class, the link with industrial relations has become more tenuous, indeed almost nonexistent.

In addition to the three major fields which currently make up the core of the interdisciplinary study of labor there are additional small interdisciplinary institutional groups. Labor studies in the United States grew out of labor education. It focuses on essentially the same phenomena as industrial relations but considers its mission to be more specifically prolabor. Despite ideological differences there is a significant amount of overlap and communication between labor studies and industrial relations in the United States. New International Labor Studies focuses largely on labor problems in the third world. There are essentially no ties between it and industrial relations. Instead it draws significantly from the political economy literature and Marxist research generally.

Although its conceptual apparatus was developed more than twenty years ago, the Social Relations of Production is still in its infancy as an institutional field. It would appear to have more in common with the New International Labor Studies than with any of the other groups.

Summary and Outlook

Labor has been the central focus of academic research and teaching for about a hundred years now. As with other developing fields, this period has been characterized by paradigm competition (Adams 1983). Each group of scholars addressing some part of the labor universe has approached it with a particular set of concepts and values that illuminate part of the phenomena of interest but cast other parts into the shadows.

Industrial relations, which came into existence as a distinguishable field in the years after World War II, seemed to be the institution which would unite these efforts and bring about a holistic and unified understanding of relations between labor and management. That was clearly the intent of the founders.

In a book written in the mid-1960s, Milton Derber (one of the original members of the IRRA), undertook to review the state of labor research in the United States at that time. He claimed anything having to do with labor as the domain of industrial relations, which he conceived of as "a field of knowledge and study in which all of the traditional social sciences, as well as law and engineering, intersect at different points and in different degrees" (p. 3). He reviewed labor research under the following headings: labor history, union-management relations, public policy, the labor market, organizational behavior and interpersonal relations, foreign labor, and international comparisons and industrial society (p. 72). He concluded that, although the volume of research had expanded significantly in the post-World War II era, there remained "considerable ambivalence as to how best to interrelate the several social sciences in the field" (p. 142). Instead of research developing additively and systematically he concluded that "knowledge has grown in a purely haphazard and unrelated manner" (p. 148).

This review suggests that not much has changed in the past twenty-five years. Despite some partial cross fertilization, the general picture is one of isolated tribes of labor researchers carrying out their work either in ignorance of, or in deliberate disregard for, the work of other groups. As a result the research is not generally additive and little or no progress has been made towards a coherent and comprehensive understanding of labor. No doubt to many labor researchers this situation is not one of concern. Many are convinced that their way to knowledge about labor is superior to that of others or they are satisfied with the progress they are making in their part of the forest and are unconcerned with the overall pattern. For others, though, making holistic sense of the broad phenomena of labor is a high priority. Because of this concern the unity theme continues to reappear in the literature.

To the extent that making overall sense of labor is a worthwhile pursuit, one may ask what may be done to move towards that goal. During the 50s, 60s, and 70s, many of those concerned about this issue tried to designate a core focus or theoretical structure which would unite this diverse field. Kingsley Laffer (1974) suggested bargaining relationships; John Dunlop (1958) and Alan Flanders (1965) hoped that rules and job regulation would provide the unifying glue; Gerald Somers (1969) made a plea for the concept of "exchange relations." None of these proposals resulted in the achievement of significant progress towards unity. It seems that a different approach is needed. Instead of a unifying theory or unifying theme, what may be needed is a symbol which will stand for the totality of labor research.

At present there exists no generally accepted term to designate the broad expanse of labor research. Although, as the discussion above demonstrated, some have tried to define industrial relations in that way it is now clear that industrial relations has come to be thought of as a field that focuses on a small part of the labor universe. Therefore a different encompassing term is needed. Since so many academic fields have gone to Latin to find a name, that strategy is worth consideration.[16]

Because it is an *ology,* sociology is able successfully to embrace scholars from a broad range of ideologies who utilize widely different conceptual schemes to organize research into a wide variety of social phenomena. Instead of many separate fields sociology has many subfields. When they train to be sociologists young scholars are expected to survey the full range of subfields making up the broad field. When later they report their research findings they are expected to know about relevant developments in other subfields and to demonstrate that they understand the implications of those developments for their own research. It seems to me beyond contention that labor as a broad field would be better off if the same relationships and expectations were in place. There is no theory that unifies sociologists, there is only a unifying name, a unifying symbol. Much the same may be said of economics and psychology.

I conclude from these considerations that labor research needs to become an *ology.* In his 1930 book on work through the ages, Tilgher used the term *Homo Faber* (man the maker or man the creator as opposed to *homo sapiens,* man the thinker) to designate his central character. That phrase suggests a new name for the field. Since industrial relations has not been accepted as a unifying concept, how about "Faberology," the science of human beings as makers and creators?

Notes

1. Thoughtful comments on an earlier draft of this essay were received from Kevin Hince, Noah Meltz, Braham Dabscheck, John Goodman, Jean Boivin, Nick Blain, George Strauss, Arie Shirom, and Hoyt Wheeler. I am, of course, entirely responsible for the finished product. It is extraordinary how, throughout history, "scientific discoveries" have

been made simultaneously by two or more researchers working seperately. One theme addressed in this essay is an example of that phenomenon. I began work on this project during the summer of 1990. At the annual meeting of the Industrial Relations Research Association which was held in Washington, D.C. at the end of 1990 I found out that Bruce Kaufman of Georgia State University was working on a book on the same topic. In July of 1991, I completed a draft of this essay and sent it around to colleagues for comments. In October, Kaufman completed a draft of his book. The theme on which we agree is that although the Industrial Relations Research Association was set up after World War II in order to foster interaction between scholars of many disciplines who were interested in the concept of "labor" it has become an organization dominated by the problems and imagery of institutional labor economics. That theme became a major issue at the annual meeting of the IRRA held early in 1991. In his presidential address, Jim Stern made several recommendations for revising the structure and operating procedures of the association in order to overcome problems indicated by the new analysis.

2. The phrase is from Kochan 1980, 1. "In its broadest sense, industrial relations is an interdisciplinary field that encompasses the study of all aspects of people at work."

3. Research by Bruce Kaufman (1993) indicates many important developments in the early 1920s. Not only was the Princeton industrial relations section set up but also, in 1920, the University of Wisconsin established a Bureau of Commercial and Industrial Relations in its extension division and an area of specialization in industrial relations was created within the department of economics. The University of Pennsylvania's Wharton School of Business and Commerce set up the Industrial Research Unit whose research program focused primarily on industrial relations and the University of Chicago appointed Paul Douglas as professor of industrial relations.

4. This was also the objective in other English-speaking countries. Laffer, writing on Australia in the early 1970s argues that the "industrial relationsist" must "have a fairly good knowledge of . . . labor economics, industrial law, organization theory, and trade unionism" and should be able "to relate these to one another in his studies." (p. 65). Noting that most professors of industrial relations at that time had been trained as economists or law scholars or sociologists and had "come to industrial relations subsequently" he put great faith in graduates who "start off as industrial relationsists" to "integrate the various strands."

5. Whatever it may have done in fact, Noah Meltz attempts to demonstrate in this volume that if properly applied it could function as lynchpin holding together the various alternative ways of focusing on people at work.

6. Among industrial relationists there has always been ambiguity about the nature and scope of the field. Depending on who is asked and the context in which the question is posed definitions of the field varying from the study of "all aspects of people at work" to "the study of collective bargaining" may be implied. Thus, contrary to the evidence presented here that the founders of the IRRA considered industrial relations to embrace the broadest range of labor issues and that the industrial relations schools and institutes conceived of their mandate to provide a broad curriculum of labor and labor management subjects, Strauss and Feuille in an article published in one of the leading U.S. industrial relations journals in 1978 state unequivocally that "during the forties and fifties . . . industrial relations centered heavily on collective bargaining" (p. 260).

7. Among the universities where there was such a name change in the 1980s were Purdue, Columbia, Pennsylvania, Georgia State, and Loyola of Chicago.

8. Labeling any group of researchers is always problematic. Thus, in a recent article, Jacoby (1990) includes a much broader group of scholars in the category neoinstitutional labor economist than I do here.

9. "History" has never appeared as a separate academic occupation in the IRRA. Throughout much of the twentieth century most historical work on labor issues was done by economists (McNulty).

10. For many years the *British Journal of Industrial Relations* BJIR carried a cover page which declared that it was "A Journal of Research and Analysis covering every aspect of Industrial Relations: Industrial Sociology, Industrial Psychology, Labor Economics, Labor Law, Manpower Planning, Personnel Policy, Systems of Remuneration, Collective Bargaining, Organizational Theory, Conflict Theory, International Studies, Government Policies, Work Behaviour and Industrial Relations Theory."

11. Among the universities which established new graduate degree programs in industrial relations in the 1980s and early 1990s were the University of Toronto, Queen's University, McMaster University, the University of Alberta, and the University of Quebec at Hull. In contrast, Cappelli (1991) states that no new industrial relations programs were established in the United States in the 1980s.

12. The CIRA membership directory does not provide data on faculty affiliation. A physical count of entries in the 1991 directory produced the following data on departmental affiliation:

	No.	Percentage
Business Administration:	68	49
Industrial Relations		
Institutes/Schools	32	23
Economics	7	5
Law	8	6
Other Social Science:	6	4
Unable to classify:	19	13
Total	140	100

University administrators were excluded, as were students.

13. Among the new journals that came into existence were *Labor and Industry,* the *Australian Bulletin of Labor* and *The Economic and Labor Relations Review.* See the discussion in Jenkins, et al. 1991.

14. In their widely used textbook, Dabscheck and Niland say that there is a "broad consensus among scholars and practitioners alike that industrial relations fundamentally concerns the many ways people behave in the context of work, both as individuals and as members of groups." (*Industrial Relations in Australia,* p. 13). Deery and Plowman also state that "in its broadest sense industrial relations is about the behavior and interaction of people at work." (*Australian Industrial Relations,* p. 3).

15. To an extent the term took on an ideological patina. It was often used with the understanding that the individual being referred to was sympathetic with values implicit in Marxist analysis. See the discussion in Noel (1987).

16. Employment relations is a term favored by some (see, e.g., Wheeler 1988). It has been adopted by at least one institution (Georgia State University) which previously used the term industrial relations. There is also a British journal *Employee Relations.*

Works Cited

Adams, R. J. 1977, *Dunlop After Two Decades: Systems Theory as a Framework for Integrating the Field of Industrial Relations,* McMaster University Faculty of Business Working Paper, Hamilton, Canada. A version of this paper under the title "Integrating Disparate Strands" will appear in J. Barbash and N. Meltz, eds.,

Forthcoming, *Theory, Research and Teaching of International Industrial Relations*, Lewiston, NY: Edwin Mellen Press.

_____. 1983, "Competing Paradigms in Industrial Relations," *Relations Industrielles*, vol. 38, no. 3, pp. 508-26.

_____. 1991, "An International Survey of Courses in Comparative Industrial Relations," in *Teaching Comparative Industrial Relations*, ed. M. Bray, Sydney: Australian Centre for Industrial Relations Research and Teaching, pp. 43-51.

Adams, T. S., and H. L. Sumner. 1905, *Labor Problems, A Textbook*, New York: Macmillan.

Ader, E. B. 1966, *Socialism*, Woodbury, NY: Barron's Educational.

Bain, G. S., and H. Clegg. 1974, "A Strategy for Industrial Relations Research in Great Britain," *British Journal of Industrial Relations*, vol. 12, no. 1, pp. 91-113.

Barbash, J. 1989, "Equity as Function: Its Rise and Attrition," in Barbash and Barbash, eds. 1989, *Theories and Concepts in Comparative Industrial Relations*, Columbia, SC: University of South Carolina Press.

_____. 1991, "John R. Commons and the Western Industrial Relations Tradition," in *Comparative Industrial Relations, Contemporary Research and Theory*, ed. R. J. Adams, London: Harper Collins.

Barbash, J., and K. Barbash. 1989, *Theories and Concepts in Comparative Industrial Relations*, Columbia, SC: University of South Carolina Press.

Barrett, B., E. Rhodes, and J. Beishon. 1975, *Industrial Relations and the Wider Society*, London: Collier Macmillan.

Beer, M., B. Spector, P. Lawrence, D. Q. Mills, and R. Walton. 1985, *Human Resources Management: A General Manager's Perspective*, New York: Free Press.

Berridge, J., and J. Goodman. 1988, "The British Universities Industrial Relations Association: The First 35 Years," *British Journal of Industrial Relations*, vol. 26, no. 2, pp. 155-77.

Boivin, J. 1989, "Industrial Relations: A Field and a Discipline," in Barbash and Barbash, eds., *Theories and Concepts in Comparative Industrial Relations*.

Boyd, R. E., R. Cohen, and P. C. W. Gutking. 1987, *International Labor and the Third World*, Aldershot, England: Gower Publishing.

Braverman, H. 1974, *Labor and Monopoly Capital*, London: Monthly Review Press.

Bray, M., and C. R. Littler, "The Labor Process and Industrial Relations: Review of the Literature," *Labor and Industry*, vol. 1, no. 3, pp. 551-87.

Cappelli, P. 1985, "Theory Construction in IR and Some Implications for Research," *Industrial Relations*, vol. 24, no. 1, pp. 90-112.

_____. 1991, "Is There a Future for the Field of Industrial Relations in the United States," in R. Lansbury, ed., *Industrial Relations Teaching and Research: International Trends*, Sydney: Australian Center for Industrial Relations Research and Teaching at the University of Sydney.

Cohen, R. 1987, "Theorizing International Labor," in Boyd, et al., eds., *International Labor and the Third World*.

Commons, J. R., D. Saposs, H. Sumner, E. Mittelman, H. Hoagland, J. Andrews, and S. Perlman. 1918, *The History of Labor in the United States*, New York: Macmillan.

Commons, J. R. 1894, *Social Reforn and the Church*, New York: Thomas Y. Crowell.

_____. 1924, *The Legal Foundations of Capitalism*, Madison, WI: University of Wisconsin Press.

Cox, R. 1971, "Approaches to a Futurology of Industrial Relations," *International Institute of Labor Studies Bulletin*, no. 8, pp. 139-64.

_____. 1987, *Power and Production, Towards a Political Economy of the World's Work*, New York: Columbia University Press.

Dabscheck, B., and J. Niland. 1981, *Industrial Relations in Australia*, Sydney: Allen and Unwin.

Deery, S., and D. Plowman. 1985, *Australian Industrial Relations*, 2nd ed., Sydney: McGraw-Hill.

Derber, M. 1967, *Research in Labor Problems in the United States*, New York: Random House.

Donovan Commission. 1968, *Royal Commission on Trade Unions and Employers' Associations*, London: HMSO.

Dunlop, John T. 1958, *Industrial Relations Systems*, New York: Henry Holt.

Dwyer, R., M. Galvin, and S. Larson. 1977, "Labor Studies: In Quest of Industrial Justice," *Labor Studies Journal*, Fall, pp. 95-131.

Edwards, P. K. 1990, "The Politics of Conflict and Consent; How the Labor Contract Really Works," *Journal of Economic Behaviour and Organization*, vol. 13, pp. 41-61.

Fashoyin, T. 1991, "Recent Trends in Industrial Relations Research and Theory in Developing Countries," in R. J. Adams, ed., *Comparative Industrial Relations*, London: Harper Collins.

Flanders, A. 1965, *Industrial Relations: What Is Wrong with the System?*, London: Faber.

Form, W. 1979, "Comparative Industrial Sociology and the Convergence Hypothesis," *Annual Review of Sociology*, vol. 5, pp. 1-25.

Godard, J. 1990, "The Pedagogies and Ideologies of Business School IR Teachers," *Teaching and Research in Industrial Relations*, ed. A. Ponak, Proceedings of the 27th Conference of the Canadian

Industrial Relations Association held in Victoria, British Columbia, June 3-5.

_____. 1993, Forthcoming, "Beyond Empiricism: Towards a Reconstruction of Industrial Relations Theory and Research," *Advances in Industrial and Labor Relations.*

Gouldner, A. 1954, *Patterns of Industrial Bureaucracy*, New York: Free Press.

Griesinger, D. 1990, "The Human Side of Economic Organization," *Academy of Management Review,* vol. 15, no. 3, pp. 478-99.

Grossman, J., and W. T. Moye. 1982, "Labor History in the 1970's: A Question of Identity," in T. A. Kochan, D. J. B. Mitchell, and L. Dyer, eds., "Appraising a Decade's Research: An Overview," *Industrial Relations Research in the 1970s: Review and Appraisal,* Madison, WI: Industrial Relations Research Association.

Guest, D. 1987, "Human Resource Management and Industrial Relations," *Journal of Management Studies,* vol. 24, no. 5, pp. 503-21.

Harrod, J. 1987, *Power, Production and Unprotected Work,* New York: Columbia University Press.

Hebert, G., H. Jain, and N. Meltz, eds. 1988, *The State of the Art in Industrial Relations,* Kingston and Toronto: Canadian Industrial Relations Association.

Hince, K. 1991, "Industrial Relations Teaching and Research in New Zealand," in R. Lansbury, ed., *Industrial Relations Teaching and Research: International Trends*, Sydney: Australian Center for Industrial Relations Research and Teaching at the University of Sydney.

Hoxie, R. 1917, *Trade Unionism in the United States,* New York: Appleton.

Hyman, R. 1975, *Industrial Relations: A Marxist Introduction,* London: Macmillan.

Industrial Relations Research Association. 1990, *Membership Directory,* Madison, WI: IRRA.

International Industrial Relations Association. 1989, *Membership Directory,* Geneva: IIRA.

Jacoby, S. M. 1990, "The New Institutionalism: What Can It Learn from the Old?" *Industrial Relations,* vol. 29, no. 2., pp. 316-59.

Jenkins, L., R. Lansbury, and M. Westcott. 1991, "Industrial Relations Teaching and Research in Australia: Extending the Boundaries," in R. Lansbury, ed., *Industrial Relations Teaching and Research.*

Kaufman, B. 1993, *The Origin and Evolution of the Field of Industrial Relations in the United States,* Ithaca, NY: ILR Press.

Kelly, L. 1987, "Industrial Relations at Queen's: The First 50 Years," *Relations Industrielles,* vol. 42, no. 3, pp. 475-99.

Kerr, C. 1984, "A Perspective on Industrial Relations Research—

Thirty-six Years Later," *Proceedings of the Thirty-Sixth Annual Meeting of the Industrial Relations Research Association*, Madison, WI: IRRA.

_____. 1988, "The Neo-classical Revisionists in Labor Economics (1940-1980)—R.I.P.," *How Labor Markets Work*, B. Kaufman, ed., Lexington, MA: Lexington Books.

_____, and L. Fisher. 1964, "Plant Sociology: The Elite and the Aborigines," *Labor-Management and Industrial Society*, C. Kerr, ed., Garden City, NY: Doubleday.

Kerr, C., F. Harbison, J. Dunlop, and F. Myers. 1960, *Industrialism and Industrial Man*, Cambridge, MA: Harvard University Press.

Klare, K. E. 1978, "Judicial Deradicalization of the Wagner Act and the Origins of Modern Legal Consciousness, 1937-41," *Minnesota Law Review*, vol. 62, no. 3, pp. 265-39.

Kochan, T. 1980, *Collective Bargaining and Industrial Relations*, Homewood, IL: Irvin.

Kochan, T., and T. Barocci. 1985, *Human Resources Management and Industrial Relations*, Boston, MA: Little, Brown.

Kochan, T., R. McKersie, and P. Cappelli. 1984, "Strategic Choice and Industrial Relations Theory," *Industrial Relations*, vol. 23, no. 1, pp. 16-39.

Kochan, T. A., D. J. B. Mitchell, and L. Dyer. 1982, "Appraising a Decade's Research: An Overview," in *Industrial Relations Research In the 1970s: Review and Appraisal*, eds. T. Kochan, D. Mitchell, and L. Dyer, Madison, WI: Industrial Relations Research Association.

Kuhn, T. 1962, *The Structure of Scientific Revolutions*, Chicago: University of Chicago Press.

Laffer, K. 1974, "Is Industrial Relations an Academic Discipline?" *Journal of Industrial Relations*, March, pp. 62-73.

Lansbury, R. 1991, *Industrial Relations Teaching and Research: International Trends*, Sydney: Australian Centre for Industrial Relations Research and Teaching at the University of Sydney.

Lester, R. 1977, *Report on the State of the Association*, Madison, WI: Industrial Relations Research Association.

_____. 1986, *The Industrial Relations Section of Princeton University, 1922-1985*, Princeton, NJ: Princeton University Department of Economics.

McNulty, Paul. 1980, *The Origin and Development of Labor Economics*, Cambridge, MA: MIT Press.

McPherson, W., and M. Derber. 1948, "The Formation and Development of the IRRA," in *Proceeding of the First Annual Meeting of theIndustrial Relations Research Association*, Cleveland, OH: IRRA.

Meltz, N. M. 1989, "Industrial Relations: Balancing Efficiency and

Equity," in Barbash and Barbash, eds., *Theories and Concepts in Comparative Industrial Relations.*

Morris, R. 1987, "The Early Uses of the Industrial Relations Concept," *Journal of Industrial Relations*, December, pp. 532-38.

Morton, D. 1988, "Labor and Industrial Relations History in English-Speaking Canada," in Hebert et al., eds., *The State of the Art in Industrial Relations.*

Munck, R. 1988, *The New International Labor Studies, An Introduction*, London: Zed Books.

Munsterberg, H. 1913, *The Psychology of Industrial Efficiency*, Boston: Houghton Mifflin.

Noel, A. 1987, "Accumulation, Regulation, and Social Change: An Essay on French Political Economy," *International Organization*, vol. 41, no. 2, pp. 303-33.

Norton, S. D., and D. Gustafson. 1982, "Industrial/Organizational Psychology as Applied to Human Resources Management," *Professional Psychology*, vol. 13, no. 6, pp. 904-917.

Parsons, M. D. 1990, "Labor Studies in Decline," *Labor Studies Journal*, vol. 15, no. 1, pp. 66-81.

Roberts, B. C. 1977, "The Study of Industrial Relations," *LSE*, November, pp. ii-2.

Rose, M. 1988, *Industrial Behaviour, Theoretical Development Since Taylor*, 2nd ed., London: Allen Lane.

Roy, D. 1952, "Quota Restriction and Goldbricking in a Machine Shop," *American Journal of Sociology*, vol. 57, no. 5, pp. 427-42.

Schatz, R. Forthcoming, "From Commons to Dunlop: Rethinking the Field and Theory of Industrial Relations," in *Defining Industrial Democracy: Work Relations in Twentieth-Century America*, eds. H. Harris and N. Lichtenstein, Cambridge: Cambridge University Press.

Schmitter, P. 1974, "Still the Century of Corporatism?" *Review of Politics*, January.

Simpson, I. H. 1989, "The Sociology of Work: Where Have the Workers Gone?" *Social Forces*, vol. 67, no. 3, pp. 563-81.

Somers, G. 1969, "Bargaining Power and Industrial Relations Theory," in *Essays in Industrial Relations Theory*, ed. G. Somers, Ames, IA: Iowa State University Press.

Stone, K. "The Post War Paradigm in American Labor Law," *Yale Law Journal*, vol. 90, no. 7, pp. 1511-80.

Strauss, G., and P. Feuille. 1978, "Industrial Relations Research: A Critical Analysis," *Industrial Relations*, vol. 17, no. 3, pp. 259-77.

Strauss, G. 1989, "Industrial Relations as an Academic Field: What's Wrong with It?" in Barbash and Barbash, eds., *Theories and Concepts in Comparative Industrial Relations.*

_____. Forthcoming, "Present at the Beginning: Some Personal Notes on OB's Early Days and Later," in *Management Laureates: A Collection of Autobiographical Essays,* ed. A. Bedeian, Greenwich, CT: JAI Press.

Thompson, M. 1973, "Applying a Theory of the Future of Industrial Relations to North America," *Labor Law Journal,* August, pp. 564-72.

Tilgher, A. 1930, *Work: What It Has Meant to Men Through the Ages,* New York: Harcourt Brace.

Warner, W., and J. O. Low. 1947, *The Social System of the Modern Factory,* New Haven, CT: Yale University Press.

Webb, S., and B. Webb. 1897, *Industrial Democracy,* London: Longmans.

_____. 1920, *A History of Trade Unionism,* London: Longmans.

Wheeler, H. 1988, "A Proposal for Renaming Our Field of Study "Employment Relations," *UC Forum,* vol. 1, no. 1, p. 5.

Whyte, W. F. 1987, "From Human Relations to Organizational Behavior—Reflection on the Changing Scene," *Industrial and Labor Relations Review,* vol. 40, no. 4, pp. 487-501.

Williamson, O. 1985, *The Economic Institutions of Capitalism,* New York: Free Press.

Winchester, D. 1991, "The Rise and Fall of Golden Ages: The British Experience of Industrial Relations Research and Teaching," in R. Lansbury, ed., *Industrial Relations Teaching.*

Witte, E. E. 1949, "Where We Are in Industrial Relations," *Proceedings of the First Annual Meeting of the Industrial Relations Research Association,* Champaign, IL: IRRA.

Woods, H. D., J. Crispo, and G. Dion. 1968, *Canadian Industrial Relations: The Report of the Task Force on Labor Relations,* Ottawa: Privy Council Office.

Wren, D. A. 1987, *The Evolution of Management Thought,* 3rd ed., New York: John Wiley.

Industrial Relations Systems as a Framework for Organizing Contributions to Industrial Relations Theory

Noah M. Meltz

Introduction

In his pioneering volume, *Industrial Relations Systems,* Dunlop (1958) develops a framework for understanding industrial relations phenomena. The intention of the 1958 volume was to provide a theoretical base for industrial relations through which hypotheses could be tested and research results accumulated. Industrial relations was to be a separate discipline " . . . on the same logical plane as economics" (Dunlop 1958, 5-6). This volume has led to a significant and continuing debate in the industrial relations litera-

The author wishes to thank the School of Industrial Relations, Queen's University, Kingston, Ontario, where this chapter was written while the author was a visiting research associate. The author would also like to thank Roy Adams, Elizabeth Dalzell, Viatour Larouche, and Frank White for their comments and Eva and Oscar Hollander for their assistance.

ture on whether this is really a useful model for understanding industrial relations (IR) phenomena (Meltz 1991, Adams 1992a).

The purpose of this chapter is to demonstrate that Dunlop's *Industrial Relations Systems* (IRS) model, when combined with subsequent modifications by Barbash (1984), Craig (1990), and Kochan, Katz and McKersie (1986) provides a framework for understanding IR phenomena and for reconciling the unitarist, pluralist, and Marxist approaches or paradigms.

The chapter begins by discussing the context of industrial relations, followed by a presentation of a systems-type framework that is adapted from Dunlop (1958) and that incorporates a number of the subsequent developments. The chapter continues by demonstrating how this framework can be applied to understand industrial relations phenomena and what the framework cannot do. The unitarist, pluralist, and Marxist approaches are considered to show how they fit within the systems framework.

The Context of Industrial Relations

The scientific method of approaching the explanation and prediction of physical phenomena is through controled experiments, whereby scientists find and subsequently verify certain relationships in the physical world, termed natural laws. In the case of social phenomena, it is extremely difficult to conduct controled experiments because time can't be held constant and the past can't be repeated.

In addition, researchers would not be permitted to expose the subjects (humans) to the negative consequences that might follow from controled experiments. Social scientists usually are not permitted to have widely different rates of inflation within a country in order to study their impacts. Instead, we attempt to simulate control through comparisons of similar situations through the use of cross-sectional and longitudinal analysis.

Of the social sciences, economics, among others, has determined some phenomena which exist and can be predicted. However, even the "laws" of economics are subject to the qualification of all other things being equal, something which rarely occurs. The result is that predictions on the basis of these laws have to take into consideration the particular circumstances and the weights of the various developments which are occuring at the same time.

Industrial relations phenomena are difficult to understand and especially difficult to predict because so many things are happening simultaneously and each of these developments can interact with the other things to produce differing outcomes. The following is a specific example. In 1978, negotiations between the United Steelworkers of America and the International Nickel (INCO) Company in Sudbury, Canada, were at a standoff. The company was demanding some changes in practices which the union regarded as "takebacks." The company had more than a year's supply of nickel, which meant that the plant could be closed for more than a year and INCO could still meet its customers' needs. The director of the union district urged the president of the local to accept the company's terms. In such circumstances we should have expected (or predicted) that there would be a settlement without a strike. Instead the local went on a strike that lasted eight-and-a-half months and ended in a settlement with a contract that was almost the same as the last prestrike offer.

Was the 1978-1979 INCO strike the result of irrational and unpredictable union leadership decisions that defy scientific explanation or prediction? The answer is no. The negotiations at INCO took place against a background of mutual distrust and open hostility. Long strikes were the order of the day. The subsequent round of negotiations ended with an agreement after a three-and-a-half month strike. At that time there was a six-month stockpile of nickel. Even though the 1978-79 strike produced almost no gains for the union, the president of the local was subsequently elected director of the district, defeating the former director who had urged acceptance of the company's offer without a strike.

To understand such developments we need a framework that can take into consideration the various factors and their weights in the particular situations. Clearly we are dealing with judgements that can vary from researcher to researcher. However, an appropriate framework should be able to assist in the analysis of such situations and enhance the possibility of predicting the outcomes. An enhanced ability to analyze and possibly even predict some outcome may enable the parties to avoid or mitigate some of the more extreme outcomes.

Is the role of industrial relations to avoid or mitigate extreme outcomes or to simply explain and possibly predict what will happen? This too is a subject of debate within IR. I believe, along with Barbash, that many professionals in the field of industrial relations, and certainly the pioneers in the field, have seen their role as that of changing outcomes by attempting to balance equity and efficiency considerations, (Barbash 1989, Meltz 1989a.). To do this industrial relationists (to use Laffer's 1974 term) need a framework for analysis and, where possible, prediction. Experience in the field is clearly of enormous value, but there has to be in addition a scientific approach which accumulates, builds on, and contributes to the insights gained through experience. The systems framework is a starting point for scientific analysis.

The Systems Framework

Although there have been many variations adapting and building on Dunlop's original (1958) IR systems framework (see Meltz 1991, footnote 2, 18-19), we will confine this article to the presentation of three: Barbash (1984), Craig (1990), and Kochan, Katz, and Mckersie (1986). Our purpose is not to critique any of these but rather to show that the systems frameworks can assist in understanding IR problems and the alternative approaches which have been put forward.

Figure 1 shows a detailed framework adapted from Dunlop (1958), Barbash (1984), Craig (1990), and Kochan, Katz, and McKersie (1986) and presents what is intended to be a three-dimensional diagram of the determinants of employment relationships. The third dimension is discussed below in terms of various levels of aggregation such as local/municipality, regional (such as state/provincial), national, and even international. In this chapter we use the term framework rather than model. The choice is deliberate. We believe that the term model implies a set of hypotheses which can be tested. A framework for analysis provides a mechanism for understanding industrial relations phenomena by identifying the major elements which shape IR developments. Each of these elements, in turn, is the product of forces which can themselves be understood only after the application and testing of relevant theories (Adams 1988). As a result, the environmental elements are presented only in outline form whereas the industrial relations system itself includes much more detail because that is the focus of the framework.

Dunlop (1958) intended that his framework be in the form of a model so that hypotheses could be formulated and tested and the results accumulated in a body of research. For example, what impact does monopoly in the product market have on the industrial relations system of the organization which has the monopoly? Barbash (1984) incorporates internal bargaining which takes place within both management and trade unions. He also sees management focusing on efficiency or cost discipline, while unions focus on equity as well as price, effort, and power. Craig's (1990) formulation and that of Kochan, Katz, and McKersie (1986) are deliberately set out as frameworks rather than testable models since the intention is that testable hypotheses are to be found within specific components of the framework and not through the framework itself. As a result, Craig and Kochan, Katz, and McKersie can be said to have generalized Dunlop's original model in differing dimensions. Alternately Dunlop's model can be viewed as intended to be a testable part of the more general IR systems framework.

The five major components of the industrial relations systems (IRS) framework are

1. The actors, including their goals, values (ideology), power, and history
2. The environmental context in which they interact
3. The mechanisms through which and within which they interact (what Dunlop termed procedural rules
4. The outcomes of the interaction for both organizations and workers (what Dunlop termed substantive rules)
5. The feedback or short-term and long-term implications for the actors themselves and for society as a whole by way of the environmental context.

The diagram is intended to be three dimensional, with the third dimension being the various levels of organizational decision-making which are suggested by Kochan, Katz, and McKersie (1986). Each of these components will be discussed in turn.

Figure 1. Industrial Relations Systems Framework of Employment Relationships

Inputs →

External Environment	Internal to the Actors	Actors	Level of Strategic Chores by the Actors			Interaction Mechanisms
			1. Long Term Strategy and Policy Making	2. Collective Bargaining and Personnel Policy	3. Workplace and Individual/Organization Relationships	
Ecological Physical Surroundings Natural Resources Climate	Goals	Employees and Their Organizations (Unions, Assoc.) (Equity)	Political Strategies Representation Strategies Organizing Strategies Planning with Mgmt. or Govt.	Collective Bargaining Strategies Internal Bargaining	Contract Administration Worker Participation Job Design and Work Organization	**Collective Bargaining:** Certification Negotiation Conciliation Mediation Fact Finding Arbitration of Interest and Right Disputes Creative Bargaining Inquiry Commissions Strikes and Lockouts Union-Management Committees Workers on Board of Directors Works Councils Regional and National Bipartite and Tripartite Boards
Economic Product Market Labor Market Macro (see also legal) Fiscal and Monetary Policies	Values					
Technological	Power	Employers and Their Hierarchy (Efficiency)	Business Strategies Investment Strategies Human Resource Strategies Planning with Unions and/or Govt.	Personnel Policies Negotiations Policies Internal Bargaining	Supervisory Style Worker Participation Job Design and Work Organization	**Human Resource Management Policy:** Including: Planning Staffing Development and Training Maintenance Incl. Compensation
Political Political System Levels of Government and Their	External Directed Efforts: Lobbying and Other Participation in the Political Process					
	History					

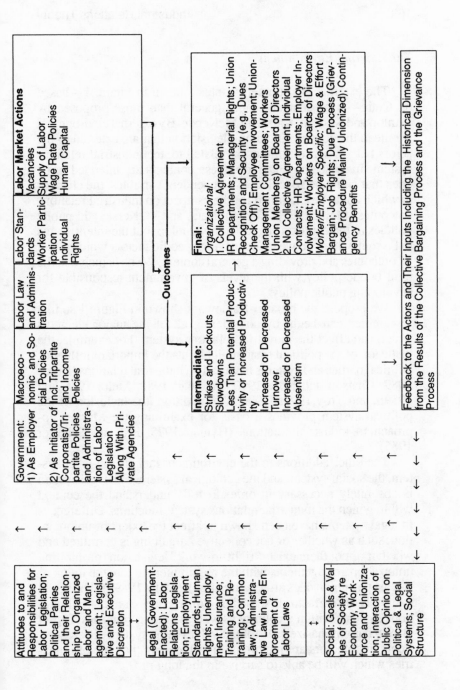

The External Environment

The external environment context shown in Figure 1—based on Craig—is broader and more general than those proposed by Dunlop and Kochan, Katz, and McKersie. By external environment we mean the contexts including legislation that are external to the actors but are part of, or closely related to, the industrial relations system. In the case of Dunlop, these contexts are intended to be ones that could be specified as independent variables, the changes in which could be examined for their impact on industrial relations outcomes (Meltz 1991). Kochan, Katz, and McKersie add public policies to the contexts suggested by Dunlop, but the intent seems to be somewhere between identifying specific factors which affect IR outcomes and providing a general context. We have included the term public policy with the levels of government responsible for developing public policy.

We propose the broader framework shown in Figure 1 so that researchers can begin by considering all of the major elements which can affect the industrial relations system. For example, the inclusion of the political system highlights the important influence political parties and systems have had on industrial relations (Bruce 1989, Chaison and Rose 1990, Freeman 1988, Meltz 1985 and 1989b, and Troy 1990a, 1990b). In addition, the inclusion of the political system provides a basis for examining the Marxist approach to industrial relations (Hyman 1975, Erd and Scherrer 1985).

The other additions to the environment include the legal system, the social system, and the ecological system. The legal system is absolutely necessary in order to fully understand the context within which the industrial relations system functions. Differences in legal systems have been shown to affect the extent of unionization, such as whether or not collective bargaining is permitted and whether or not there exists "right-to-work" legislation (prohibiting union shop arrangements with the requirement to join the union or at least pay union dues after being hired) (Meltz 1989b). The social system is also a factor in explaining differences in industrial relations systems within a country as well as among countries. Lipset (1990) has emphasized the role of values in IR system differences. Ecological factors are important in influencing the type of industries which will be able to survive in the long run.

Although the framework in Figure 1 begins with the broad contextual factors, this is not to preclude a narrower focus and a more analytical approach once the major elements have been identified. For example, industry-level studies would likely focus on the aspects which Dunlop and Kochan, Katz, and McKersie identify once the role of the general contextual factors had been established. This general context is a starting point for more specific analysis.

This approach to the context has another advantage. The systems which are shown in the environmental context in Figure 1 are also associated with particular disciplines, enabling linkages between industrial relations and these other disciplines. Ecological systems relate to such disciplines as geology and geography. The other systems relate respectively to economics, political science, law, sociology, and psychology. The inclusion of history introduces the discipline of history (Hebert, Jain, and Meltz 1988).

Dunlop and Kochan, Katz, and McKersie identify technology as a separate environmental factor, whereas Craig includes technology under the economic system. We have separated technology since its impact is important as an independent factor and the disciplines to which it relates are as much engineering and science as they are economics.

The Actors

All IRS frameworks identify three main actors: labor, management, and government. Dunlop (1958) is explicit in referring to workers and their organizations, the hierarchy of management, and government and its agencies. Craig (1990) focuses on labor as organized (unionized) labor, while Kochan, Katz, and McKersie are explicit in dealing only with unions. Kochan, et al., are also explicit in identifying levels of industrial relations activity and decision-making. They identify three levels: long-term strategy and policy making; collective bargaining and personnel policy; and workplace and individual/organization relationships. We will use the original Dunlop approach of considering the workers as both individual employees and as members of informal and formal groups including trade unions.

Each of these levels of organization could be subdivided. For example, a distinction could be made between policies that are decided in head offices that are located outside a country and local operations offices. (For a discussion of the various considerations of levels, see Adams 1992a.) More levels could also be added if the organizational activities were divided into different geographical levels, both among countries and within a country, such as all of the plants/offices of a firm and those located in a state/province, region, municipality, or a single local plant or office. Nevertheless, the three tiers do identify conceptually different levels of decision-making within an organization, whether the organization is in the private or public sector, a trade union, or a branch of the government.

The goals, values, and power are Craig's terms, which include the distribution of power in the larger society and the ideology (a set of ideas and beliefs held by the actors), as identified by Dunlop, and the values and business strategies as identified by Kochan, Katz, and McKersie.

The Levels of Strategic Choices and the Interaction Mechanisms

There are two primary aspects of the mechanisms by which the actors interact with the environmental context. The first portion of the interaction mechanism describes the three levels of decision-making by the three actors as developed by Kochan, Katz, and McKerzie. The three levels are long-term strategy and policy making; collective bargaining and personnel (human resource management) policy; and workplace and individual/organization relationships. Traditionally, in industrial relations in North America, the middle tier has been the major focus for the interaction mechanisms among the actors. This is the tier where decisions are made about strategy relating to collective bargaining and human resource management. The lower portion of the three tiers relates to practices at the workplace and decisions relating both to formal and informal groups and to individual workers.

In North America the upper portion, strategic planning, largely takes place without any formal interaction mechanisms. In other areas, such as some countries in Europe and Asia with a corporatist tradition, there are formal mechanisms for political bargaining at the national level (Adams 1989). Occasionally, there may be some interaction among the actors at the strategic level initiated by a federal government or a provincial or state government. Some countries also require worker participation on corporate boards of directors where strategic corporate decisions are often made.

The second portion of the interaction mechanism in Figure 1 describes the traditional means by which differences between organized labor (unions) and management are resolved at the bargaining table: the negotiation process; conciliation officer and board (mediation); fact-finding; other approaches to deal with bargaining impasses; arbitration of interest (terms of an agreement) and rights (grievance) disputes; and special enquiry commissions. In addition there is the day-to-day interpersonal relations to satisfy social and psychological needs both for individuals covered by collective agreements and for individual employees not covered by a collective agreement. For such employees the individual contract of employment, which the law presumes to be freely negotiated, is fundamental to the relationship between the employer and the employee. Individual employees may also have recourse to grievance mechanisms.

The second portion of the interaction mechanism also includes human resource management (HRM) practices (such as planning, recruitment, selection, compensation, benefits, training, etc.; see Dunlop forthcoming and Hills in this volume) and labor market aspects such as internal labor markets (Doeringer and Piore 1971). The explicit inclusion of human resource management in the framework may also have a positive long-run impact in helping to bring IR and HRM back together after the separation of the two in the mid-1950s (See Kaufman 1993, and the chapters by Adams, "All Aspects of People at Work," and Hills in this volume).

The upper portion, strategic planning, largely takes place without any formal interaction mechanisms. Occasionally there may be some interaction among the actors at the strategic level initiated by the federal government or a provincial or state government.

The Outcomes

There are two types of outcomes of the interaction of the actors and the environmental context. The first type of outcome includes the terms and conditions of employment, called worker-oriented outputs by Craig and substantive rules by Dunlop. The second type of outcome includes the formal and informal understanding of the relationship between the parties in the near future. This understanding may be for a specified period in a collective agreement or for an unspecified period if there is no collective agreement. If the understanding is part of a collective agreement, then it may set out management rights and union recognition and security, which Craig calls organizational outputs, as well as the procedures for resolving disputes between the parties during the period of the understanding (grievance procedure). Dunlop refers to the latter as procedural rules.

There are also the outcomes from understandings reached between individual workers and management when there is no union. In this case there will be no formal bargaining but terms and conditions of work are established by employers taking into consideration external and internal labor market considerations, and there is normally an expected period to which they apply. These individual terms and conditions are often said to be determined by human resource management policies, but HRM policies can be said to apply whether or not there is a union. HRM policies would be developed in the middle tier of decision-making by employers.

For Kochan, Katz, and McKersie the performance outcomes relate to employers, employees, labor unions, and society, through decisions taken at the three levels. The scope of the particular decisions depends on the level under consideration. The decision in the middle tier will include the aspects just presented as the outcomes of the collective bargaining process. The decisions at the lower tier relating to the workplace include both individual relationships, which have been noted, and organization relationships which include both collective aspects when there is a union and organization considerations that apply in any situation when there are a number of employees.

The upper level, or the long-term strategy formulation, is not present in either of the Craig or Dunlop frameworks. In this case the specific outcomes include decisions relating to investment in future plant location, and future relationships with unions, such as whether the organization will attempt to operate new locations or even existing locations without a union. Above the level of the firm, multiemployer bargaining with trade unions (both formal and informal) may set constraints within which corporate decisions must be taken.

Implications of the Outcomes for the Environment and the Actors

Both Craig and Kochan, Katz, and McKersie add feedback loops to their systems, implying that the outcomes will have an impact on the environment and the actors. The explicit inclusion of feedback is to provide a dynamic element for the understanding of industrial relations phenomena. Dunlop's framework implicitly includes a feedback component but the other two make it explicit and we have included feedback in Figure 1.

In addition, we have connected the feedback to the historical dimension in order to emphasize the role of the historical context in the industrial relations system. Past history influences current decisions by all of the actors. The outcome of the current interactions among the actors can add to or change the historical context that will affect the actors and their interactions in the future. Kochan, Katz, and McKersie include history in their model as an intervening variable between the external environment and the actors. We have added the history of the relationships among the actors as an internal input along with the goals, values, and power.

An aspect of the feedback, but one which moves primarily from the actors to the environmental context, deals with the efforts by the actors to influence the outcomes of the political process through specific spending decisions by government, policy decisions, or through efforts to introduce or change legislation. We have included the government as initiator of public policies relating to corporatist/tripartite policies with the government as administrator of labor legislation since this role seems to be separable from the government as the initiator of labor legislation. The former role seems to involve strategic decision-making closely related to that of unions and management.

Applying the IR Systems Framework

The IR systems framework set out in Figure 1 is intended to be applied in several stages depending on the problem or issue being considered. The issue under consideration provides the starting point for the analysis. The researcher would identify the primary level of focus within the organization and the types of decisions at that level as set out in the three tier interaction mechanism. The next step would be to use the environmental context as a checklist to consider their possible effects on the actors at the levels being considered.

For example, Kochan, Katz, and McKersie are concerned with the causes of the decline in union representation within the American workforce. In this particular case the major environmental systems are economic and legal, although the political is relevant to the abortive efforts of the Carter administration in the United States in the late 1970s to change the legal system as it relates to certifying and decertifying unions. Another relevant political action was the Reagan administration's decertification of the air traffic controlers during their illegal strike in 1981 (see Adams 1992b). Along with the environmental context are the actions taken by the actors, both employers and unions in the long-term strategy area.

If the concern is a particular labor relations situation, such as the continuing difficulties in the Canadian Post Office, then the focus will be primarily on the strategic choices by the actors and the impact of technological change as well as the turbulent history of the relations between the actors. For most of the history the management and government actors were synonymous. Recently the Post Office became a Crown Corporation which is somewhat separated, but the government still dominates labor relations decision-making.

An alternative approach is to begin with a particular change in one or more factors in the environmental systems. For example, what impact would the changes being considered in labor legislation in Ontario have on the incidence and duration of strikes in Ontario. One of the changes being considered is an antistrikebreaking provision that would prevent the use of replacement workers or managers from other branches of the organization to continue operations during a strike. A study of the impact of the possible changes would include examining the effects of the antistrike-breaking legislation in the Province of Quebec (see Gunderson, Melino, and Reid 1990). Other starting points could include the possible impact of a Canada-U.S.-Mexican free-trade agreement on trade union density in Canada and the United States. At the organization level, changes in technology could be examined, such as the impact of the use of parttime versus split shifts for bus drivers in the Toronto Transit Commission.

Whatever the starting point, the application of the framework would involve considering the possible implications of and for the various components that are relevant in the entire system. In particular the emphasis would be on the central elements within the industrial relations system: the actors, the mechanisms for the interactions among the actors, the outcomes, and the feedback.

The IR System and the Unitarist Approach

The unitarist approach to industrial relations looks at the relations between management and individual workers where there is said to be a commonality of purpose between the two (Fox 1986).

As can be seen from Figure 1, the unitarist approach can be included within the IR systems framework because the labor actor includes workers both as individual employees and as organized employees. To take the unitarist approach, consideration would only be given to those elements of the framework which involve employees as individuals or as unorganized groups (whether formal or informal). This means that all of the interaction mechanisms relating to collective bargaining and contract administration would be omitted, such as negotiations, mediation, strike resolution, etc. Grievance arbitration in most cases would not be considered, although some nonunion organizations have introduced grievance mechanisms (Kepler 1990, McCabe 1990). In a comment to the author, Roy Adams observes that the very act of creating a grievance mechanism in a nonunion organization may be an admission by management that the interests of employees and management are not unitary. Similarly, the outcomes which include collective aspects such as union recognition and union security would be excluded, although again there could be some informal or even formal understanding concerning various types of employee representation.

All of the environmental factors would apply with the exception of the direct application of labor relations legislation. Even here, labor relations legislation is relevant in the sense that if employees became dissatisfied with their employment relations they might decide to attempt to change to a collectivist approach.

The internal inputs of goals, values, and power would apply to the management and would also apply to individual employees. The historical dimension would apply as well because the ability of the organization to avoid collective decision-making would be influenced by the history of the relations between management and employees with respect to the treatment they have received in terms of consistency, fairness, etc., (Barbash 1989). The fact that IBM and DOFASCO (a Canadian firm) have successfully practiced the unitary approach to employee relations involves consistency, fairness, competitive wages and benefits, and mechanisms to solve employee relations problems. Traditions and social values are also important in determining the extent of unionization in organizations. Adams (1989) points out that in Scandinavia people join and stay in the unions because it is the normal thing to do rather than as a response to deficient managerial practices.

Some (North American) organizations have establishments which are unionized and establishments which are not unionized. Some of the differences may have arisen from strategic decisions to open nonunion "greenfield" sites, and some may have arisen from acquisition programs. In either case organizations may be taking a unitary perspective in some of their locations and a pluralist approach in others. By pluralist we mean nonunitary or situations in which at least some of the employees at a location are represented by a bargaining agent. In these situations the IR systems framework can help to identify considerations that are relevant to both unionized establishments and those in which no collective bargaining takes place, as well as the factors which may influence in which direction the organization may proceed. For example, the United Auto Workers was able to defeat the attempt by the Big Three auto firms to operate plants without collective bargaining mechanisms in the Southern United States (Kochan, Katz, and McKersie 1986), but unions in other industries have not been as successful.

While some managers may see the world through a frame of reference in which the goals and interests of management and labor in the firm are essentially the same, industrial relationists (both pluralist and radical) assume that labor and management have separate and distinct interests whether employees are organized or not (Fox 1986). Those managers who have a unitary frame of reference would combine the employee and employer rows in Figure 1. A radical or pluralist perspective would see separate rows whether or not the employees were covered by a collective agreement.

Whether we are dealing with a "pure" unitary situation or a mixed system in which some employees have collective representation and some do not, the IR systems framework should be a valuable tool of analysis.

The Marxist and Socialist Approaches

In contrast to the unitary approach, the Marxist approach posits a class system with an inevitable conflict that will ultimately result in the overthrow of the capitalists by the workers. For Marx, trade unions were to be in the vanguard in the overthrow of the capitalists. Their (the unions') role was to concentrate on the overthrow of the economic and political system rather than simply or only attempting to improve the working conditions of employees (Hyman 1975, Scheinstock 1980, Shalev 1980, Erd and Scherrer 1985).

The focus on the overthrow of the economic and political system distinguished the Marxists from the socialist reformers, such as the Webbs, who saw unions as both making improvements in the working conditions of employees as well as influencing government legislation to set minimum standards of employment for all workers (Marshall and Perlman 1972, 3-58).

More recent Marxist writings have softened the immediate goal of the overthrow of the economic system, but the focus is still on the inevitability of class conflict. Both IR pluralists and Marxists who do labor relations research posit fundamental labor-management conflict. The difference is that the pluralists see collective bargaining and other institutions of labor-management interaction as being able constructively to funnel the conflict; Marxists see these institutions as means of cooling out conflict to the detriment of labor.

The IR systems framework can accommodate both the Marxist and the socialist approaches. In both cases the political and economic systems are important but for the Marxists they are the exclusive focus, especially the political system which is the end in itself. For the socialists the political system is more of a means acting through the legal system to introduce reforms in setting minimum employment standards and also providing the means whereby workers could legally join unions (Morton and Copp 1984). Socialists were also interested in expanding, through democratic methods, government ownership of particular means of production, such as banks, and major manufacturing sectors, such as steel. In addition, the socialists were concerned with the outcomes of the relations between unions and management.

In terms of Figure 1, the Marxist approach concentrates on the relationship between the actors and the environment. In particular, the focus is on the relationship between unions and the political system on the one hand, and management (the capitalists) and the government on the other hand. The government is viewed as being the handmaiden of the capitalists. Whereas the usual systems model shows the direction of causation as being from the environment to the actors (Craig 1990), in the case of the Marxist approach the direction of the causation would be the other way, that is toward the left side of Figure 1, literally and, it might be said, figuratively.

The socialist approach has causation going both ways in terms of the relationship between organized labor and the political system. The unions, either through political lobbying and/or through participation in labor parties, attempt to either form governments or at least influence governments to pass legislation that would favor employees. There might be aspects of the legislation which would affect the mechanisms of interaction, although the focus would also be on the outcomes, particularly the wages and conditions of employment. Depending on the particular socialist approach, greater or lesser efforts would be made to affect the outcomes.

A variant of the Marxist and socialist approaches is that called political economy. The hallmark of the political economy approach is that it retains the essential nature of the class conflict, but sees a more gradual approach to the reconciliation of the conflicts inherent in the capitalist system (Giles 1989, Giles and Murray 1987, 1992). This approach as well can be encompassed within the systems framework because it is focusing on the role of government and its agencies in intervening in the workplace. For the political economy approach, the government actor is an extension of the political system and has a major impact on the outcome of the IR system.

As a summary comment it can be said that the Marxist and socialist approaches to labor relations, as well as the variant termed political economy, can be examined and applied within the industrial relations systems framework set out in Figure 1.

Concluding Comments

While there has been considerable debate concerning the use-fulness of the systems framework, it has been suggested that the framework can be used in a variety of approaches, with the most recent being the strategic choice model developed by Kochan, Katz, and McKersie (1986). It has also suggested that the IR systems framework can encompass the widely divergent unitarist and Marx-ist approaches as well as the socialist and political economy varia-tions.

The framework can be used to distinguish between a general description, where the researchers use the framework to identify the major elements on which they want to focus, and an analytical approach where particular aspects of the framework are used in the form of testable hypotheses along the lines which were originally suggested by Dunlop (1958). The approach, of essentially building on the systems framework, has been followed by Kochan, Katz, and McKersie (1986) in their analysis of the transformation of the American industrial relations system.

I expect there will be disagreement with what has been pre-sented here. But I hope there will be discussion and particularly an application of the framework in the spirit of advancing the disci-pline of industrial relations.

Works Cited

Adams, R. J. 1992a, "Integrating Disparate Strands: an Elaborated
    Version of Systems Theory as a Framework for Organizing
    the Field of Industrial Relations," in J. Barbash and N. M. Meltz,
    eds., *Theory, Research and Teaching in International Industrial
    Relations,* Lewiston, NY: The Edwin Mellen Press.
_____. 1992b, "The Role of the State in Industrial Relations," in
    D. Lewin, O. Mitchell, and P. Sherer, eds., *Research Frontiers in
    Industrial Relations,* Madison, WI: Industrial Relations Research
    Association.
_____. 1989, "Industrial Relations Systems: Canada in Compara-
    tive Perspective," in J. C. Anderson, M. Gunderson, and A. Ponak,
    Union-Management Relations in Canada, 2nd ed., Don Mills,
    Ontario: Addison Wesley Publishers, pp. 437-464.

_____. 1988, "Desperately Seeking Industrial Relations Theory," *The International Journal of Comparative Labor, Law and Industrial Relations*, vol. 4.

Barbash, J. 1984, *The Elements of Industrial Relations*. Madison, WI: University of Wisconsin Press.

_____. 1989, "Equity as Function: Its Rise and Attribution," in J. Barbash and K. Barbash, eds., *Theories and Concepts in Comparative Industrial Relations*, Columbia, SC: University of South Carolina Press, pp. 113-122.

Bruce, P. 1989, "Political Parties and Labor Legislation in Canada and the U.S.," *Industrial Relations*, vol. 28, no. 2 , pp. 115-141.

Chaison, G. N., and J. B. Rose. 1990, "Continental Divide: The Direction and Fate of North American Unions," in *Advances in Industrial and Labor Relations*, D. Lewin, D. Lipsky, and D. Sockell, eds., Westport, CT: JAI Press.

Craig, A. 1988, "Mainstream Industrial Relations in Canada," in G. Hebert, H. Jain, and N. M. Meltz, eds., *The State of the Art in Industrial Relations*, Kingston, Ontario: Industrial Relations Centre, Queen's University and Centre for Industrial Relations, pp. 9-43.

_____. 1990, *The System of Industrial Relations in Canada*, 3rd ed., Scarborough, Ontario: Prentice-Hall, chap. 1, pp. 1-19.

Doeringer, P., and M. Piore. 1971, *Internal Labor Markets and Manpower Analysis*, Lexington, MA.: Heath.

Dunlop, J. 1958, *Industrial Relations System*, New York: Henry Holt and Co.

_____. Forthcoming, "Organizations and Human Resources, Internal and External Markets," in C. Kerr and P. Staudohar, eds., *Labor Economics and Industrial Relations*, Stanford, CA: Stanford University Press.

Erd, R., and C. Scherrer. 1985, "Unions—Caught between Structural Competition and Temporary Solidarity: A Critique of Contemporary Marxist Analysis of Trade Unions in Germany," *British Journal of Industrial Relations*, vol. 23, no. 1 , pp. 115-131.

Fox, A. 1986, "Industrial Sociology and Industrial Relations," *Royal Commission on Trade Unions and Employers' Associations*, Research Paper No. 3, London: Her Majesty's Stationery Office.

Freeman, R. B. 1988, "Contraction and Expansion: The Divergence of Private Sector and Public Sector Unionism in the United States," *Journal of Economic Perspectives*, vol 2, no. 2, pp. 63-88.

Giles, A. 1989, "Industrial Relations Theory, the State and Politics," in J. Barbash and K. Barbash, eds., *Theories and Concepts in Comparative Industrial Relations*. Columbia, SC: University of South Carolina Press, pp. 123-154.

Giles, A., and G. Murray. 1987, "The Rise and Fall of the Systems

Approach: Implications for an Understanding of Canadian Industrial Relations," Canadian Industrial Relations Association Annual Meetings.

_____. 1992." Industrial Relations Theory and Political Economy: Why Is There No State of the Art?" in J. Barbash and N. M. Meltz, eds., *Theory, Research and Teaching International Industrial Relations,* Lewiston, NY: The Edwin Mellen Press.

Gunderson, M., A. Melino, and F. Reid. 1990, "The Effects of Canadian Labor Relations Legislation on Strike Incidence and Duration," *Labor Law Journal,* vol. 41, no. 8, pp. 512-517.

Hebert, G., H. Jain, and N. M. Meltz. 1988, *The State of the Art in Industrial Relations,* Industrial Relations Centre, Queen's University at Kingston and Centre for Industrial Relations, University of Toronto.

Hyman, R. 1975, *Industrial Relations: A Marxist Introduction,* London: Macmillan Press, pp. 9-31.

_____. 1982, "Comments on Collective Bargaining and Industrial Relations, by Thomas A. Kochan," *Industrial Relations,* vol. 21, pp. 100-113.

Kaufman, B. 1993, Forthcoming,*The Origins and Evolution of the Field of Industrial Relations in the United States,* Ithaca, NY: IRL Press.

Kepler, M. J. 1990, "Nonunion Grievance Procedures: Union Avoidance Technique or Union Organizing Opportunity?" *Labor Law Journal,* vol. 41, no. 8, pp. 557-563.

Kochan, T. A., H. C. Katz, and R. B. McKersie. 1986, *The Transformation of AmericanIndustrial Relations,* New York: Basic Books.

Laffer, K. 1974, "Is Industrial Relations an Academic Discipline?" *Journal of Industrial Relations,* vol. 16, no. 1, pp. 62-73.

Lipset, S. M. 1990, *Continental Divide: The Values and Institutions of the United States and Canada,* New York: Routledge

Marshall, R., and R. Perlman. 1972, *An Anthology of Labor Economics: Readings and Commentary,* Toronto: Wiley, pp. 3-58.

McCabe, D. M. 1990, "Corporate Nonunion Grievance Procedures: Open Door Policies—A Procedural Analysis," *Labor Law Journal,* vol. 41, no. 8, pp. 551-557.

Meltz, N. M. 1985, "Labor Movements in Canada and the United States," in T. A. Kochan, ed., *Challenges and Choices Facing American Labor,* Cambridge, MA: The MIT Press, pp. 315-337.

_____. 1989a, "Industrial Relations: Balancing Efficiency and Equity," in J. Barbash and K. Barbash, eds., *Theories and Concepts in Comparative Industrial Relations,* Columbia, SC: University of South Carolina Press, 109-113.

_____. 1989b, "Interstate vs Interprovincial Differences in Union Density," *Industrial Relations*, vol. 28, no. 2, pp. 142-158.

_____. 1990, "Unionism in Canada, U.S.: On Parallel Tread-mills?" *Forum for Applied Research and Public Policy*, vol. 5, no. 4 , pp. 46-52.

_____. 1991, "Dunlop's Industrial Relations Systems After Three Decades," in R. J. Adams, ed., *Comparative Industrial Relations, Contemporary Research & Theory*, London: Harper-Collins Academic, pp. 10-20.

Morton, D., and T. Copp. 1984, *Working People: An Illustrated History of the Canadian Labor Movement*, rev. ed. Ottawa: Deneau.

Schienstock, G. 1981, "Towards a Theory of Industrial Relations," *British Journal of Industrial Relations*, vol. 191, pp. 170-189.

Shalev, M. 1980, "Industrial Relations Theory and the Comparative Study of Industrial Relations and Industrial Conflict," *British Journal of Industrial Relations*, vol. 18, no. 1, pp. 26-41.

Troy, L. 1990a, "Is the U.S. Unique in the Decline of Private Sector Unionism?" *Journal of Labor Research*, vol. 11, no. 2, pp. 111-143.

_____. 1990b, "Future Paths Different for Private and Public Unions," *Forum for Applied Research and Public Policy*, vol. 5, no. 4, pp. 37-45.

Integrating Industrial Relations with the Social Sciences

Stephen M. Hills

As a long-standing student of industrial relations (IR), I have tried to overcome three "great divides" that hinder the development of a relatively integrated view of the field. They are:

1. A division between a macro view of industrial relations as negotiation among abstract "actors"—labor, management, and government—and a micro view of the relationships that individuals have with each other in the workplace;
2. A division between a Marxist and a non-Marxist worldview; and
3. A division with regard to the main policy problems addressed by IR theory—the allocation of "human resources" (i.e., policies to encourage economic efficiency) or the establishment of worker industrial rights (i.e., policies to encourage workplace equity and justice).

These divisions within the field run deep and can, in fact, cause a student to believe that an integrated view of IR is impossible. The thesis of this essay is that a degree of integration *is* possible by a

The author wishes to acknowledge the helpful research assistance of Frank Borgers and the comments on earlier drafts of Roy Adams, Roy Lewicki, Steve Mangum, and Hoyt Wheeler.

better conceptualization of how various IR theories complement each other, how they apply to the workplace, and how they are linked to the social science disciplines.

My years of teaching graduate IR theory have convinced me that an explicit focus on the social sciences is highly desirable. The most important advantage is that the employment relationship can be emphasized rather than a specific institution like the labor union. The influence of unions may rise and fall in a particular country while the employment relationship maintains its importance to economic activity. Secondly, by treating "classic" theories according to the separate disciplines most closely associated with them, students gain an appreciation for the assumptions, biases, and special contributions brought to the field from each separate social science area. The approach also forces students (as well as their instructors) to differentiate the parts of each discipline that are particularly applicable to IR from the parts that are not. Few students today can become renaissance persons due to the tremendous expansion, elaboration, and testing of theory in each of the social sciences. If for no other reason than time, boundaries need to be set. Establishing boundaries for the field also demands that the student define what the term "industrial relations" means. The definition, in turn, helps link various social science theories to the pragmatic problems of the workplace. Finally, an emphasis on the social sciences delays, at least temporarily, the student's own tendency to specialize in just one set of social science theories, thereby creating a potential for true interdisciplinary thinking.

A good conceptualization of industrial relations is important for making explicit the special contributions of each of the social sciences. But I believe it should satisfy several specific criteria—ones that have not necessarily been met in the past.

The conceptualization should be readily applicable to the everyday activities of the work place. IR theory (from the pluralist and radical perspectives) starts with the premise that an inherent conflict characterizes employment relationships—at the very least "tensions" exist at the workplace (Barbash 1984). Though an IR system can be imagined in which the representatives of labor, management, and government establish the rules of the game, the system still consists of a myriad of regulations affecting individual employment relationships (Dunlop 1958). A total IR system can certainly be envisioned for a given country, but it is hard to conceptualism anything similar to the measurable flows of consumption, investment, or government expenditure so important to the study of macroeconomics. [1]

As a result it is probably best to build IR theory from the bottom up, starting with the key elements of an individual's employment relationship and then expanding one's focus to the work unit, the firm, government, and society as a whole.[2]

The conceptualization should clearly show the impact of government policy on the workplace. Application of IR theory has typically occurred in countries with mixed economies where market forces are important but where government policy regulates the market significantly. The conceptualization should provide some answer to why IR theory has been applied under these circumstances. It should also clarify the way in which government policy affects individual employment relationships.

The conceptualization should provide some common ground for debate between Marxist and non-Marxist theorists. Politically, a tremendous change toward pragmatic testing of various economic policies has occurred in countries previously committed to Marxist ideology. A corresponding pragmatism in conceptualization in IR theory would be highly desirable, incorporating ideas in common to both Marxist and non-Marxist scholars. A concept that is used by both groups alike is "control." A conceptualization that emphasized control processes but allowed for different interpretations of control would therefore be quite desirable.

The conceptualization should illustrate, at least to some degree, the dynamics of the negotiation process. Negotiation is a key process in virtually all the employment relationships analyzed by IR theory. And it is increasingly being incorporated into theory that derives from several of the social sciences: economics, political science, psychology, and sociology. Consequently, a better understanding of the negotiation process for individuals and groups should enhance our understanding of the dynamics of the entire IR system.

The conceptualization should be readily linked to the social sciences. If the conceptualization includes an emphasis on negotiation, a strong link to the social sciences is automatically established due to the ongoing interest in the topic across the disciplines. If the conceptualization is specific enough in terms of workplace activities, it can also provide a strong connection to the social sciences. Social scientists, after all, are concerned with predicting all types of individual and group behavior. Still, a particular social science may emphasize one set of workplace activities more than another. Making these special emphases explicit can be quite helpful to students.

Conceptual frameworks used regularly in IR only partly meet the above criteria. Some have conceptualized the employment relationship quite well in a unionized setting but have ignored nonunion settings. Some are macro and ignore the day-to-day activities of the individual employment relationship. Others are micro and ignore the structure of power in society. Theory has tended to be either Marxist or non-Marxist, a part of the ideological debate over the "best" system where little common ground is possible.

Students who are critical of IR as a field often claim that it is largely "atheoretical." If they are right, it is pointless to elaborate on the above contentions. The problem would be lack of theory, not its nature. But Adams (1988) argues that the field of IR relies on quite a number of theories: IR systems theory, bargaining theory, conflict theory, dual labor market theory, theories of internal labor markets, theories of union-management participation, theories to predict individual worker preferences for unionization, theories to understand the determinants of job satisfaction, and theories to "explain the appearance of unions as well as union growth, structure, ideology, strategy, militancy and role in industrial society" (Adams 1988, 6).

How well do the theories enumerated by Adams fit our criteria? Note how many of the theories predict individual behavior toward unions or the tactics and activities of unions themselves. Theories of union growth (Ashenfelter and Pencavel 1969, Stepina and Fiorito 1986), union bargaining structure (Dunlop 1944, Freedman and Fulmer 1982, Mitchell 1980, Ready 1990, Ross 1948), and union militancy (Becker and Olson 1986, Kaufman 1982, Olson 1986) concern themselves with important work place activities, but they ignore the activities that occur in nonunionized firms. They are focused on the union as an institution and not on the employment relationship. Theories of union joining behavior and labor management participation are broader, however. A theory of why individuals join unions is implicitly a theory of why they do not—it is derived from the nature of the employment relationship (Farber and

Saks 1980, Hamner and Smith 1978, Hills 1985, Touraine 1986). Theories of labor management participation and job satisfaction (Hirschman 1970, Freeman 1980, Hamner et al. 1986, Kochan et al. 1985) also derive from the employment relationship and can be applied in either a union or a nonunion setting. They have both macro and micro implications. They, in fact, meet most of our criteria for elements of a good conceptual framework, but they may or may not provide a particularly good meeting ground for Marxists and non-Marxists. If, however, a theory of participation were to encompass the control processes of the firm or if theories of job satisfaction were broad enough to include the concept of alienation, debate would be possible.

Bargaining theory (Dunlop 1944, Ross 1948) and internal labor market theory (Doeringer and Piore 1971) both meet the criterion for focus on the dynamics of workplace relationships. Like the theories considered above, however, neither provides much common ground for debate between radical and more traditional scholars. Bargaining assumes a pluralism of power between the parties to the bargain, an assumption class theory rejects. Internal labor market theory places emphasis on the skills acquired by individuals through long tenure with firms, a proposition that is at odds with the Marxist emphasis on division of labor, deskilling, and the reserve army of the unemployed. Dual labor market theory, on the other hand, has offered interesting ground for theorists of opposing ideologies to debate. The dual labor market division of jobs into two types—those with long run potential, high earnings, and good opportunities for training and those with high turnover, low pay, and little opportunity for training—can be consistent with a "free market" view of the world as long as individuals choose freely among good and bad jobs. If, however, the people who apply for each type of job are screened such that only a particular kind of person (or class) is admitted to each sector of the labor market, a more radical view of the market prevails (Averitt 1968, 1988, Beck et al. 1978, Tolbert et al. 1980). Dual labor market theory encourages debate between Marxists and non-Marxists about control over the hiring process (Beck et al. 1980, Hauser 1980). The theory applies equally well in the union and nonunion sectors of the economy, it spells out the dynamics of the hiring process, and it has strong links, both to sociology and to economics. It has both macro (labor market) and micro (firm level hiring) implications. Thus, for one set of workplace activities the theory meets our criteria well.

John Dunlop's application of systems theory to IR (Dunlop 1958) has provided an enduring conceptual framework for the field, particularly when comparing the industrial relations practices of one country with another (Kerr et al. 1960, Dunlop et al. 1975). Control over the system is vested in a web of rules negotiated among labor, management, and government, the actors in the system. The potential dynamic of class relationships is not explicitly included in the framework, however. The framework is also quite macro in outlook, and the lack of emphasis on specific workplace activities makes it hard to connect it with each of the separate social science disciplines (but see Meltz's essay in this volume).

Conflict theory, on the other hand, complements systems theory by its emphasis on the dynamics of conflict generation and its resolution (Coser 1956, Dahrendorf 1959, Simmel 1955, Wheeler 1985). Conflict theory is easily applied to both workplace and societal levels, and it affords ample ground for Marxists and non-Marxists to debate. It is central to negotiation. It, in fact, meets all our criteria and might well be incorporated into an overall conceptual scheme linking IR to the social sciences.

A Conceptual Framework Linking IR to the Social Sciences

As previously stated, an overall conceptual scheme for industrial relations should "build IR theory from the bottom up, starting with the key elements of an individual's employment relationship and then expanding [its] focus to the work unit, the firm, government, and society as a whole." But to simplify, it would be desirable to categorize the day-to-day activities that occur in the workplace. Each of the categories can then be linked to the social sciences since the activities included in each one are the subject matter for the social scientist's modeling and research. A simple, though inclusive, classification results in four main categories: activities surrounding the education, training, and development of human resources; activities related to the allocation of individuals to specific jobs in a variety of work organizations; activities that affect how individual energies are utilized once people have been matched with jobs; and activities that influence the way in which work effort is maintained over time—more simply, the development, the allocation, the utilization, and the maintenance of human resources.

Each of the four human resource activities can occur within the confines of the business firm, within a local labor market, or within the larger economic community. The negotiations that take place in each overall area of activity are what shape the individual's work environment. The activities and negotiations that occur, in turn, establish the boundaries for the field of industrial relations. Viewed in this way, the conceptualization already begins to bridge both macro and micro views of the world—the first "divide" noted above.

The various activities that comprise the employment relationship have been staked out, but to stop here would leave the conceptualization descriptive and static. The dynamics of industrial relations thought revolve around the problem of who or what controls the employment relationship. On the one hand, there are those who argue that the employment relationship can and should be controled impersonally through a competitive, free market. In such a system, individuals make decisions about the development, allocation, utilization, and maintenance of their human resources, but very little control is assumed for government or for the managers of individual firms. Government is assumed to play a small role in the economy, and business firms are envisioned to be small in size, competing vigorously with each other, some succeeding because of the choices they make in response to market signals, others failing because they ignore the information they receive from the market.

On the other hand, a different view prevails if we assume that a system of monopoly capitalism takes the place of the free market system. In this case, the locus of control does not solely reside in the market, but rather is shared with large, powerful firms. In the competitive, free market system, the firm served as an agent for fulfilling the interests and desires of individuals. The firm created the jobs from which individuals could choose. If an individual were to try out a job and find it unsatisfactory, a switch could readily be made to another firm that would, in turn, serve as an agent for the individual's satisfaction in work, income, and wealth. But if the firm grows large and powerful and becomes immune to market constraints (i.e., becomes a monopoly), it may no longer serve as an agent for the desires of the individuals who work within it. Instead, it may serve primarily the interests of those who own or control the firm. It will create for itself an independent locus of control so that the market is not exclusively in control of the employment relationship. By explicitly recognizing two potential centers of control, the conceptualization seeks to bridge, at least in part, the gap between Marxists and non-Marxists—the second important divide within the field of IR.

The structure of control in industrial societies shapes the negotiation that individuals can undertake with regard to their own employment relationships. In a competitive, free market system, very little negotiation is possible since small firms simply create specific jobs that are required to create a product or provide a service. Individuals look over the jobs available and more or less take them or leave them. Also, in a world of monopoly capitalism, individuals have little room for negotiation. An individual's power to negotiate is relatively small compared to the power of the firm. But negotiation is possible if individuals, through agents that they or governments create (labor unions or works councils, for example), resist the concentration of control either in the market or in the hands of a monopoly firm's owners or management.

If the locus of control over the employment relationship is centered either in the market or in the firm, individuals will seek out or create agents to protect themselves from the negative consequences of centralized control. Control that is concentrated in the market, is problematic because technological developments often require rapid changes in the four human resource activities. New products may require quite different skills for employees. Some products may no longer be demanded, firms will die, and employees will have to find new jobs. An unregulated, free market system demands that such changes be made quickly and, at times, painfully. Control that is concentrated in the firm is also problematic because it restricts the choices that individuals can make and requires change according to the dictates of the employer.

Some of the agents that could help to ease the pain of adjustment to change in the employment relationship are the following: a council of elected employees that asks management to transfer and retrain the present workforce rather than discharge old and rehire new employees; a labor union that establishes contractual agreements for lay-offs such as severance pay and a procedure for laying off least senior workers first; or a government that supports the establishment of labor unions, requires the election of works councils or regulates by law the way in which lay-offs are to occur. In each case the agent is transparent in the process of negotiation, reflecting the interests of individuals. The agent is also a collective, thereby increasing an individual's ability to control the employment relationship —control that would otherwise accrue to the firm or to the market.

Unfortunately, agents who always represent the individual interests of constituents belong to the academic's ideal world. In reality, the protective agents that employees create may, at times, represent the interests of those who direct and work in the institutions that have been built—labor union leaders, government civil servants, etc. A new potential locus of control over the employment relationship has been created, one from which individuals may, in turn, also need protection. One way to achieve such protection is to return to the market as the basic means of control, eliminating a union-controlled employment system (e.g., hiring hall in North America) for example, and allowing employers to select their workforce from the labor market without requiring that union members alone be hired. Another means of protection is for one agent to control another—for government to require that labor unions use democratic procedures in the election of officers, for example, and if they do not, for a government agency to manage union affairs temporarily. Conversely, public employees themselves may unionize to protect themselves from the power of government.

To summarize the argument so far — industrial relations is the study of negotiation between the firm and groups of individuals (or their agents) about control over the employment relationship. The negotiation deals with 1) the specific problems of developing, allocating, using, and maintaining human resources and 2) the degree to which market forces should be allowed to influence a firm's decisions.

Figure 1 shows the interaction among various centers of control over the employment relationship and the four functional areas that comprise employment related activities. For each functional area, lines radiate out from a market-centered locus of control to several other potential centers of control. Negotiation between workers and

Figure 1. Human Resource Activity

Development, Allocation, Utilization, or Maintenance by Center of Conrol

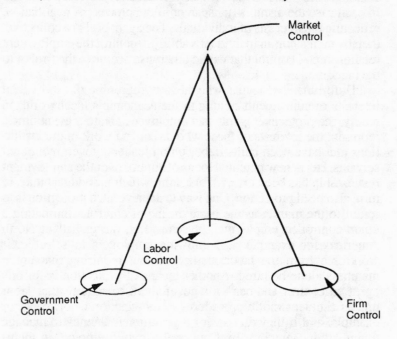

employers determines whether control will be concentrated in only one center or whether control will be shared among several other centers of control. Negotiation in each of the functional areas is not totally independent since societal values underlie the negotiations across all functional areas. In all areas, industrial relations pluralists advocate a system of shared control.

If government or labor served only as agents for individuals, they would be transparent in Figure 1. No lines would be drawn to show separate centers of control for either of them. Instead, government or labor "agents" would simply assist individuals in negotiating a system of control that was neither totally centered in the firm nor in the market. The results of negotiation would be shown somewhere in the middle of the axis that connects the firm to the market, a position of shared control. As drawn, however, Figure 1 shows that both government and labor may also vie for control over the employment relationship and potentially could acquire complete control. If either gained total control, what would be the consequence?

A centralization of control over the employment relationship in government has, in the past, usually been associated with authoritarianism, a situation that precludes negotiation altogether. Communist central planning exemplifies this type of control, but it is also an arrangement that has been strongly resisted—as witnessed by the dramatic events occurring in Eastern Europe and the Soviet Union. Experience with communist central planning shows that if government is to retain an agency function and further the interests of individual employees, it must be strongly democratic to check abuse of its far reaching authority.

Whether democratic or not, government control over the employment relationship may restrict unduly the firm's ability to respond to the market. Employers may be required to hire those sent them by government agencies and to maintain them in employment for life. Individuals may lose the choice over jobs that market-directed control over the employment relationship would provide, and employers may sacrifice production efficiency, thereby reducing growth in the economic system.

Control over the employment relationship that was concentrated wholly in union leaders' hands would have many of the same results described for the case of government. Unions should therefore also be democratic to avoid abuse of authority and to retain their agency functions. Though total control over the employment relationship by labor is theoretically possible, real-life examples are hard to find. We do, however, find situations where government and labor join forces to exercise joint control over the employment relationship—Juan Peron's corporatist government in Argentina, for example.

When, at the other extreme, control rests exclusively in the market, negotiation over a comprehensive employment relationship is not as important as is the process of prescribing jobs and contracting for them to be filled. To understand how an employment relationship is established, the free market economist does not examine how individuals or groups negotiate conflict, but rather looks to how markets help resolve conflict. For the free market economist, the worker joins a firm (a group, in other words) only after marketing individually developed skills; the skills are fitted into the production process once the individual accepts a job that best uses those skills. Individuals work out potential conflicts *for themselves* by making careful choices in the market, and they ultimately choose jobs that are a compromise between the needs of the employer (as set out in a detailed job description) and their own needs. Workers must know in advance what the choices are, make rational decisions, contract with employers to fill the requirements of specific jobs, and then accommodate to them. If economic circumstances change, the employer may change job requirements. Employees must then recontract to fill the new positions or quit and search the market for new jobs, where once again they will be contracted to adjust to the needs of the employer. When control is vested totally in the market, employers search intermittently for prospective employees who are willing to accept predetermined jobs and then to accommodate to them.

As in the case where control is concentrated in government, individuals may strongly resist the concentration of control in the market. When markets operate without regulation, individuals are often unable and unwilling to accept the constant accommodation required of them and will negotiate institutional protection. They will seek out long-term employment contracts with individual firms —either detailed, written agreements or simple implicit under-standings. They will organize unions. They will lobby government for protective legislation and social insurance. The institutional protections thus created will surround each impersonal job descrip-tion with a set of very personal expectations and understandings, established by groups in the defense of individual interests. Man-agement and unions reach understandings about the proper pace of work, about appropriate ways to carry out work, and about the conditions under which work will be done. Government legislation creates norms for health and safety and for treatment of minorities. When offering long-term employment contracts, firms may ask employees to be flexible about future job assignments in exchange for job security. All such negotiated understandings and agreements create an ever-changing employment relationship that takes the place of the fixed, contractually determined jobs envisioned by free market theory. The ever-changing and negotiated employment re-lationship is derived from a world of shared control between government and the market, between the labor union and the market and between the firm and the market.

Marxist scholars describe the outcome of yet a third extreme where control is held almost exclusively by capitalist firms. Marxist scholars argue that the market system does not adequately resolve conflict because imbedded in the system is the influence of social class. Since members of the upper class have disproportionate power in the market, they can restrict the choices of others (i.e., they have control over the market). The job choices of individuals no longer represent a compromise between the interests of consumers and the preferences of job seekers. Instead, the best jobs are reserved for the upper classes. Upper class members also have disproportionate control within the firm. Lower class members of society must either accept work roles with limited autonomy and control or join the ranks of the unemployed. Class conflict results and with it comes a profound crisis for the entire economic system. Political behavior is the result, but with an aim to overturn the economic and social system.

IR's normative issues arise in relationship to policy: Should capitalist firms be dismantled in an attempt to eliminate class control? Do individuals need protection from market control, from firm level control, from the control of labor unions and from government control? Or should individuals be primarily responsible for managing their own human resources? Under what circumstances should firms be restricted in the management of the human resources they control? Should a labor union control all the human resource decisions of the firm? The answers to such questions are reached societally, but due to strong beliefs about control, IR scholars will often not remain totally neutral. Understanding the reasons why does much to close the third major divide in the field —a division of opinion about policy.

IR pluralists argue that none of the extremes of control need occur, but the alternatives suggested may reflect either a reformist or radical view of the world. Reformists argue that total market control should yield to a system where control is shared with groups of individuals who, in turn, create institutions that help to shape the work environment (Commons 1917, Perlman 1949, Webb and Webb 1897). Individuals may, however, become controlled by the very institutions they create (Jacoby 1985). Government planning agencies, social insurance bureaucracies, large firms that

provide long-term employment security, labor unions and government regulatory agencies may themselves begin to assume a significant degree of control over the lives of individual employees. This
control, if too great, likewise will be resisted, thus limiting the
authority of public officials, labor union leaders, or private management (Storey 1983). IR pluralists argue that the control of the
market should not be totally replaced by government (or any other
agent's) control over all areas of economic activity. Shared control
is, instead, the objective.

Radicals argue that the control of powerful firms is more a
threat to individuals than the control of the market system *per se*.
And the control of monopoly firms will be resisted, not so much by
building protective institutions as by revolutionary action (Gorz
1967, Burawoy 1978). Monopoly capitalism may be replaced by a
system of central planning, but if so, that system of control will also
be resisted and transformed, leading to yet a better system. Though
both radical and reformist reasoning differ significantly from each
other, they share a common interest in control, and in both, a
sociological and political perspective complements the economics
of the market.

The Importance of the Functional Activities

A discussion of reformist and radical policy alternatives has
already established a connection between IR and the social sciences, but to make the link more formal, the specific activities
comprising each of the four functional groupings should be made
more explicit. The reason—research in the social sciences is directed at specific behaviors that must be related to equally specific
activities in the employment relationship. An enumeration of such
activities should, nevertheless, retain the overall idea that activities
occur in the context of alternative centers of control. One of the key
ways in which IR, as conceived by pluralists, distinguishes itself
from the separate social sciences is its argument for the desirability
of shared control.

IR pluralists and radicals argue that too much control in the
hands of management is highly undesirable. The most vocal of
these, as we have already seen, are the Marxists with their emphasis
on class divisions and conflict. IR scholars also address the degree

to which control should be centered in government or labor. Some advocate industrial democracy as an alternative to centralized planning and others, union democracy as a requirement for meeting the needs of union members. Many IR scholars also argue that too heavy a reliance on market control is to be avoided, the institutionalist school of thought is representative of this type of market critique. By advocating such policies, IR scholars make explicit a set of values regarding the employment relationship, namely that too heavy an emphasis on any one center of control is not good. Within the traditional social science disciplines, however, many scholars are reluctant to make similar value judgements, preferring instead to associate individual and group behavior with its antecedents while leaving policy to the politicians.

In Figures 2 through 5, examples of specific activities are enumerated for each category of workplace activity but in such a way that potential centers of control can be recognized.[3] For activities that are nearest to each center of control, the possibility for negotiation is minimized, but for those in the middle, negotiation over a wide range of issues is likely. Since IR scholars are generally interested in the activities that have a high potential for negotiation, they will value most the social science research that is directed at the activities listed in the middle range of each "axis of control."

Human Resource Development: Specific Activities and
Related Social Science Theory

The activities listed in Figure 2 focus on processes for acquiring job related skills, but the ways in which skills are acquired involve decisions by individuals, by their agents (government or unions, for example), and by firms. In a market-driven economy, as we saw above, firms may simply advertise for the skills they need, post a price, and wait for skilled individuals to respond. For the individual in a market-controlled situation, career development consists of a set of choices over time, made in response to market signals. This set of activities is illustrated as number five in Figure 2—unregulated and unsubsidized individual choice of training.

The "value system" of most industrial relationists does not support control concentrated in the market alone. An unregulated and unsubsidized market that is changing rapidly can create an intolerable degree of uncertainty for individuals, particularly when information about new job opportunities and careers is incomplete. Government-subsidized compulsory education is the first departure from a completely market-controlled career development system, thereby guaranteeing that the workforce will have at least a minimum level of general skill to be used in making adjustments to market changes.[4] Government may also subsidize the costs of gaining job information by way of a public employment service, specialized training, and economic development planning. The progression to full government control is illustrated by specific activities four, three, two and one in Figure 2.

Enumeration of human resource development activities, as is done in Figure 2, clarifies not only the type of social science theory that is critical for IR scholars but also some of the reasons for its importance. The economist's human capital theory is clearly important for any type of career development based on market choice, but it is important for students of IR, not so much for understanding the processes of unregulated, free choice, as it is for understanding market imperfections and obstacles to choice. The inadequacies of the market lead to a negotiated solution to human resource development that lies somewhere between total market and total government control.

The social science theory required for mid-range human resource activities shown in Figure 2 (activities two, three, and four) can be derived from the research and thinking of institutional economists, but it is less well developed than IR theory that is focused on allocational activities, to which we will turn next. A well-developed theory that applied to middle range activities would rely both on conflict theory and theories of negotiation. Conflict theory specifies that conflict originates under conditions of cooperation or shared activity, but the parties to conflict have mutually exclusive objectives that cannot be achieved simultaneously (Schmidt and Kochan 1971). In the case of human resource development, neither the shared activity, the mutually exclusive objectives, nor the institutions that would be expected to negotiate a settlement have been spelled out in a well developed theoretical framework. Theory has not been developed, for example, to analyze tri-partite negotiations over the training provided to individuals at the local level of the United States economic system (the Private

Industry Councils) or of the Swedish system (the Labor Market Board).[5] Instead, the presumption seems to be that, under certain types of political conditions, subsidized training services will be offered, possibly in response to perceived imperfections in the market. Human capital theory is assumed to be sufficient to understand the choices that individuals subsequently make among various types of subsidized and unsubsidized services. IR theory, according to our conceptual framework, should cast doubt on this assumption and ask how individuals improve their chances for access to training through negotiation.

Career development takes on a very different connotation if individuals are employed by large firms and if we examine the sharing of control between firms, labor unions (if they exist), and the market. The degree to which individual preferences are reflected in this type of career development is clearly a matter for negotiation and is reflected in the progression of human resource activities depicted in Figure 2 as we move from total market to total firm control. In the case of a firm with a highly developed internal labor market, a human resource planning department may determine successors for specific jobs, controling the promotion process throughout the firm. Training is provided for specific individuals in anticipation of promotion. Individuals, on the other hand, would prefer open competition for jobs based on a system of bidding that has clear criteria to determine the minimum requirements for a job vacancy. By knowing in advance which jobs were most likely to become vacant, individuals could train for them, thereby anticipating the jobs to which they aspired. The final shape of the firm-wide training system is, thus, a matter for negotiation. If firms give general training, they will provide individuals with the means to resist managerial control. Thus firms would be expected to prefer specific training programs, while individuals would prefer more general training. The conflict in interests sets the stage for negotiation.

A conflict of interests may also characterize union apprenticeship programs. Many apprenticeship programs are jointly directed by labor unions and employers, but in some cases such as the construction industry in the US, union control over apprenticeship has led to conflict between the interests of individual union members and public policy. The requirement to hire only union-trained apprentices allows a craft union to restrict the supply of skilled workers, raise wages, and, in some cases, discriminate by race and gender. But if some individuals are excluded from training, government may attempt to control or bypass the apprenticeship system and increase directly the numbers of women and minorities represented by the crafts. Human capital theory is not as useful in understanding the interests of unions in apprenticeship as is organizational theory that emphasizes power relationships and organizational structure and control.

The theory underlying firm level negotiation of development activities is more developed than was true for government. Human capital theory differentiates between general training and firm-specific training, allowing us to identify managerial interests and control in providing specific training. The theory of internal labor markets differentiates between ports of entry where the external labor market exercises control and internal job ladders where individual and collective negotiation are critically important. Theories of human resource planning apply statistical models to the flows of people through various job positions in the organization and focus on the training required to facilitate such flows. Less emphasized, however, has been theoretical treatment of the power structure within the firm and its effect on negotiations over the human resource development activities of the firm or the labor union. Though better developed than theory dealing with government subsidized education and training, theories of conflict, negotiation, and control over firm level human resource development activities could still benefit from additional elaboration.

Human resource development activities shown in Figure 2 (definition of symbols).

1. Centralized government economic development planning with government-financed training institutions supplying a fixed number of trained persons per year to be placed in government sponsored projects.

2. Government-financed compulsory education with individual choice of field based on individual preferences and potential future earnings.

3. Government-guaranteed loans to individuals who choose specific training programs within broad areas deemed to be acceptable (for example, guaranteed loans for college or university training).

Figure 2. Development Activities

Arranged by center of control.

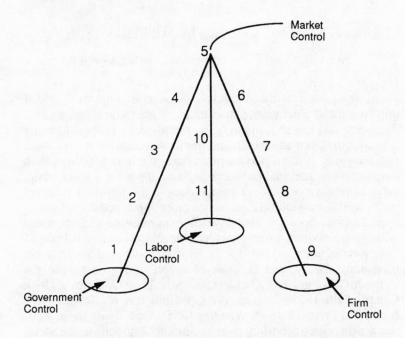

4. Government-financed assistance in providing information about present and future job openings (so that individuals know what training to obtain privately).

5. Unregulated and unsubsidized individual choice of training programs as offered by private firms. (Individual career development).

6. Firm-sponsored training programs offered to employees. Programs that combine firm specific training with general training that is transferable through the market.

7. Firm-sponsored, firm-specific training.

8. Firm-directed promotions, work experience, and career development.

9. Indentured servants.

10. Joint apprenticeship programs — firm, union, and government
11. Union-sponsored apprenticeship with requirement to hire union-approved apprentices alone.

Human Resource Allocation and Utilization: Specific Activities and Related Social Science Theory

A brief look at the activities included in Figures 3 and 4 (allocation and utilization) shows that here are the areas of greatest theorizing and research in the field of industrial relations. In many countries the labor union is an important institution for each of these two activities. It often plays a prominent role in negotiation, both in establishing national public policy and at the local level where bargaining may occur over compensation, the terms of employment, working conditions, grievance procedures, and the introduction of new technology. To analyze human resource allocation and utilization activities, IR scholars have developed an ample body of theory about unions—theories of union structure and governance, bargaining theory, and theories of union joining behavior, for example (Dunlop 1990, Kochan 1980, Strauss 1977, Zeuthen 1930, Chamberlain 1951, Stevens 1963, Walton and McKersie 1965, Block and Premack 1983, Wheeler 1985). Underlying these theories are theories of conflict, thereby linking IR directly to the social sciences where this topic is examined—sociology in particular but also political science and psychology. When unions are not a strong factor in negotiation, IR scholars have developed theories that apply to managerial activity alone in the areas of compensation, performance appraisal, employee motivation, job satisfaction, etc. All these theories underlie the conceptual framework presented in the illustrations.

Figure 3 spells out a number of human resource activities that we would associate with the allocational functions of the market, of the firm, and of the government. At the top of the illustration (activity number six) are the familiar job-matching activities that we associate with free, competitive markets. Standard economic theory explains both wage rate determination and the mobility of individuals across jobs. But listed down each of the "control axes" are activities that depart to one degree or another from the free market situation. The activities listed on the axis connecting government and market control, for example, range from a simple government subsidy of the costs of information about new jobs to mandated hiring quotas. The theory underlying activity number five is still derived from neoclassical economics with the assumption of imperfect information in the market. The role of government is to provide such information, but standard economic theory still applies. As we move further toward government control over the employment relationship, economic theory is less applicable than other theories. Policies of affirmative action and comparable worth rest on an assumption that social relationships are more important for wage rate determination than is the market. The concept of a "fair wage" and the assumption that negotiated wage rates are required to remedy discrimination are key elements in a theory that lies directly in the range of interest of IR scholars. Further down the control axis are hiring quotas that could be viewed as part of government's agency function (though a strongly coercive one) to protect the interests of specific subgroups of citizens. But if government exercises an independent control over the employment relationship and it is no longer perceived as a legitimate agent for all its citizens, then quotas could also be viewed a means by which subgroups achieve their own control over employment relationships *through* government. Quotas would thus be appropriately depicted on the control axis in a position close to total government control.

Job search theory undergirds a free market view of job matching and provides some of the rationale for government subsidy of the costs of search, but under some special formulations it can also be considered IR theory. Job search theory, at least as developed by economists, is a simple extension of human capital theory (Lippman and McCall 1976). As such, it incorporates little of the flavor of negotiation that is characteristic of pluralist IR theory. But job search theory can also be approached more sociologically. Information about new job possibilities can derive from informal networks that differ by race and gender, for example. Also, job information may accrue to an individual naturally due to the characteristics of the first jobs. Some jobs may be rich in information about other work opportunities while other jobs yield very little information (Granovetter 1974). Theory based on informal informational networks could allow for negotiation to achieve more favorable positions in the informal networks. Since labor unions or more informal self-help support groups may be key to achieving favorable outcomes in the negotiation of job information, their activities should be accounted for in job search theory.

In its sociological form, job search theory underlies the labor union activities shown under number twelve of Figure 3. In Figure 3, the agency functions of the labor union are reflected both in activities number twelve and thirteen. But other examples further down the control axis show how agency functions are converted to activities that reinforce the union organization itself, culminating in mandatory membership provisions and union control of hiring. This is not to say that individual union member interests cannot also be served as in the hiring hall, which serves a useful function as a private employment service for union members. Organization theory as well as theory directed at the need for specialized employment services helps us understand why closed shops and hiring halls are supported by union members and leaders alike under specific institutional conditions.

Along the government/market control axis are activities to which public sector theories of negotiation apply, activities that occur when government is in control as employer, directly negotiating compensation and allocating individuals across jobs. To some degree, theories developed for private sector bargaining have simply been transferred to the public sector. But because of the non-profit nature of public sector employment, theories of tri-partite bargaining (Kochan 1974, Derber 1988), or theories of dispute resolution that focus on alternatives to the strike, have also been developed. In many of these theories the important question is who ultimately has managerial control over a negotiated contract—whether the vaguely defined concept of "government" is sufficient or whether a specialized bargaining agency within government or the electorate broadly defined should be considered to be "in control."

Middle range theories along the market/management control axis for allocational activities are closely associated with the idea of internal labor markets, markets created within the firm by rules restricting the hiring of new employees from outside the firm. In the conceptual framework developed here, unions arise out of resistance to total market or total firm level control. If firms are small and competitive, they do not typically develop internal labor markets, and they have little independent control over individuals. In modern capitalist economies, however, large bureaucratic firms have developed, and individuals have sought protection both from the firm's power and from the insecurity of the market through their own agents—labor unions. Unions demand written rules for promotion, for lay-offs, and for hiring or re-hiring. They help to create an internal labor market in which managerial flexibility over allocation and utilization of labor is controled. Management prefers flexibility—systems for promotion and compensation that preserve managerial judgment, while employees often prefer systems with clearly specified criteria for promotion. Other conflicts occur over compensation, efficiency, and job security.

To understand and predict the behavior shown in the range of activities depicted along the management control axis of Figure 3, a mix of market theory and more sociological theory is required. The existence of internal labor markets allows concepts of fairness, equity, and interpersonal comparisons of compensation to influence the movement of individuals from job to job within the firm. But the external labor market still exercises influence since employees are free to leave the firm under any other circumstances than slavery, the extreme point in firm level allocative control.

Allocational activities are concerned with how people move from job to job over time and the incentives that are required to influence their movement (i.e., their compensation). Utilization activities are concerned with the best fit of individuals to jobs at any one point in time. Good utilization of human resources, when viewed at the level of the firm, means choosing the proper mix of labor and capital to achieve maximum productivity. Good utilization of human resources, when viewed from the level of the national economy, means operating an economic system at full employment, managing the system so that all those who want to are also able to work. Utilization activities become of concern to IR scholars when groups of individuals or their agents negotiate over the means by which maximum productivity and full employment are to be achieved. At the plant level, employees and managers negotiate continuously, though informally, over work effort, the adjustment of work organization to technical change, and the way in which labor and capital are combined. At the national level, labor unions and labor political parties may pressure government to reduce the level of unemployment, to pursue specific kinds of trade policy, and to influence the rate of technological advance. Figure 4 shows in detail various examples of the negotiations that can occur, again arranged according to the proximity of the negotiation to each center of control. Notice how strongly utilization activities are associated either with management or with government. The utilization of human resources is more closely associated with the overall direction of the firm than any of the other human resource functions. Thus, in a free market system, decisions about utilization will fall heavily to management. In a socialist-planned economy, decisions would likewise fall to government. But in neither is labor likely to achieve total control. At most, labor's influence would be felt through joint labor-management committees or "featherbedding" rules that retained employees even when technological change had undermined their usefulness in the production process. Thus, in Figure 4, no examples are given for total labor control over the utilization of human resources.

On the far left control axis of Figure 4 are activities that we generally associate with the term "industrial policy," the extremes being government control over the entire economic system and full market control in which any form of industrial policy is absent. Macroeconomic theory provides the arena in which debate over industrial policy occurs. Is monetary policy sufficient to control the path of the economy over time, or are other forms of government intervention desirable or even necessary to achieve a consistent level of full employment? Given full employment, who will control *changes* in the employment relationship caused by new technology? As was true for other human resource functions, IR scholars tend to be skeptical that the activities shown under number five in Figure 4, by themselves, will produce an ideal utilization of the workforce. Rather, some form of industrial policy and some type of human control over the firm's use of labor in the firm will be desirable. IR theorists argue that firm level control over the utilization of labor does not necessarily restrict productivity and may enhance it (Freeman and Medoff 1984). Many also believe that job redesign, works councils, and joint labor management control over the introduction of new technology could increase job satisfaction and labor productivity. The result is an evergrowing body of theory and research directed at the negotiation of labor utilization in business firms.

Human resource utilization activities are the subject matter for much research in human resource management (HRM). But the choice of topics to be investigated and the assumptions regarding control can create serious divisions between scholars interested in the traditional topics of unions or collective bargaining and scholars interested in such topics as worker motivation, staffing, and effective management of the workforce. The latter topics may assume that the firm maintains a high degree of control over its workforce. But we argue here that IR scholars, pluralists especially, reject an assumption of a high level of control either for the firm or for the market. Total firm level control over the employment relationship should be no more acceptable to a society than total government control. Human resource management scholars who agree with this important assumption must, therefore, recognize the potential for negotiation over the utilization of human resources. If recognized, the divisions between HRM and other IR research topics can be bridged.

Human resource allocation activities shown in Figure 3 (explanation of symbols).

1. Government-controlled placement on all jobs. Government-designed compensation schedule.

2. Government-imposed hiring quotas and rules for determining compensation for race and gender groups in the private and public sectors.

3. Government-designed policies for pay based on the "comparable worth" of all public-sector jobs.

4. Government-regulated affirmative action policies for selection, promotion, and pay within the public and private sectors.

5. Government-subsidized occupational projections, wage and salary information, and job placement services.

6. Unregulated market guided choice of jobs and establishment of compensation through forces of supply and demand.

7. Internal job-posting system where internal applicants compete freely with external applicants. Formalized job evaluation and performance appraisal for promotion and pay. Compensation based on a schedule that may be the result of a union contract.

Figure 3. Allocation Activities

Arranged by center of control..

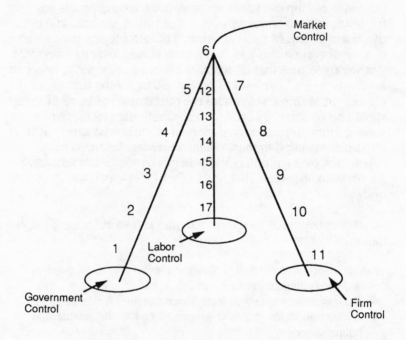

8. Internal job-posting system where internal applicants are given first consideration for all but low-level positions. Formalized job evaluation and performance appraisal for promotion and pay. Compensation based on a schedule that may be the result of a union contract.

9. Firm level screening and job placement based on criteria that are not necessarily job related.

10. Upper level positions filled only "from within" with no formalized criteria for promotion and pay and no job posting.

11. Slavery.

12. Union-acquired information on job openings through contractually demanded job postings or through informal networks.

13. Union-demanded system of promotions from within.

14. Agency Shop (a regulation that all employees must provide financial support to the union).
15. Union Shop (a regulation that all employees must become union members as a condition of employment).
16. Closed Shop (a regulation that management may only hire union members).
17. Hiring Hall (a regulation which requires that employees may only be hired through a union-operated employment exchange. Usually the exchange is available only to union members).

Human resource utilization activities shown in Figure 4 (explanation of symbols).

1. Centralized government control over investment decisions, technological change, and the way in which labor is combined with capital.
2. Governmental guidance over industrial "restructuring." Subsidies to selected firms which, without assistance, would go bankrupt.
3. Government research on the effects of technological change and the best ways of easing labor force adjustment problems to that change.
4. Money market, public expenditure, and federal tax policies aimed at achieving full employment.
5. Policy of steady growth in the money supply to match growth in the economy. No antirecession policies by either the banking system or the federal government. Market adjustment to prevailing economic conditions occurs through decisions made by firm level management.
6. Work rules and job design jointly determined between employees and management to increase workforce satisfaction and productivity. Works councils.
7. Objective procedures to settle alleged arbitrary supervision and enforcement of work rules.
8. Gain sharing compensation systems where workforce initiated suggestions for use of labor results in higher wage rates and higher profit.
9. Quality circles, advisory to management, where suggested changes in work rules and job design result in higher productivity and profit.

Figure 4. Utilization Activities

Arranged by center of control.

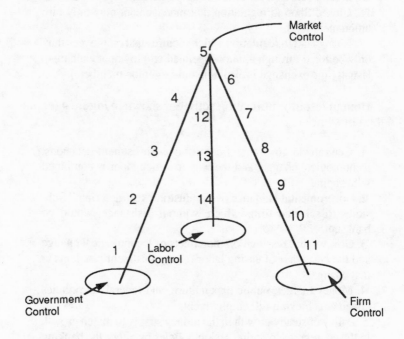

10. Mandated work rules and job design. No formalized dispute resolution procedures.

11. Informally determined work rules under managerial control. No objective dispute resolution procedures.

12. Union contracts try to slow technological change and specify transfer policies and criteria for lay-offs.

13. Works councils jointly determine with management job design, adjustment to technological change, and staffing changes.

14. "Featherbedding" is used to resist technological change and protect the structural integrity of the union.

Human Resource Maintenance Activities

Taken in more or less chronological order, human resource maintenance activities are considered last, preceded as they are by development activities that often occur at the beginning of one's worklife, allocational activities that occur when first finding a job, and utilization activities that occur continuously over a lifetime of employment. Maintenance activities sustain the employment relationship over time by preserving an employee's skills and health, both while employed and unemployed. Control is reflected on the government side by the degree to which the maintenance function is provided through guaranteed employment in government-sponsored jobs or guaranteed participation in government sponsored insurance. On labor and management's side, it is reflected by the degree to which funds are controlled for such things as private pensions and health insurance.

Economics is the social science discipline most closely linked to government sponsored human resource maintenance activities. Economists examine the effects of receipt of unemployment insurance on the duration of unemployment. They calculate the costs of workplace safety regulations. They have examined the effects of public pension programs on the national rate of savings and the projected costs of a national system of health insurance. Yet none of this research incorporates the ideas of conflict and negotiation so critical to pluralist IR theory. Little of John R. Commons' (1934) framework for analysis of unemployment insurance or the employment service remains in present-day theories. Commons analyzed the philosophies of the various parties who helped propose unemployment insurance legislation in Wisconsin and concluded that an important role existed for collective action and negotiation in first establishing services to job seekers. After determining that some sort of unemployment insurance should be enacted, Wisconsin lawmakers created a state-level advisory committee, which included business representatives who opposed the original unemployment insurance plan. The advisory committee negotiated the final legislative provisions and the plan for administering the program. Bargaining, in this case, allowed a controversial social innovation to occur "without legal compulsion" (Commons 1934, 850). The Commons example demonstrates that if conflict, negotiation, and collective action are to be incorporated into theory that applies to the maintenance function, stronger ties will be needed with political science and sociology, thus deemphasizing the purely economic side of maintenance activities. Job seekers in the United States sometimes join self-help groups to assist in maintaining themselves during job search of long duration. To some extent, such self-help groups serve as agents for job seekers, pooling information on job search tactics and job leads. But their assistance is largely individual, providing emotional support to individual job seekers and trying to place individuals higher on the queues of prospective job applicants. To my knowledge, the existence of such groups has not been incorporated into theories of job search or explanations of how individuals maintain themselves psychologically during long bouts with unemployment. How such groups are used and the extent of their effectiveness would be particularly good topics for research. If self-help groups were found to lobby for more job creation activities, they could be treated in the theory developed here as agents who negotiate more favorable positions for all individual job seekers in the market.

Social science theory that can be used to analyze the activities of labor and management in their various maintenance activities is as follows: economic analysis of individual behavior in response to the various monetary incentives of unemployment insurance, economic analysis to predict the average expected age of retirement; and demographic analysis that predicts the future demands on pay-as-you-go systems of retirement. Yet in all these examples, the individual is the unit of analysis and little emphasis is placed on collective activity or negotiation. Useful though this social science research may be, it is of less interest to IR scholars. Political action that supports or opposes government financing of old age pensions, on the other hand, does involve negotiation. Where taxes are transferred from one generation to another, an older generation of citizens must negotiate with the next for financing of the retirement system. In this area, IR scholars bring insight for understanding the potential for conflict, bargaining, group solidarity, and conflict resolution. Private pension plans, privately supplemented unemployment compensation, and job-sharing plans are also negotiated under circumstances that are best understood through the combined sociological and economic analysis that is familiar ground for IR scholars.

Figure 5. Maintenance Activities

Arranged by center of control.

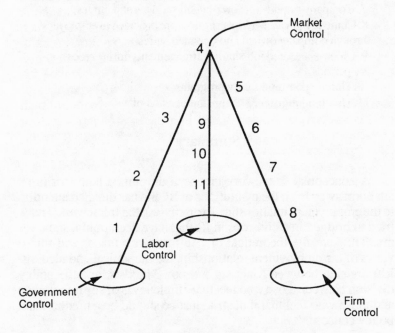

Human resource maintenance activities shown in Figure 5 (explanation of symbols).

1. Government-controlled plant committee provides all benefits. Workforce is permanently attached to the firm for life.
2. Government provides social insurance: pensions, unemployment compensation, worker's compensation, health insurance.
3. Government regulates health and safety. Regulates private insurance carriers. Regulates private firms in providing advance notice of lay-offs and in making adjustments to unfavorable economic conditions. Establishes a minimum wage.
4. Unregulated private firms sell social insurance services to individuals. Companies adjust to economic conditions free of government regulation. No minimum wage.

5. Employee assistance programs provide information and referrals to employees for health needs and in preparation for lay-offs.

6. Private firms sell group social insurance services to company.

7. Company provides its own health services and clinics.

8. Company towns. Multiple services are provided to employees through company owned and operated stores.

9. Union-sponsored job-sharing arrangements during recessionary periods.

10. Union-sponsored safety programs.

11. Union-administered health and pension plans.

Summary

A conceptual framework has been developed here that turns attention away from the institutions of IR and has directed attention to the employment relationship. In discussing the framework, I have tried to bridge three divisions in IR that have been troublesome for me. They are the theoretical division between macro and micro views of the employment relationship, the theoretical and ideological division between Marxists and non-Marxists, and the policy division between those who feel that efficiency is of key importance and those who feel that industrial justice should be a predominant policy concern.

Bridging Divisions in Macro and Micro Theory

The conceptual framework presented here envisions negotiation on all aspects of the employment relationship—the development, allocation, utilization, and maintenance of human resources. But it also envisions negotiation at several different levels. Negotiation is first required to establish the set of societal rules that, in turn, will set the boundaries for all other negotiations. One such set of rules creates a free market system since the market is neither automatic nor necessarily a natural outgrowth of economic activity. Laws that establish private property rights exemplify such rules. In the labor market, however, persuasive arguments have been made that a purely free market has never existed and would not be acceptable even if it did (Polanyi 1944). Labor unions, protective legislation, and government-sponsored social insurance give evidence that full control of economic life vested solely in the market is indeed unacceptable in most industrialized countries. Yet in Eastern Europe and the Soviet Union, equally strong societal voices are demanding that control should likewise not rest exclusively in government. And an elaborate body of regulatory legislation in industrialized societies attests to the desire to limit the power of the firm, particularly when it has sufficient size to operate independently of the market. If unions develop as a way of countering the power of the firm, rules may be enacted to limit the power of individual unions vis a vis their members. Citizens of most industrialized countries have, sooner or later, demanded that a negotiated set of rules govern economic life, one that does not grant undue control to the market, the government, unions, or firms.

Is there a dynamic at work in the IR system that propels it toward one or another center of control? Marxists argue, yes, that control over time will accumulate in the hands of a select few— owners of large, monopoly firms. The downsizing and decentralization of authority in many large firms runs counter to such a prediction, but power and control may not be measured by such trends alone. Will control gradually be subsumed by increasingly authoritarian governments as Heilbroner (1974, 1980) has predicted? The rapid demise of systems of central planning and the rise of democratic forms of governance cast doubt on this possibility, but history also shows that authoritarian systems cannot be easily dismissed. Does the breakdown of Communist forms of control over economic life and the internationalism of the world economy mean that the market, in its pure and unregulated form, will emerge as the principle control center for economic activity? Polanyi (1944) argues that the economic insecurity of such an arrangement precludes its acceptability over a long period of time even though transitional time periods may impose considerable hardship on the workforce.

The theoretical framework developed here suggests another dynamic at work in industrial relations systems. The dynamic starts with the creation of a freely functioning, unregulated market system. In this system, both individuals and firms seek to avoid the pressures of the market. Firms react to the insecurity of the market by growing in size and power, attempting to create relatively stable market environments for themselves. Individuals react to market insecurity by creating agents to negotiate protective rules on their behalf (government agencies or labor unions, for example). Agents may also represent individuals in negotiating protection from the control of business enterprises. But as agents grow in influence, they also gain potential for control, thereby extending the dynamic. Individuals may then choose to move policies back in the direction of market control or they may negotiate protection from one agent through another. The dynamic represents a constant movement back and forth between centers of control, with an aim to negotiate some arrangement of shared control.

I believe that in the long run, shared control is the norm for IR systems, but that at present we are experiencing a period of painful change in many systems similar to the industrial revolution itself. Globalization is rapidly eroding the traditional institutional forms of protection to which workers have become accustomed, just as the industrial revolution destroyed the protective institutions of feudalism. The protective institutions that industrial relations scholars have examined in such detail have been based on our concept of what constitutes a society or a nation state. But the nation state is being weakened by the demands of separate societal groups within it and superseded by the demands of an international economy. Under such circumstances, it is difficult to envision new protective institutions that address both the diversity of peoples in the world and the common need for protection from "pure capitalism." Even though it is uncertain what form they will take, I have no doubt that new institutions will be built, ones that, internationally, achieve negotiated protection from the market, from authoritarian states, and from powerful, profit-seeking firms. This is a major implication of the conceptual framework developed in this chapter and a consistent underlying assumption within the field of industrial relations. It is also true, however, that strong forces exist from time to time, pushing the IR system in the direction of total firm, market, or government control. Carefully constructed institutions can prevent the undesired consequences of control centered in the firm, the market, or government, but historically, the building of such institutions has required much effort and sacrifice on the part of individual workers.

Once societal rules are negotiated and their dynamics are understood, consideration can turn to the negotiation of an individual's own autonomy and control. A major assumption here is that autonomy and control do not automatically accrue to an individual as part of a market-determined employment contract. Rather these must be negotiated, either through representatives of government, labor unions, or other employee-directed institutions. Negotiation is for joint control over the employment relationship.

Where control is shared between the firm and the market, IR scholars have identified sources of conflict among individuals, their employers and the market. The market demands efficiency from business firms, a demand they, in turn, pass on to individuals. The market may create uncertainty, both for firms and individuals, particularly in times of rapid technological change. As a consequence, individuals will often negotiate a slower and more predictable pace of change. In all these cases, IR scholars examine the institutional methods through which negotiation takes place.

Where control is shared between the government and the market, the instruments of social and industrial policy are not clearly delineated in institutional terms. Where control is shared between the firm and the market, labor unions, employee associations, or shifting coalitions of groups of employees within the firm convey employee interests in the process of negotiation. Interests of the firm are fairly clear and immediate—to survive in the market, to maintain efficiency, to make a profit. Where control is shared between government and the market, as is true in an economy with some form of industrial policy, the situation is more complicated. Market-dictated needs for efficiency are not automatically conveyed to individuals through government, even when government serves as employer since the "public interest," not the profit motive drives government economic activity. When government establishes an industrial policy, the needs of the market are more diffuse and less immediate than in the case of the private firm—the need for a workforce well trained in general skills, for example, or the need for a long range international trade strategy. IR scholars have not spelled out as clearly the inherent conflicts that exist among individuals, governments, and the market as they have the case of shared control between the firm and the market. The institutions that could mediate such conflicts have been even less well examined. We know that bargaining between labor unions and business firms has some fairly predictable kinds of outcomes and varies predictably depending on whether negotiations take place at the national, industry, or local level (Weber 1967, Hendricks and Kahn 1982, 1984, Mishel 1986). But similar predictions would be difficult to make for the negotiation that occurred in the United States between community action agencies and local or state government officials during former President Johnson's War on Poverty or between the federal and state governments over the design of public sector employment programs. The theory on which to base predictions is not well developed. The theory is still quite closely aligned with standard neoclassical economics where the search for and acceptance of a contracted job is more important than the negotiated environment in which the contracts are finalized.

Divisions between Marxists and non-Marxists

By envisioning our conceptual framework as a Marxist would and then contrasting it with the image of a non-Marxist, a quick summary of key assumptions about control can be compiled. We have already noted the dynamics that are assumed by Marxists, namely that control will be increasingly concentrated at the firm level while weakened for government and for the market. Simultaneously, the range of possibilities for individuals to negotiate a degree of personal control will become increasingly circumscribed as labor unions and other mechanisms for bargaining grow weaker as well. The shift in power is not benign. It may occur as a function of technological change, the internationalization of the world economy, or the growing concentration of wealth in the hands of individuals with increasingly valuable professional skills. But subsequently, class interests will cause those in control to maintain their position in society at the expense of others.

Non-Marxists agree that a variety of forces may shift control toward firms and even toward the owners of a relatively small number of powerful firms. But they do not see the shift as inevitable or irreversible. From a non-Marxist viewpoint, institutions can and will be constructed to negotiate a structure of control that is shifted toward the market and/or toward government. The shift in control, in turn, will give individuals more leeway to negotiate greater autonomy for themselves.

The recent repudiation of Communist interpretation of Marxist thought in a variety of countries does not mean that Marxist ideas will no longer be debated by social scientists. Marxist thought should be distinguished from Marxist political dogma. As already indicated, however, the debate can be well framed and perhaps some divisions can be overcome by considering alternative centers of control within the IR system and the stability of the system over time.

Policy Divisions

By focusing on the employment relationship, the conceptual framework of this chapter reveals a theoretical connection among IR scholars who focus attention on the labor market, on the inter-actions between labor unions and business firms, and on the indi-vidual activity that occurs within the firm, whether unionized or not. All three groups of scholars have very different ideas about policy, but their similarities are more evident if government, the market, and the firm can be seen as alternative centers of control for economic activity. The institutional economist, focusing on the labor market, is in a broad way dealing with the potential for shared control among the government, the individual and the market. Similarly, the student of collective bargaining or labor law is examining the shared control that can exist among the market, the labor union and the firm.

The conceptual framework also reveals differences in theoret-ical orientation among various IR scholars but it associates these differences with the separate social sciences that contribute to IR theory. An IR scholar interested in human resource development, for example, could examine the rates of return to various kinds of training, basing analysis mainly on the neoclassical theory of human capital. But the analysis could also examine why training has the impact that it does. Is it due to the credential itself or to an enhancement of skill? If credentialism is important, how do people negotiate favorable positions in the queue for training or for em-ployment? If queues are based on race and gender, is it possible to renegotiate positions in the queue? The latter set of questions does not assume that the market is the sole center for control, and it places considerable emphasis on the process of negotiation. Thus, the analysis distances itself from mainstream economic theories of labor market behavior. The analysis fits squarely in an IR tradition of skepticism about human capital theory, with its assumption that control be centered in the market. IR pluralists argue that some form of shared control, with government serving in the defense of individuals, will be more likely.

While some IR scholars focus their research attention on issues close to the market, others are interested in the nonmarket behavior of individuals as they do their daily work inside the confines of large firms. While the former may be skeptical of mainstream economic theory, the latter may challenge the traditional assumptions of psychology. For IR scholars interested in human resource management, psychological theories of motivation and individual behavior will explain only some aspects of organizational life. Legal regulation, collective demands for control over promotions and transfers, and conflict among groups that comprise a highly heterogeneous workforce introduce the concepts of negotiation, control, and ideas about fairness that are familiar aspects of IR theory.

Some students of human resource management may, of course, ignore the more macro aspects of conflict and control that influence the degree of individual or collective negotiation that is possible within the firm. To the extent they do, their theory and research will have a strongly individualistic bias that, to me, does not reflect the concerns of IR scholars. The same can be said for economists who ignore the potential for conflict, control, and negotiation in labor markets. To stay within the theoretical framework set out in this chapter, IR scholars trained in psychology should work, at least to some degree, at the boundary of psychology and sociology. Also, those trained in economics should pay careful attention to the views of sociologists and political scientists. IR theory is not complete if it focuses its attention exclusively on the individual while ignoring the structure of control in the firm and in society as a whole. In Richard Hyman's words, "Industrial relations is the study of the processes of control over work relations, and among these processes, those involving collective worker organization and action are of particular concern" (Hyman 1975). Because we have adopted four potential centers of control for the IR system, Hyman's definition need not be interpreted as Marxist or non-Marxist. It is neither macro nor micro, and it need not imply any particular bias with regard to policy. It serves as a convenient way to conclude our peculiar view of the employment relationship — one that links specific activities of human resource development, allocation, utilization, and maintenance to the social sciences, but in the context of control over the economic system.

Notes

1. The concept closest to the macroeconomist's C, I, G, or M would be power. If we had good ways to measure the power of the actors in the IR system and could influence power predictably by manipulating national legislation, then a fairly good macro model could be created.

2. The same point was made earlier by Somers (1968).

3. The activities are merely illustrative and definitely do not include all activities that could be envisioned under each subheading of the employment relationship.

4. This, of course, is only one of the reasons for compulsory education financed by government.

5. This is despite the fact that Private Employment Councils in the United States typically involve informal negotiating among groups that may differ in their interests regarding training.

Works Cited

Adams, A. V., and J. Krislov. 1974, "New Union Organizing: A Test of the Ashenfelter-Pencavel Model of Trade Union Growth, *Quarterly Journal of Economics*, vol. 88, pp. 304-11.

Adams, R. J. 1988, "Desperately Seeking Industrial Relations Theory," *The International Journal of Comparative Labor, Law and Industrial Relations*, vol. 4, 1988.

Ashenfelter, O., and J. H. Pencavel. 1969, "American Trade Union Growth: 1900-1960," *Quarterly Journal of Economics*, vol. 83, no. 3, pp. 434-68.

Averitt, R. T. 1968, "The Business Organization of the US Industrial System," in *The Dual Economy*, New York: W. W. Norton.

_____. 1988, "The Prospects for Economic Dualism: A Historical Perspective," in G. Farkas and P. England, eds., *Industries, Firms, and Jobs: Sociological and Economic Approaches*, New York: Plenum Press.

Barbash, J. 1984, *The Elements of Industrial Relations*, Madison, WI: University of Wisconsin Press.

Beck, E. M., P. M. Horan, and C. M. Tolbert II. 1978, "Stratification in a Dual Economy: A Sectoral Model of Earnings Differentiation," *American Sociological Review*, vol. 43, pp. 704-20.

_____. 1980, "Social Stratification in Industrial Society: Further Evidence for a Structured Alternative," *American Sociological Review,* vol. 45, pp. 712-19.

Becker, B. E., and C. A. Olson. 1986, "The Impact of Strikes on Shareholder Equity," *Industrial and Labor Relations Review,* vol. 39, no. 3, pp. 425-38.

Block, R. N., and S. L. Premack. 1983, "The Unionization Process: A Review of the Literature," in *Advances in Industrial Relations,* vol. 1, Greenwich, CT: JAI Press, pp. 31-70.

Burawoy, M. 1978, "Toward a Marxist Theory of the Labor Process: Braverman and Beyond," *Politics and Society,* vol. 8, pp. 247-312.

Chamberlain, N. W. 1951, *Collective Bargaining,* New York: McGraw-Hill.

Commons, J. R. 1917, *Labor and Administration,* New York: Macmillan.

_____. 1961[1934], *Institutional Economics,* Madison, WI: University of Wisconsin Press.

Coser, L. A. 1956, *The Functions of Social Conflict,* Glencoe, IL: Free Press.

Dahrendorf, R. 1959, *Class and Class Conflict in Industrial Society,* Stanford, CA: Stanford University Press.

Derber, M. 1988, "Management Organization for Collective Bargaining in the Public Sector," in B. Aaron, J. M. Najita, and J. L. Stern, *Public Sector Bargaining,* Washington, DC: Bureau of National Affairs, Inc., pp. 90-123.

Doeringer, P., and M. Piore. 1971, *Internal Labor Markets and Manpower Analysis,* Lexington, MA: Heath.

Dunlop, J. T. 1944, *Wage Determination under Trade Unios,* New York: Macmillan.

_____. 1958, *Industrial Relations Systems,* New York: Holt.

_____. 1990, "The Management of Labor Unions," in *The Federation and the Constituent National Unions,* Lexington, MA: D. C. Heath.

Dunlop, J. T., F. Harbison, C. Kerr, and C. Myers. 1975, *Industrialism and Industrial Man Reconsidered,* Princeton, NJ: Inter-University Study of Human Resources in Economic Development.

Farber, H. S., and D. Saks. 1980, "Why Workers Want Unions," *Journal of Political Economy,* vol. 88, no. 2, pp. 349-69.

Freedman, A., and W. E. Fulmer. 1982, "Last Rites for Pattern Bargaining," *Harvard Business Review,* vol. 60, no. 2, pp. 30-48.

Freeman, R. B. 1980, "The Exit-Voice Tradeoff in the Labor Market: Unionism, Job Tenure, Quits, and Separations," *Quarterly Journal of Economics,* vol. 94, pp. 643-73.

Freeman, R. B., and J. Medoff. 1984, *What Do Unions Do?* New York: Basic Books.

Gorz, A. 1967, *Strategy for Labor: A Radical Proposal*, Boston: Beacon Press.

Granovetter, M. 1974, *Getting a Job*, Cambridge, MA: Harvard University Press.

Hamner, W. C., and F. J. Smith. 1978, "Work Attitudes as Predictors of Unionization Activity," *Journal of Applied Psychology*, vol. 63, no. 4, pp. 415-21.

Hamner, W. C., H. Tove , and R. N. Stern. 1986, "A Yo-Yo Model of Co-operation: Union Participation in Management at the Rath Packing Co," *Industrial and Labor Relations Review*, vol. 39, no. 3, pp. 337-60.

Hauser, R. M. 1980, "Comment on Stratification in a Dual Economy," *American Sociological Review*, vol. 45, pp. 701-12.

Heilbroner, R. 1974, *An Inquiry into the Human Prospect*, New York: Norton.

_____. 1980, *An Inquiry into the Human Prospect: Updated and Reconsidered*, New York: Norton.

Hendricks, W., and L. Kahn. 1982, "The Determinants of Bargaining Structure in U.S. Manufacturing Industries," *Industrial and Labor Relations Review*, vol. 35, no. 2, pp. 181-95.

_____. 1984, "The Demand for Labor Market Structure: An Economic Approach," *Journal of Labor Economics*, vol. 2, no. 3, pp. 412-38.

Hills, S. M. 1985, "The Attitudes of Union and Nonunion Male Workers Toward Union Representation," *Industrial and Labor Relations Review*, vol. 38, no. 2, pp. 179-94.

Hirschman, A. O. 1970, *Exit, Voice, and Loyalty*, Cambridge, MA: Harvard University Press.

Hyman, R. 1975, *Industrial Relations: A Marxist Introduction*, London: Macmillan.

Jacoby, S. 1985, *Employing Bureaucracy: Managers, Unions, and the Transformation of Work in American Industry 1900-1945*, New York: Columbia University Press.

Kaufman, B. E. 1982, "The Determinants of Strikes in the United States, 1900-1977," *Industrial and Labor Relations Review*, vol. 35, no. 4, pp. 473-90.

Kerr, C., J. T. Dunlop, F. Harbison, and C. Myers. 1960, *Industrialism and Industrial Man*, Cambridge, MA: Harvard University Press.

Kochan, T, A., H. C. Katz, and R. B. McKersie. 1986, *The Transformation of American Industrial Relations*, New York: Basic Books.

Kochan, T. A., H. C. Katz, and N. R. Mower. 1985, "Worker Participation and American Unions," in T. A. Kochan, ed., *Challenges and Choices Facing American Labor*, Cambridge, MA: MIT Press, pp. 271-306.

Kochan, T. 1974, "A Theory of Multilateral Bargaining in City Governments," *Industrial and Labor Relations Review*, vol. 27, pp. 525-42.

_____. 1980, "Collective Bargaining and Organizational Behavior Research," in *Research in Organizational Behavior*, vol. 2, Greenwich, CT: JAI Press.

Lippman, S., and J. McCall. 1976, "The Economics of Job Search: A Survey," *Economic Inquiry*, vol. 14, no. 2, pp. 155-89.

Marx, K. 1986, *The Essential Writings of Karl Marx*, F. L. Bender, ed.

Mishel, L. 1986, "The Structural Determinants of Union Bargaining Power," *Industrial and Labor Relations Review*, vol. 40, no. 1, pp. 90-104.

Mitchell, D. J. B. 1980, *Unions, Wages, and Inflation*, Washington, DC: Brookings Institution.

Olson, C. A. 1986, "Strikes, Strike Penalties, and Arbitration in Six States," *Industrial and Labor Relations Review*, vol. 39, no. 4, pp. 539-51.

Perlman, S. 1949, *A Theory of the Labor Movement*, New York: Kelley.

Polanyi, K. 1944, *The Great Transformation*, New York: Farrar and Rinehart.

Ready, K. J. 1990, "Is Pattern Bargaining Dead?" *Industrial and Labor Relations Review*, vol. 43, no. 2, pp. 272-79.

Ross, A. M. 1948, *Trade Union Wage Policy*, Berkeley, CA: University of California Press.

Schmidt, S., and T. Kochan. 1971, "Industrial Conflict: Toward Conceptual Clarity," *Administrative Science Quarterly*, vol. 17, no. 3, pp. 359-70.

Simmel, G. 1955, *Conflict*, trans. K. H. Wolff, Glencoe, IL: Free Press.

Somers, G. 1968, *Essays in Industrial Relations Theory*, 1st ed., Ames, IA: Iowa State University Press.

Stepina, L. P., and J. Fiorito. 1986, "Toward a Comprehensive Theory of Union Growth and Decline," *Industrial Relations*, vol. 25, no. 3, pp. 248-64.

Stevens, C. 1963, *Strategy and Collective Bargaining Negotiations*, New York: McGraw Hill.

Storey, J. 1983, *Managerial Prerogative and the Question of Control*, London: Routledge and Kegan Paul.

Strauss, G. 1977, "Union Government in the U.S.: Research Past and Future," *Industrial Relations*, vol. 16, no. 2, pp. 215-42.

Tolbert, C. M. II, P. M. Horan, and E. M. Beck. 1980, "The Structure of Economic Segmentation: A Dual Economy Approach," *American*

Journal of Sociology, vol. 85, pp. 1095-1116.

Touraine, A. 1986, "Unionism as a Social Movement," in S. M. Lipset, *Unions in Transition,* San Francisco: Institute for Contemporary Studies, pp. 151-76.

Walton, R. E., and R. B. McKersie. 1965, *A Behavioral Theory of Labor Negotiations,* New York: McGraw Hill.

Webb, S., and B. Webb. 1897, *Industrial Democracy,* London: Longmans Green.

Weber, A. 1967, "Stability and Change in the Structure of Collective Bargaining," in L. Ullman, ed., *Challenges to Collective Bargaining,* Englewood Cliffs, NJ: Prentice-Hall.

Wheeler, H. 1985, *Industrial Conflict: An Integrative Theory,* Columbia, SC: University of South Carolina Press.

Zeuthen, F. 1930, *Problems of Monopoly and Economic Welfare,* London: Routledge & Sons.

Industrial Relations and Theories of Interest Group Regulation

Braham Dabscheck

Industrial relations is usually, if not popularly, viewed as a discipline devoted to the study of the interactions or relationships that occur between employers and workers. In seeking to gain an understanding of the nature of various worker-employer relationships it is crucial, of course, to have knowledge of the various factors or variables which are relevant in shaping such relationships. While recognizing that external variables are important in approaching an understanding of employer-worker relationships, the above definition, however, contains a strong connotation that industrial relations involves the interaction of only two actors, and that the focus of research should be located where such interactions apparently occur, namely at the workplace.

Unfortunately, or fortunately, not all employer-worker relationships manifest themselves at the workplace; nor do they occur in splendid isolation free of the involvement of other interest groups and institutions which either have an interest, or become involved, in industrial relations. The particular institution (or should it be institutions) which is of interest here is that of the *state*. For good or for bad the *state,* or rather various factions or fractions of the state, becomes involved with, participates in, and seeks to determine both procedural and substantive issues associated with the real world of industrial relations.

The nature or role of the state[1] has been a lacuna or source of controversy within the social sciences. There have been a series of vigorous debates concerning the state and the functions or role that it performs. At the risk of simplifying a complex and challenging literature, some writers have perceived the state to assume functions akin to that of an umpire at a sporting contest. With this approach the state seeks to ensure that various participants observe the "rules of the game" and dispenses discipline or punishment (justice?) to transgressors. This approach begs the question of how such rules are created, and what is the role of the "league" which presumably appoints and determines the functions to be performed by umpires. Alternatively, the state is an arena where interest groups struggle with each other for their place in the sun. Other theorists have perceived the role of the state as acting to serve the interests of the powerful (capital), to provide a cloak of legitimacy for social systems wracked by inequalities of wealth and power. Engels, for example, asserted "the executive of the modern state is but a committee for managing the common affairs of the whole bourgeoisie" (quoted in Hyman 1975, 121). Finally, the state may be perceived as being autonomous, possessing goals and objectives separate from other institutions in society.[2] It is only in the last decade or so that industrial relations scholars have attempted to reach an understanding of the state's role.[3]

This chapter will focus on a particular literature that has developed concerning the role of the state and will explore its applicability and usefulness in enhancing our knowledge of industrial relations. The literature is loosely described as theories of regulation.[4] This literature mainly stems from North America and combines writings from law, economics, politics, and administration. The idea of regulation was originally associated with the Progressive movement which swept the United States at the beginning of the twentieth century. Progressives held the view that government should bring into being agencies, staffed by independent experts, to divine solutions to the various problems associated with the management of society.[5]

Australia was also influenced by North American Progressivism at the beginning of this century and similarly turned to regulatory agencies and experts to devise solutions to a variety of social and economic problems (Roe 1984).

Theories of regulation have particular relevance to students of industrial relations where agencies have been created to regulate various aspects of worker-employer relationships. Several writers have made use of such writings in examining the activities of agencies which regulate occupational health and safety (Kelman

1980, Gunningham 1984, Braithwaite 1985, Grabosky and
Braithwaite 1986, Rees 1988, Carson 1989), antidiscrimination and
equal employment opportunity (Grabosky and Braithwaite 1986,
Ronfeldt 1989) and the determination of wages and employment
conditions. The attraction of theories of regulation is that they help
to provide insights into the nature of the interaction that occurs
between various parts of the state and other institutions involved in
industrial relations.

This chapter will be concerned with providing a survey of
various theories of regulation and assessing their usefulness with
respect to the study of industrial relations.[6] In doing this the chapter
will draw on the experience of Australian industrial tribunals which
regulate relationships between unions and employers to illustrate
or highlight various issues.

Industrial Tribunals and Australian Industrial Relations

Two interesting aspects associated with the operation of regulatory agencies in North America will be presented to provide a
point of departure concerning industrial tribunals in Australia. First,
persons appointed to regulatory agencies are invariably appointed
for a fixed period, usually seven years. Second, the regulatory
decision-making processes seemingly occur in private; only those
with a direct and immediate interest in regulation are seen to have
any input into the various machinations associated with regulation.[7]
The implication of these two features is that short-term appointees
who conduct the affairs of a regulatory agency away from the gaze
of the public will become dominated and subservient to the interest
groups that they regulate.

Neither of these features of North American regulation, however, are present in the case of Australian industrial tribunals. First,
the various personnel who work on Australian industrial tribunals
have tenure to age sixty five. In 1904, when the Commonwealth
Court of Conciliation and Arbitration was created[8] tenure was set
at seven years. Legislative amendments in 1926 witnessed the
granting of life tenure. In 1956, tenure was reduced to age seventy,
and to sixty five in 1972. Furthermore, only a few members of the
federal tribunal have resigned before reaching their majority, and

only one person has suffered the indignity of "being removed" from office.[9]

In addition, the Australian Constitution provides the federal tribunal with unique protection from external interference and direction. The major power available to the Commonwealth government, with respect to industrial relations, is Section 51, paragraph XXXV. It states that

> The parliament shall, subject to this Constitution, have the power to make laws for the peace, order and good government of the Commonwealth with respect to . . .
>
> Conciliation and Arbitration for the prevention and settlement of industrial disputes extending beyond the limits of any one state.

This section of the Constitution provides the Australian (Commonwealth) government with an indirect power. It is undoubtedly the only national government in the world which does not enjoy a direct industrial relations power, with respect to the private sector. The Constitution forces the Australian government to delegate powers of conciliation and arbitration to industrial tribunals who are charged with the responsibility of settling and preventing interstate industrial disputes. Subject to other powers in the Constitution, the Australian government cannot directly legislate on such issues as wages, hours of work, working conditions, and so on. If it is desirous of achieving certain industrial relations outcomes, it is forced, like other parties, to argue its case before the federal tribunal.[10]

For example, the Australian government cannot institute wage and price controls and undoubtedly is the only national government in the world deprived of such powers. If it was desirous of introducing controls on wages, as part of a comprehensive incomes policy, it would be required to make appropriate submissions to the federal tribunal, which has the consitutional authority to either accept or reject such submissions. Or alternatively, the federal tribunal could decide to operate incomes type policy controls on wages, notwithstanding the oppostion of the Australian government, as occurred between 1975 and 1981 when the Liberal National Party Coalition government of Malcolm Fraser was in power (Dabscheck 1989a, 28-32).

The Constitutional protection afforded to the federal tribunal and the tenure provisions enjoyed by its members enable the persons so appointed to regard their work on the tribunal as fulfilling a life-time career. The federal tribunal does not constitute a stepping stone towards glittering prizes that beckon in the distance. The federal tribunal, or its personnel,[11] have scope, and it may even be suggested that it is encouraged, to develop its own solutions to the various problems associated with industrial relations regulation.

Second, industrial tribunals conduct their affairs in a very public and open way. Australia experiences a great deal of interest and discussion concerning industrial relations. Industrial relations issues are continually the subject of broad public debate. The different pieces of legislation which govern the operation of industrial tribunals at both the Commonwealth and state level are continually being amended and altered. The major piece of legislation at the Commonwealth level has been changed almost ninety times since 1904! Governments are continually commissioning reports or conducting inquiries concerning industrial relations. Decisions of industrial tribunals are closely picked over and studied by unions, employers, governments, and other interested parties. Comments and criticisms are continually directed at industrial tribunals concerning the wisdom or folly of their decisions. The Australian media, both print and electronic, devote much time and attention to industrial relations developments in general, and industrial tribunals in particular. Australia's well-known passion for sport is probably the only other area of social life which attracts more attention and interest than that of industrial relations!

In short, industrial tribunals are subject to continuous critical scrutiny, both by the parties whose relationships they regulate and by other parties and interest groups. Industrial tribunals are under an unremitting pressure to perform, to find and justify solutions to the never-ending problems associated with the real world of industrial relations regulation. Given these introductory comments concerning industrial tribunals in Australia, this chapter will proceed to survey various competing theories of regulation.

Public-Interest Theory

Public interest theory sees governments creating regulatory bodies following a breakdown or crisis in the operation of the economic or social system. Regulatory bodies are designed to either control the activities of a monopolist, prevent cut-throut competition among a group of small producers, or overcome problems associated with externalities. In the words of Owen and Braeutigan (1978, 20) "the victims of economic change should not be placed at the mercy of the impersonal market, but should be protected by a mechanism that provides economic justice." In crisis situations governments could conceivably take over the task or service provided by the economic agents in question. They could presumably nationalize the industry or activity of concern. The creation of regulatory agencies represents a compromise between market capitalism and the perceived needs for government intervention. The creation of regulatory bodies traditionally follows a broad-based campaign urging governments to do something about the particular issue in question. It is maintained that the public interest will be served by the creation of a regulatory agency, and society will be protected from the abuses and disasters resulting from the free or untrammelled operation of market forces.

Industrial tribunals were created in Australia during the period 1890 to 1910 in response to the so-called crisis engendered by a depression and strikes of the 1890s.[12] The creation of industrial tribunals resulted from the work of middle class intellectuals, of lawyers and politicians, who believed that the state had a duty and responsibility to create machinery to regulate relationships between workers and employers. Neither unions nor employers played any real part in the formation of these embryonic tribunals (Macintyre 1989). The employers of that era expressed strong and unremitting hostility to the formation of such bodies which they perceived would interfere with freedom of contract.

Two related arguments are advanced to support the technique of regulation as a means of promoting the public interest. First, a regulatory body is free from political interference. If a government sought to control economic agents through a government department, for example, the Minister concerned would be subjected to incessant lobbying by interest groups, and might find it expedient to bow to such pressures. Regulatory agencies, so it is claimed, take government intervention "out of politics," and insulate decision making from the pressure of special interest groups. Second, regulatory agencies will be staffed by experts, who, free from the pressure of political life, make decisions in a clear and dispassionate manner. Regulators, so it is claimed, interpret and enforce the common good.

Various members of industrial tribunals in Australia have consistently maintained that they make decisions in accordance with the needs or dictates of the public interest. Henry Bournes Higgins,[13] the second President of the Commonwealth Court of Conciliation and Arbitration from 1907 to 1921, maintained, in an oft-quoted passage, that industrial tribunals would usher in (Higgins 1915, 13-14)

> a new province for law and order . . . the process of conciliation, with arbitration in the background, is substituted for the rude and barbarous processes of strike and lockout. Reason is to displace force; the might of the State is to enforce peace between industrial combatants as well as between other combatants; and all in the interests of the public.

William Jethro Brown,[14] President of the Industrial Court of South Australia from 1916 to 1927, stated in the South Australian Industrial Reports (hereinafter SAIR) that

> In Industrial Courts, the Judge is impelled . . . to consider how a particular award may affect the parties in a particular industry, the class interests of employers and employees at large, and the welfare of the community. What I wish to stress here is that *the good of the community is the supreme factor* in the formulation of principles by an Industrial Court. (2 SAIR 46)

Jethro Brown also claimed that (3 SAIR 242-3) "an Industrial Court is primarily an organ of the community for promoting distributive justice." He also likened industrial tribunals to (2 SAIR 215) "an intelligence department of the Government," and argued that they (3 SAIR 249) "should lead rather than be swayed by public opinion."

Similar views concerning the role of industrial tribunals have been expressed by William Raymond Kelly, President of the South Australian Industrial Court from 1930 to 1941, and a Judge of the Commonwealth Court of Conciliation and Arbitration from 1941 to 1956, being Chief Judge from 1949.[16] He claimed that

> the interests of the community must, so far as the Court is concerned, always be allowed a voice in the discussion of what is a fair contribution on the part of any section of it to the industrial life of the whole . . . the tribunal whose decision has the sanction of the law is to that extent the chosen mouthpiece of the community. The determination is tantamount to an expression by the community itself of what it recognizes to be fair . . . the voice of the . . . people must be heard by this Court in the legislation by . . . Parliament. The Court must also constitute itself, within, the legislation, the mouthpiece of the community whose particular interest is committed to its care. (15 SAIR 364-65)

While members of industrial tribunals have perceived themselves to be champions of the public interest, they have simultaneously claimed that they hand down decisions which are immune from biases and value judgements. For example in the 1952-53 *Standard Hours and Basic Wage* case (77 Commonwealth Arbitration Reports [hereinafter CAR] 506-09), it was claimed that

> The Arbitration Court is neither a social nor an economic legislature . . . it is not the function of the Court to aim at such social and economic changes that may seem to be desirable to members of the tribunal . . . The Court is not a social or an economic legislature and . . . theories and policies should play no part in its determinations.[17]

It is interesting to speculate how, industrial tribunals, in seeking to champion the public interest could manage to exclude social or economic theories from their thinking and deliberations. William Jethro Brown has pointed out that members of industrial tribunals like to maintain the fiction that it is the "law," rather than they, that makes decisions. He has wryly noted that (Brown 1906, 291):

Lest they should innovate prematurely or capriciously, they have affected as a profession of faith that they cannot innovate at all . . . and, in so far as they have innovated, they have sought to conceal the fact from themselves as well as the public.

Two major criticisms have been leveled at the public interest theory of regulation. The first concerns the proposition that regulation can take government intervention "out of politics." As the section above on Australian industrial relations maintained, industrial relations is a very public activity with numerous interest groups placing pressure on industrial tribunals to secure the realization of their respective goals.

Second, there is the problem of defining what is meant by the public interest. The statutes that govern regulatory agencies usually do not attempt to define the public interest, or to the extent that they do the term is defined vaguely or in broad terms. The meaning which should be placed on the public interest is left to the regulators themselves to discern. In this sense, it could be argued, that legislation is so designed as to provide regulators carte blanche to discover and define the public interest. In saying this, however, it should be noted that Section 90 of the (Commonwealth) *Industrial Relations Act* 1988 provides a definition of the public interest. In reaching decisions the Industrial Relations Commission is required to have regard to

1. The objects of the Act,[18] and
2. The state of the national economy and the likely effects on the national economy of any award or order that the Commission is considering, or is proposing to make, with special reference to likely effects on the level of employment and on inflation.

Barkin has pointed to problems associated with defining the public interest. He maintains (Barkin 1971, 96) that

Absolutely no public has its own static interest any more than an absolute reality with unvarying truth exists. Publics are ways of conceiving activities, and interests are means of indicating the value assigned to them by their participants and others. No such thing as *the* public activity, *the* society, or *the* public interest exists. The public interest as such, the claim of a specific group that its interests should be recognized and shared by all other groups, is a myth.

While acknowledging the veracity of Barkin's analysis, it is still necessary to reach an understanding of the function that the myth of the public interest performs for those who inhabit regulatory agencies. Its essential function is to provide a form of legitimacy for the decisions made by regulators. The myth of the public interest provides a shield to ward off criticism and attack. For those who criticise the "impartial, unbiased, public interest" decisions of a regulatory agency face the counter charge that they are partial and biased, motivated by nothing more than naked self-interest.

Life-Cycle Theory

Bernstein (1955)[19] examined the operation of a number of North American regulatory agencies. His research provides one of the earliest and most trenchant criticisms of regulation.[20] According to Bernstein, regulation amounted to nothing more than special interest groups manipulating government intervention to further their own interests. Bernstein maintained that (1955, 156) "a commission finds its survival as a regulatory body dependent heavily on its ability in reaching a modus operandi with the regulated groups. . . . The limits of regulatory policy tend to be set by the acceptability of regulatory policies to the dominant parties in the interest." In Bernstein's hands regulation is a sham, a confidence trick played by the state and special interest groups on an unsuspecting and gullible public. Bernstein postulated that regulatory agencies had a natural life cycle, evolving through four phases. They were gestation, youth, maturity, and old age.

The gestation phase is the period in which the problem or crisis emerges, reformers campaign for government action, and a regulatory body is ultimately created. Reformers and special interest groups engage in a battle over the legislation creating the regulatory body. Bernstein found that (1955, 76) "agitation for regulation rarely produces a first statute that goes beyond a compromise between the majority favoring and the powerful minorities opposing regulation." The resulting legislation is vague and ambiguous;

it does not provide clear guidelines for the persons appointed to the regulatory body. The lack of such guidelines, however, may enhance the ability of persons so appointed to develop and experiment with their own solutions concerning the various issues associated with regulation. In the case of Australian industrial tribunals, as has already been noted above, politicians are forever amending the statutes which govern their operation.

Once established the regulatory body takes on the task of regulation with youthful zest and vigor. In this youthful phase it interprets its functions broadly, displaying initiative and ingenuity in attempting to promote *its* version of the public interest. It is confronted, however, by two major problems. First, its policies, procedures, and administration are underdeveloped and untested. Second, special interest groups are well organized (their organizational capability has probably been enhanced in response to the demands for regulation) and strenuously resist the regulatory body. Either decisions which antagonize special interest groups will be challenged in a superior court, or Parliament will be lobbied for legislative changes to restrict the activities of the regulatory body. Industrial tribunals in Australia have been attacked on these two flanks.

At various times, members of industrial tribunals have been involved in some very public and celebrated clashes with the parties and governments of the day. Probably the most famous example is the acerbic exchanges which occurred between Higgins and Prime Minister William Morris Hughes concerning the latter's attempt in 1920 to introduce special tribunals, which Higgins claimed would undermine the work of the Commonwealth Court of Conciliation and Arbitration (Higgins 1920, Lee 1980). At the time of writing the Industrial Relations Commission is involved in a very public clash with the Hawke Labor government and the Australian Council of Trade Unions concerning the approach to wage determination and the implementation of enterprise bargaining.[21]

In addition, the High Court of Australia has handed down decisions which have served to restrict and limit the decision-making ability of the federal tribunal.[22] Higgins, for example, bitterly complained about the High Court reducing the effectiveness of the federal tribunal in the following terms (4 CAR 42):

> At present the approach to the . . . Court is through a veritable
> Serbonian bog of technicalities; and the bog is extending . . .
> these decisions as to the limits of the Court's power, with all the
> corollaries which they involve, will make it impracticable to
> frame awards that will work will entail indeed, a gradual paral-
> ysis of the functions of the Court. Yet this Court, if it be trusted
> and unless it can be trusted it ought not to exist shows magnifi-
> cent promise of usefulness to the public. It is in a position to solve
> problems which cannot be solved, to settle disputes which cannot
> be settled, by any tribunal except one that has authority in all
> parts of Australia. . . . I am . . . duty bound . . . to make known
> the obstacles and dangers which confront the Court, and before
> it is too late.

Following the attacks of special interest groups the regulatory
agency enters its third phase, that of maturity. It adopts a cautious
and circumspect approach to the various problems associated with
regulation. It is not prepared to confront special interest groups, and
shapes its policies to protect itself from attack and criticism. According to Bernstein (1955, 87), in this phase

> Its functions are less those of a policeman and more that of a
> manager of an industry. . . . The commission becomes accepted
> as an essential part of the industrial system . . . standards of
> regulation are determined in the light of the devices of the
> industry affected. It is unlikely that the commission, in this
> period will be able to extend regulation beyond the limits accept-
> able to the regulated groups.

The regulatory agency then enters into its fourth and final
phase, that of old age. It loses vitality and initiative, being unable
to resist the demands of special interest groups. Bernstein claims
that it interprets (1955, 92) "its primary mission . . . [as] the
maintenance of the status quo in the regulated industry and its own
position as recognized protector of that industry." In this phase, the
regulatory agency is viewed as serving no useful purpose, and the
reasons justifying its creation and continued operation are increasingly questioned.

Two major criticisms can be directed at Bernstein's life-cycle theory. First, Sabatier has suggested that Bernstein's theory is unscientific. He claims that (1975, 304)

the unspecified time span of Bernstein's cycle of decay makes his thesis inherently nonfalsifiable. If the theorist does not specify a deadline for decay to occur then the maintenance of a vigorous program over an extended period of time or the rejuvenation of an old agency . . . cannot be introduced as conclusive evidence to deny the thesis.

Second, regulatory agencies oscillate between passive and active periods. Williams, for example, has pointed out that (1976, 324) "some agencies were never "young" while others discovered their youth in old age." Moreover, changes in the leadership of a regulatory agency may, in all probability, be associated with the development of new and different approaches to regulation. As a new leader settles into the job, she or he, will bring an individual style, approach, or agenda to regulation. In the case of Australian industrial relations the last four Presidents (or Chief Judges) of the federal tribunal have employed markedly different approaches to industrial relations regulation. Sir William Raymond Kelly, in his period of stewardship (1949 to 1956), employed a strict legal approach to the work of the tribunal, an approach which emphasized conservatism concerning the granting of wage rises and other concessions. Sir Richard Kirby (1956 to 1973) adopted a more pragmatic, flexible, or accommodative approach to the various issues associated with industrial relations regulation.[23] Under the presidency of Sir John Moore (1973 to 1985), the federal tribunal employed a centralized system of wage determination in which wage rises were linked to movements in prices, i.e., a system of wage indexation.[24] Finally, under the leadership of Mr. Justice (Barry) Maddern (1985 onwards), the federal tribunal has sought to enhance the productive performance of Australian industry and enterprises under the auspices of the structural efficiency principle.[25]

The information contained in the above paragraph may be criticized on the grounds that the federal tribunal adopted new programs to satisfy, to use Bernstein's words, "the dominant parties" involved in regulation. In each case, however, such policies were pursued despite, at times, trenchant and bitter opposition. Kelly was looked on with scorn, if not derision, by his contemporaries (Dabscheck 1983). Kirby clashed on several occasions with Prime Minister John Gorton (d'Alpuget 1977). Sir John Moore pursued wage indexation notwithstanding consistent opposition from the Fraser Coalition government and private employers (Dabscheck 1989a). Reference has already been made to the clashes between Maddern and the Hawke Labor government and the Australian Council of Trade Unions.[26]

Capture Theory

Regulation, and regulatory agencies, have been trenchantly criticized by neoclassical economists.[27] In 1962, Stigler and Friedland examined the impact of the regulation of electric utilities in various American states before 1937. They were unable to discover any effect of regulation and implicitly concluded that such regulation was a waste of time (Stigler and Friedland 1970). In a pioneering article, Stigler (1971) revised his "no effect" hypothesis to one where regulators are captured to serve the needs of the special interest groups they are supposed to regulate.[28] In the words of Breyer and MacAvoy (1974, 125) "an agency has been captured by the industry it regulates when that industry consistently obtains favourable decisions."

The conventional supply and demand framework of economists is applied by Stigler to the phenomenon of law making. Laws are not made in a vacuum; they result from the interaction of politicians and special interest groups. Stigler's central thesis is (1971, 3) "that, as a rule, regulation is acquired by the industry and is designed and operated primarily for its benefit." Special interest groups use the coercive power of the state to increase their income, either by controling entry or through appropriate price manipulation.[29] Stigler argues that (1971, 8) "when an industry receives a grant of power from the state, the benefit to the industry will fall short of the damage to the rest of the community."

Stigler's theory can be summarized as follows: politicians are akin to entrepreneurs seeking to maximize their chances of future electoral success. They *supply* programs and support legislation which enhances their ability to win votes and raise money to finance election campaigns. Special interest groups *demand* programs which promote their sectarian interests. They are more aware of the costs and benefits of regulation and are better informed and more able to lobby politicians than the public at large. The benefits of regulation are concentrated, whereas the costs (incurred by the general public) are diffused. The superior organization and lobbying effectiveness of special interest groups ensures that regulation will serve their interests, rather than the amorphous needs of society as a whole.

Presumably, capture theorists would illustrate the saliency of their position by pointing to the example of Mr Justice Powers, a member of the Commonwealth Court of Conciliation and Arbitration from 1913 to 1926 (being President between 1921 and 1926), as an industrial relations regulator who had been captured by employers. He sought, and subsequently obtained, a knighthood for resisting demands by unions and workers for improvements in wages and working conditions (McQueen 1983, 161). More generally, however, Australian capture theorists have maintained that industrial tribunals have been dominated by, and subservient to, unions. In the mid-1980s a group known as the "New Right" trenchantly criticized industrial tribunals on the basis that they had been captured by unions.[30] This claim has somewhat intrigued union officials and members who have traditionally viewed industrial tribunals as nothing more than a "boss's court." The current clash between Mr. Justice Maddern and the Australian Council of Trade Unions should also be remembered.

Three major criticisms can be leveled at capture theory. Goldberg (1976) argues that capture theorists have failed to comprehend an essential feature of regulation. He argues that regulation is analogous to a situation of long-term or administered contracts. While parties enter into an agreement, an agreement which involves continuous transactions into the future, they have not agreed on the details and specifics of future trading. "By attempting to analyse regulation within a discrete transaction framework, (neoclassical) economists have suppressed the most significant aspect of the regulatory arrangement and this has led to an overstatement of the case against regulation" (Goldberg 1976, 427). In Goldberg's hands regulators act as a broker between producers and consumers "enforcing and revising the rules under which individual transactions take place" (1976, 429). He also argues that most economic activities subject to regulation are inherently complex and intricate, a point which critics of regulation dismiss too readily. "Many of the problems that arise in regulated industries would arise if the industries were not under the jurisdiction of a regulatory agency" (Goldberg 1976, 444). The world of industrial relations is one of ongoing or continuing relationships. Industrial tribunals can be viewed as brokers, administering, revising, and enforcing the long-term contracts that exist between unions and employers. Goldberg's analysis reduces the applicability of Stigler's capture theory to the study of industrial relations regulation.

Second, Stigler's analysis focuses on the relationship between special interest groups, who demand, and politicians, who supply, regulation. While this may constitute a theory of politics it is far from clear that he has developed a theory of regulation. Stigler has failed to provide any discussion or examination of the mechanics of regulation of how regulators confront the tasks and responsibilities assigned to them. While politicians may simply be pawns in the hands of powerful interest groups, it needs to be established that regulators are equally hapless and passive. As has been discussed above, regulators are not given clear or exact guidelines on how to pursue their functions; regulators have scope to develop their own approach in solving the various problems associated with regulation. Regulators may be more independent, and display more initiative, than envisaged by Stigler. Examples have already been provided concerning the personnel of Australian industrial tribunals developing their own schemes, often in opposition to the parties and government(s), in responding to industrial relations problems. William Alfred Foster, a member of the federal tribunal between 1945 and 1962,[31] even went as far to describe himself and his colleagues as the "economic dictators of Australia" (quoted in Perlman 1954, 32). A rather odd comment from a passive instrument of special interest groups!

Third, Stigler assumes that the interests of the regulated are uniform. He does not consider situations where regulators are confronted by well-organized interest groups with conflicting goals. As has already been pointed out, Australian industrial relations is a very public affair, involving a never-ending struggle between unions, employers, governments, and other interest groups.[32] These groups are continually examining and commenting upon the decisions of industrial tribunals, searching for the means to obtain favorable decisions. In the 1952-53 *Standard Hours and Basic Wage* case, the Commonwealth Court of Conciliation and Arbitration pointed out (77 CAR 477, at 507) that

> application[s] before the Court must be determined in accordance with ... principles. They must thus be determined regardless of the dissatisfaction of an unsuccessful party. It is really impossible to settle a dispute in a way that satisfies all parties; it is frequently impossible to arrive at a just settlement which satisfies even one of the parties to the dispute.

The history of Australian industrial relations is one in which industrial tribunals hand down decisions which sometimes favor unions, sometimes favor employers, sometimes favor governments, and sometimes favor no one in that all of the parties are upset with the tribunal's decision. The problem confronting Stigler is that it is difficult to understand how industrial tribunals can be captured by one group and then another, and then by no one.

Bargaining or Activist Theories

Both Bernstein and Stigler stress the dominance of special interest groups, and the virtual irrelevance of regulators, in their respective examinations of regulation. Other writers have not been equally convinced that the world of regulation is one of a simple command obey relationship between dominant interest groups and hapless captured regulators. Rather, regulators have been imbued with varying degrees of assertiveness or independence.

Williams, for example, maintains that regulators have their own notions of how issues and problems associated with regulation should be approached.[33] He argues that "the exercise of pressure and influence is not entirely one way . . . the atmosphere or environment of regulation is sometimes as much conditioned by commissioners as by the regulated interests" (Williams 1976, 324).

Joskow (1974) examines why regulatory bodies adopt different techniques or approaches to regulation, and how such approaches are diffused to different regulatory jurisdictions. Changes in the economic and social environment of regulatory bodies induce them to develop new techniques of regulation. Joskow argues that (1974,

297) "regulatory agencies seek to minimise conflict and criticism appearing as signals from the economic and social environment in which they operate, subject to the binding legal and procedural constraints imposed by the legislation and the courts."

Joskow distinguishes between two different models of regulation. The first is a passive or equilibrium model in which the regulatory body is in harmony with its environment. "Equilibrium is characterized by a well-established organizational structure and regulatory procedures that are well defined and used repetitively and predictably" (Joskow 1974, 297). Regulation is seemingly trouble-free and there is little pressure or incentive to change established procedures.

The second is an evolutionary or innovative model. Following changes in the regulatory environment, such as continuing or increasing inflation, pressure is placed on regulators to develop a new approach to regulation. Signals in the economic and social environment indicate that past approaches have broken down. New techniques are needed to solve problems of the moment. Regulatory bodies innovate in an attempt to discover a new equilibrium.

Both federal and state governments create agencies to regulate various economic activities. Hence, there are a number of regulatory agencies performing similar functions, operating in different jurisdictions. More then one hundred industrial tribunals operate in Australia at both the federal and state level.[34] Joskow distinguishes between regulatory agencies which are leaders, and others which are imitators. Leaders experiment with different approaches in searching for a new equilibrium. The imitators closely watch these experiments and, if successful adopt them in their own jurisdictions. As Joskow explains (1974, 325), "The imitators are constantly monitoring the activities of the leaders during this disequilibrium situation. As the leaders adopt new techniques of regulation we will see the imitators adopting them also, usually citing the leading commissions as precedent for their decisions."

Industrial tribunals oscillate between passive and innovative phases. New approaches to industrial relations regulation are usually developed following significant changes in the broader social and economic environment. The notion of leaders and imitators can be applied to industrial tribunals. The tribunals keep an eye on each other as they search for solutions to the numerous issues surrounding industrial relations regulations. The (major) federal tribunal has assumed a de facto leadership role in Australia; other tribunals tend to emulate its approach to industrial relations regulation.[35] Since the mid-1970s, there has been a concerted attempt to increase the degree of cooperation and coordination between federal and state tribunals.[36]

Wilson (1971, 1974, 1978, 1980) has developed a model of regulation which explicitly highlights the independence, or activism, of regulators. Regulators operate in an environment which can be either supportive or hostile. Attacks can be mounted by special interest groups, politicians, superior courts, and the media. The potential hostility of the environment is a constant fact of regulatory life. Executives of regulatory agencies devote much of their time and energy to protecting the agency from critics and rivals. "Whatever they wanted to accomplish when they took office, it is not long before they come to see their day as dominated by the need to react to the environment and to view the environment as composed of real and potential threats" (Wilson 1978, 200). Regulators seek to gain control over their environment by increasing the autonomy of their agency.[37] Wilson argues (1978, 165) that

> The only way . . . crisis orientation can be minimized is by devising some way of assuring the autonomy of the agency. An agency is autonomous to the degree it can act independently of some or all of the groups that have the authority to constrain it. Autonomy is acquired by eliminating rival organizations that might wish to perform some or all of the same tasks as one's own bureau and acquiring sufficient goodwill and prestige as to make attacks on oneself or one's agency costly for one's critics.

Wilson's theory can be applied to the operation of Australian industrial tribunals. Industrial tribunals devise strategies to increase their autonomy and independence. Decisions are designed to protect themselves from political attack and appeals to superior courts. Moreover, members of industrial tribunals have sought to inculcate their values and beliefs into the operation of Australian industrial relations. Starting with Higgins and his "new province for law and order," going through to Maddern's structural efficiency principle, various industrial relations regulators have devised schemes and blueprints to solve industrial relations problems. In doing this, however, they have taken cognizance of the constraints of the environment and the expectations of the parties. They have sought to steer the parties into what they regard as a just and equitable system of industrial relations. In developing solutions, industrial tribunals seek to influence, cajole, push, or bully the parties to accept their interpretation of how to approach the problems associated with industrial relations regulation. Industrial tribunals engage in a continuing struggle with the parties to win their endorsement, if not acceptance, of their principles.

Industrial tribunals are involved in a balancing act, an act which is more complicated than balancing the completing claims of special interest groups. They balance the expectations of the parties with their interpretation of what the problems of the moment require. Dressed in the garb of impartiality they seek to bring their version of justice and reason to the world of industrial relations. It is as if industrial tribunals are seeking to lead the parties down an *ideal* path of regulation.

Wilson's analysis is also interesting because of the notion of regulators seeking to influence (or do we dare say *capture?*) the decision-making of special interest groups. It could be argued that industrial tribunals have taken over, or restricted, some of the functions performed by employers and unions.[38] Some commentators have maintained that the parties have become overly reliant or dependent on industrial tribunals. Howard, for example, has claimed (1977, 269-70) that "perhaps the Australian labor movement . . . is a labor movement in form and intention, rather than in tactic and achievement . . . where they have developed to meet a bureaucratic need (i.e., servicing industrial tribunals), as the Australian experience seems to be, perhaps unions themselves, in general, are industrial cosmetics." Scherer has also developed this line in perceiving (1976, 1) "unions [as] agents of the arbitration system." He argues that "federally registered trade unions are in fact government agencies. They are organizations established under the Conciliation and Arbitration Act[39] to carry out the purposes of that Act."

Australian Industrial Tribunals: "Stirring Up Peace"

This chapter has been concerned with exploring the role of the *state*[40] in industrial relations. It has attempted to do this by focusing on theories of regulation and assessing the usefulness of this literature in the context of the operation of industrial tribunals in Australia. Public interest, life cycle, capture and bargaining/activist theories of regulation were examined. The major conclusion of the chapter is that bargaining/activist theory provides the clearest insight into gaining an understanding of the role of industrial tribunals in Australia. Industrial tribunals are perceived as developing their own solutions to problems associated with industrial relations regulation. Industrial tribunals struggle, not only with the parties that they regulate, but also with governments, superior courts and other tribunals,[41] in attempting to gain acceptance or endorsement for the schemes or programs that they develop.

In 1913, Edmund Barton, Australia's first Prime Minister from 1901 to 1903, and a member of the High Court from 1903 to 1920, described Henry Bournes Higgins, in his capacity as President of the Commonwealth Court of Conciliation and Arbitration, as "stirring up peace" (Quoted in Rickard 1984, 274). Higgins was fearless in defending and developing the role of his tribunal in seeking to establish "a new province for law and order."

The history of industrial tribunals in Australia has been one of controversy and struggle. Their actions and decisions have been closely scrutinised by the parties, governments, superior courts and other interested parties. Industrial tribunals continually find themselves propelled to the centre stage of Australian society in the never ending search for an industrial relations nirvana. They have found themselves caught between a rock and a hard place, damned if they do and damned if they don't. Despite, or because of, such pressures industrial tribunals, or rather successive generations of tribunal personnel, have sought to devise solutions to the various problems associated with industrial relations regulation. They have found themselves embroiled in "stirring up peace" as they have sought to convince the parties of the wisdom of following their lead down an ideal path of industrial relations regulation.

Notes

1. The state is not monolithic. It contains many and varied institutions; such institutions struggle and complete with each other for resources, influence, and power.

2. For a review of theories of the state, see Head 1983.

3. The most obvious example would be those writers who have employed a corporatist, or neocorporatist framework. Also see Dabscheck 1983, Zeitlin 1985, Dabscheck 1989b, Giles 1989, and Keller 1990.

4. It should not be confused with French Regulation theory which provides a radical neo-Marxist analysis of society. For a recent review of this literature, see Jessop 1990.

5. For further information on progressivism, see Mowry 1946, Mowry 1958, Kolko 1963, Lasch 1966, Gould 1974, Trebing 1984, and Trebing 1987.

6. The survey will be an updating and adaption of Dabscheck 1983, chapter 1.

7. Both Marcus 1984 and Dethrick and Quirk 1985 demonstrate that in the 1970s and 1980s regulation became a more public affair.

8. Over the years there have been four changes to the name of the major federal industrial relations tribunal. From 1904 to 1956, it was called the Commonwealth Court of Conciliation and Arbitration; between 1956 and 1973, the Commonwealth Conciliation and Arbitration Commission; between 1973 and 1989, the Australian Conciliation and Arbitration Commission; and since 1989, the Australian Industrial Relations Commission.

9. Or rather, was not reappointed following her (Commonwealth) *Industrial Relations Act* 1988 when the Australian Industrial Relations Commission replaced the Australian Conciliation and Arbitration Commission. For details, see Kitay and McCarthy 1989, and Kirby 1989.

10. State governments are not as constrained in their relationships with their respective tribunals. For further discussion concerning the role of the Constitution and its interpretation by the High Court, see McCallum, Pittard, and Smith 1990.

11. There have been several examples of tension between various members of the tribunal concerning the best or most appropriate policy which should be pursued at a particular point in time.

12. For a fuller examination of the origins of industrial tribunals in Australia, see Macintyre and Mitchell 1989.

13. For details of Higgins' career see Higgins 1915, Higgins 1919, Higgins 1920, Lee 1980, McQueen 1983, Callaghan 1983, and Rickard 1984.

14. See Dabscheck 1983 and Roe 1984 for further details concerning Jethro Brown.

15. His emphasis.

16. For an examination of Kelly's approach to industrial relations regulation, see Dabscheck 1983.

17. See Isaac 1989 for a recent restatement of such a view.

18. Which are: (a) to promote industrial harmony and cooperation among the parties involved in industrial relations in Australia; (b) to provide a framework for the prevention and settlement of industrial disputes by conciliation and arbitration in a manner that minimizes the disruptive effects of industrial disputes on the community; (c) to ensure that, in the prevention and settlement of industrial disputes, proper regard is had to the interests of the parties immediately concerned and to the interests (including the economic interests) of the community as a whole; (d) to facilitate the prevention and prompt settlement of industrial disputes in a fair manner and with the minimum of legal form and technicality; (e) to provide for the observance and enforcement of agreements and awards made for the prevention and settlement of industrial disputes; (f) to encourage the organization of representative bodies of employers and employees and their registration under this Act; (g) to encourage the democratic control of organizations, and the participation by their members in the affairs of organizations; and (h) to encourage the efficient management of organizations.

19. Also see Bernstein 1961 and Bernstein 1972.

20. For another, see Kolko 1963.

21. See Dabscheck 1990 for a discussion of various issues associated with enterprise bargaining in the Australian context.

22. See McCallum, Pittard, and Smith 1990 for an examination of the High Court's role.

23. For additional information concerning Kirby's approach to industrial relations regulation, see Kirby 1965, Kirby 1970, and d'Alpuget 1977.

24. See Vernon 1986 for further information concerning Sir John Moore's period as president. Also see Kitay 1984.

25. See *National Wage Case* decisions August 1988, August 1989, and April 1991.

(National wage cases play a prominent role in the Australian system of wage determination and industrial relations regulation. They provide a forum in which the federal tribunal determines both the level of, and/or the procedures for determining wages of workers under its jurisdiction—state tribunals invariably emulate the national wage case decisions of the federal tribunal—consistent with their perception of the industrial relations and economic needs of Australia. In the 1970s and 1980s, there were periods when approximately 90 percent of wage rises resulted from decisions of the federal tribunal in national wage cases. National wage cases are something of an Australian institution and are reproduced in Commonwealth Arbitration Reports).

26. It is conceivable that Bernstein could be still correct here if we perceived the federal tribunal to be "the dominant party" involved in

250   Industrial Relations Theory

regulation. Such a conclusion, however, would result in the complete rejection of Bernstein's life-cycle theory.

27. They are supported, however, by institutional economists. See, for example, Trebing 1984, and Trebing 1987.

28. Also see Peltzman 1976.

29. Stewart has pointed out that this approach to regulation (1983, 1553) "posits and enforces a vision of society in which citizens use government power to prey on one another."

30. See Dabscheck 1989a for a critical examination and rejection of this view.

31. For further details concerning Foster, see Sharp 1963 and Larmour 1985.

32. Presumably industrial tribunals should be included as one of these other interest groups.

33. Also see Meidinger 1987.

34. Within each jurisdiction there is a mainstream tribunal, such as the Australian Industrial Relations Commission, and a number of specialist tribunals with responsibility for a particular sector or group of workers.

35. In some cases state legislation compels them to do so.

36. For details see the *Australian Journal of Labour Law* (May 1990) which is devoted to "Joint State-Federal Arrangements in the Settlement of Industrial Disputes."

37. Niskanen (1971) has perceived regulatory bodies as being imperialistic organisations seeking to maximize their budgets. This begs the question, however, of the reason, or rationale, for such budget maximization.

38. See Callus, Moorehead, and Buchanan (1991) for a recent and extensive empirical examination of employer and union organization at the workplace.

39. Now, of course, if would be the *Industrial Relations Act* 1988.

40. See footnote 1.

41. And other relevant regulatory agencies or arms of the state.

Works Cited

Barkin, D. 1971, *American Pluralist Democracy: A Critique*, New York: Van Nostrand Reinhold Company.
Bernstein, M. H. 1955, *Regulating Business by Independent Commission*, Princeton, NJ: Princeton University Press.
_____. 1961, "The Regulatory Process: A Framework for Analysis," *Law and Contemporary Problems*, vol. 26, pp. 329-346.
_____. 1972, "Independent Regulatory Agencies: A Perspec-

tive on their Reform," *The Annals of the American Academy of Political and Social Science,* vol. 400, pp. 14-26.

Braithwaite, J. 1985, *To Punish Or Persuade: Enforcement of Coal Mine Safety,* Albany, NY: State University of New York Press.

Breyer, S. G., and P. W. MacAvoy. 1974, *Energy Regulation by the Federal Power Commission,* Washington, DC: Brookings Institution.

Callaghan, P. S. 1983, "Idealism and Arbitration in H. B. Higgins' New Province for Law and Order," *Journal of Australian Studies,* no. 13, pp. 56-66.

Callus, R., A. Moorehead, M. Cully, and J. Buchanan, 1991, *Industrial Relations At Work: The Australian Workplace Industrial Relations Survey,* Commonwealth Department of Industrial Relations, Canberra: AGPS.

Carson, W. G. 1989, "Occupational Health and Safety," *Labour and Industry,* vol. 2, no. 2, pp. 301-316.

d'Alpuget, B. 1977, *Mediator: A Biography of Sir Richard Kirby,* Carlton: Melbourne University Press.

Dabscheck, B. 1983, *Arbitrator At Work: Sir William Raymond Kelly and the Regulation of Australian Industrial Relations,* Sydney: George Allen and Unwin.

_____. 1989a, *Australian Industrial Relations in the 1980s,* Melbourne: Oxford University Press.

_____. 1989b, "A Survey of Theories of Industrial Relations," *Theories and Concepts in Comparative Industrial Relations,* eds. J. Barbash and K. Barbash, Columbia, SC: University of South Carolina Press.

_____. 1990, "Enterprise Bargaining: A New Province for Law and Order?," *The Australian Quarterly,* vol. 62, no. 3, pp. 240-255.

Dethrick, M., and P. J. Quirk. 1985, *The Politics of Deregulation,* Washington, DC: Brookings Institution.

Giles, A. 1989, "Industrial Relations Theory, the State and Politics," in Barbash and Barbash.

Goldberg, V. P. 1976, "Regulation and Administered Contracts," *Bell Journal of Economics,* vol. 7, no. 2, pp. 426-448.

Gould, L. L., ed. 1974, *The Progressive Era,* Syracuse, NY: Syracuse University Press.

Grabosky, P., and J. Braithwaite. 1986, *Of Manners Gentle: Enforcement Strategies of Australian Business Regulatory Agencies,* Melbourne: Oxford University Press.

Gunningham, N. 1984, *Safeguarding The Worker: Job Hazards and the Role of the Law,* Sydney: Law Book Co.

Head, B. W. 1983, "State and Economy: Theories and Problems," in *State and Economy in Australia,* ed. B. W. Head, Melbourne: Oxford University Press.

Higgins, H. B. 1915, "A New Province for Law and Order I," *Harvard Law Review*, vol. 34, no. 2, pp. 13-39.

_____. 1919, "A New Province for Law and Order II," *Harvard Law Review*, vol. 32, no. 3, pp. 189-217.

_____. 1920, "A New Province for Law and Order III," *Harvard Law Review*, vol. 34, no. 2, pp. 105-136.

Howard, W. A. 1977, "Australian Trade Unions in the Context of Union Theory," *The Journal of Industrial Relations*, vol. 19, no. 3, pp. 255-273.

Hyman, R. 1975, *Industrial Relations: A Marxist Introduction*, London: Macmillan.

Isaac, J. E. 1989, "The Arbitration Commission: Prime Mover or Facilitator," *The Journal of Industrial Relations*, vol. 31, no. 3, pp. 407-427.

Jessop, B. 1990, "Regulation Theories in Retrospect and Prospect," *Economy and Society*, vol. 19, no. 2, pp. 153-216.

Joskow, P. L. 1974, "Inflation and Environmental Concern: Structural Change in the Process of Public Utility Price Regulation," *Journal of Law and Economics*, vol. 17, no. 2, pp. 291-327.

Keller, B. K. 1990, "The State as Corporate Actor in Industrial Relations Systems," *The Journal of Industrial Relations*, vol. 32, no. 2, pp. 254-268.

Kelman, S. 1980, "Occupational Safety and Health Administration," in *The Politics of Regulation*, ed. J. Q. Wilson, New York: Basic Books.

Kirby, M. 1989, "Justice Staples and the Politics of Australian Industrial Arbitration," *The Journal of Industrial Relations*, vol. 31, no. 3, pp. 334-371.

Kirby, R. 1965, "Some Comparisons between Compulsory Arbitration and Collective Bargaining," *The Journal of Industrial Relations*, vol. 7, no. 1, pp. 1-17.

_____. 1970, "Conciliation and Arbitration in Australia: Where the Emphasis?," *Federal Law Review*, vol. 4, pp. 1-29.

Kitay, G. B. 1984, *Federal Conciliation and Arbitration in Australia 1967-1981*, Ph.D. Thesis, Australian National University.

Kitay, J., and P. McCarthy. 1989, "Justice Staples and the Politics of Australian Industrial Arbitration," *The Journal of Industrial Relations*, vol. 31, no. 3, pp. 310-333.

Kolko, G. 1963, *The Triumph of Conservatism: A Reinterpretation of American History, 1900-1916*, New York: Free Press.

Larmour, C. 1985, *Labor Judge: The Life and Times of Judge Alfred William Foster*, Sydney: Hale and Iremonger.

Lasch, C. 1966, *The New Radicalism in America*, New York: Alfred A. Knopf.

Lee, M. 1980, *The Industrial Peace Act 1920: A Study of Political Interference in Compulsory Arbitration*, M.Ec. Thesis, Sydney University.

Macintyre, S. 1989, "Neither Capital Nor Labour: The Politics of the Establishment of Arbitration," in S. Macintyre and R. Mitchell, eds., *Foundations of Arbitration: The Origins and Effects of State Compulsory Arbitration 1890-1914*, Melbourne: Oxford University Press.

Marcus, A. A. 1984, *The Adversary Economy: Business Responses to Changing Government Requirements*, Westport, CT: Quorum Books.

McCallum, R. C., M. J. Pittard, and G. F. Smith. 1990, *Australian Labour Law: Cases and Materials*, Sydney: Butterworths.

McQueen, H. 1983, "Higgins and Arbitration," in E. L. Wheelwright and K. Buckley, eds., *Essays in the Political Economy of Australian Capitalism*, vol. 5, Sydney: Australian and New Zealand Book Co.

Meidinger, E. 1987, "Regulatory Culture: A Theoretical Outline," *Law and Policy*, vol. 9, no. 4, pp. 335-386.

Mowry, G. E. 1946, *Theodore Roosevelt and the Progressive Movement*, New York: Hill and Wang.

Mowry, G. E. 1958, *The Era of Theodore Roosevelt: 1900-1912*, London: Hamish Hamilton.

Niskanen, W. A. 1971, *Bureaucracy and Representative Government*, Chicago: Aldine-Atherton.

Owen, B. M., and R. Braeutigan. 1978, *The Regulation Game: Strategic Use of the Administrative Process*, Cambridge, MA: Ballinger.

Peltzman, S. 1976, "Toward a More General Theory of Regulation," *Journal of Law and Economics*, vol. 19, no. 2, pp. 211-240.

Perlman, M. 1954, *Judges in Industry: A Study of Labour Arbitration in Australia*, Melbourne: Melbourne University Press.

Rees, J. V. 1988, *Reforming the Workplace: A Study of Self-Regulation in Occupational Safety*, Philadelphia: University of Pennsylvania Press.

Rickard, J. 1984, *H. B. Higgins: The Rebel as Judge*, Sydney: George Allen and Unwin.

Roe, M. 1984, *Nine Australian Progressives: Vitalism in Bourgeois Social Thought 1890-1960*, St. Lucia: University of Queensland Press.

Ronfeldt, P. 1989, *Racial Discrimination in Employment: The Impact of the Anti-Discrimination Act (NSW) 1977-1987*, Industrial Relations Research Centre Monograph, Kensington: University of New South Wales.

Sabatier, R. 1975, "Social Movements and Regulatory Agencies: Toward a More Adequate and Less Pessimistic Theory of "Clientele Capture," *Policy Sciences*, vol. 6, no. 3, pp. 301-342.

Scherer, P. 1976, "The Arbitrator as Manager of Discontent" (mimeo),
    47th ANZAAS Congress, Hobart, 10-14 May.
Sharp, I. G. 1963, "Alfred William Foster," *The Economic Record*, vol.
    39, no. 85, pp. 107-115.
Stewart, R. B. 1983, "Regulation in a Liberal State: The Role of Non-
    Commodity Values," *The Yale Law Journal*, vol. 2, no. 8, pp.
    1537-1590.
Stigler, G. J. 1971, "The Theory of Economic Regulation," *Bell Jour-
    nal of Economics and Management Science*, vol. 2, no. 1, pp. 3-21.
Stigler, G. J., and C. Friedland. 1970, "What Can Regulators Regulate?
    The Case of Electricity," in *The Crisis of Regulatory Commissions:
    An Introduction to a Current Issue of Public Policy*, ed. P. W.
    MacAvoy, New York: Norton.
Trebing, H. M. 1984, "Public Utility Regulation: A Case Study in the
    Debate over Effectiveness of Economic Regulation," *Journal of
    Economic Issues*, vol. 17, no. 1, pp. 223-250.
_____. 1987, "Regulation of Industry: An Institutionalist Ap-
    proach," *Journal of Economic Issues*, vol. 21, no. 4, pp. 1707-1737.
Vernon, T. 1986, *The Australian Conciliation and Arbitration Commis-
    sion under Sir John Moore, B.Com.* Honours Thesis, University of
    New South Wales.
Williams, R. J. 1976, "Politics and the Ecology of Regulation," *Public
    Administration* (London), vol. 54, pp. 319-331.
Wilson, J. Q. 1971, "The Dead Hand of Regulation," *Public Interest*,
    no. 25, pp. 39-58.
_____. 1974, "The Politics of Regulation," in *Social Responsibil-
    ity and the Business Predicament*, ed. J. W. McKie, Washington, DC:
    Brookings Institution.
_____. 1978, *The Investigators: Managing FBI and Narcotics
    Agents*, New York: Basic Books.
_____, ed. 1980, *The Politics of Regulation*, New York: Basic
    Books.
Zeitlin, J. 1985, "Shop Floor Bargaining and the State: a Contradictory
    Relationship," in *Shop Floor Bargaining and the State: Historical
    and Comparative Perspectives*, eds. S. Tolliday and J. Zeitlin,
    Cambridge: Cambridge University Press.

Theorizing Industrial Relations: The Dominance of Logical Positivism and the Shift to Strategic Choice

Viateur Larouche and Michel Audet

Although industrial relations research has mushroomed in recent decades, many authors have argued that it is theoretically underdeveloped. There has, nevertheless, been a substantial amount of writing which may be classified as theoretical or at least conceptual in nature (Adams 1988). Using a model developed to classify and assess social scientific theories (Burrell and Morgan 1979), the aim of this article is to chart patterns of industrial relations theorizing. The first part of the article reviews the Burrell and Morgan scheme with respect to its applicability to the social sciences generally. The second part describes a modified version of the model designed to classify theoretical contributions to industrial relations. The next part of the paper reviews the use of significant analytical patterns by industrial relations theorists before and after 1980. Finally, conclusions about the weight of both older and more recent patterns of analysis applied to industrial relations are offered.

We would like to express our thanks to Roy J. Adams and Braham Dabscheck for their thoughtful comments on an earlier version of the article. The final product is, of course, entirely our responsibility.

A Social Sciences Model

Burrell and Morgan (1979), propose that social theories, to which industrial relations belongs, may usefully be classified in terms of four key constructs or paradigms[1] based upon assumptions about two dimensions: *the nature of society and the nature of social science.* Investigating assumptions with regard to the nature of society, the authors discovered that most problems could be described in terms of a regulation versus radical change continuum. Regulation is concerned with the explanation of society in terms of its underlying unity and cohesiveness and the need for order in human affairs. Radical change, however, is mainly concerned with the explanations of deep-seated structural conflict, modes of domination, and structural contradictions which its theorists see as characterizing modern society. It is preoccupied with the struggle for emancipation from structures which limit and stunt potential; its theorists tend to dwell on the issue of deprivation, both material and psychic; it is concerned with potential rather than actuality, with alternatives to the status quo.

Analyzing the nature of social science, two additional perspectives are identified: objective and subjective. The objective dimension treats the social world as if it were a hard, external, objective reality. Scientific endeavor is likely to focus upon relationships and regularities among the various elements which comprise society. The primary concern, therefore, is the identification and definition of societal elements and the discovery of different ways to express the relationships between them. The important methodological issues are thus the concepts themselves and their measurement, and the discovery of underlying regularities.This perspective expresses itself most forcefully in a search for universal laws which explain and govern the reality that is being observed.

The alternative view of the social world stresses the importance of subjective experience in the creation of society. Its main concern is with the way people create, modify, and interpret the world in which they are placed. (See the Godard chapter in this volume for additional discussion of this perspective.) Emphasis is sometimes placed on the explanation and understanding of what is unique and particular, rather than on what is general or universal. In methodological terms this approach stresses the relativistic nature of the social world. A fundamental proposition of those who follow this approach to the acquisition of knowledge is that humans are limited by their senses and instruments in knowing reality. Critics sometimes claim that, rather than being an alternative means of scientific inquiry as its supporters claim, it is instead the antithesis of science.

The relationship between the two dimensions described above allows the authors to develop a coherent model which yields four different constructs (paradigms): humanist, structuralist, interpretative, functionalist. Table 1 provides an illustration of the links which exist between the dimensions used and the characteristics related by these four main paradigms.

The *humanist paradigm* is defined by its concern to develop radical change from a subjective standpoint. This construct emphasizes the importance of challenging the limitations of existing social arrangements.One of the most basic notions underlying this concept is that the consciousness of man is dominated by ideological superstructures (typically learned unconsciously) with which he interacts with perceived objects. The ideological constructs often lead to "false conciousness," which inhibits true human fulfilment. This approach, then, seeks to reveal these false constructs in order to oppose what it sees as inhumane and unethical behavior.

The *structuralist paradigm* focuses on the fact that contemporary society is characterized by fundamental conflicts which generate radical change through political and economic crises. It is through such conflicts and changes that the emancipation of individuals from the social structures in which they live is seen as forthcoming. This approach concentrates upon structural relationships within a realistic social world. It emphasizes that radical change is built into the very nature and structure of contemporary society, and it seeks to provide explanations of the basic interrelationships within the context of total social formations.

The *interpretative paradigm* insists on understanding the world "as it is," which means understanding the fundamental nature of problems on the level of subjective experience. It focuses on explanation within the realm of individual conciousness, on subjectivity within the frame of reference of the participant as opposed to the observer of action.Those who accept this conception, are concerned with understanding the essence of the everyday world.Their analytical framework aims at issues relating to the nature of the

Table 1   Paradigms Used in Analysis of Social Theory
(Main Characteristics)

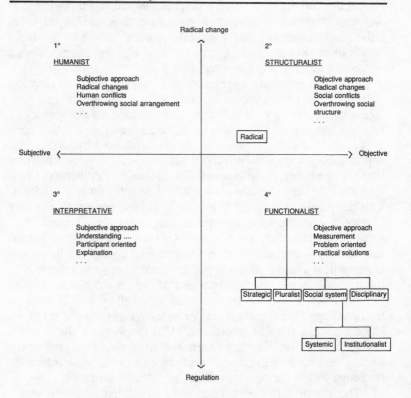

Burrell and Morgan's Paradigms and Industrial Relations

Burrell and Morgan[2] stress that "most organization theorists, industrial sociologists, psychologists and industrial relations theorists approach their object from within the bounds of the functionalist construct". They also point out that some authors approach their object from within the bounds of the structuralist concept.

The Functionalist Paradigm

Burrell and Morgan identified five broad categories of functionalist defined in terms of analytical approaches. In order to give an industrial relations orientation to those categories,[3] we suggest they be identified as follows:

1. Disciplinary (multi or pluri) approach.
2. Institutional approach.
3. System approach.
4. Pluralist approach.
5. Strategic approach.

Disciplinary (multi or pluri) Approach

Those who use this approach in studying industrial relations assume that labor problems are complexes which must be studied using the methodology of different disciplines such as sociology, law, psychology, economics, history, and so on. This approach was originally developed to integrate those disciplines and build a new theory, one which would have characterized industrial relations. Unfortunately interdisciplinary efforts at theory building did not progress very far. Today, more often than not, we encounter the paradox of multidisciplinary approaches which apply one discipline at a time to any given industrial relations topic. The great hope that an industrial relations theory would emerge through synthesis and breakdown of the conventional knowledge barriers was never realized (see, e.g., Adams in this volume).

Institutional Approach

This approach focuses on documenting the history, origins, and development of labor institutions (trade unions, employee's associations, and governmental labor agencies). Its practitioners offer detailed descriptions of labor institutions and the structures and operations which characterize them. As Kochan (1988) points out, they are also interested in describing the legal framework and the mechanisims they use (such as collective bargaining, mediation) to solve problems.They do the same with current issues confronting practitioners and policymakers, working in the field of industrial relations. Such an approach is, of course, mainly inductive and normative.

System Approach

The concept of system has been defined by many in such fields as biology, physics, psychology, sociology, and so on, as a set of components interacting within a boundary possessing the property of filtering both the kind and rate of flow into and out of the system (Peterson 1971). Craig (1983), applying the system approach to industrial relations, explains that a system consists of four basic components:

1. Internal inputs as summarized by the concepts of goals, values, power of the participants (actors) in the system, which are conditioned by the flow of effects from environmental subsystems (external inputs)
2. The processes or complex of private and public activities for converting inputs into outputs
3. The outputs, comprising the material, social, and psychological rewards employees receive in rendering their services
4. A feedback loop through which the outputs flow directly into the industrial relations system itself and also into the environmental subsystem. The outputs which flow through the feedback loop can shape the subsequent goals, values and power of the actors in the industrial relations system as well as influence the actors in other environmental

subsystems whose activities may be affected by certain outputs.

Users of this approach first try to build a model which integrates the main components of industrial relations, and to clarify the relationships which exist between the components (variables) of the system. To do so, they often use disciplinary approaches (deductive or inductive, statistical, quantitative, etc.) which help them both to develop and test hypotheses.

Pluralist Approach

Under this approach, industrial relations is mainly concerned with the notion that employees and employers bring expectations to their work roles which are partially shaped by societal values, cultural heritage, and experience. Consequently, while workers bring a variety of their own needs and goals to the workplace, they also accept (to varying degrees) the legitimacy of management's right to organize work and direct the workforce. In such a context, employee-employer relationships are characterized by power relations. Facing that reality, the pluralist approach suggests that there are plural interests in the economy which result in conflicts that need to be resolved within the context of organizations.

This framework applies to both procedural and substantive issues within organizations. Conflict of interest may arise not only over the objective conditions of employment but also over the means used to make decisions at the workplace. Whenever authority relations exist, there is a potential for conflict, since differences over the scope and exercise of authority, power, and control are bound to arise. Thus, this approach focuses on the fact that industrial relations problems must be studied by taking into account the dimension of opposing forces and that solution must involve some degree of compromise.

Strategic Approach

The strategic approach originated from doubts expressed over the ability of the system approach to explain recent changes in the labor world of the United States (Dimmock and Sethi 1986). By proposing this "new" approach, Kochan, McKersie, and Cappelli (1984) were not concerned with presenting an entirely new theory of industrial relations or with totally rejecting the system framework, but with incorporating into the latter a new dimension of strategic choice or an elaboration of the system approach (see, e.g., Meltz in this volume).

With increasing regularity, strategic choice has been used in both economics and organizational theory. Although the literature offers various definitions of strategy, as used among game theorists the term stands for the concrete actions or rules for choosing actions in a conflict situation; for some, strategy is "high level" or "long-term" planning, while for others it is only the broad gauging of issues of "mission" (Kochan et al., 1984). It deserves to be stated that at both the level of the firm and the level of labor management, the relationship between strategy and structure is dynamic and interactive (Gospel 1983).

In short, to apply this approach one needs to be familiar with business strategy (decision-making) models which integrate product changes in response to changing consumer demand, capital, technology, labor, etc. (Dimmock and Sethi 1986).

The Structuralist Paradigm

Many scholars study their object in the bounds of the structuralist paradigm which means they used a radical approach which maintains that a class stuggle is inevitable because the means of production are controlled by the capitalist class. Of course, this way of thinking overlooks the flexibility of the capitalist system, in which unions have acquired a consumptionist function which bolsters the economy, and therefore are regarded as positive institutions in society (Hameed 1982). The methodologies used are drawn mainly from sociology, economics, politics, and history. For the most part its descriptions are treated dialectically (Zeitlin 1985).

Industrial Relations (Objects)

The different approaches used by industrial relations writers are not applied to the same object. Reviewing the literature, it is possible to indentify six broad definitions of what constitutes "the reality" of industrial relations phenomena. These objects are not totally mutually exclusive, nor are they exhaustive.

1. Labor relations and collective bargaining.
2. Rules and the rule-making process.
3. Resolution of conflict.
4. Power conflict.
5. Employment relationships (including both human resources management and labor relations).
6. Human resources management.

Labor Relations and Collective Bargaining

Authors of this group maintain that industrial relations include all relationships between organized labor, management, and collective bargaining as compromise of different labor interests, such as unions, management, and the public. They believe industrial relations as a field of inquiry should focus on protective labor legislation and union organization. They share the basic assumption that conflict of interest does arise out of the nature of capitalism, but that the means for resolving it can come from within the capitalist system, through workers' organizations, union-employer accommodation, and periodic compromises (Kochan 1980).

Rules and the Rule-Making Process

This is how Dunlop characterized industrial relations. He argued that the discipline was framed by four basic constructs: actors, environnemental constraints, ideology, and rules. Dunlop visualized three actors in the system: labor, management, and governmental agencies. The environmental constraints were technology, market, budget, and the locus of power in the broader social system. Ideology was a shared understanding among the actors. As its product this approach emphasized a set of procedural and substantive rules (Hameed 1975a). Some authors have modified Dunlop's definition of industrial relations. For example, Craig (1983) remarks that these rules are intended to allocate rewards to employees for their services and compensation for the conditions under which such services are rendered.

Resolution of Conflict

The conflict resolution school takes an essential element of industrial relations, bargaining, as a mechanism for the resolution of conflict. Although conflict between organized labor and management is inherent to the system, it is not regarded as irresolvable. Authors who espouse this point of view regard industrial relations as the study of labor conflict, but within a solvable framework.

Power Conflict

Conflict is the essence of industrial relations because industrialization generates stratifications which in turn generate tensions among the people stratified. Technology, scale, organization, efficiency, and uncertainty generate tensions of command and subordination, competitiveness, and exploitation at work as well as economic insecurity. Here industrial relations is mainly concerned with power relations (between capital and labor) and the struggle of labor and management to consolidate and strengthen their respective positions in order to influence the structure and working conditions of industrial labor. Here conflict is the key ingredient of industrial relations. This field of study investigates which power positions capital and labor hold in conflict over the structures of work and how far the organized working class has advanced in its struggle for the abolition of a condition which they, as wage-workers are obliged to accept as dictated by others (Schienstock 1981).

Employment Relationships

According to Heneman and Yoder (1965), industrial relations must study employment behavior and relationships at micro and macro levels, individuals and groups (unions), labor marketing, labor relations, personnel management, workers' participation in entreprise decision-making, solution of labor conflicts, and so on. It is a discipline which studies human behavior as a relationship

among individuals, both formal and informal and between public
and private groups which interact in a work-related environment to
reach a compromise over the allocation of rewards (Hameed
1975a). As seen here industrial relations has two major components: labor relations and human resources management, (Boivin
1987). Adams (1992) goes further by proposing that IR is about
much more than labor relations and human resources management.
As indicated by research reported in industrial relations publications, it is also about various labor market issues (unemployment,
immigration, employment standards) which do not fit into either of
those categories.

Human Resources Management

Some industrial relations writers believe their discipline should
focus strictly on the management of human resources, which means
all the managerial dimensions of the work pattern of an individual.
This definition of the discipline does not include all aspects of the
relationship between organized labor and business but only those
aspects relevant to enterprise management.

For these writers industrial relations should be concerned with
managerial aspects of the individual as they earn monetary and
nonmonetary rewards, develop a work-oriented perception and
motivation, communicate and participate in the structure and processes of formal and informal groups at work, abide by work
regulations imposed both by management and government, and
receive various work-related benefits such as unemployment and
worker compensation and retraining allowances, and finally retirement benefits (Hameed 1975b).

Methodology

The purpose of this section is to provide a description of current
analytical patterns and their characteristics in terms of the approaches and objects defined above. Before proceeding with our
exercise however, some points warrant further emphasis. First, the
approaches we will apply to classify authors are based on broad
categories which are not necessarily mutually exclusive. The same

author may appear in different categories; for example, many
authors using the system approach to integrate results of research
in industrial relations, also apply disciplinary methodology to study
problems in industrial relations. Even if such authors have been
closely associated with one approach, we must recognize that they
may also have been indentified with another. Second, categorizing
authors is always a risky enterprise. Some clearly express how they
see industrial relations and what approach they think should be
applied to study its various aspects. Others express their point of
view less clearly or are not yet at a point where they can articulate
it. Finally, the same author may at different times express different
perspectives on the meaning of industrial relations and the right
approach to it.

   An extensive review of the literature resulted in the identification of 158 theoritical articles, chapters of books, and other material
(between 1897 and 1988) which significantly focused on "what
industrial relations is . . . " These articles were analyzed and
categorized in accordance with the analytical patterns identified
above.

Industrial Relations: The Significant Patterns . . .

Disciplinary Approach: Labor Relations and Collective Bargaining

   The industrial relations literature reveals that authors who
apply the disciplinary approach see industrial relations in terms of
labor relations, collective bargaining, and other related topics.
Among these writers are Bacharach and Lawler 1980, 1981;
Barbash 1979; Behrend 1963; Chamberland 1951; Chamberland
and Kuhn 1965; Commons 1934; Derber 1964, 1969; Farnham and
Pimlott 1979; Garbarino 1966; Laffer 1968, 1974; Palmer 1983;
Somers 1969; Strauss and Feuille 1978; and Winchester 1983.

   With regard to this aproach we have also identified a group of
authors who advocate that industrial relations be defined more
broadly in terms of employment relationships, including both labor
relations and human resources management (Adams 1983, 1988;

Barbash, 1964; Capelli 1985; Sen and Hameed 1988; Shimmin and Singh 1973; and Wheeler 1985, 1986).

Institutionalist Approach: Labor Relations and Collective Bargaining

The great majority of industrial relations authors who applied the institutional approach to industrial relations illustrated it through the labor relations and collective bargaining framework. This, the predominant framework, was chosen by Allen 1971; Barbash 1988; Barkin 1980; Caire 1973; Clark 1987; Deery and Plowman 1985; Flanders and Clegg 1954; Gill and Concannon 1977; Hameed and Sen 1987; Maurice, Sellier, and Silvestre 1979; Perlman 1928; Richardson 1954; and Webb and Webb 1897.

The same analytical approach was sometimes used by others who considered industrial relations in terms of employment relationships (Barbash 1986; Dion 1986; Hale 1986; and Hébert, Jain, and Meltz, 1988).

System Approach: Rules and Employment Relationship

The reviewed literature shows that the system approach was very frequently used (or at least mentioned) as the one which should be applied to industrial relations. As indicated by Schienstock (1981), this approach devotes most attention to how regulation of industrial relations involving employers, employees, and governmental agencies is arrived at and how such regulation is adapted to the prevailing contextual situation. An impressive group of authors have applied the systems approach to industrial relations in the framework of the rules concept: Blyton Dastmalchian, and Adamson 1987; Cox 1971; Craig 1966, 1983, 1988; Crispo 1978; Dabscheck 1980, 1981, 1983, 1987; Dunlop 1958, 1976; Fatchett and Whittingham 1976; Geare 1977; Goodman et al. 1975; Gunderson, 1988; Hameed 1982; Jain 1975; Jamieson 1957; Krislov 1987; Lumley 1979; Margerison 1969; Nayar 1985; Poole 1986; Purcell and Earl 1977; Singh 1976, 1978; Walker 1969, 1976; Wood et al. 1975; and Wood 1978.

Under the same approach, a second group of industrial relations authors (as important as the first) advocated that the key concept of industrial relations was employment relationships. These are Adams 1992 and "All Aspects . . . " in this volume; Anderson 1979; Anderson and Gunderson 1982; Bélanger, Petit, and Bergeron 1983; Bemmels and Zaidi 1986; Blain and Gennard 1970; Boivin 1987, 1989; Giles and Murray 1988; Hameed 1975a, 1988; Hanlon 1985; Henneman 1967, 1968, 1969; Heneman and Yoder 1965; Larouche and Deom 1984; Owen and Finston 1964; Parker and Scott 1971; Peach and Kuechele 1985; Shiron 1985; and Weiss 1980.

Within this approach there was a smaller, third group who regarded industrial relations as the domain of labor relations and collective bargaining. These are Beaumont and Harris 1988; Davidson 1973; Dominguez 1971; Gill 1969; Hartman 1973; Philips, 1981; and Thompson 1988.

Finally, within the same approach, we encounter authors interested in studying industrial relations through the resolution of conflict (Crouch 1972 and Eldridge 1968) and through human resources management (Dolan and Schuler 1987; Gospel 1983; and Peterson 1971).

Pluralist Approach: Rules and Resolution of Conflict

Among those who applied the pluralist approach to study industrial relations, a first group have done so in the framework of the rules concept. These are authors like Bain and Clegg 1974; Clegg 1972, 1979; Flanders 1968, 1970; and Kerr 1955, 1960, 1986.

Another group of industrial relations theorists applied the same analytical approach to a different industrial relations content, the resolution of conflicts: Fox 1971, 1973, 1974; Hills 1988; and Strauss 1977.

Finally, we find theorists who advocated this approach but defined industrial relations in terms of labor relations and collective bargaining: Clegg 1975 and Kerr 1978.

Strategic Approach: Human Resources Management

Scholars who advocate the strategic approach are mainly interested in seeing industrial relations in terms of human resources management. Although they do not deny employment relationship, based on labor relations and human resources management, as the key concept of industrial relations, they maintain that industrial relations theorists and practitioners should concentrate their energy on one of those two elements, i.e., human resources management.

The authors who adhere to this line of thought are Beer et al. 1984; Brewster and Connock 1985; Dimmock and Sethi 1986; Kochan 1988; Kochan, Mackersie, and Cappelli 1984; Kochan and Barocci 1985; Kochan, Mitchell, and Dyer 1982; Kochan, Katz, and McKersie 1986; Lewin 1987; Reshef and Murray 1988; Sethi and Dimmock 1987; Strauss 1984; Thurley and Wood 1983; and Timberley 1980.

Radical Approach: Power conflict

The radical approach is mainly concerned with a Marxian analysis, and its users claim that industrial relations must concentrate on the study of power conflict. Its supporters are Armstrong, Goodman, and Hyman 1981; Braverman 1974; Bray 1981; Burawoy 1979; Frenkel 1977; Friedman 1977; Guille 1984; Hyman 1975, 1978, 1979; Hyman and Brough 1975; Kirkbride 1985; Korpi 1981; Korpi and Shalev 1979; Marsden 1982; Oostermeyer 1978; Shalev 1980; Stark 1980; Storey 1983; and Strinati 1982.

Importance of Analytical Patterns

The examination of a number of contemporary theoretical articles on the analysis of industrial relations reveals a breadth of analytical patterns. This multiplicity becomes evident (Table 2) as soon as one examines the range of issues treated by different authors using different approaches. As shown in Table 2, the most used approach is the system one. Among the different objects authors maintain to characterize industrial relations, the most frequently

Table 2. Analytical Patterns Used By Industrial Relations Theorists (N = 158)

Approaches Object	Disciplinary (multi or plury)	Institution	System	Pluralist	Strategic	Radical	Total
Labor Relations & Collective Bargaining	17	13	7	2	–	–	39
Rules & Rule-making process	–	–	31	8	–	–	39
Resolutions Conflict	–	–	2	6	–	–	8
Power Conflict	–	–	–	–	–	19	19
Employment Relationship	9	4	23	–	–	–	36
Human Resources Management	–	–	3	–	14	–	17
Total	26	17	66	16	14	19	158

used by authors are 1) *labor relations and collective bargaining,* 2) *rules and the rule-making process,* and 3) *employment relationship.*

Because our review of literature covers an important period of time (from the Webbs 1897 to Lewin 1987), we thought it would be worthwhile to look at the material from two specific periods (before 1980 and after 1980) to determine whether the authors accorded the same importance to the proposed patterns (Table 3).

Our classification of the articles which we reviewed leads us to conclude that research in industrial relations has been and continues to be carried out primarily within the functionalist tradition of research. This means that industrial relations is firmly focused on regulation and is used to approach subject matter from an objective point of view. This construct, according to Burrell and Morgan, is

Table 3. Analytical Patterns Used by Industrial Relations Theorists Before 1980 and After 1980 (N = 158)

BEFORE 1980				AFTER 1980			
RANK	PATTERN	N	%	RANK	PATTERN	N	%
1°	System – Rules	19	23.0	1°	System – Employment relations	14	18.6
					Strategic – Human Resources Management	14	18.6
					System – Rules	12	16.0
					Radical – Power Conflict	9	12.0
2°	Disciplinary – Labor Relations and Collective Bargaining	13	15.6	2°	Institutional – Labor Relations and Collective Bargaining	6	8.0
					Institutional – Employment Relations	5	6.6
					System – Labor Relations and Collective Bargaining	4	5.3
					Disciplinary – Labor Relations and Collective Bargaining	4	5.3
					Disciplinary – Employment Relations	3	4.0
3°	Radical – Power conflict	10	12.0	3°	System – Human Resources Management	2	2.6
					Pluralist – Rules	1	1.3
					Pluralist – Resolution of Conflict	1	1.3
4°	System – Employment Relations	9	10.8				
	Institutional – Labor Relations and Collective Bargaining	8	9.6				
	Pluralist – Rules	7	8.4				
	System – Labor Relations and Collective Bargaining	5	6.0				
	Pluralist – Conflict Resolution	4	4.8				
5°	Disciplinary – Employment Relations	3	3.6				
	Pluralist – Labor Relations and Collective Bargaining	2	2.4				
	System – Conflict Resolution	2	2.4				
	System – Human Resources Management	1	1.2				
TOTAL:		83	100.0			75	100.0

characterized by a concern for providing explanations of the status quo, social order, consensus, social integration, solidarity, need satisfaction, and actuality. It approaches these general concerns from a standpoint that tends to be both realist and positivist.

Within the functionalist category there are several separate, although overlapping, approaches to the study of industrial relations. For several decades industrial relations theorists were concerned primarily with union-management relations and with collective bargaining. As a means of conceptualizing union-management relations, John Dunlop's IR systems achieved dominance and it continues to attract a large number of adherents. More recently, however, its utility has been challenged.

Kochan and his colleagues from MIT (1984) found it to be deficient in that (according to their analysis which is challenged by Meltz in this volume) it compelled a focus on union-managment relations and collective bargaining at the expense of other aspects of labor-management interaction. They found that much industrial relations decision-making in the United States had shifted from the collective bargaining arena to the top management level and to the shop-floor level in both unionized and nonunionized firms. To capture this change they made use of the concept of strategic choice. During the 1980s, there was a significant shift within the functionalist category away from the application of the systems model to the use of the strategic choice framework and to the use of the concept of human resource management which more capably captured labor-management interaction at the point of production than did models which highlighted union-management relations.

The shift added vigor to a minority radical-structuralist approach in industrial relations. According to Dimmock and Sethi, "perhaps the most fundamental issue is whether the system theory has any continuing relevance as an explanatory vehicle. In so far that it rests on structural functionalist assumptions it is. . . largely out of theoretical alignment with the necessary treatment of ideology and power in terms of strategic choice. Notions of systems maintenance appear inappropriate when applied to industrial relations in the face of managerial strategies" (751).

One of the most remarkable finds of our research is the almost total void of subjectivist research on industrial relations. As reviewed by Godard (and briefly in the introductory essay by Adams in this volume) interpretational and humanist research has expanded significantly in the social sciences in recent years. To this point, however, it has made little or no impact on industrial relations.

Notes

1. A paradigm is: A universally recognized scientific achievement that for a time provides model problems and solutions to a community of

practitioners. "Paradigms," "problematics," "alternative realities," "frames of reference," "forms of life" and "universe of discourse" are all related conceptualizations although, of course, they are not synonymous (Burrell and Morgan 1979).
2. For a discussion about paradigm, see E. Guba (1990).
3. According to Burrell and Morgan, the functionist concept (paradigm) focuses on four categories of theories which are 1) objectivism 2) social system with structural functionalist and the systems theory 3) integrative theory, and the 4) interactive theory.

Works Cited

Adams, R. J. 1983, "Competing Paradigms in Industrial Relations," *Relations ndustrielles,* vol. 38, no. 3, pp. 508-531.

_____. 1988, "Desperately Seeking Industrial Relations Theory," *The International Journal of Comparative Labor Law and Industrial Relations,* vol. 4, no. 1, pp. 110.

_____. 1992, "Integrating Disparate Strands: An Elaborated Version of Systems Theory as a Framework for Organizing the Field of Industrial Relations," in J. Barbash and N. M. Meltz, eds., *Theory Research and Teaching in International Industrial Relations,* Lewiston, NY: The Edwin Mellen Press.

_____. "'All Aspects of People at work,' Unity and Division in the Study of Labor and Labor Management," this volume.

Allen, V. L. 1971, *The Sociology of Industrial Relations: Studies in Method.* London: Longman.

Anderson, J. 1979, "Bargaining Outcomes: An IR System Approach," *Industrial Relations,* vol. 18, no. 2, pp. 127-143.

Anderson, J., and M. Gunderson. 1982, "The Canadian Industrial Relations System," in Anderson and Gunderson, eds., *Union-Management Relations in Canada,* Ontario: Don Mills, pp. 1-26.

Armstrong, P. J., J. F. B. Goodman, and J. D. Hyman. 1981, *Ideology and Shop-floor Industrial Relations,* London: Croom Helm.

Audet, M., and V. LaRouche. 1988, "Paradigmes, écoles de pensée et théories en relations industrielles," *Relations Industrielles,* vol. 43, no. 1, pp. 3-31.

Bacharach, S., and E. J. Lawler. 1980, *Power and Politics in Organizations,* San Francisco: Jossey-Bass.

_____. 1981, *Bargaining, Power, Tactics and Outcomes,* San Francisco: Jossey-Bass.

Bain, G. S., and H. A. Clegg. 1974, "A Strategy for Industrial Relations Research in Great Britain," *British Journal of Industrial Relations,* vol. 12, no. 1, pp. 91-113.

Barbash, J. 1964, "The Elements of Industrial Relations," *British Journal of Industrial Relations*, vol. 11, no. 1, pp. 66-78.

_____. 1979, "Collective Bargaining and the Theory of Conflict," *Relations Industrielles*, vol. 34, no. 4, pp. 646-660.

_____. 1986, "The New Industrial Relations," *Labor Journal*, vol. 37, no. 8, August, pp. 528-533.

_____. 1988, "The New Industrial Relations in the US: Phase II," *Relations Industrielles*, vol. 43, no. 1, pp. 32-42.

Barkin, S. 1980, "European Industrial Relations. A Resource for the Reconstruction of the American System," *Relations Industrielles*, vol. 35, no. 3, pp. 439-445.

Beaumont, P. B., and R. I. D. Harris. 1988, "Sub-System of Industrial Relations: The Spatial Dimension in Britain," *British Journal of Industrial Relations*, vol. 26, no. 3, pp. 397-407.

Beer, M., B. Spector, P. R. Lawrence, D. Quinn Mills, and R. E. Walton. 1984, *Managing Human Assets*, New York: Free Press, pp. 15-38.

Behrend, H. 1963, "The Field of Industrial Relations," *British Journal of Industrial Relations*, vol. 1, no. 3, pp. 383-394.

Belanger, L., A. Petit, and J. L. Bergeron. 1983, *La gestion des ressourceshumaines: une approche globale et intégrée*, Chicoutimi: Gaetan Morin, ed., pp. 19-41.

Bemmels, B., and M. Zaidi. 1986, *Industrial Relations: The Minnesota Model*, Minneapolis: University of Minnesota, (working paper 86-09).

Blain, A. N. J., and J. Gennard. 1970, "Industrial Relations Theory: A Critical Review," *British Journal of Industrial Relations*, vol. 8, no. 3, pp. 389-407.

Blyton, P., A. Dastmalchian, and R. Adamson. 1987, "Developing the Concept of Industrial Relations Climate," *The Journal of Industrial Relations*, June, pp. 207-217.

Boivin, J. 1987, "Les relations industrielles: une pratique et une discipline," *Relations Industrielles*, vol. 42, no. 1, pp. 179-195.

Boivin, J., and J. Guilbault. 1989, *Les relations patronales-syndicales*, Chicoutimi: Gaetan Morin ed.

Braverman, H. 1974, *Labor and Monopoly Capital*, New York and London: Monthly Review Press.

Bray, M. 1981, *The Labor Process: A New Approach to the Study of Industrial Relations?* Department of Industrial Relations (Working Paper), Sydney: University of New South Wales.

Brewster, C., and S. Connock. 1985, *Industrial Relations: Cost Effective Strategies*, London: Hutchinson.

Burawoy, M. 1979, *Manufacturing Consent*, Chicago: University of Chicago Press.

Burrell, G., and G. Morgan. 1979, *Sociological Paradigms and Organizational Analysis,* London: Heinemann.

Caire, G. 1973, *Les relations industrielles,* Paris: Dalloz.

Capelli, P. 1985, "Theory Construction in Industrial Relations and some Implications for Research," *Industrial Relations,* vol. 24, no. 1, pp. 90-112.

Chamberland, N. 1951, *Collective Bargaining,* New York: McGraw Hill.

Chamberland, N., and J. W. Kuhn. 1965, *Collective Bargaining,* New York: McGraw-Hill, pp. 113-130.

Clarke, O. 1987, "Industrial Relations Theory and Practice," *Relations Industrielles,* vol. 42, no. 1, pp. 196-202.

Clegg, H. A. 1972, *The System of Industrial Relations in Great Britain,* Oxford: Blackwell.

_____. 1975, "Pluralism in Industrial Relations," *British Journal of Industrial Relations,* vol. 13, no. 3, pp. 309-316.

_____. 1979, *The Changing System of Industrial Relations in Great Britain,* Oxford: Blackwell.

Commons, J. R. 1934, *Institutional Economics: Its Place in the Political Economy,* New York: Macmillan.

Cox, R. W. 1971, "Approaches to a Futurology of Industrial Relations," *International Institute of Labor Studies,* Bulletin no. 8, pp. 141-142.

Craig, A. W. 1966, "A Model for the Analysis of Industrial Relations," in H. C. Jain, ed., *Canadian Labor and Industrial Relations Public and Private Sectors,* Toronto: University of Toronto Press.

_____. 1983, *The System of Industrial Relations in Canada,* Scarborough: Prentice-Hall Canada.

_____. 1988, "Les relations industrielles au Canada: Aspects principaux," in G. Hébert, H. C. Jaim, and N. M. Meltz, eds. *L'état de la discipline en relations industrielles au Canada,* (monographie no.19), Montréal: Ecole de relations industrielles, Université de Montréal, pp. 13-55.

Crispo, J. 1978, *The Canadian Industrial Relations System.* Toronto: McGraw-Hill Ryerson.

Crouch, C. 1972, *Class Conflict and the Industrial Relations Crisis,* London: Heinemann.

Dabscheck, B. 1980, "The Australian System of Industrial Relations: An Analytical Model," *The Journal of Industrial Relations,* vol. 22, pp. 196-218.

_____. 1983, "Of Mountains and Routes Over Them: A Survey of Theories of Industrial Relations," *The Journal of Industrial Relations,* vol. 25, no. 4, pp. 485-507.

_____. 1987, "New Right or Old Wrong? Ideology and Industrial Relations," *The Journal of Industrial Relations,* vol. 29, no. 4, pp.

425-450.

Dabscheck, B., and J. Niland. 1981, *Industrial Relations in Australia,* Sydney: Allen and Unwin.

Davison, R. B. 1973, "Industrial Relations Theory: A View from the Third World," *Labor Law Journal,* vol. 24, no. 8, pp. 543-550.

Deery, S., and D. Plowman. 1991, *Australian Industrial Relations,* 3rd ed., Sydney: McGraw Hill.

Derber, M. 1964, "Divergent Tendencies in Industrial Relations Research," *Industrial and Labor Relations Review,* vol. 17, pp. 598-611.

_____. 1969, "Industrial Democracy as an Organizing Concept for Theory of Industrial Relations," in G. Somers, ed., *Essays in Industrial Relations Theory,* Ames, IA: Iowa State University Press, pp. 177-190.

Dimmock, S., and A. S. Sethi. 1986, "The Role of Ideology and Power in Systems Theory: Some Fundamental Shortcomings," *Relations Industrielles,* vol. 41, no. 4, pp. 738-757.

Dion, G. 1986, *Dictionnaire canadien des relations du travail,* Québec: Presses de l'Université Laval.

Dolan, S., and R. Schuler. 1987, *Personnel and Human Resource Management in Canada,* St. Paul, MN: West Publishing Co., pp. 10-11.

Dominguez, J. R. 1971, "An Analysis of the Industrial Relations System in a Collective Society," *British Journal of Industrial Relations,* vol. 9, no. 1, pp. 21-32.

Dunlop, J. T. 1958, *Industrial Relations Systems,* New York: Henry Holt & Co.

_____. 1976, "Structural Changes in the American Labor Movement and Industrial Relations System," in Rowan, ed. *Reading in Labor Economics and Labor Relations,* Homewood: Irwin.

Eldridge, J. E. T. 1968, *Industrial Dispute,* London: Routledge and Kegan Paul.

Farnham, D., and J. Pimlott. 1979, *Understanding Industrial Relations,* London: Cassel.

Fatchett, D., and W. M. Whittingham. 1976, "Trends and Developments in Industrial Relations Theory," *Industrial Relations Journal,* vol. 7, no. 1, pp. 50-61.

Flanders, A. 1968, "Collective Bargaining: A Theoretical Analysis," *British Journal of Industrial Relations,* vol. 6, no. 1, pp. 2-25.

_____. 1970, "Industrial Relations: What is Wrong with the System?," in *Management and Unions, The Theory and Reform of Industrial Relations,* London: Faber & Faber, pp. 83-129.

Flanders, A., and H. A. Clegg. 1954, *The System of Industrial Relations in Great Britain,* Oxford: Basil Blackwell.

Fox, A. 1971, *A Sociology of Work in Industry*, London: Collier-
Macmillan.
_____. 1973, "Industrial Relations: A Social Critique of Pluralist
Ideology," in Child, ed., *Man and Organisation*, London: Allen and
Unwin, pp. 185-233.
_____. 1974, *Beyond Contract: Work, Power and Trust Rela-
tions*, London: Faber & Faber.
Frenkel, S. J. 1977, *Industrial Relations Theory, a Critical Discussion*,
Department of Industrial Relations (Research Paper no. 3),
Sydney: University of New South Wales.
Friedman, A. 1977, *Industry and Labor*, London: Macmillan.
Garbarino, J. W. 1966, "The Industrial Relations System," in *Designing
Education for the Future: An Eight- State Project* (from the first
project publication): Prospective Changes in Society by 1980,
Denver, CO.
Geare, A. I. 1977, "The Field of Study of Industrial Relations," *The
Journal of Industrial Relations*, vol. 19, no. 3, pp. 274-285.
Giles, A., and G. Murray. 1988, "Towards an Historical Understanding
of Industrial Relations Theory in Canada," *Relations Industrielles*,
vol. 43, no. 4, pp. 780-812.
Gill, C. G., and H. M. G. Concannon. 1977, "Developing an Explana-
tory Framework for Industrial Relations Policy within the Firm,"
Industrial Relations Journal, vol. 7, no. 4, pp. 13-21.
Gill, J. 1969, "One Approach to the Teaching of Industrial Relations,"
British Journal of Industrial Relations, vol. 7, no. 2, pp. 265-271.
Goodman, J. F. B., E. G. A. Armstrong, A. Wagner, J. E Davis, and S. J.
Wood. 1975, "Rules in Industrial Relations Theory: A
Discussion," *Industrial Relations Journal*, vol. 6, no. 1, pp. 14-30.
Gospel, H. F. 1983, "New Managerial Approaches to Industrial Rela-
tions: Major Paradigms and Historical Perspective," *The Journal of
Industrial Relations*, vol. 25, no. 2, pp. 162-176.
Guba, E., ed. 1990, *The Paradigm Dialog*, San Mateo, CA: Sage Publi-
cations.
Guille, H. 1984, "Industrial Relations Theory: Painting by Numbers,"
Journal of Industrial Relations, vol. 26, pp. 484-495.
Gunderson, M. 1988, "Economie du travail et relations industrielles,"
in Hébert, Jain, and Meltz, eds., *L'état de la discipline en relations
industrielles au Canada* (monographie no. 19), Montréal: École
de relations industrielles, Université de Montréal, pp. 55-88.
Gurdon, M. 1978, "Patterns of Industrial Relations Research in Aus-
tralia," *Journal of Industrial Relations*, vol.20, no. 4, pp. 446-462.
Hale, M. 1986, "The New Industrial Relations in A Global Economy,"
Labor Law Journal, vol. 37, no. 8, pp. 539-543.

Hameed, S. 1975a, "An Integrated Theory of Industrial Relations," in Hameed, ed., *Canadian Industrial Relations*, Toronto: Butterworth and Co., pp. 11-21.

_____. 1975b, "Perspective of Industrial Relations," in Hameed, ed., *Canadian Industrial Relations*, Toronto: Butterworth and Co., pp. 1-11.

_____. 1982, "A Critique of Industrial Relations Theory," *Relations industrielles*, vol. 37, no. 1, pp. 15-30.

_____. 1988, "A Theory of Responsive Bargaining," in Sen and Hameed, eds.,*Theories of Industrial Relations*, Littleton, MA: Copley Publishing Group, pp. 105-118.

Hameed, S., and J. Sen. 1987, "A Power Theory of Third Party Intervention in Labor Management Relations," *Relations Industrielles*, vol. 42, no. 2, pp. 243-256.

Hanlon, M. D. 1985, "Unions, Productivity and the New Industrial Relations: Strategic Considerations," *Interfaces*, vol. 15, no. 3, pp. 41-53.

Hartman, H. 1973, *Structure and Process in Industrial Relations*, Paper presented to the Third World Congress of International Industrial Relations Association.

Hébert, G., H. C. Jain, and N. M. Meltz. 1988, "L'état de discipline en relations industrielles: quelques interrogations et notions de base," in Hébert, Jain, and Meltz, eds., *L'état de la Discipline en Relations Industrielles au Canada* (monographie no. 19), Montréal: Ecole de Relations Industrielles (Université de Montréal), pp. 1-13.

Heneman, H. G. 1967, "Conceptual System of Industrial Relations," *Manpower and and Applied Psychology*, vol. 1-2, pp. 95-101.

_____. 1968, "Contributions of Industrial Relations Research," *Manpower and Applied Psychology*, vol. 2, no. 2, pp. 5-16.

_____. 1969, "Toward a General Conceptual System of Industrial Relations: How Do We Get There?" in Somers, ed., *Essays in Industrial Relations Theory*, Ames, IA: Iowa State University Press, pp. 39-55.

Heneman, H. G., and D. Yoder. 1965, "Industrial Relations Systems," in Heneman and Yoder, eds., *Labor Economics*, Cincinnati: South-Western Publishing Co., pp. 93-116.

Hills, S. 1988, "Organizational Behavior and Theoretical Models of Industrial Relations," in Sen and Hameed, eds. ,*Theories of Industrial Relations*, Littleton, MA: Copley Publishing Group, pp. 92-104.

Hyman, R. 1975, *Industrial Relations: A Marxist Introduction*, London: Macmillan.

_____. 1978, "Pluralism, Procedural Consensus and Collective Bargaining," *British Journal of Industrial Relations*, vol. 16, no. 1, pp. 16-40.

_____. 1979, "La théorie des relations industrielles: une analyse matérialiste," *Sociologie du travail*, vol. 21, no. 4, pp. 418-438.

Hyman, R., and I. Brough. 1975, *Social Values and Industrial Relations*, Oxford: Basil Blackwell.

Jain, H. C. 1975, *Canadian Labor and Industrial Relations*, Toronto: McGraw-Hill, Ryerson.

Jamieson, S. 1957,*Industrial Relations in Canada*, Toronto: Macmillan.

Kerr, C. 1955, "Industrial Relations and the Liberal Pluralist," in IRRA, ed., *Proceedings of the Seventh Annual Meeting*.

_____. 1978, "Industrial Relations Research: A Personal Retrospective," *Industrial Relations*, vol. 17, no. 2, pp. 131-142.

Kerr, C., F. Harbison, J. T. Dunlop, and C. Myers. 1960, *Industrialism and Industrial Man*, Cambridge, MA: Harvard University Press.

Kerr, C., and P. Staudohar, eds., *Industrial Relations in a New Age*, San Francisco: Jossey-Bass.

Kirkbride, P. 1985, "Power in Industrial Relations Research: A Review of Some Recent Work," *Industrial Relations Journal*, vol. 16, no. 1, pp. 44-56.

Kochan, T. A. 1988, *Collective Bargaining and Industrial Relations*, 2nd ed., Homewood IL: Irwin.

Kochan, T. A., D. J. B. Mitchell, and L. Dyer. 1982, "Appraising a Decade's Research: An Overview," in Kochan, Mitchell, and Dyer, eds., *Industrial Relations Research in the 1970's: Review and Appraisal*, Madison: IRRA.

Kochan, T.A., R. B. McKersie, and P. Cappelli. 1984, "Strategic Choice and Industrial Relations Theory," *Industrial Relations*, vol. 23, no. 1, pp. 17-39.

Kochan, T. A., and T. A. Barocci. 1985, *Human Resource Management and Industrial Relations: Text, Readings and Cases*, Boston: Little Brown and Co., 1985.

Kochan, T. A., H. C. Katz, and R. B. McKersie. 1986, *The Transformation of American Industrial Relations*, New York: Basic Books, 1986.

Korpi, W. 1981, "Sweden: Conflict, Power and Politics in Industrial Relations," in Doeninger, ed., *Industrial Relations in International Perspective: Essays on Research and Policy*, London: Macmillan.

Korpi, W., and M. Shalev. 1979, "Strikes, Industrial Relations and Class Conflict in Capitalist Society," *British Journal of Sociology*, vol. 30, no. 2, pp. 164-187.

Krislov, J. 1987, "Are There Industrial Relations Sub-Models?" *Industrial Relations Journal*, vol. 18, no. 3, pp. 201-210.

Kuhn, T. 1970, *The Structure of Scientific Revolution*. Chicago: University of Chicago Press.

Laffer, K. 1968, "Les relations professionnelles—Enseignement et étendue du sujet: une expérience australienne," *Bulletin de l'Institut*

international d' études sociales, vol. 5, pp. 10-30.
_____. 1974, "Is Industrial Relations an Academic Discipline?,"
  The Journal of Industrial Relations, vol. 16, no. 1, pp. 62-73.
Larouche, V., and E. Déom. 1984, "L'approche systémique en relations
  industrielles," *Relations industrielles,* vol. 39, no. 1, pp. 114-144.
Lewin, D. 1987, "Industrial Relations as a Strategic Variable," in M.
  Kleiner, R. N. Block, M. Roomkin, S. W. Salsburg, eds., *Human
  Resources and the Performance of the Firm,* Madison, WI: IRRA,
  pp. 1-43.
Lumley, R. 1979/80, "A Modified Rules Approach to Workplace Indus-
  trial Relations," *Industrial Relations Journal,* vol. 10, no. 4, pp.
  49-56.
Margerison, J. 1969, "What Do We Mean By Industrial Relations—A
  Behavioral Science Approach," *British Journal of Industrial
  Relations,* vol. 7, no. 2, pp. 273-286.
Marsden, R. 1982, "Industrial Relations: A Critique of Empiricism,"
  Sociology, vol. 16, no. 2, pp. 232-250.
Maurice, M., F. Sellier, and J. J. Silvestre. 1979, *The Social Foun-
  dation of Industrial Power,* Cambridge, MA: M.I.T. Press.
Nayar, M. 1985, "Effectiveness of Industrial Relations System at the
  Enterprise Level," *Indian Journal of Industrial Relations,* vol. 21,
  no. 1, pp. 1-15.
Oostermeyer, I. 1978, *Richard HYMAN and Industrial Relations The-
  ory: A Radical Alternative on a Radical Dilemma,* Sydney:
  University of New South Wales (Discussion Paper in Industrial
  Relations).
Owen, W. V., and H. V. Finston. 1964, *Industrial Relations,* New York:
  Appleton-Century-Crofts, pp.9-18.
Palmer, G. 1983, *British Industrial Relations,* London: Allen and
  Unwin.
Parker, S. R., and M. H. Scott. 1971, "Developping Models of Work
  Place Industrial Relations," *British Journal of Industrial Relations,*
  vol. 9, no. 2, pp. 214-225.
Peach, D. A., and D. Kuechele. 1928, *The Practice of Industrial Rela-
  tions,* Toronto: McGraw Hill-Ryerson.
Perlman, S. 1928, *A Theory of the Labor Movement,* New York: Mac-
  millan.
Peterson, R. 1971, "A System Approach to Industrial Relations," *Per-
  sonnel Administration,* vol. 34, no. 4, pp. 34-40.
Phillips, C. E. 1986, *Labor Relations and the Collective Bargaining
  Cycle,* Toronto: Butterworths.
Poole, M. *Industrial Relations: Origins and Patterns of National
  Diversity,* London: Routledge and Kegan Paul.
Purcell, J., and G. M. Earl. 1977, "Control Systems and Industrial Rela-

tions," *Industrial Relations Journal*, vol. 8, no. 2, pp. 41-54.

Reshef, Y., and A. I. Murray. 1988, "Toward a Neoinstitutionalist Approach in Industrial Relations," *British Journal of Industrial Relations*, vol. 26, no. 1, pp. 85-97.

Richardson, J. H. 1954, *An Introduction to the Study of Industrial Relations*, London: George Allen and Unwin.

Schienstock, G. 1981, "Toward a Theory of Industrial Relations," *British Journal of Industrial Relations*, vol. 19, no. 2, pp. 170-189.

Sen, J., and S. Hameed. 1988, "State of Industrial Relation & Discipline," in Sen and Hameed, eds., *Theories of Industrial Relations*, Toronto: Butterworth and Co., pp. 1-8.

Sethi, A. S., and S. J. Dimmock. 1987, "Un modèle transactionnel de relations industrielles," *Travail et Société*, vol. 12, vo. 2, pp. 345-367.

Shalev, M. 1980, "Industrial Relations Theory and the Comparative Study of Industrial Relations and Industrial Conflict," *British Journal of Industrial Relations*, vol. 18, no. 1, pp. 26-43.

Shimmin, S., and R. Singh. 1973, "Industrial Relations and Organizational Behavior: A Critical Appraisal," *Industrial Relations Journal*, vol. 4, no. 3, pp. 37-43.

Shirom, A. 1985, "The Labor Relations System: A Proposed Conceptual Framework," *Relations Industrielles*, vol. 40, no. 2, pp. 303-323.

Singh, R. 1976, "Systems Theory in the Study of Industrial Relations: Time for a Reappraisal?," *Industrial Relations Journal*, vol. 7, no. 3, pp. 59-71.

_____. 1978, "Theory and Practice in Industrial Relations," *Industrial Relations Journal*, vol. 9, no. 3, pp. 57-64.

Somers, G. G. 1969, "Bargaining Power and Industrial Relations Theory," in Somers, ed., *Essays in Industrial Relations Theory*, Ames, IA: Iowa State University Press, pp. 39-55.

Stark, D. 1980, "Class Struggle and the Transformation of the Labor Process," *Theory and Society*, no. 9, pp. 89-130.

Storey, J. 1983, *Managerial Prerogative and the Question of Control*, London: Routledge and Kegan Paul.

Strauss, G. 1977, "The Study of Conflict: Hope for a New Synthesis Between Industrial Relations and Organizational Behavior?," *Reprint no. 417*, University of California, pp. 329-337.

_____. 1984, "Industrial Relations: Time of Change," *Industrial Relations*, vol. 23, no. 1, pp. 1-15.

Strauss, G., and P. Feuille. 1978, "Industrial Relations Research: A Critical Analysis," *Industrial Relations*, vol. 17, no. 3, pp. 259-277.

Strinati, D. 1982, *Capitalism, the State and Industrial Relations*, London: Croom Helm.

Thompson, M. 1988, "Applying a Theory of the Future of Industrial
    Relations to North America," in Sen and Hameed, eds., *Theories
    of Industrial Relations,* Toronto: Butterworth and Co., pp. 78-92.
Thurley, K., and S. Wood, eds. *Industrial Relations and Manage-
    ment Strategy,* Management and Industrial Relations Series,
    Cambridge: Cambridge University Press.
Timberely, S. 1980, "Organisation Strategies and Industrial Relations,"
    Industrial Relations Journal, vol. 11, no. 5, pp. 38-45.
Walker, K. F. 1969, "Facteurs stratégiques des systèmes de relations
    professionnelles," *Bulletin de l'Institut International d'Etudes
    Sociales,* vol. 6, pp. 205-229.
_____. 1976, "Toward a Useful General and Comparative Theory
    of Industrial Relations," in IIRA *,Proceeding of the 4th World
    Congress,* Geneva.
Webb, S., and B. Webb. 1897, *Industrial Democracy,* England:
    Longmans.
Weiss, D. 1980, *Relations industrielles,* 2nd ed., Paris: Sirey.
Wheeler, H. 1985, *Industrial Conflict: An Integrative Theory,* Charles-
    ton, SC: University of South Carolina Press.
_____. 1986, "Industrial Relations from a Natural Science Per-
    spective," *Labor Law Journal,* vol. 37, no.8, pp. 544-548.
Winchester, D. 1983, "Industrial Relations Research in Britain," *Brit-
    ish Journal of Industrial Relations,* vol. 21, no. 1, pp. 100-113.
Wood, S. J., A. Wagner, E. G. A. Armstrong, J. F. B. Goodman, and J.
    E. Davis. 1975, "The Industrial Relations System Concept
    as a Basis of Theory in Industrial Relations," *British Journal of
    Industrial Relations,* vol. 13, no. 3, pp. 291-308.
Wood, S. 1978, "Ideology in Industrial Relations Theory," *Industrial
    Relations Journal,* vol. 9, no. 4, pp. 42-56.
Zeitlin, 1985, *Shop Floor Bargaining and the State,* in Tolliday and
    Zeitlin, eds. , Cambridge: Cambridge University Press.

Theory and Method in Industrial Relations: Modernist and Postmodernist Alternatives

John Godard

Introduction

Though the disciplinary status of industrial relations (IR) has always been a somewhat precarious one, it has become especially uncertain over the past decade, particularly in the U.S., where the decline in union density and the growth of human resources management as a distinctive field have increasingly threatened to marginalize the traditional "mainstream" focus upon labor unions and collective bargaining (see Weber 1987, Strauss 1989, Kaufman 1992, Adams 1992). In response, scholars have variously called for a broadening of the field to encompass "all aspects of people at work" (Adams 1993), for the development of closer associations with related social science disciplines (Stern 1992), for a reexamination of the theoretical and value premises underlying the field (Kaufman 1992), and for greater emphasis upon developments and

Roy Adams, Marie Sickmeier, Barb Townley, and Bob Sass all made valuable comments on an earlier draft of this article.

issues of relevance to practitioners and policy makers (Stern 1992). Generally absent, however, has been serious consideration of more fundamental issues concerning the nature and purpose of social science theory and research, as raised in the philosophy and sociology of science literature.[1] These issues, and the alternatives they suggest, are critical for how scholars define the meaning and purpose of IR theory and research and, ultimately, for how they come to understand and go about analyzing their subject matter (Cohen 1987). As such, they are of central importance for any attempt at restructuring the field.

The purpose of this article is thus to introduce various issues, debates, and alternatives advanced in the philosophy and sociology of science literature as they pertain to the study of IR and, in so doing, to argue for an alternative conception of the nature and purpose of the field, one which recognizes the limits to "science," is more critically oriented and, most important, exhibits greater tolerance for theoretical and methodological diversity. The paper begins by addressing the underpinnings and assumptions of the "scientific method" as it is conventionally understood, discussing the application of this method to IR. It then introduces the "social action" critique of this method, the alternative conception of social science it entails, and its applicability to the field. Next, a further approach, referred to as "theoretical realism," is proposed as a preferred alternative for IR theory and research. Finally, the analysis turns to the currently fashionable "postmodernist" critique of social science in general and its implications for a restructuring of IR.

The Scientific Method

As the universe was depersonalized, beauty (and in time, even moral goodness) came to be thought of as "subjective." So truth is now thought of as the only point at which human beings are responsible to something nonhuman. A commitment to "rationality" and "method" is thought to be a recognition of this responsibility. The scientist becomes a moral exemplar, one who selflessly expresses himself again and again to the hardness of fact.

Richard Rorty 1991: 35

One of the defining features of the modern era has been its faith in science. This faith has perhaps been strongest in the physical sciences and their ability to enhance our understanding and ultimately control over the physical world, but it has also become widespread in the social sciences (see Giddens 1990, 38 *passim*). In both cases, the predominant assumptions would appear to have been twofold: 1) that some logical order of things seems to exist; 2) that it is possible to study this logical order in a detached, objective manner. For present, the former can be referred to as "rationalis," and the latter as "objectivism."

Out of these assumptions has developed a relatively common conception of the "scientific method," variously referred to as logical empiricism, logical positivism, and even "modernism" (McCloskey 1985). Under this conception, there exists what one author has referred to as an "arch of knowledge" (Oldroyd 1986), characterized by two types of research: inductive and deductive. Inductive research is intended to generate theory, with scholars engaging in systematic observation and then inducing general laws, based upon this observation. Deductive research on the other hand is intended to test empirical hypotheses that have been deduced from these laws. Thus, scientific research moves from the empirical to the theoretical (induction) and then from the theoretical back to the empirical (deduction), resulting in a gradual increase in theoretical sophistication and knowledge over time. Since Thomas Kuhn's *The Structure of Scientific Revolutions* was first published in 1962, scholars have come to acknowledge that this may involve more of a dialectical than an evolutionary process, as new "paradigms" emerge to challenge and ultimately supplant old ones. Yet the general assumption would still appear to be that the accumulation of knowledge is progressive over time and that each generation of scholars builds from agreed-upon foundations—something referred to as "foundationalism."

Along with the accumulation of knowledge is a gradual shift away from inductive research and the use of qualitative data towards more highly specified deductive research and the use of quantitative data. Ideally, hypotheses can be derived and stated mathematically, and concepts can be measured precisely and analysed statistically. To the extent that a field of knowledge has progressed to this point, it is considered to be advanced; to the extent that it has not, it is considered to fall short of the scientific ideal.

Until recent decades, the field of industrial relations would *by these criteria* be considered almost prescientific. Research was primarily qualitative, and while scholars might induce certain general conclusions, these conclusions were seldom intended to generate theory. Moreover, though research was often premised upon underlying assumptions and arguments, these bore little resemblance to the common conception of scientific theory. Deductive theory was rarely developed or used; the main attempt at theory development (Dunlop's system theory) and subsequent modifications of it (e.g., Craig 1975) served more as frameworks for organizing knowledge and determining what, in effect, would be considered as falling within the mainstream of the field. This was in stark contrast to two contiguous disciplines, economics and social psychology, both of which had become highly quantitative and mathematical, conforming much more closely to the scientific ideal at least in appearance.

Beginning in the mid-1970s, things began to change, particularly in the United States. First, economists and social psychologists increasingly came to apply their methods to the study of topics traditionally considered within the mainstream of the field. Second, and more important, a "new generation" of industrial relations scholars, trained in the quantitative methods of economics and social psychology, emerged and came to a position of some dominance. These developments essentially formed the basis for Tom Kochan's *Collective Bargaining and Industrial Relations: From Theory to Policy and Practice,* first published in 1980. The following excerpts from the first two paragraphs of this book nicely capture the hopes and expectations of the new generation of industrial relations scholars in particular:

> The teaching of collective bargaining has traditionally reflected the highly descriptive orientation of research in the field. . . . As yet, the field has not successfully made the transition from the descriptive to [a] more analytical approach. The study of collective bargaining is still, therefore, in what Thomas Kuhn has called its "preparadigm" stage of development.
>
> The central purpose of this book is to integrate the advances in theory building and empirical research from the behavioral sciences and economics with the strong institutional base from

which the study of collective bargaining and union management relations has evolved (1980: vii, viii).

The Kochan book generated a considerable amount of discussion within the field (see Ashenfelter et al. 1982). It is now in its second edition (with Harry Katz as coauthor), and the "new generation" is rapidly becoming an old one, with a sizeable offspring of its own (some of whom have remained in the fold, others of whom have not). Indeed, it would appear that "economic" and "behavioral" research have come to dominate more-or-less the mainstream of the field in the U.S. Though scholars cannot agree upon what exactly distinguishes one from the other (see Kaufman 1989, Lewin, Mincer, and Cummings 1989), they subscribe to the "scientific method" as commonly understood.

Both economic and behavioral research have contributed substantially to the field. Yet, to date, they have fallen far short of the "promise" of the scientific ideal. Large quantities of multivariate research have been published, but there have been surprisingly few consistent findings (at least relative to inconsistent ones). As such, it would appear that few really substantive research questions have been resolved satisfactorily, whether these questions pertain to union organizing and growth (see Chaison and Rose 1991, Wheeler and McClendon 1991), union membership attitudes and participation (Gallagher and Strauss 1991), strike activity (Godard 1992b), union "effects" (see Gunderson 1989), the effectiveness of employee involvement schemes (see Guest 1990, Godard 1991), or the role of strategic choice processes (see Lewin 1987).

It is readily argued that these failings will be gradually remedied, as scholars develop "better" theory and acquire "better" data (see Blalock 1987). After all, science entails the *progress* of knowledge, and in any case the application of the scientific method is still relatively new to the field. Yet similar problems have characterized economic and behavioral research in general (see Blaug 1980, McCloskey 1985, Webster and Starbuck 1988). More important, there are a number of quite compelling arguments to suggest that the problem may lie with logical empiricism itself and that it is the assumptions underlying logical empiricism which may be to blame at least in part for many of the difficulties which have come to plague the field. Of particular note are the criticisms levelled under the social action approach.

The Social Action Approach

Proponents of the social action approach do not take issue so much with the broader assumptions of rationalism and objectivity underlying the "scientific method" as they do with belief that deductive theory and multivariate research are appropriate for the study of social phenomena. At the heart of the social action critique is the argument that there is a fundamental difference between the subject matter of the physical sciences and that of the social sciences: where the physical sciences study inanimate objects incapable of making conscious choices, the social sciences study human subjects with a will and volition of their own. Thus, where the behavior of the former can be studied in accordance with their objective physical properties and is determined by external, causal forces, the behavior of the latter must be studied in accordance with essentially subjective motives and belief systems and is determined by conscious and unconscious choice processes. It follows that, though the behavior of physical objects is subject to universal laws and can (ideally) be predicted with a high degree of certainty based upon these laws, the behavior of human beings is not subject to such laws and cannot be predicted with a high degree of certainty. If behavior does appear to be readily predicted, it is only because individuals choose to behave in certain ways under certain conditions. Thus, the task of the social sciences is to analyse not the "objective" but rather the "subjective," seeking to explain and understand behavior with reference to underlying motives and meaning systems rather than to predict and control it.

In addition to this fundamental difference is a further difference: where the subject matter of the physical sciences involves an objectively constituted physical reality, the subject matter of the social sciences involves a subjectively constituted social reality. When individuals act, they generally take into account the expected actions of others, basing these expectations upon shared or "intersubjective" rules and understandings that have come to be established over time. Moreover, the "reality" in which they find themselves involves ongoing processes of action and interaction, subject to these intersubjective rules and understandings. Thus, this reality is in effect socially constructed. It has no objective ontological status of its own, but is instead continually produced, reproduced, and changed over time, consisting of complex, dynamic, and reciprocal social relations and processes. Even if we could hope to obtain reasonable measures of these processes and relations, it would be mistaken to think that their associations could be modelled with any degree of precision or that we could identify with any certainty various "dependent" and "independent" variables. As a result, attempts to do so almost invariably require the imposition of researchers' own definitions, preconceptions, and meanings and hence are highly subjective despite the appearance of objectivity.

Taken seriously, the social action critique thus engenders a call for hermeneutic research, through which scholars concern themselves primarily with the motives and meanings underlying social action, on the assumption that these motives and meanings are at the heart of social phenomena. Particularly influential in this respect has been Anthony Giddens' *New Rules of the Sociological Method* (1976), which suggests in essence that individuals act in accordance with socially established rules, norms, and understandings, yet in so doing they reproduce and ultimately change these rules, norms, and understandings. Thus, it is essential to establish what these rules, norms and understandings are, and how they are "produced" and "reproduced."[2] Arguably, some of the major contributions of industrial and organizational sociologists to the study of IR have been more-or-less consistent with this method. In North America, for example, one could identify the Hawthorne studies and much of the early "human relations" research addressing the role of informal rules and understandings in the workplace (see Whyte 1948, Roy 1954). One could also identify work associated with the early "institutional" school in organizational sociology particularly Gouldner's *Wildcat Strike* (1965). In Britain, the early work of the Tavistock Institute comes to mind, as do a number of subsequent studies of strike activity, most notably Batstone et al. the *Social Organization of Strikes* (1975). Generally, however, truly hermeneutic research has been a rarity in the mainstream of the field, and the social action critique has served more as a basis for rejecting the determinism of the scientific method and, along with this, justifying qualitative research methods.

One problem with the social action approach, and for that matter, qualitative research in general, is that its proponents have not developed alternative standards of objectivity and theoretical adequacy. With respect to the former, scholars have thus been subject to the criticism that their work is unduly impressionistic, grounded more in their interpretations and preconceived notions than in objective "fact." With respect to the latter, they have been subject to the criticism that their work is theoretically weak, failing adequately to explain systematic variation in social phenomena. In essence, this has left social action analysis open to the broader criticism that it is not sufficiently "scientific," for it fails to conform to the two maxims of science identified earlier: objectivity and rationalism. Disciples of the social action approach do no see these attributes as failings but rather as fundamental limits to human inquiry.

Theoretical Realism: The New Scientific Method?

Not surprisingly, there has been considerable debate between proponents of logical empiricism and proponents of the social action approach, as these approaches represent fundamentally opposite conceptions of the nature and purpose of social science and hence of the appropriate methods of social analysis. One of the more common responses to this debate has been to recognize the legitimacy of both methods and/or to argue that each has a place in social science, depending upon the research question or "interests of knowledge" at hand (Apel 1984, Habermas 1971). Thus, the scientific method is of value when attempting to predict variation in measurable phenomena; the social action approach is of value when attempting to understand why specific phenomena occur (or do not occur). Yet while this response is to be welcomed for the intellectual tolerance it engenders, it fails to address the criticisms levelled at either approach.

Theoretical realism may be viewed as an attempt to transcend this debate by proposing an alternative conception of the scientific method one which accounts for social action processes and the role of volition but conforms more closely to the maxims of rationalism and objectivity. According to theoretical realists (see especially Keat and Urry 1975, Bhaskar 1978, Outhwaite 1987), social action occurs subject to relatively enduring economic and social-structural arrangements (e.g., established laws and institutions). These arrangements do not strictly determine action, but they constitute the objective reality within which it takes place, and hence are reflected in the motives and meaning systems of the actors. In this sense, they serve as "generative mechanisms" which underlie or give rise to action, as manifest not in the form of determinate outcomes but rather in the form of "empirical tendencies." Thus, under the realist philosophy of science, there is need to go beyond surface appearances and explanations and identify these underlying mechanisms if one is to develop an adequate theoretical basis for understanding and explaining observed empirical phenomena. For example, a theoretical realist approach to explaining strike activity (see Godard 1992b) would begin by discussing the nature of the employment relation and the sources of conflict which underlie it. It would then argue that these serve as "generative mechanisms" which give rise to strike activity, and that strike activity constitutes a "natural empirical tendency" in capitalist economies because of underlying conflicts. Finally, it would argue that, though the actual manifestation of this conflict in the form of strike activity may vary in accordance with specific circumstances (e.g., managerial practices) and that it depends upon the conscious choices of workers and their agents, neither provides an adequate explanation for strike activity, for strikes would be far less likely to occur and indeed might not occur at all if it were not for the nature of the employment relation itself. In other words, under this approach, both observed empirical associations and the choices of actors are ultimately explained by underlying "generative mechanisms" and can be adequately analysed only with reference to these mechanisms.

As should be apparent, theoretical realism ascribes a central role to theory and in this sense conforms to the modernist belief that a logical order can be identified. It also entails a belief that there exists a concrete "reality" within a given system and that this reality can be objectively analysed. However, it proceeds from a somewhat different conception of science than does logical empiricism. First, where logical empiricism seeks to develop theory for the sake of prediction and control, theoretical realism seeks to develop theory more for the sake of understanding and explanation. Thus, where the former views theory as instrumental to empirical analysis and is concerned with making specific predictions, the latter views empirical analysis more as instrumental to theory and is concerned more with enhancing general understanding.

Second, where the scientific method involves processes of induction and then deduction, theoretical realism involves processes of retroduction. That is, scholars reject the careful, systematic induction advocated by logical empiricism as a route to theory and instead begin by developing abstracted, often speculative arguments or postulates about underlying generative mechanisms. They then determine the adequacy of these postulates for explaining their subject matter, and reject, modify, or build upon these postulates accordingly.

Third, where proponents of the scientific method generally adhere to the principle of falsification and embrace empirical analysis (or at least pretend to) as the sole basis for modifying or rejecting a theory, theoretical realists concern themselves more with a theory's overall plausibility. For theoretical realists, empirical facts and evidence are important for establishing plausibility, but they are rarely if ever sufficiently conclusive. As such, much depends upon the characteristics of the theory itself, especially its general explanatory power, its internal logical consistency, and its "independence" from the phenomena to be explained (see Caldwell 1982, Isaac 1988, 68).

Finally, while the scientific method proceeds from the assumption that the world can (and should) be precisely modelled and measured and that theory should ultimately provide a mirror of reality, theoretical realists view the world as far too complex to model and measure with much precision, considering theories as idealized abstractions which rarely if ever bear a direct correspondence to observed data. This need not entail a rejection of nomological analysis and multivariate research, but it does entail a rejection of the logical empiricist assumptions which typically underlie the use of these methods (Godard 1993a). For theoretical realists, attempts to construct elaborate causal models and to obtain precise empirical measures represent both an exercise in futility and a misunderstanding of the subject matter at hand, for causal models can provide at best only crude representations of complex social processes, while empirical measures are often little more than crude indicators of complex social phenomena. Thus, while these methods can be of value for illustrating and garnering support for a theory, they must be employed and interpreted with considerable caution, and they should be given far less weight than is typically given them by logical empiricists.

To a large extent, these arguments coincide with arguments in the philosophy of science which address the actual practice and conventions of science. Most notable here are the work of Kuhn (1962) and Lakatos (1978), both of whom, in essence, have viewed the practice of science as a social process in which adherents to particular "paradigms" (Kuhn) or "scientific research programs"(Lakatos) are primarily concerned with enhancing the plausibility of these paradigms/scientific research programs, and in which observed data often play only a limited role. But also of note are recent attempts to defend logical empiricism by arguing that critics proceed from an unduly rigid idealization of its underlying assumptions. For example, one prominent sociological theorist has argued as follows:

> What, then, is positivism? My views relax, somewhat, the criteria of deductive rigor, prediction, and falsification, while rejecting any assumption that positivism is a deductive enterprise ... Much of what constitutes a deductive science is, in reality, folk reasoning ... The real question is, does a theory increase understanding? .... Falsification is not a lock-step procedure, but rather a more fluid process of negotiating and assessing plausibility ... Abduction, or the simultaneous use of abstract concepts and data, is often involved in generating the creative ideas of theory (J. Turner 1992: 158-59).

This would seem to be far closer to a rejection of logical empiricism in favor of theoretical realism than a defense of it, and though the author stops short of acknowledging the importance of underlying causal factors, one of his colleagues, in the same volume, makes the following observation: "Any sufficiently rich theory in the natural or social sciences uses theoretical terms or postulates unobservable entities and mechanisms" (D'Amico 1992, 143). The problem may thus be that many scholars practice some variant of theoretical realism while at the same time adhering to the assumptions of logical empiricism. The result is more than likely confusion rather than clarity.

If the realist conception of theory and method appears to be closer to the actual practice of science, then it may also be more-or-less consistent with the implicit understandings and methods of many theorists in industrial relations. But it is by far-and-away most exemplified by work done in the "radical/political economy" tradition, which is directly informed by an attempt to explain empirical events and developments as manifestations of underlying conflicts and contradictions. Most notable in this respect is the labor process perspective, which links managerial strategies and the organization of work to the conflicts which underlie the employment relation (see Braverman 1974, Bowles 1985, Knights and Wilmott 1990, Littler in this volume). But it is applicable to a number of the topic areas normally considered within the purview of IR, especially if broadly defined (Godard 1993a).

Theoretical realism is of value not just because it suggests an alternative conception of theory, but also, and more important to the present analysis, because it suggests that social (including industrial relations) research can adhere to the "scientific" standards of rationalism and objectivism without having to adhere to the often unrealistic and counterproductive assumptions and strictures of the "scientific method" as conventionally understood (see Pawson 1988, 6). In essence, it overcomes the limitations of both logical empiricism and the social action approach and, in so doing, provides a far more promising basis for theory and method than at present underlies much of the work in the "mainstream" of the field.

At the same time, theoretical realism has not stood immune from criticism. One criticism is that it is unduly "reductionist" and "deterministic," for it attempts to reduce everything to a single underlying cause (i.e., the "generative mechanism"), and even though it may allow some role for social action, it does not adequately allow for the multiplicity of factors which can explain social phenomena (Laclau and Mouffe 1985, Resnick and Wolfe 1987). Yet this criticism is by no means fatal. In essence, all theoretical realism argues is that analysis should both inform and be informed by an underlying theoretical explanation for observed phenomena. This explanation need not be all-encompassing, though it should be sufficiently powerful that it provides a useful starting point or "point of entry" for the analysis and understanding of the phenomena in question. Thus, for example, to argue that underlying labor-capital conflicts serve as the primary explanation for why strikes occur is not to suggest that all strikes can be directly attributed to these conflicts or that no strikes would occur in their absence. Rather, it is only to suggest that recognition of these conflicts provides the most powerful "point of entry" for analyzing strike activity.

Perhaps the more serious criticism of theoretical realism has to do with its underlying assumptions: that social phenomena *can* in fact be understood in some "objective" sense and that some sort of underlying rationale for these phenomena can be identified. These assumptions have been extensively criticized by postmodernists, who in so doing do not just reject theoretical realism as an approach to science, but who also reject the very assumptions of science itself.

The Postmodernist Challenge: Is the Jig Up?

It is difficult enough to grasp postmodernism let alone characterize it, for, by its very nature, it is highly diverse and fragmented.[3] Indeed, any attempt to characterize it is contrary to the method of postmodernism itself, for postmodernists seem to celebrate diversity over uniformity, creativity over orthodoxy, and autonomy over conformity. More important, they are "antirepresentational," believing that there can be no such thing as a singularly accurate representation of knowledge. Nonetheless, postmodernism would appear at present to represent a major new development in the social sciences, and it may have especially important implications for Industrial Relations.

To begin, postmodernism can be viewed as a rejection of the institutions and the ideologies which came to dominate in the modern era. Underlying this rejection would seem to be a more fundamental rejection of the instrumental rationality which has formed the underlying ethos of modern cultures. For postmodernists, this ethos has served primarily as a rationalizing myth which has made dissent illegitimate and served to justify relations of domination and control in modern institutions. The problem is not with the institutions themselves, but with the very cultural assumptions which underlie them and their instrumental premises. In essence, postmodernism is the antithesis to modernism:

> Post-modernists criticize all that modernity has engendered: the accumulated experience of Western civilization, industrialization, urbanization, advanced technology, the nation state, life in the "fast lane." They challenge modern priorities: career, office, individual responsibility, bureaucracy, liberal democracy, tolerance, humanism, egalitarianism, detached experience, evalua-

tive criteria, neutral procedures, impersonal rules, and rationality (Rosenau 1992, 5).

Central to the rejection of modernism is a rejection of the modernist faith in science. To postmodernists, there can be no claim to objectivity, for knowledge is always in the final instance a creation of our minds, expressed in the form of language, which in turn entails socially established linguistic conventions. Attempts to establish an objective "truth"[4] or to "climb outside of our minds" and provide a neutral representation of the world "out there" are thus futile and ultimately undesirable. This "antirepresentationalism" is perhaps best expressed by Richard Rorty, who, though not himself a postmodernist, has contributed substantially to the postmodernist attack on science:

We need to make a distinction between the claim that the world is out there and the claim that truth is out there. To say that the world is out there, that it is not our creation, is to say, with common sense, that most things in space and time are the effects of causes which do not include human mental states. To say that truth is not out there is simply to say that where there are no sentences there is no truth, that sentences are elements of human languages, and human languages are human creations (Rorty 1989, 5).

Postmodernists also reject the modernist belief in rationalism. Not only does the subjectivity of knowledge mean that a logical order cannot be established, attempts to do so both devalue the richness of everyday life experiences and deny the self-understandings and personal (i.e., subjective) knowledge of individuals and their communities (see Rosenau 1992, 83). Theory represents an attempt to impose an order which would not otherwise exist, and ultimately an attempt to oppress others, for theory and power are closely interconnected (Aronowitz 1988). For the most radical postmodernists,

Theory conceals, distorts, and obfuscates; it is "alienated, disparate, dissonant," it means to "exclude, order, and control rival powers"; it is ideological and rhetorical, although claiming to be scientific. It is overbearing, seeking "stable ground" and aiming to "anchor a sovereign voice." Theory . . . is, then, considered as little more than an "authoritarian weapon" (Rosenau 1992, 81-82).

Along with the rejection of the objectivity and rationality assumptions of science is a rejection of foundationalism, for according to postmodernists questions of fact, truth, correctness, validity, and clarity can neither be posed nor answered (Fish 1989, 344). In short, therefore, postmodernists appear to reject social (and natural) science itself: there can be no such thing as a "true" theory, for a logical order of things cannot be identified; there can be no such thing as objective research, for research is inherently a subjective process; and, there can be no such thing as "truth," at least beyond that of personal knowledge. Indeed, for many postmodernists, science and the modern enterprise in general have not only failed us, they have turned against us, in essence placing us in a Weberian "iron cage"[5] which stifles diversity, creativity, and autonomy, and expunges emotions, values, and aesthetics from the realm of "rational" discourse.

Does the rejection of social science as it is conventionally understood mean that there is no place at all for theory and research? For more radical postmodernists, it does. But for others it means simply that social analysis has a different focus and role. For these postmodernists, both theory and research are of value if they enable others to interpret or understand daily life without making a particular claim to rationality or objectivity (see Rosenau 1992, 83 *passim*). Thus scholars can continue to do social analysis, and "to engage in representationally dependent activities of description, explanation, and theory construction, even though in more modest forms" (Rosenau 1992, 105). The critical point, however, would seem to be that scholars should not pretend to be engaging in science, but instead should admit that they are essentially engaged in storytelling. At best, they can present arguments (not facts), and it is up to the reader/listener to choose which arguments to believe and which not to believe.[6] Where scholars do not do this, and instead pretend to be presenting an objective analysis, it is important to "deconstruct" their analysis, revealing the hidden arguments and assumptions which underlie it and what the implications of these arguments and assumptions are for the conclusions reached. Thus, where theoretical realists essentially criticize scholarly analysis for not adequately developing underlying arguments, postmodernists criticize them for not making these arguments sufficiently explicit. The difference, of course, is that theoretical realists believe that these arguments can capture an underlying reality, while postmodernists believe that they are purely subjective and can be no more than that. Thus, where the former embrace rationalism and objectivity, the latter do not.

Individually, many of the arguments associated with postmodernism may not seem entirely new. A number coincide with the social action critique of logical empiricism. But collectively they pose a major challenge to the social sciences and to the institutions of modernity in general, with important implications for the field of Industrial Relations. In particular, the postmodernist critique of social science suggests that "the jig is up"—that, regardless of intent, the methodological pretense and the claims to objective knowledge which have become characteristic of much of the field (especially in North America) amount to little more than forms of intellectual terrorism (especially where logical empiricism is involved). There can be no one set of standards for either the conduct or the evaluation of scholarly work, but instead "only an absence of knowledge claims, an affirmation of multiple realities, and an acceptance of divergent interpretations" (Rosenau 1992, 137). Attempts to develop a true theory, or to claim generalizable research findings, or to make prescriptions for policy or practice all of which have been central to the field are "logocentric," claiming to represent an objective reality yet grounded in self-constituted logic which is circular, self-serving, and self-satisfying (Rosenau 1992, xii).

Does this mean that the field of industrial relations as currently constituted is little more than a sham? Are scholars engaging in elaborate processes of deception of both themselves and others, pretending all manner of objective knowledge but guilty of no true learning? The answer is "yes" to the extent that scholars do in fact engage in these processes. It is "no" to the extent that scholars are aware of the limits to their work and consciously acknowledge these limits. Undoubtedly, there are far more scholars falling into the former category than into the latter, though in their hearts the overwhelming majority probably fall somewhere in between. Indeed, the inability of the field to develop adequate general theory, or to claim many generalizable research findings, or to provide clear policy prescriptions, is (to postmodernists) a "good thing" (though the periodic handwringing and navel gazing associated with it is not). More important, much of the scholarly output of the field could probably be considered as the telling of stories. Even if these stories *are* typically cloaked under the facade of scientific objectivity and are intended to be "true," most involve a "storyline" (central argument), build upon this storyline through the selective analysis and interpretation of available information (data), reach a "climax" (findings), and then proceed to a "denouement" (conclusion).

Under the postmodernist critique, therefore, the major problem with the field would seem to be one of attitude as much as it is one of method, having to do with how scholars view their work as much as how they actually do it. Rather than pretending to represent facts or to have discovered some theoretical truth, scholars should view their work as what it is: the telling of stories. For more radical postmodernists, these stories need not (in fact should not) claim any purpose or relevance (as, arguably, is often the case both in the field and in the social sciences in general). But it is also consistent with the postmodernist critique to view theory and research as playing more of an intellectual/educative role than an informational/technical one, stimulating individuals to think for themselves and to develop their *own* knowledge, rather than discouraging thoughtfulness by imposing a pregiven order of knowledge upon them (see Godard 1992b).[7] Ideally, doing so involves a movement away from a concern over "facts" to one which is much more closely oriented to values and aesthetics (see Rose 1991, 163-168). For postmodernists, however, this process must also ultimately entail the making of personal choices, based upon the heart (i.e., feeling) more than the head (i.e. reason), and it must not entail attempts to impose these choices on others.

The ideal of postmodernism is to liberate us from the strictures of modernism, and in this respect it has a great deal to offer. Yet the postmodernist critique of science and the alternative it suggests suffers from some important problems of its own. First, it risks reducing social inquiry to little more than an intellectual game, in which scholars take little responsibility for the implications of their work, and in which more concrete problems and issues experienced by people in the world "out there" are either denied or ignored. Intellectual freedom and debate are no doubt laudable, but unless they bring with them some sort of personal commitment they are meaningless. Similarly, leaving it up to the reader to choose is to be encouraged, but the failure of an author to commit to a definite position may only result in confusion, especially if the reader is looking to the author for guidance.

The second problem is the claim that the commitment to a particular position involves a form of deception, for the truth can never be objectively established. The problem with this argument is that, from establishing that we cannot be absolutely certain of the truth, postmodernists make the leap of faith (or logic) that there is no point attempting to establish what the truth might be. Surely our mental processes and linguistic conventions are not so distorted that we cannot attempt a reasoned approximation to the truth, especially if we take care to allow for and attempt to exorcise our personal biases to the extent possible. Surely we can find some sort of intersubjective consensus from which to act (see Habermas 1987). Even if this consensus is "wrong" (which postmodernists would resist claiming) and has unintended consequences, surely it is preferable to anarchism, chaos, or simply paralysis.

Third, the claim that no logical order of things can be established and may not exist, thereby defeating the purpose of theory, is unduly pessimistic. It may well be that no singular logic can be identified, and that no singular "generative mechanism" exists; but, it is certainly possible to identify enduring structural relations and to attempt to establish the implications of these relations for observed social phenomena.

What, then, are we to make of postmodernism? It seems that, if there is any overriding theme in the postmodernist literature, it is the critique of instrumental reason and the strictures it almost invariably brings with it (Rosenau 1992, 129-130). What it is that postmodernists really seem to be rebelling against are the myths which often underlie these strictures, and ultimately the Weberian "iron cage" that appears to have developed as modernity has advanced. For postmodernists, instrumental reason and calculative rationality have been employed as little more than legitimating devices to defend relations of domination and oppression, and science has been their handmaiden. But this does not call for a rejection of either instrumental reason or of science. Rather, it calls for a *subordination* of instrumental reason (means) to moral reason (ends)[8] and a more thoroughgoing appreciation of the potentiality as well as the limits to social science. Instead of "anti-modernism," a truly postmodern approach would be to go *beyond* the assumptions of rationally and objectivity. Doing so would require a recognition that what passes for "science" in many respects represents a form of storytelling, and that it is essential that different stories be heard. In this respect, the intellectual tolerance and educative orientation suggested by the postmodernist critique are essential to a truly postmodern approach. But such an approach involves more than storytelling and intellectual tolerance. Ideally, it also involves an attempt to influence the reader and ultimately the subject matter itself (what Anthony Giddens refers to as the "double hermeneutic": 1976). It should make us less rather than more complacent, recognizing that the issues and problems experienced by individuals and groups are *real* issues and problems, and that a failure to address them in a systematic way through empirical research and theoretical explanation is, if anything, to condone oppression rather than contribute to it. In short, if we are to view our work as storytelling, we should also make our stories as convincing and relevant as possible. This requires a critical rather than a complacent orientation, but it also requires that rationalism and objectivity remain central to our work, if only as unattainable ideals.

Conclusion

This article has weaved its way through a rather complex and difficult set of issues and debates in the philosophy and sociology of science. What can be concluded from this journey? Following from the postmodernist critique of science, there is need of increased intellectual debate and tolerance in the field. Corresponding to this, there is also need for the field to play more of an intellectual/educative role than an informational/technical one (see Godard 1992b) one which appeals to the experiences of others (e.g., practitioners) and encourages rather than stifles thoughtfulness and intellectual flexibility. Yet, at the same time, this should not entail a rejection of science or of the assumptions associated with it. Rather, it should entail a reorientation in the way science is practiced, away from the unrealistic and often counterproductive strictures of the "scientific method" (a/k/a logical empiricism, positivism, or "modernism"), towards a more critically oriented, theoretical realist approach, under which scholars search for underlying causes or explanations of observed phenomena, employ either hermeneutic *or* quantitative research methods, yet acknowledge the limits to both and hence the importance of interpretation and debate. Such an approach would entail a recognition by scholars of their responsibility to take a position on various issues and to argue for this position, while at the same time recognizing the legitimacy of alternative perspectives.[9] The result would be more dialogue and less dogma, thereby providing practitioners and policymakers with a basis for making decisions rather than attempting to impose decisions upon them. Doing so suggests a shift away from the prescriptive role often assumed under the scientific method, but it makes considerable sense in a world where increasing complexity and uncertainty has rendered this role less and less tenable.

Notes

1. Two exceptions are Capelli (1985) and Godard (1993a). This article draws extensively on, but goes beyond, the latter.

2. For present purposes, I am oversimplifying Giddens' work, which, in particular, places considerable emphasis on the role of power. See Giddens 1976 and Cohen 1987.

3. This section draws extensively from Rosenau 1992.

4. Some argue that more local, personal, or community forms of truth are possible, rejecting only the notion of a broader, universal truth. Others reject the notion of truth altogether (see Rosenau 1992, 80).

5. I am referring to the work of Max Weber, who argued that the growth of instrumental rationality as the dominant ethos of Capitalist economies and the concomitant pervasiveness of bureaucracy would on the one hand result in improved material conditions, but on the other hand leave individuals disenchanted, with a sense of meaningless and powerlessness, unable to exert control over their life situations and lacking any sense of moral purpose or reason. For a discussion of this, see Habermas 1984.

6. Indeed, true postmodernists reject attempts to convince others that any particular view is best (Rosenau 1992, 137).

7. This is consistent with the postmodernist belief that it is necessary to "decentre" the author and instead privilege the reader (see Rosenau 1992, 170).

8. This is generally consistent with the argument of Jurgen Habermas, who argues that it is possible to arrive at an intersubjective agreement as to truth, and that this agreement will entail a subordination of instrumental

reason to moral reason. For a discussion and critique of this position, see Antonio 1989.

9. This is essentially the position taken in my forthcoming book, *Industrial Relations, The Economy, And Society* (1993b).

Works Cited

Adams, R. J. 1993, "All Aspects of People at Work," this volume.

Antonio, R. J. 1989, "The Normative Foundations of Emancipatory Theory,"*The American Journal of Sociology*, vol. 94, pp. 721-748.

Apel, K. 1984, *Understanding and Explanation*, Cambridge, MA: MIT Press.

Aronowitz, S. 1988, *Science as Power*, Minneapolis: University of Minnesota Press.

Ashenfelter, O., L. L. Cummings, M. Derber, C. Kerr, G. Strauss, R. Hyman, T. A. Kochan. 1984, "A Review Symposium: Collective Bargaining and Industrial Relations," *Industrial Relations*, vol. 21, pp. 73-122.

Batstone, E., J. Boraston, and S. Frankel. 1978, *The Social Organization of Strikes*, Oxford: Basil Blackwell.

Bhaskar, R. 1978, *A Realist Philosophy of Science*, Hassocks, England: Harvester Books.

Blalock, H. 1987, *Basic Dilemmas in Social Science*, Beverley Hills, CA: Sage.

Blaug, M. 1980, *The Methodology of Economics*, Cambridge: Cambridge University Press.

Bowles, S. 1985, "The Production Process in a Competitive Economy," *American Economic Review*, vol. 75, pp. 16-36.

Braverman, H. 1974, *Labor and Monopoly Capital*, New York: Monthly Review Press.

Caldwell, B. 1982, *Beyond Positivism: Economic Methodology in the Twentieth Century*, London: Allen and Unwin.

Capelli, P. 1985, "Theory Construction in IR and Some Implications for Research," *Industrial Relations*, vol. 24, pp. 90-112.

Chaison, G., and J. Rose. 1991, "The Macrodeterminants of Union Growth and Decline," in G. Strauss et al., eds., *The State of the Unions*, Madison, WI: IRRA, pp. 3-46.

Cohen, I. 1987, "Structuration Theory and Social Praxis," in A. Giddens and J. Turner, eds., *Social Theory Today*, Stanford, CA: Stanford University Press.

Craig, A. 1975, "A Framework for the Analysis of Industrial Relations Systems," in B. Barrett, E. Rhodes, and J. Beishon, eds., *Industrial Relations and the Wider Society*, London: Collier-Macmillan.

D'Amico, R. D. 1992, "Defending Social Science Against the Postmodern Doubt," in S. Seidman and D. G. Wagner, eds., *Postmodernism and Social Theory*, Cambridge, MA: Blackwell.

Fish, S. 1989, *Doing What Comes Naturally*, Durham, NC: Duke University Press.

Gallagher, D., and G. Strauss. 1991, "Union Membership Attitudes and Participation," in G. Strauss et al., eds., *The State of the Unions*, Madison, WI: IRRA, pp. 139-174.

Giddens, A. 1976, *New Rules of the Sociological Method*, London: Hutchinson.

_____. 1990. *The Consequences of Modernity*, Stanford University Press, Stanford, CA.

Godard, J. 1991, "The Progressive HRM Paradigm: A Theoretical and Empirical Examination," *Relations Industrielles*, vol. 46, pp. 378-400.

_____. 1992a, "Strikes as Collective Voice: Towards An Integrative Theory of Strike Activity," *Proceedings of the 44th Annual Meetings of the IRRA*.

_____. 1992b, "Education vs Training in Business Schools: The Case of IR," *Canadian Journal of Administrative Sciences*.

_____. 1993a, "Beyond Empiricism: Towards a Reconstruction of IR Theory and Research," *Advances in Industrial and Labor Relations*.

_____. 1993b, *Industrial Relations, the Economy, and Society*, Toronto: McGraw-Hill Ryerson.

Gouldner, A. 1965, *Wildcat Strike*, New York: Harper.

Guest, D. E. 1991, "Human Resource Management and the American Dream," *Journal of Management Studies*, vol. 27, pp. 377-397.

Gunderson, Morley. 1989, "Union Impact on Compensation, Productivity, and Management of the Organization," in J. Anderson et al., eds., *Union-Management Relations in Canada*, Toronto: Addison-Wesley.

Habermas, J. 1971, *Knowledge and Human Interests*, Boston: Beacon Press.

_____. 1984, *The Theory of Communicative Action*, vol. 1, trans. T. McCarthy, Boston: Beacon Press.

_____. 1987, *The Philosophical Discourse of Modernity*, Boston: Beacon Press.

Hodgson, G. 1988, *Economics and Institutions*, Philadelphia: University of Pennsylvania Press.

Isaac, J. C. 1988, *Power and Marxist Theory*, Ithaca, NY: Cornell University Press.

Kaufman, B. 1989, "Models of Man in Industrial Relations Research," *Industrial and Labor Relations Review*, vol. 43, no. 1, pp. 72-88.

_____. 1992, "Strategic Choices Facing IR and the IRRA," *Proceedings* of the 44th Annual Meetings of the IRRA.

Keat, R., and J. Urry. 1975, *Social Theory as Science*, London: Routledge and Kegan Paul.

Kochan, T. A. 1980, *Collective Bargaining and Industrial Relations*, Homewood, IL: Irwin.

Knights, D., and H. Wilmott, eds. 1990, *Labor Process Theory*, London: The Macmillan Press, London.

Kuhn, T. 1962, *The Structure of Scientific Revolutions*,Chicago: University of Chicago Press.

Laclau, E., and C. Mouffe, 1985, *Hegemony and Socialist Strategy*, London: Verso.

Lakatos, I. 1978, *The Methodology of Scientific Research Programs*, Cambridge: Cambridge University Press.

Lewin, D. 1987, "Industrial Relations as a Strategic Variable," in Kleiner, M., R. Block, M. Roomkin, and S. Salsberg, eds., *Human Resources and Firm Performance*, Madison, WI: IRRA.

Lewin, D., J. Mincer, and L. L. Cummings. 1989, "Models of Man in Industrial Relations Research: Discussion," *Industrial and Labor Relations Review*, vol. 43, no. 1, pp. 89-102.

McCloskey, D. N. 1985, *The Rhetoric of Economics*, Madison, WI: University of Wisconsin Press.

Oldroyd, D. 1986, *The Arch of Knowledge*, New York: Methuen.

Outhwaite, W. 1987, *New Philosophies of Social Science*, London: Routledge and Kegan Paul.

Pawson, R. 1989, *A Measure for Measures*, London: Routledge.

Resnick, S., and R. Wolfe, 1987, *Knowledge and Class: A Marxian Critique of Political Economy*, Chicago: University of Chicago Press.

Rose, M. A. 1991, *The Post-Modern and the Post-Industrial*, New York: Cambridge University Press.

Rosenau, 1992, *Post-Modernism and the Social Science*, Princeton, NJ: Princeton University Press.

Rorty, R. 1989, *Contingency, Irony, and Solidarity*, Cambridge: Cambridge University Press.

_____. 1991, *Objectivity, Relativism, and Truth*, Cambridge: Cambridge University Press.

Roy, D. 1954, "Efficiency and the Fix," *American Journal of Sociology*, vol. 60, pp. 255-66.

Stern, J. 1992, "Presidential Address," Proceedings of the 44th Annual Meetings of the IRRA, Madison, WI.

Strauss, G. 1989, "Industrial Relations as an Academic Field: What's Wrong With It?," in J. Barbash and K. Barbash, eds., *Theories and Concepts in Comparative Industrial Relations*, Columbia, SC: University of South Carolina Press.

Turner, J. 1992, "The Promise of Positivism," in S. Seidman and P. G. Wagner, eds., *Postmodernism and Social Theory,* Cambridge, MA: Blackwell.

Weber, A. 1989, "Industrial Relations and Higher Education," in D. J. B. Mitchell, ed. ,*The Future of Industrial Relations,* Los Angeles, CA: Institute of Industrial Relations (UCLA).

Webster, J., and W. Starbuck. 1988, "Theory Building in Industrial and Organizational Psychology," in G. Cooper and I. Robertson, eds., *International Review of Industrial and Organizational Psychology,* vol. 3.

Wheeler, H., and J. McClendon. 1991, "The Individual Decision to Unionize," in G. Strauss et al., eds., *The State of the Unions,* Madison, WI: IRRA, pp. 47-84.

White, S. K. 1988, *The Recent Work of Jurgen Habermas: Reason, Justice, and Modernity,* Cambridge: Cambridge University Press.

Whyte, W. F. 1948, *Human Relations in the Restaurant Industry,* New York: McGraw Hill.

Wood, Ellen Meiksins. 1986, *The Retreat From Class,* London: Verso

Industrial Relations Theory: A Political Economy Perspective

Craig R. Littler

Introduction

An initial and fundamental problem of industrial relations theorizing is this: what is being theorized; what is the nature of the problematic? There has been a range of answers and the nature of the answer defines the core and boundaries of industrial relations at a point in time. In terms of theoretical fruitfulness not all of the answers have been of equal weight. Extensive social and economic changes typically have acted to stimulate intellectual debate creating various nodes of theorizing. Three of these nodes are discussed below.

1. *The emergence of mass unionism.* Clearly, unionism was a developing process in reaction to industrialism and increasing concentrations of labor. But, more than that, unionism was changing in the latter part of the nineteenth century from the reassuring postures of the craft unions to the street marches and revolutionary songs of the semiskilled and unskilled unions. What sense could be made of this? How were unions to be incorporated within society and the body politic? These were among the most pressing issues at the beginning of industrial relations writings.

For the Webbs, the issue was that of incorporation of the new unions; the creation of a socially efficient unionism. For the nineteenth century radical writers, the issue was that of the significance of trade unions in terms of political transformation. Industrial relations was a subset of a concern with the dynamics of the capitalist mode of production.

2. *The processes of restructuring and rebuilding post-WWII resulted in the Dunlopian systems perspective on industrial relations.* The difference between this and the first node is that a broader range of institutions and actors are considered relevant and that the interactions are treated as a "system" with a significant degree of relative autonomy from the economic or political systems. Many writers have given lip service to a systems perspective and then reverted to an institutional geography approach in practice. Nevertheless, the research directions of industrial relations, especially in the United States, have been largely bound by the Dunlopian systems perspective (Strauss 1989).

There continued to be a political economy perspective on trade unionism during the 1950s and 1960s, but it made very little theoretical progress in my view.

3. *The rapid decline of trade unions in the United States and the transformation of employment relations since the 1960s and 1970s.* This condition has given rise to two key texts—Kochan, Katz, and McKersie (1984) and Freeman and Medoff (1984).[1] Understanding unionism is still the principal focus, but now it is done from a perspective of the long-term decline of unions.

The political economy perspective on labor relations shifted and developed during the 1970s and 1980s: the principal focii were not trade unions themselves, but the changing nature of work organization and societal regulation which gave rise to the notion of "industrial relations" in the first place. These focii created a burgeoning labor process and regulation literature.

It will be seen from the above that limited theoretical cohesion has been achieved within the literature on industrial relations (see Adams in this volume). I want to argue in this chapter that underlying the above definitions of varying problematics is a basic divide between an exchange paradigm and a political economy paradigm. I will examine the basic nature of the exchange paradigm and contrast it with a political economy paradigm which underlies some of the perspectives above. The chapter will then examine the major research directions within the political economy paradigm and consider their implications in connection with industrial relations theory. The article concludes by considering future research needs.

The Exchange and Political Economy Paradigms

The exchange paradigm involves a number of assumptions at a broad level of abstraction. In essence, the exchange paradigm treats the mutual trading of money and services between employers and employees as a subset of the more general category of transactions between buyer and seller (see Alchian and Demsetz 1972). As such, firms and individuals are treated as rational maximizers engaged in constrained optimization of profits on the one hand and utilities on the other. Involved in this set of exchange processes is the idea that the process is choice-theoretic: in the final analysis all economic phenomena and behavior are explicable in terms of choices made by individual agents such that institutions reflect the preferences and constraints of the individuals involved. Unions, for example, are assumed to represent the interests of the median voter. These choices are constrained and are subject to imperfect information conditions, but choices they are. The market is seen as acting as a control mechanism.

What does the exchange paradigm omit and does it matter? Clearly, any abstract system of ideas will simplify and omit some aspects of reality. Consequently, to point the finger of omission is not convincing in itself. It only matters if the omissions can be shown to lead to serious failures of explanation and analysis. The political economy argument is that this can be shown to be so for the exchange paradigm. Moreover, from the perspective of labor relations scholars, the argument is that the problematics of industrial relations are specfically affected by these omissions of exchange theory.

What are the omissions? One key point is that economic exchanges, particularly those involving labor, are not just about short-term profit or utility maximization, but about longer term reproduction of patterns of power. The relations are political as much as they are economic. This is a particularly important issue in connection with comparative industrial relations and building comparative models. Thus the perspective should be power-theoretic not just choice-theoretic. Exchange theory tends to assume more or less homogenous units—firms and households—operate within more or less given technological and market conditions and try to improve their economic lot within the constraints of those conditions. The basic model of perfect competition assumes that power is so evenly and thinly distributed that its influence can be neglected. In contrast, political economy theory assumes that the greater the power of a social group, the more effective that group is as a cause of social structures. Markets are social structures, therefore certain economic agents will be able to reap special benefits in and through the market mechanism. This idea can be handled to some degree within the exchange paradigm in terms of monopolistic or oligopolistic forms of market. However, there are broader issues involved. Some patterns of choice will be systematically excluded and these systematic exclusions result in the reproduction of power inequalities. Moreover, this reproduction is conflictual and never secure and this fact is an essential element in the nature of the system.

The above arguments are particularly pertinent in connection with the employment relationship and the wage-labor nexus. While exchange theory has recognized that labor is a peculiar type of commodity, this idea has not been developed theoretically. In contrast, the political economy perspective assumes that employers as buyers of units of labor can only purchase time from individuals and their availability for work, not work itself, nor work effort, nor motivation. This long-standing labor/labor power distinction (i.e., between labor power as a saleable commodity and labor as a productive factor) has been explored recently by heterodox labor economists such as Leibenstein (1982). By making simple assumptions which are common in the political economy literature (e.g., employment contracts are necessarily incomplete, principal-agent relations in the firm and the possibility of joint adversarial choices by employees and managers), Leibenstein (1982, 97) is led to conclusions which are decidedly peculiar from a neoclassical perspective:

> Firms operate within, and not on, their production frontier. For a given output, costs are generally not minimized. Innovations are not introduced when it optimally pays to do so. Firm equilibrium is not Pareto optimal. Less output is not necessarily

Figure 1. The Exchange Paradigm. A Conceptual Map

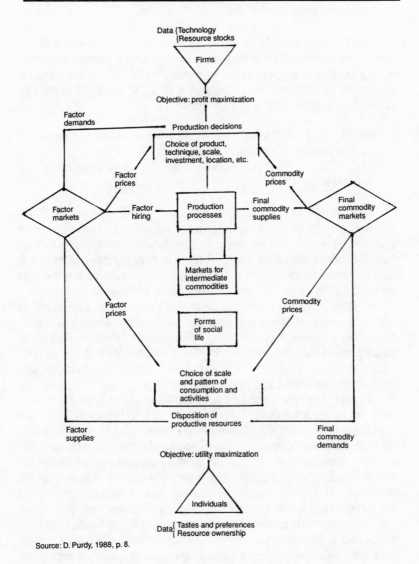

Source: D. Purdy, 1988, p. 8.

312 Industrial Relations Theory

associated with more desired leisure. Firms do not necessarily maximize profits.

Such conclusions have led to a rediscovery of the firm and the employment relationship by some contemporary economists after a long period of neglect (see Putterman 1986, 24). The exchange paradigm is summarized in Figure 1 and the political economy paradigm is summarized in Figure 2.

> **Note:** Fig. 2 only "K" refers to the the institutions of capital and capital-holders as a category or group(s).
> "L" refers to wage and domestic laborers as a category or group(s).

One thing to note immediately from comparing Figures 1 and 2 is that they involve different forms of abstraction. Both represent conceptual maps and as such involve levels of abstraction and simplification. However, Figure 1 has a psychological reality to the participants involved. For example, profit maximization (or satisficing) is built into the management information system of firms. However, this is not the case with the processes depicted in Figure 2—few, if any, managers are consciously aiming to reproduce "the relations of production." It certainly is not built into the management information system. Such structuration goes on "behind the backs" of the participants. It is an outcome characteristic of a system of social and economic relations.

Figure 2 involves the key notion of "forms of appropriation." In order to unpack this idea it is useful to turn to Weber (1947). The argument is that all groups, including economic ones, can be "open" or "closed." But economic groups tend to become closed and this closure occurs around economic advantages and opportunities. In other words, there is pressure towards monopoly inherent in all economic development—an argument that Adam Smith would have recognized. The next step is the idea of "appropriation." This refers to a specific mode of access to economic (and other) advantages and is an attempt to put the commonsensical ideas of "property" or "ownership" into a broader context. Appropriation equals the conversion of advantages into rights. Appropriation can be contrasted with unstable forms of access to resources, such as squatting or force majeure. Forms of appropriation (whether non-

Figure 2. The Political Economy Paradigm: A Conceptual Map

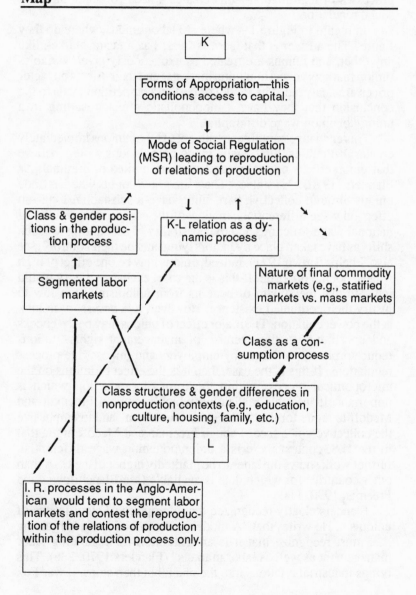

inheritable property, nonalienable property, or "free" property) involve rights but these are never absolute and require continual processes of legitimation—this creates a need for some mode of social regulation.

In regard to Figure 1—where are labor unions, where do they figure? The answer is that labor is treated as a factor market, like any other, and unions are treated as exogenously given variables (union markets versus nonunion markets) and their effects on factor prices are analyzed. The model of perfect competition leads to the conclusion that they have a monopolistic effect, resulting in a union/nonunion wage differential.

This exchange paradigm treatment of labor unions immediately creates difficulties. First, many industrial relations writers believe that union effects on real wage levels are limited or minimal. As Flanders (1970, 239) stated, "There are grave doubts whether trade unions through collective bargaining have a substantial long-run effect on wage differentials, in view of the comparative rigidity of national wage structures and the possibility of accounting for such shifts as have taken place by factors lying outside their control" (see also, Phelps Brown 1971). Indeed, unions may be one effect of high wages, not the opposite. If this is the case, exchange theory would indicate that the stream of benefits from unionism is too low to justify their continued existence. However, it is necessary to look at the power equation. The major effect of unions may be the checks and constraints to the exercise of management rights—unions reduce arbitrary treatment by employers and impose due process regulations. If this is the case, then it is the effect of unions on the micropolitical process within the form of production which is important. It was this realization which prompted Freeman and Medoff to argue for the "two faces of unionism" and to emphasize the collective voice face. Though Freeman and Medoff argue that in the U.S. context there is a union/nonunion wage differential, further work shows the latter to be markedly higher in the USA than other countries for which data is available (see Blanchflower and Freeman 1990, 11).

Flanders clearly recognized the micropolitical significance of unionism. He writes that "A modern view of collective bargaining . . . must recognize that it is an institution for regulating labor management as well as labor markets" (Flanders 1970, 236). This brings industrial relations into the plant, but then stops. It was Fox who attempted to bridge this obvious gap. Fox was one of the few mainstream industrial relations writers who attempted to analyse the task structures of work organization and indicate their labor relations significance—this was a critical step. In his book *Beyond Contract* (1974), Fox attempted to synthesize notions of high trust dynamics and low-trust dynamics as intertwined work processes and industrial relations processes. This work should be familiar to readers and I do not propose to set out the arguments in detail here. The critical point is the perceived need to analyze labor processes in order to explain the development of industrial relations. This idea is examined in the next section.

Fox's *Beyond Contract* was published in 1974, the same year as Braverman's work *Labor and Monopoly Capital*. In many ways *Beyond Contract* was a fumbling attempt at synthesis which failed; *Labor and Monopoly Capital* was a startling direct account which was oversimplistic and wrong—but the latter grabbed the intellectual market.

Over the past twenty years there have been two major intellectual projects within the political economy tradition directly bearing on industrial relations: first, the labor process literature and second, the regulation program of research. These two bodies of research are reviewed and assessed in the following sections.

The Contributions of Labor Process Literature

Between 1974 and 1984, much of the literature and research within the political economy paradigm focussed on the labor process. I have reviewed this literature in several publications (e.g., Littler 1990a). I have already indicated that the exchange paradigm has given very little attention to the nature of the firm, work organization, and changes within management structures. In contrast, labor process theory starts from the management end of the spectrum. It is concerned with a critical analysis of managerial processes. Consequently, industrial relations processes are seen as derived processes of broad trends. What labor process literature has sought to do is to construct a typology of managerial systems at a general level of abstraction. These managerial control structures are defined in terms of the processes of job design, the structure of managerial control and the employment relationship (Littler 1982).

For example, a common typology and sequence (though not one I would endorse) is that of traditional managerial systems: Taylorism/Fordism, neo-Fordism, and flexible specialization. Each of these types of managerial systems has been subject to considerable debate and definitional problems. In particular, there has been the issue of level of abstraction. Some writers, including Burawoy (1983), have tended to slide from the careful analysis of management systems at the point of production to attempts to characterize entire epochs of capitalism.

According to some writers, the types of managerial systems of labor process theorizing involve particular configurations of capital/labor relations, specific dynamics which can give rise to particular forms of industrial relations. For example, this is an argument pursued by John Mathews (1989). He argues that the major features of "Fordist industrial relations" involved 1) the centrality of money wage rates, with payment by task performed; 2) narrow definition of job categories; 3) adversarial industrial relations; 4) lack of skill-based career paths; and 5) the formalization of industrial relations procedures, with limited roles for enterprise-based delegates (Mathews 1989, 140, 148, 155-6). These features are contrasted with those of "post-Fordist industrial relations" involving, amongst other elements, flexible specialization. (Refer to Table 2 in this article and Mathews, 148-9).

These kinds of linkages are simplistic, overgeneralizing and they ignore the institutional context of industrial relations. Nevertheless, they do indicate some of the theoretical thrust of the literature: patterns of industrial relations are the outcome of the dynamics of capitalist production structures. I will qualify this point in a moment, however, let me turn to another critical issue first.

What underlies the changes in managerial systems? One answer is the changes in the nature of technologies or technoeconomic paradigms (Freeman and Perez 1986). For example, Bell (1972) and Blackburn, Coombs, and Green (1985) suggested that automation can be seen as a three-dimensional space constituted by three categories of production process. The argument is that all production processes consist of three different functional activities: 1) the transformation of workpieces, such as the shaping, cutting, drilling of metal, wood, etc; 2) the transfer of workpieces between work stations; and 3) the coordination and control of 1 and 2. These three activities can be mechanized or manual and a high level of automa-

Table 1. Engineering model of evolution of production processes

Date	Primary mechanization (a)	Secondary mechanization (b)	Tertiary mechanization (c)
1850			
	beginning		
1875			
1900	spreading across sectors and maturing	beginning	
1925	technically		
1950	continuing but increasingly likely to occur together with secondary or tertiary mechanization	significant diffusion and increasing technical maturity Further diffusion restricted by product markets	beginning in some industries and slowly becoming more flexible
1975			flexibility increasing

Source: P. Blackburn, R. Coombs, and K. Green, *Technology: Economic Growth and the Labour Process,* Macmillan, Basingstroke, 1985, p. 37.

tion in one area does not necessarily imply a high level in the other two. Moreover, they are not just analytic distinctions, because it is further suggested that there have been three phases of mechanization which have been the successively dominant form over the past 100 years or so across most industries. The first of these phases (primary mechanization) ran from the middle of the nineteenth century to the end of that century and placed the emphasis on using power-driven decentralized machinery to accomplish transformation tasks. The second phase (secondary mechanization) ran from roughly the start of World War I to the 1950s, and placed the emphasis on using machinery to accomplish transfer tasks. The third phase (tertiary mechanization), which began during WWII and is still continuing, has placed the emphasis on using machines to achieve control functions. Given these ideas, it is possible to outline an "engineering model" of change which focuses on the metalworking industries. Thus, Table 1 sketches such a model of development.

There is one key question implicit in Table 1; namely, what drives the shift from one form of mechanization to another? The shift from one predominant mode of mechanization to another is associated with "bottlenecks" and with diminishing returns in relation to existing paths of development. In other words, the "bottlenecks" are not simply technological problems but profit problems. Thus, the rapid increase in the productivity of late nineteenth century machine tools resulted in increasing levels of competition and declining profit opportunities until new process or product technologies were brought on stream. In the event, the major innovations centered around the automation of transfer systems as well as new products. The secondary phase of mechanization, typified by assembly-line methods and Fordism, solved some of the problems of synchronization and production imbalances by mechanical handling technologies and, in so doing, created competitive advantages for firms like Ford's. These technologies created the mass production industries which, however, faced a restricted diffusion potential because of variations and fluctuations in many product markets, making dedicated automation impossibly expensive. Thus a new bottleneck arose from the problems of extending assembly-line production beyond the mass production industries without control innovations which permitted flexibility. However, this only mattered when profit levels were declining, as they did in the 1970s. It is in this context that information technology becomes significant.

The shift from one form of automation to another is determined by systematic changes in profit opportunities (as has been said) but also by extensive changes in military imperatives. It was the First World War and the Second World War which significantly affected the move towards secondary forms of automation. Similarly, it was the Cold War which fuelled the research and development (R&D) expenditure for the diffusion of tertiary forms of automation. To put it crudely, in terms of hardware, Table 1 indicates the shift from Winchester rifles to tanks to radar arrays controlling missile deployments (Littler 1991a).

The idea of a link between an ideal type sequence of managerial forms and technology systems is, in my view, incorrect. It constitutes a confusion over levels of abstraction. Managerial forms, Taylorism, Fordism, etc., represent a range of possibilities which tend to coexist across a range of industries and firms. In order to understand the dynamics of change, it is necessary to construct a sequence at a higher level of abstraction than that of "managerial systems." This has been the goal of a number of writers who are discussed in the next section.

One criticism which has been leveled at the labor process literature is that it confines itself too much to the shop-floor level. This criticism is an oversimplification. Labor process literature focuses on production forms or managerial strategies which lead to generalizations across a set of firms within one industry or across industries. Nevertheless, it is the case that labor process writing tends to neglect the role of the state (see Littler 1987, 1-7). As has been frequently pointed out, collective bargaining has more than an intraplant significance; it carries a societal and political significance. As Muller-Jentsch argues, "Collective bargaining is a central integrating mechanism of capitalist society in that it seeks to divorce economic from political struggles and to channel class conflict into conflicts of interest with pragmatic outcomes" (Muller-Jentsch 1982, 7). In other words, it has a social regulatory function. These issues have been addressed by regulation theory.

Regulation Theory and Industrial Relations

As we have seen, much of the labor process literature tended to focus on the microlevel, on technology and managerial strategies. However, there is an overlapping literature which is concerned with the broader picture, with the framework of the present. The literature on structures of accumulation and regulation theory constitutes an attempt to locate changes in technology, management practices, and employment systems within a broad historical and comparative framework.

The regulation literature involves an attempt to recast the logic of capitalist power relations on a nondeterminist basis. Most contemporary writers would reject the essentially nineteenth-century ideas that the logic of capitalist economic development involves a

Table 2. New Phase of Capitalist Development — Three Interpretations

	Regulation Theory	Flexible Specialization	Japanization
Assumptions			
Earlier Phase	Fordism—broadly defined	Mass Production	Taylorism
Timing	Post-1970s. Not in place yet.	1970s onwards.	1970s onwards.
Diffusion	Core economies outwards.	Pattern of diffusion not clear. Some suggestion that semi-core economies (e.g., N. Italy) are important.	Cultural barriers to diffusion. Geographic focus, or Japanese firms necessary as conduits of transfer
Key Features			
Job Design	Breakdown of traditional job demarcations. Multi-skilling.	New craft worker. Upgrading & multivalent skills	Multi-skilling & continuous training.
Management Control	No clear statement	"Managerial Reform" Organic organization. [No clear statement].	Dynamics of JIT & TQC.
Employment Relationship	Increasingly segmented labor force.	Greater tendency to forms of participation & worker involvement.	Job security & internal labor markets.
Market Structure	"Post-Fordist." Some fragmentation of markets	Breakup of mass markets. Unstable market conditions. Small firms important.	Continuation of mass markets with some niche markets. Large corporations important.
Technology Base.	Not necessarily technology-based. Technological configuration not yet clear.	FMS & new technology.	Not technology based. Management systems crucial
Assessment	Regulation theory tends to be agnostic about the successor to Fordism.	Intrinsically unlikely. Lack of empirical data. Nothing to say about nonmanufacturing	Considerable empirical data. Limited nonmanufacturing literature.

continual decline in real wage levels (the immiserization thesis), increasing levels of deskilling (the Braverman thesis), declining rates of profit, or a continual tendency towards working class organization and class revolution. Purdy (1988, 106) spells out the contemporary view:

> . . . both as individuals and groups workers confront a host of potential interests which will often be incompatible, and amongst which there is no compelling overarching principle of choice comparable to the univalent standard employed by the enterprise. . . . It follows that the teleological view of the workers' movement as heading towards a long-run socialist destiny is without foundation. And even assertions of broad sociological tendency are open to grave doubt.

If we reject such teleological ideas as empirically and theoretically untenable, then what framework of long term change is acceptable? There have been three broad attempts to define the 1970s as a watershed decade for the core capitalist economies leading to a qualitative shift in production relations; these are the regulation theorists, the flexible specialization thesis, and the Japanization debates. The extent to which these various conceptualizations focus on industrial and employment relations varies, but all carry significant implications for labor relations. The assumptions and key ideas of these three theories are summarized in Table 2.

The ideas of each of the three types of theory set out in Table 2 are considered in what follows. First, if we consider the ideas of the regulation theorists, then one basic assumption continues to be that the capitalist economies are subject to periodic and systemic crises that are qualitatively different from conventional business cycles. However, there is the rejection of the classical Marxist idea that the outcome of crises will be the breakdown of capitalism as a world economic system. The present period (the 1990s) is identified as a phase of structural crisis, but what is the nature of that crisis?

One key idea of regulation theory is that of the mode of social regulation (or MSR) as a maintenance mechanism. A specific ensemble of regulatory mechanisms is termed the mode of social regulation. It can be argued that associated with the MSR are specific systems of industrial relations and labor regulation. This form of argument is summarized in Table 3.

Table 3. Phases of Regulation and Systems of Industrial Relations

(Based on core economies and manufacturing development.)

	1850s-1890s	1890s-1939		1945-1973	1974-Present
		Emerging Intensive Accumulation			
		Upswing Phase 1890s-1914	Crisis Phase 1918-1939		
Nature of Accumulation System	Extensive Accumulation			Intensive Accumulation (Fordist Regime)	Emergent New System. Japanization? Flexible accumulation?
Mode of Social Regulation (MSR)	Competitive Capitalism		Crisis of competitive capitalism	Monopolistic capitalism (Fordist-Keynesian MSR)	Crisis of monopolistic capitalism. MSR unclear.
System of Labor Regulation & Ind. Relations	Neo-classical labor market conditions. Employer strategies characterized by labor cheapening, wage cuts and attempts to lengthen the working day. Emergence of mass unions. Collective bargaining at national, or regional, level. Control of apprenticeship system by craft unions.		Decline of unions, esp. in the inter-war years. Emergence of "human relations."	Multi-segmented labor market with many firm-specific ILM's in core economies. Public sector unions reinforcing ILM's in public service.	Decline of unions, including public sector unions. Emergence of HRM.

One implication of Table 3 relates to the "nesting" and linkages of levels of analysis. The argument is that industrial relations can never be conceptualized as simply institutional geography. Instead, systems of industrial relations are part of broader patterns of labor regulation, which, in turn, are part of modes of social regulation, which, in turn, are part of a regime of accumulation.[3] While there are no simple matching processes (there is more than one way to skin a cat), there is a functional concordance between the accumulation system, the MSR, and the mode of labor regulation. In other words, the nature of the industrial relations system is constrained by factors external to itself in a systematic way. (For an overview of regulation theory, see Jessop 1990.)

The flexible specialization thesis advanced by Piore and Sabel (1984) has been subject to considerable debate. Piore and Sabel argue that the era of flexibility or "flexible specialization" represents a new configuration of demand and supply that is qualitatively different from that of mass production. What is the core of their argument?

First, they perceive industrial history in terms of two divides. The first industrial divide constituted the shift from craft production to Fordism (or mass production). The second industrial divide constituted the qualitative shift from Fordism to the new era of flexible specialization. What is an "industrial divide"? Essentially it is defined as a technological design space on a macro scale. Piore and Sabel define it as "The brief moments when the path of technological development itself is at issue . . . "(p. 5). In other words, an industrial divide is a point in time when a society has an opportunity to choose between a future based on one technological paradigm as opposed to another.

Their ideas assume long-term and extensive change in markets, creating niche markets with differentiated products. The argument is that there is a particular production regime arising from the changing product markets and task structures. Fordism implies mass production and dedicated mechanization while flexible specialization involves computer-aided manufacturing, robotics, and programmable technology. Fordism is predicated on large organizations; flexible specialization is associated with smaller firms. In addition, Fordism involves a particular set of industrial relations— confrontational at a collective level, or if collective organization is absent, then there is widespread worker alienation at an individual level (see Mathews 1989). Flexible specialization involves increased participation. Why is this? The nature of the technology is such that it is more costly to have worker alienation and sporadic disputes. This hypothesized tendency towards increased consultation and participation does not derive from employer paternalism but arises out of the nature of the production regime.

It can be seen from Table 2 that flexible specialization is virtually the flip-side of Fordism. Large corporations are replaced by decentralized production and increasing numbers of small firms. Markets become fragmented with extensive "niche" production. In terms of skill trends, a phase of deskilling is replaced by one of upgrading and cooperative industrial relations.

What are the prime movers of this industrial "flipover"; what are the basic dynamics? The nature of the causal links in the flexible specialization thesis are left ambiguous in Piore and Sabel. In a critical discussion of the flexible specialization thesis, Bramble (1988) attempts to mark out the basic linkages in connection with the "first" and "second" industrial divides. The primary variables are the nature of the market interacting with the pattern of competition (large firm versus small firm) and available technology. Piore and Sabel deny that they are technological determinists (pp. 261-2). For instance, in relation to the Second Industrial Divide, they argue that:

> If the computer appears to be the cause of industrial flexibility,
> this is probably less because of its applications than because,
> malleable as it is, it has helped to crystallize the vision of a
> flexible economy just as the costs of rigidity were becoming
> obvious (Piore and Sabel 1984, 262).

Nevertheless, they accept an independent dynamic to technology and the notion of "technological paradigm" is used throughout the book.

These configurations of market and technology shape the production regime which influences skill trends and employee relations. Whether extensive skill upgrading and managerial high trust strategies are essential to successful competition in the new market conditions is not totally clear. This issue is raised by a number of critics in attempting to reinterpret the flexible specialization thesis (e.g., see Bramble 1988). A number of trenchant criticisms of Piore and Sabel have been raised (e.g., Williams et al. 1987, Elam 1990, Pollert 1991) such that by 1992 it is widely regarded as requiring major theoretical rethinking.

The third aspect of Table 2 relates to the Japanization thesis which attempts to comprehend the new phase of capitalist development in terms of the diffusion of Japanese management and industrial practices. The literature on Japanization is vast and, as I have argued elsewhere (Littler 1990b), the Western literature has changed over time in critical ways. During the 1970s, the Japanese management literature tended to focus on single techniques (e.g., quality control circles) and to be "quick-fix" in its orientation. From the mid-1980s, the literature broadens out to a significant degree. It is no longer focused so much on a single technique, as on production systems in general. This shift is important because it supplies the potential to provide a grounded analysis of the new phase of capitalist development on the assumption that Japanese management practices are generalizable in the same way that Fordist practices diffused. (Refer to Table 2. I will not attempt to deal with the culturalist versus structuralist debate in this article.)

So far, this potential has not been fully realized; the elements of Japanization have not been integrated into a single model. Nevertheless, most of the recent literature tends to take the Just-in -Time (JIT) production system as the key. If we accept this perspective, then what are the dynamics of JIT? Ignoring for the purposes of this article the issues around machine and material utilization, then the existing research indicates that the impacts of JIT concerning human resources are as follows:

1. Increased multiskilling and upgrading of jobs;
2. Team working;
3. Increased work intensity;
4. Enhanced job securitry associated with functional flex-ibility, but with a tendency to core/periphery employment relations;
5. Enhanced point of production worker leverage because of the absence of buffer stocks plus limited suppliers and short supply chains (see Juredini 1991); and
6. A dynamic towards nonunionism or weak enterprise unions arising from the above (point 5) e.g., see Oliver

1991. (For a most useful Japanese analysis of the dynamics of enterprise unions, see Kawanishi 1989).[4]

From an industrial relations perspective, the last two points are crucial. The decline of unions in many Western economies is seen to be linked to the emergence and diffusion of new production methods and, therefore, is likely to continue. This is the most important labor relations issue to emerge from the analyses of Japanese management methods. Up to the present, it is not possible to be dogmatic about the new phase of capitalist development emerging (and consolidating?) during the 1990s. The developments and issues are too close to the front of our face ("what is in front of one's face, is furthest from one's brain"—Chinese saying). However, if we take the experience of the earlier part of this century as a guide to present analysis, then some points are clear. First, it was the experience and practice of specific management methods (e.g. Taylorism, Fordism) which was most critical, not the proponents of general philosophies of "rationalization" (see Littler 1982, 102). Secondly, the spread of new production methods depended on dominant economic power and mechanisms of diffusion. If we take these basic points into consideration, then it suggests that flexible specialization is the ungrounded philosophy of the 1990s; that regulation theory may help us to understand the broader trends beyond the production chain, but that it is an in-depth analysis of Japanese management practices which will provide keys to understanding the political economy of the 1990s and beyond.[5.]

Conclusions

In this article I have argued that there remains a lack of theoretical cohesion within industrial relations. Moreover, this situation has not been helped by the fact that much of the work by economists, sociologists, and labor historians towards understanding work relations has not been integrated within mainstream labor relations. The labor process literature has permitted a broad understanding of work relations which can help to underpin a revitalized industrial relations. In essence, labor process research attempted to delineate and explain in terms of basic dynamics long-term trends in work organization (including skill patterns) and management structures.

Underlying the differing perspectives of mainstream industrial relations are two paradigms—the exchange paradigm and the political economy paradigm (the two faces of industrial relations). I examined some of the key assumptions of the exchange paradigm and concluded that the omissions were critical for industrial relations analyses. Industrial relations does not just constitute a set of economic choices and exchanges. On the contrary, industrial relations is economic, juridical, and political. As such, the subject area requires the broader perspectives derived from a political economy paradigm. These were discussed and the specific contributions of the labor process literature were examined. The labor process literature has tended to focus on microlevel work relations, while the regulation-type literature examines the macro picture. The contributions of the regulation literature were assessed.

A range of scholars agree that the present period constitutes a qualitative break from the 1945-73 period, but there is no clear agreement on the nature of the change and the most useful form of conceptualization. This arena of debate is critical in terms of the framework of future industrial relations. Apart from regulation theory, there are two broad sets of conceptualizations which have been put forward—flexible specialization theory and Japanization ideas. Both sets of ideas were briefly discussed. It was concluded that the diffusion of Japanese management methods is likely to continue such that the analysis of Japanization is key. The decline of U.S. models of management is likely to accelerate greatly during the course of the 1990s, leaving Japan as the major source of contemporary management ideas.

What of the future? Will human resources management eclipse traditional industrial relations by the end of the 1990s (see Adams and Poole chapters in this volume)? If industrial relations remains as the camp follower of labor relations institutions, then the answer to this question is likely to be yes. Industrial relations cannot sustain itself as a limited and practical subdiscipline arising from the late nineteenth and early twentieth century attempt to integrate the industrial working class in Northern Europe and North America. It is essential that it recasts itself as the focii of employment relations broadly conceived. Theoretical reinvigoration is critical to the future of industrial relations. It is hoped that this book can be a useful step in that direction.

Notes

1. The primary focus of Freeman and Medoff is on the social utility of unions. However, underlying much of the discussion is a concern about the decline of unionism (e.g., see Chapter 15).

2. Writers such as Boyer, writing from a regulation perspective, recognize this point clearly: "A key lesson to be drawn here is that importing the American model has by no means meant a gradual convergence of institutional forms of wage/labor relations. In fact, each country seems to have introduced it by adapting its national traditions, to such an extent that it is clearly wrong to claim that Fordist wage/labor relations can have only one configuration." (1988, 16).

3. The term "regime of accumulation" is sometimes used as a comprehensive term and sometimes as referring to a set of mechanisms and relations separate from the MSR. Here I have used the term "accumulation system" in the latter sense and regime of accumulation in the overarching sense.

4. Kawanishi's detailed text examines the various Japanese theories of the development of enterprise unions starting with Okochi (Part 1) and considers a number of post-1945 case studies in Parts 2 and 3. This includes a discussion of the "dynamics of atrophy"(as he calls it) of enterprise unionism.

5. One implication of the above discussion is that changes in the U.S. industrial relation system are not simply traceable to the union/nonunion wage differential as suggested by Freeman and Medoff (1984), but to union influences over labor processes during a period of a changing technoeconomic paradigm. It is difficult to explain generalized heightened employer resistance to unions during the 1970s and 1980s without considering nonwage issues. This implication, of course, requires empirical research. However, the point here is that the above ideas, even without further elaboration, carry significant implications which are not generally assessed in the IR literature. Further, industrial relations theory cannot advance without considering the basic dynamics of social and economic change. The cost of not doing so is to condemn labor relations to institutional geography or a series of nonintegrated industrial relations models. (See Littler 1991b, and Adams, "All Aspects . . .," in this volume).

Works Cited

Alchian, A. A., and H. Demsetz. 1972, "Production, Information Costs, and Economic Organization," *American Economic Review*, vol. 62, pp. 777-95.

Bell, R. M. 1972, *Changing Technology and Manpower Requirements in the Engineering Industry*, London: Sussex University Press.

Blackburn, P., R. Coombs, and K. Green. 1985, *Technology, Economic Growth and the Labor Process*, London: Macmillan.

Blanchflower, D., and R. Freeman. 1990, *Going Different Ways: Unionism in the US and Other Advanced OECD Countries*, Discussion Paper No. 5, Centre for Economic Performance, London: London School of Economics.

Boyer, R., ed. 1988, *The Search for Labor Market Flexibility*, Oxford: Clarendon Press.

Bramble, T. 1988, "The Flexibility Debate: Industrial Relations and New Management Production Practices," *Labor & Industry*, vol. 1, no. 2, pp. 187-209.

Braverman, H. 1974, "Labor and Monopoly Capital," *Monthly Review Press*.

Burawoy, M. 1983, "Between the Labor Process and the State: Changing Face of Factory Regimes under Advanced Capitalism," *American Sociological Review*, vol. 48, pp. 87-605.

Elam, M. J. 1990, "Puzzling Out the Post-Fordist Debate: Technology, Markets and Institutions," *Economic and Industrial Democracy*, vol. 11, pp. 9-37.

Flanders, A. 1970, *Management and Unions: The Theory and Reform of Industrial Relations*, London: Faber and Faber.

Fox, A. 1974, *Beyond Contract: Work, Power and Trust Relations*, London: Faber and Faber.

Freeman, C., and C. Perez. 1986, *The Diffusion of Technical Innovations and Changes of Techno-economic Paradigm*, paper for DAST Conference, University of Venice, March, 1986.

Freeman, R. B., and J. L. Medoff. 1984, *What Do Unions Do?* New York: Basic Books.

Jessop, B. 1990, "Regulation Theories in Retrospect and Prospect," *Economy and Society*, vol. 19, no. 2, pp. 152-216.

Jureidini, R. 1991, "Just-in-Time and Power Relations in the Manufacturing Chain," *Labor & Industry*, vol. 4, no. 1, pp. 23-40.

Kawanishi, Hirosuke. 1989, *Kigyobetsu Kumiai no Riron (A Theory of the Enterprise Union)*, Tokyo: Nihon Hyoronsha.

Kochan, T. A., H. C. Katz, and R. B. McKersie. 1984, *The Transformation of U.S. Industrial Relations*, Boston: Basic Books.

Leibenstein, H. 1982, "The Prisoners' Dilemma in the Invisible Hand: An Analysis of Intrafirm Productivity," *The American Economic Review,* vol. 72, pp. 92-7.

Littler, C. R. 1982, *The Development of the Labor Process in Capitalist Societies,* London: Heinemann Educational Books. Republished by Gower Press, 1986.

_____. 1987, "The Social and Economic Relations of Work: Editorial Introduction," *Labor and Industry,* vol. 1, no., 1, October, pp. 1-7.

_____. 1990a, "The Labor Process Debate: A Theoretical Review, 1974-88," in K. Knights and H. Willmott, eds., *Labor Process Theory,* London: Macmillan.

_____. 1990b, *Does Japanese Management Work in an Australian Context?* Melbourne: CIRCIT Paper.

_____. 1991a, *Technology and the Organisation of Work,* Melbourne: Deakin University Press.

_____. 1991b, "Teaching Comparative Industrial Relations: The Merits of Models," in M. Bray, ed., *Teaching Comparative Industrial Relations,* ACIRRT Monograph No. 2., Sydney: University of Sydney.

Mathews, J. 1989, *Tools of Change: New Technology and the Democratisation of Work,* Sydney: Pluto Press.

Muller-Jentsch, W. 1982, *Trade Unions as Intermediary Organisations,* Frankfurt: Institut Fur Sozialforschung.

Oliver, N. 1991, "The Dynamics of Just-in-Time," in *New Technology, Work and Employment,* vol. 6, no. 1.

Phelps Brown, E. H. 1971, *Collective Bargaining Reconsidered,* The Stamp Memorial Lecture, London: University of London:The Athlone Press.

Piore, M. J., and C. F. Sabel. 1984, *The Second Industrial Divide: Possibilities for Prosperity,* New York: Basic Books.

Pollert, A. 1991, *Farewell to Flexibility?,* Oxford: Blackwell.

Purdy, D. 1988, *Social Power and the Labor Market,* Hampshire: Macmillan Education.

Putterman, L., ed. 1986, *The Economic Nature of the Firm: A Reader,* Cambridge: Cambridge University Press.

Strauss, G. 1989, "Industrial Relations as an Academic Field: What's Wrong with It?," in J. Barbash and K. Barbash, eds., *Theories and Concepts in Comparative Industrial Relations,* Columbia, SC: University of South Carolina Press, pp. 241-260.

Webb, S., and B. Webb. 1898, *Industrial Democracy,* published by the authors.

Weber, M. 1947, *The Theory of Social & Economic Organization,* Refs. to 1964 edn., New York: Free Press.

Williams, K., T. Cutler, J. Williams, and C.Haslam. 1987, "The End of Mass Production?" *Economy and Society,* vol. 16, no. 3, pp. 405-40.

Theory Construction and Assessment: A Checklist

Roy J. Adams

Introduction

No doubt the most famous theory in the world is that of Einstein: $E=mc^2$. It relates three "variables" to each other: energy, mass, and the speed of light. It is simple, elegant, universal in time and space, precise and it suggests ways in which humankind may intervene in order to control energy. It is the quintessential theory.

While the term "theory" clearly refers to the class of phenomena of which Einstein's equation is a unit, it also refers to other schemes which are not so obviously in the same class. Consider, for example, the discussion by Joel Cutcher-Gershenfeld in this volume. He reports that as part of his course on industrial relations theory he reviews three bodies of literature: one which proceeds from the assumption that the interests of the labor and management in the employment relationship are in conflict; one which assumes that there is no inherent conflict between the interests of labor and

I am grateful for comments made on an early version of this article by Rick Hackett, Willie Wiesner, Tom Muller, and George Wesolowsky. The final product is, of course, my own doing.

management and one which assumes that some of the interests of labor and management are in conflict and some are shared. These assumptions and the implications which flow from them are sometimes referred to as theories but they are very different from Einstein's formula.[1]

Another example is the industrial relations systems idea first developed by John Dunlop and elaborated by Noah Meltz here. It is commonly referred to as a major theoretical contribution but it is largely a conceptual framework rather than a formula which relates one group of variables to another (Parsons and Shils 1962).[2] Yet another example of "theory" which is quite different from that of Einstein is "Set Theory." The theory of sets is a branch of mathematics which, in and of itself, is entirely an abstraction with no necessary relation to material objects in the "real world." Psychoanalytic theory has properties very different from those exemplified by E=mc2. It is best defined as the sum total of work produced by psychoanalytic writers such as Freud, Jung, and Adler (Marx and Hillix 1963, 1979). In Webster's New Collegiate Dictionary the number one definition of theory is "contemplation; speculation."

In this article, my intention is to focus on that subclass of theory of which Einstein's equation is an example. The term will be used to refer to any empirically grounded conceptual system containing two or more variables connected by one or more rules of interaction whose intention it is to represent a regularity in nature (Dubin 1978). No distinction is made between hypothesis and theory or between theory and law. The term theory is used here to refer both to empirical generalizations and to hypothetico-deductive systems.[3] Some simple examples are:

- If inflation increases, strikes will increase.
- If unemployment increases, union membership will decrease.
- A high level of social expenditure is associated with a low level of industrial conflict.
- If I flick the switch, the light will come on.
- If I put my foot on the sidewalk, I will not fall through to China.

Everyone operates on the basis of theories which they learn from literature or experience (Rosenberg 1988). Theories are the operating principles which allow us to get out of bed in the morning and get on with the day. Theories are anything but esoteric; they are among the most basic necessities of life. They are our way into the future. They help us to control our environment so that we can survive and with luck prosper.

There are good theories and bad theories. The latter are theories which do a poor job of fulfilling our expectations. We turn on the switch and the light does not come on. I put my foot down on what I expect to be solid ground and fall down a manhole and break my back. Unemployment increases and so does union membership.

Although we tend to think of theories as formal systems, in fact, most people operate on the basis of theories which they do not even realize that they believe in.[4] This type of theory often exists in books, articles, newspapers, and conversation implicitly or fractionally. Many statements imply theory even though the author or speaker did not consciously intend to "theorize." For example, in his book on collective bargaining, John Windmuller (1987) made these statements:

> Other things being equal, the greater the heterogeneity of constituencies and interests and the greater the range and complexity of the issues, the more difficult it will be to achieve consensus [within each side to the collective bargaining relationship] (p. 54).

> Other things being equal, publicity tends to have an adverse effect on ongoing negotiations, for example by making it difficult for the parties to retreat without loss of face from an announced position (p. 65).

> The degree of popular participation in determining an agreement to a considerable extent varies inversely with the size of the geographic area for which the bargaining is conducted (p.71).[5]

I included these quotes in an article which I published a few years ago (Adams 1988). When I sent the article to Windmuller, who has always considered himself to be a sober realist rather than an abstract theorist, he joked that, like the man who was amazed to find that he had been talking prose all of his life, here he had been creating theory all of his career.

The Theory Checklist

The checklist contains the following items:

- concept names
- theoretical definitions
- operational definitions
- statement of relations
- theoretical rationale
- operational links
    signs
    shape of relationship (e.g., linear? reversible?)
    direction (e.g., causality?)
    time effects
    dependency (e.g., necessary conditions? sufficient conditions?)
    measure
- internally consistent
- contingencies
- empirically relevant
- links compatible with knowledge
- control permitted
- scope
    geographic
    through time
- precision (e.g., exactness of predictions)
- reliability
- parsimony
- variables mutually exclusive
- falsifiable

My object in this article is to present and discuss a checklist which I have found to be useful as a means of identifying, formalizing, assessing, and extending theories such as those of Windmuller which are imbedded in descriptive discourse. The checklist may also be used as a way to assess systems which formally purport to be theories. Most of the items in the checklist are discussed in books on theory construction and research methodology (see, e.g., Babbie 1992, Adams and Schvaneveldt 1991, Nachmias and Nachnias 1987, Dubin 1978, Chavetz 1978, Hage 1972, Meehan 1968, Stinchcombe 1968). They are rules of conduct which most experienced researchers and theorists know by rote but do not often consciously think about and too often forget or ignore. The utility of the checklist is that it allows one systematically to apply a large body of such rules to any conceptual system. Doing so helps one to identify the strengths and weaknesses of the system, to see it from several angles, and thus to understand it better and to develop it further if that should seem to be warranted. For the theory builder, it is an iteration of items which need to be given conscious thought. Ideally, each element on the list should be readily identifiable in any new theory and the theorist should be able to provide an explanation for the choices that have been made.

To illustrate how it works, I will apply it to an example found in Eugene Meehan's *Explanation in Social Science* (1968). It is not an example from social science but rather from everyday life.

"The phenomenon to be explained," according to Meehan, "is a change in the amount of illumination provided by a light bulb." (p. 58). It is observed that when batteries are added to the circuit containing the bulb the amount of illumination provided by the bulb goes up.

Concept Names The theory contains six concepts. Their names are light bulb, battery, electrical circuit, illumination, number, and amount.

Statement of Relations One should be able to state succinctly any empirical theory. For the system described by Meehan, the statement would be: the amount of illumination provided by a light bulb is a direct function of the number of batteries on the electrical circuit to which the bulb is attached. Statements of relations may be made both verbally and mathematically. For example, Meehan's simple theory may be stated: $i = f(b)$.

Theoretical definition The theoretical definition is the definition in words of the concepts. In a well-specified theory, all of the theoretical definitions are clear.

- light bulb: a detachable incandescent lamp.
- battery: a connected group of electrochemical cells for the generation of electrical energy.

- illumination: to light up.
- electrical circuit: the complete path of an electric current.
- number: the (or rather one of many) dictionary definition(s) is "The, or a total aggregate or amount of units." We do not, however, have to provide such a definition. We can consider the term to be "primitive." Such terms we know through direct contact with the empirical world. To be sure that one understands fully every term in a theory one might define all of the terms in the theory back to primitives (Hage 1972). That is hardly ever done, however, because it is very tedious and the effort far exceeds the reward.
- amount: primitive term.

Note that in this theory there are two types of terms: variables and nonvariables (Hage 1972). Bulb is a nonvariable. Bulb simply is. Nothing can be bulber or bulbest or least bulb. By adding quantity we can say that there are more or fewer bulbs and thus the more complex term "quantity of bulbs" is variable.

Operational definition Empirical theories should be grounded. One needs operational rules specifying how one is to identify the concept or object from all of the other objects in the real world. Thus, an operational definition for a light bulb might be: "Find an incandescent detachable object. Screw it into a socket on an electrical circuit. If it lights up it is a light bulb." This definition has problems. The bulb might not light up because it is burnt out but someone with lots of experience would still identify it as a light bulb. Maybe the socket is defective. Operational definitions often have problems like this. The theory builder has to eliminate as many such problems as possible; the theory evaluator has to look for such problems.

Theoretical rationale All good theories should have a theoretical rationale; a reason for believing that the empirical relationship makes sense. Thus even if one were to find a well-established relationship between the number of storks flying over Cape May and the number of babies born in Boston, one would be foolish to assert the theory that storks deliver babies. In Meehan's electrical theory there is a solid theoretical rationale. Batteries produce electrical voltage and there is a well-established relationship between the amount of voltage passing through an electrical current and the amount of illumination given off by bulbs attached to the circuit.

Here is an industrial relations theory: union membership is a direct function of full employment. In fact, there is evidence from several countries that union membership increases during periods of full employment. Why? What is the theoretical rationale? There may be several but one is that during periods of full employment unions have the capacity to inflict considerable damage on employers and therefore employers are more prone to give in to union demands. Since unions are more effective during periods of full employment, individuals are more likely to find them to be attractive.

In the second example from Windmuller above, the fact that public knowledge of the position of the parties makes it difficult for them to retreat from announced positions was, in essence, a rationale for the asserted inverse relationship between publicity and effective negotiations.

Operational Links Operational links define the relationship between the variables in a theory. Links may be (initially) represented in signs. Thus in the illumination example one may say "+batteries therefore +illumination." One may also say that for each battery added, illumination will increase by one unit. In that case the relationship is linear. If we remove a battery the illumination goes down by one unit. We may say "-batteries therefore -illumination." Many discursive theories imply a linear two-way relationship where in fact there is little evidence that such a relationship exists. Or perhaps such a relationship exists over a small range and then changes. Perhaps it is really curvilinear or squiggly. For example, in some countries (those in which the unions operate social schemes such as unemployment insurance) union membership typically goes up during periods of full employment (because the unions are effective) but union membership also goes up during periods of high unemployment (because nonmembers want to gain access to unemployment insurance funds). Only at moderate levels of unemployment does membership become more or less stable (Price 1991). In short, the relationship is curvilinear. A classic example of a theory in which there is not a two way relationship is that of Herzberg's "Two-Factor Theory" of work satisfaction. The theory holds that one set of factors make workers satisfied and another set entirely produce dissatisfaction. For example, poor working conditions may elicit dissatisfaction but good working conditions are not likely to satisfy. On the other hand, workers are likely to get a sense of satisfaction from being given responsibility but the absense of responsibility is not prone to make people dissatisfied (Herzberg, Mausner, and Snyderman 1959).

The theory builder or analyst also needs to ask: Is the relationship causal? In our example, do more batteries cause more illumination? Although there are philosophical problems with the concept of causation (Blalock 1964), one may reasonably hold that causation is involved if certain conditions hold. Two variables must be demonstrably related; changes in the independent variable must occur before changes in the dependent variable and the changes must not be due to some third variable (Lazarsfeld 1959, noted in Babbie 1992, 72). One way to check this is to do a mental experiment by thinking about the effects of reversing the causal arrow. Can illumination cause more batteries? Certainly not. On the other hand the causal arrows between amount of industrial conflict and amount of inflation may go both ways.

If we find that union membership is high where social democratic parties are strongly represented then we may say that there is a positive relationship between the strength of social democratic parties and union membership density and we can predict that: given any country if the social democratic party is strong then union membership will be high.[6] From such observations may one also say: If the social democratic party wins more popular support over time, then union membership will increase over time? Rephrasing a theory presented in cross-sectional terms into a temporal theory forces one to think more deeply about the nature of the relationship and to see the phenomenon more fully.

With respect to the illumination case one may ask: Is the addition of a battery a necessary condition for more illumination, a sufficient condition, a necessary and sufficient condition, or a condition which only makes more illumination more probable? Asking such questions helps us to penetrate the relationship represented by the theory more deeply. In this case there may be something other than a battery which would cause more illumination (a lightning bolt?) and so an additional battery is not a necessary condition for more illumination. It is a sufficient condition assuming that the circuit and bulb and battery are sound.

How about the relationship between inflation and strikes? A necessary condition? One asks oneself: With inflation constant may strike rates vary? The answer is yes, certainly and thus a change in the rate of inflation is not a necessary condition for a change in the strike rate. A sufficient condition? Will the strike rate change whenever the inflation rate changes? Not necessarily. A probable condition? Yes, experience suggests that strike rates often (but not always or inevitably) do increase when the inflation rate increases and decrease in tandem with the inflation rate.

There are four basic scales of measurement: nominal, ordinal, interval, and ratio (see e.g., Babbie 1992 or Nachmias and Nachmias 1987). In constructing or assessing theories it is useful to think consciously about the explicit or implicit scale of the variables. In building theories one should (*ceteris paribus*) attempt to incorporate variables that are measured on the highest scale because it allows one to make and test more precise statements about the phenomenon.

Internally Consistent Any theory allows one to make several statements. For example, about the electrical system we may say: If more batteries are added, illumination will go up; If batteries are removed, illumination will go down; If the light bulb is removed, there is no illumination. All such statements derived from a theory must be logically consistent. They must not contradict each other. In the simple theories being discussed here logical inconsistency is not likely to occur but in some bodies of theory there are a large number of independent variables. Strikes rates and union membership density, for example, are said to have multiple and complex causes. In producing a complex theory it is easy to incorporate inconsistent statements. One common problem is the inclusion of different versions of the same variable on both sides of the equation. "Why is inflation so high? Because merchants are charging higher prices." "Why can't people find jobs? Because unemployment is at record levels."

Empirically Relevant In any good theory of the class being considered here one should be able to connect the concepts in the theory to the real world.[7] In the electrical circuit example, the theoretical and operational definitions must be sufficiently clear to allow the consumer of the theory to identify the real world objects which have been named battery, bulb, and electrical circuit. In social science this is often not too easy. Are our instructions clear enough to allow us to identify "intelligence," "job satisfaction," "the working class," "the middle class," "a trade union" (is the American Medical Association a trade union?) "neocorporatism" as opposed to "pluralism," "the new industrial relations," "Fordism" as opposed to "Toyotism," and "human resources management" instead of "personnel management?"

Poorly specified rules of correspondence between the theoretical concept and the real world object to which the theory is intended to apply are a very common failing of social science writing. On reading a theoretical proposition, one wants to evaluate it against one's own personal and vicarious experience, but if the rules of correspondence are inadequately specified that is impossible. Poorly specified rules of correspondence also frustrate meaningful dialogue. As Stinchcombe has said, "for a social theorist ignorance is more excusable than vagueness. Other investigators can easily show that I am wrong if I am sufficiently precise. They will have much more difficulty showing by investigation what, precisely, I mean if I am vague. I hope not to be forced to weasel out with, "But I didn't really mean that." Social theorists should prefer to be wrong rather than misunderstood. Being misunderstood shows sloppy theoretical work" (1968).

Links Compatible With Knowledge On essentially any social science issue there will be a body of knowledge. Any new theory should be compatible with that body of knowledge or if it is not then the burden is on the author to explain why the received wisdom is considered to be inaccurate. This is one reason why Ph.D. students developing a thesis are required to do a comprehensive literature review. For example, a superficial reading of "popular" writing might give one the impression that unions are, by nature, opposed to technological change. There has, however, been a considerable amount of professional research done on this topic. In fact unions are not typically opposed to such innovation and any theory, based on a superficial review of the subject, which contained that proposition would be a bad theory.

Control Permitted A defining characteristic of industrial relations as a field of inquiry is a concern to find means of overcoming "labor problems." Instead of searching for knowledge just for the sake of knowing, industrial relationists generally want to achieve control over some aspect of the real world. Most of those in the field want to reduce unemployment, increase productivity, and eradicate injustice and bigotry in employment relations (Godard 1990 for data on Canada). As a result, theories which permit control should be considered more valuable than ones that do not. To the extent that the theory builder has a choice, one should always choose a theoretical system which produces more control.

Meehan's electrical system provides a good deal of control. Normative propositions flow as corollaries from the theory. If you want more light, add more batteries; if you want less illumination, remove batteries. These propositions allow the theory-user to achieve control over part of the environment and thus the theory is very useful. Not all theories have this characteristic. Thus, Newtonian physics allows us to predict exactly when the sun will arise in the morning but the theory does not permit us much control over the course of the sun or the earth, at least not at present. It does allow us to adjust to the inevitable. If the sun will arise at five in the morning we may pull down the shades to sleep longer.

Marxian theory of socioeconomic evolution is like Newtonian physics. It says that the internal dynamics of capitalism will inevitably lead to its destruction.[8] Social actors (e.g., unions, political parties) may be able to speed up or slow down the process but they cannot nullify it. Marxian theory tells us that we have no control over the eventual outcome. The convergence theory of Kerr, Harbison, Dunlop and Myers (1964) is also one which does not allow the user much control. It says that as industrialism advances, social institutions will become more similar. It offers no hope and suggests no mechanism whereby the nations and peoples of the world could maintain their diversity while advancing to high levels of economic development.

Bain's theory of white-collar union growth is a good example of an industrial relations theory which does suggest considerable control (Bain 1970). It states that the density of white-collar unionism is a function of the degree of employment concentration, the degree to which employers are prepared to recognize unions representing white-collar employees and the extent of government action which promotes union recognition.

The theory suggests that industrial relations actors have a good deal of control over the dependent variable. The normative advice to trade unionists seeking higher density would be: Find ways to convince or compel employers to extend recognition and find ways to get the government to promote union recognition. The variable "employment concentration" is one which does not permit much control. There is little the union theory-user may do to accomplish more employment concentration, although the union may decide to focus its efforts on enterprises which have concentrated employment. Note that the theory does not imply advice to the union on how to get employers to extend more recognition or how to get government to promote recognition. They are problems in need of additional theoretical and empirical effort.

Scope Theory is an instrument which allows the user to travel (mentally) to unknown places and be comfortable and familiar with the surroundings. The proposition "+inflation therefore +union membership" allows me to go into any pluralist, market economy country armed with expectations about the nature of the economy. Tell me that the country is going through a period of high inflation and I will expect union membership to be on the rise. But one would not expect the same relationship to hold in a communist country such as the People's Republic of China nor in an ancient nation such as Athens in the age of Aristotle. Unlike Einstein's Theory of Relativity, our theory is limited in scope, both geographically and through time. Other things being equal, one should always prefer a theory which has more rather than less scope (Toulmin 1962, Hage 1972). With the criterion of control in mind, one would prefer to have a theory which not only explained past events but also predicted future events.

It is not uncommon for authors to offer theories which they imply to be universal, when in fact they are very limited in time and place. In the U.S., for example, researchers often incorporate the variable unionized/nonunionized into industrial relations theories. One theory, which incorporates the dichotomy, holds that there is a direct relationship between unionization and productivity (Freeman and Medoff 1985). Unionized firms are said to be more productive than nonunionized firms because unions by requiring managers to remunerate workers at rates higher than those in nonunion firms put pressure on management to find ways to produce more efficiently and effectively in order to compete. This theory, in its usual form at any rate, is primarily relevant to North America and to other countries with labor relations institutions very similar to those in Canada and the U.S. North American policy and tradition has produced a situation where the employer typically is unionized or not unionized. Collective bargaining coverage and thus the impact of collective bargaining is nearly co-terminus with union membership. But that is not the case in Europe. In the typical European country between 75 and 90% of the labor force is covered by collective agreements and union membership, which in many countries is much lower than bargaining coverage, is commonly spread fairly widely. In short, it is much more difficult in Europe than it is in North America to identify companies or plants that are either union or nonunion. Even if it is possible to locate "nonunion" companies they are likely to be covered by collective agreements and thus the applicability of the theoretical rationale of the North American theory is very dubious (Adams 1989).

Even though theories with wide scope are to be preferred over narrower ones that does not mean that small theories should be disdained. Small theories can be very useful as long as one understands the limits of their utility and does not attempt to apply them beyond those limits (Meehan 1968). Theory builders should think through the limits of their theories and ensure that theory-consumers understand them. When theorists fail to specify the bounds of their theories, they often precipitate debate at cross-purposes.

Precision The theory "+inflation therefore +union membership" is not very precise. We would like to be able to say "if rate of inflation increases by 2%, days lost due to strikes will increase 1%." Einstein's theory has this kind of precision but we are rarely able to make such precise predictions in social science, although we would certainly like to be able to do so (Toulmin 1962). Sometimes empirical econometric research will report such an exact relationship. Usually, however, what is reported is a statistical description rather than a theory. A theorist should make an effort not to confuse these two phenomena (see e.g., Ashenfelter and Pencavel 1969).

Reliability Preferably one would like to have a theory which results in a correct prediction every time a prediction is made, but rarely in social science is that level of predictability reached. Alternatively, one may ask "how many cases does this theory explain?" The more cases explained, we might reason, the more likely that it will be reliable when applied to new situations. While this sort of reasoning is generally sensible it can be problematic. Humans have the capacity to learn and therefore the capacity to change their behavior (Rosenberg 1988). Thus, it is now being suggested that, as a result of "paradigm breaks," relationships which seemed to hold reliably in one time period may not hold in a new period (Price 1991).

Parsimony The rule of thumb here is "the simpler the theory the better." It is often possible to explain the same phenomenon in several different ways. Given the choice the theorist should always choose the least complex explanation. The more complicated the theory, the more easily it is to be misinterpreted. Psychoanalytic theory, which is nothing more than the sum total of the writings of the psychoanalysts, needs to be interpreted before it can be applied and different interpreters draw different consequences from their reading of the masters (Marx and Hillix 1963). The same observation may be made of Marxian theory. It is all but impossible, on the other hand, to interpret Einstein's theory in more than one way.

Variables mutually exclusive When constructing social theories, and particularly macro theories, it is very easy to create variables which overlap or which co-vary systematically by definition. To avoid this the theorist should carefully think through the relationship of each variable to all others to be sure that they are not tapping the same thing in the world of experience.

Falsifiable Some propositions about our existence endure primarily because there is no way to demonstrate that they are not false. "Thunder is the result of angels moving furniture in heaven." Maybe! I cannot prove the statement to be false. But it is a proposition which is not very useful to me. I can not use it to make thunder happen or not happen. Neither can I make use of it to avoid inevitable thunder because I cannot observe or talk to the angels to find out when they do their housekeeping.

It is not uncommon to find untestable theory in social science. Psychoanalytic theory would seem to be in that class. According to Marx and Hillix, "nowhere is there a clear statement of what are postulates, what are theorems, what their relations are, what quantitative values are to be assigned . . . " (1963, 230). There is "a language and a set of statements available" for explaining "all sorts of behavior—dreams, forgetting, symptoms, and the genesis of given neuroses." However, "The unfortunate truth is that the *analysts' statements are so general that they can explain whatever behavior occurs*" (p. 231). In effect the "theory" boils down to "anything may happen." [9]

One of the most attractive attributes of good empirical theories is that they allow us to predict that if *a* occurs then *b* will occur but not *c*. They allow us to differentiate between courses of action. But if a theory is not falsifiable then we cannot know if it has this capacity to differentiate and its utility as a guide to the future is very suspect.

To be a useful guide, predictions from the theory should be correct considerably more often than chance. One may never prove a theory to be correct. The best that one may do is to assemble evidence that leads to a high level of confidence in the truth of the theory. Thus, it is incorrect to say that Einstein's theory is true. All that one may say is that it has proven to be a reliable instrument so far.

Contingencies In constructing theories it would be useful for the theorist to be consciously aware of the possible existence of contingencies between dependent and independent variables. For example, the theory mentioned previously that unionization (in North America) causes firms to be more productive (Freeman and Medoff 1985) is clearly not true in all cases. There is some research which suggests that unionized companies with very conflictual labor-management relations have poor productivity. Thus, instead of a direct relationship between unionization and productivity there is an important "intervening" variable which the theorist needs to incorporate.

Using the Checklist

In all social science graduate programs, students are taught how to do research. Theory building is usually taught as part of that nexus. In textbooks (and very likely in the classroom) theory building and theory assessing receive much less attention than do the techniques of data collection and analysis. That deemphasis on theory is unfortunate because theory is what the scholar deals with every day, either consciously or unconsciously.

Building and assessing theories are skills which like other skills take practice to perfect. By practicing what might be called "theory explication" —that is identifying theories embedded in discursive contexts, formalizing them, and assessing them against the check-list—one not only acquires theory building skills but also becomes a more critical reader.

The checklist presented here is very basic. There are more advanced ways of thinking about and representing perceived reality. However, if the basic skills are well learned (and it has been my experience that many social scientists either do not know them well or do not adequately apply them) then the more advanced skills may be more easily acquired.

Notes

1. They are also known as "approaches" or "paradigms" or "frames of reference."
2. Parsons and Shils (1962) identify four levels of theory: ad hoc classification systems, taxonomies, conceptual frameworks, and theoretical systems. Dunlop's Industrial Relations System is at the third level of theory within this system.
3. These distinctions are sometimes made by philosophers of science and by theoreticians in the various social and behavioral science fields. Hospers, for example, insists that empirical generalizations represent observed reality while theories consist of at least some concepts which cannot be observed (such as atoms, wave particles, and intelligence) and thus are based on contemplation rather than observation (1967, see also Hempel 1966). From such abstract, contemplative structures one may subsume empirical generalizations and deduce new propositions about reality which are referred to as hypotheses. Whether or not such distinctions are useful is a matter of debate. Constructivist theory, for example, holds that such apparently empirical concepts as *apple, tree,* and *dog* are really no more than linguistic devices not qualitatively different from *atom* or *wave length* (see e.g., Guba 1990). For the purposes of this article making the distinction is not critical.
4. "Long before the self-conscious attempts of the social scientist, common sense had provided us all with a theory about the behavior of our fellow human beings. It is a theory that we use every day to form our expectations about the behavior of one another and to explain our own behavior to one another. This implicit theory, often given the label "folk psychology" by philosophers, has always been the natural starting place for explanation social scientists have given. In fact, to the extent that social scientists, like historians, expound no explicit explanatory theory at all for the human actions they explain, they refrain from doing so because they have taken over folk psychology without even noticing." (Rosenberg 1988, 22-23).
5. This proposition was initially formulated by Shirley Lerner and quoted by Windmuller. It originally appeared in Lerner 1967.
6. Note that one observation is sufficient to formulate a theory. One may then casually "test" the theory against several familiar cases. If it seems to be true in all of those cases, then it may well be worthwhile to

formalize the theory and start down the road towards formal empirical testing.

7. This statement assumes that there is a real world that is knowable by human beings. That assumption is, by no means, fully accepted by philosophers and other students of the philosophy of science. For example, see Guba 1990 and Rosenberg 1988.

8. In the Communist Manifesto, Marx and Engels say, "The development of Modern Industry . . . cuts from under its feet the very foundations on which the bourgeoisie produces and appropriates products. What the bourgeoisie, therefore, produces, above all, is its own gravediggers. Its fall and the victory of the proletariat are equally inevitable" (Larson and Nissen 1987, 35). Marx, however, produced a great deal and much of what he wrote was, contrary to the dictum of Stichcombe about theoretical clarity, capable of more than one interpretation. As a result, in a recent textbook on sociological theory, the author argues, contrary to the quote above from the Communist Manifesto, that Marx did not think that the overthrow of capitalism was inevitable (Ritzer 1988, 22).

9. Despite being "more an art, a philosophy, and a practice than a science" psychoanalysis continues to win adherents and "its terms enrich the lay vocabulary more than the terms of any other psychological system" (Marx and Hillix 1979).

Works Cited

Adams, G. R., and J. D. Schvaneveldt. 1991, *Understanding Research Methods*, 2nd ed., New York: Longman.

Adams. R. J. 1988, "Desperately Seeking Industrial Relations Theory," *International Journal of Comparative Labor Law and Industrial Relations*, vol.4, no. 1, pp. 1-10.

_____. 1989, "Industrial Relations Systems: Canada in Comparative Perspective," eds J. Anderson, M. Gunderson, and A. Ponak, Toronto: Addison-Wesley.

Ashenfelter, O., and J. Pencavel. 1969, "American Trade Union Growth: 1900-1960," *Quarterly Journal of Economics*, vol. 83, pp. 434-48.

Babbie, E. 1992, *The Practice of Social Research*, Belmont, CA: Wadsworth.

Bain, G. S. 1970, *The Growth of White-Collar Unionism*, Oxford: The Clarendon Press.

Blalock, H. 1964, *Causal Inferences in Nonexperimental Research*, Chapel Hill, NC: University of North Carolina Press.

Chavetz, J. 1978, *A Primer on the Construction and Testing of Theories in Sociology*, Itasca, IL: Peacock.

Dubin, R. 1978, *Theory Building*, rev. ed., New York: Free Press.

Freeman, R. B., and J. L. Medoff. 1985, *What Do Unions Do?* New York: Basic Books.

Godard, J. 1990, "The Pedagogies and Ideologies of Business School IR Teachers," *Teaching and Research in Industrial Relations*, ed. A. Ponak, Canadian Industrial Relations Association, Quebec: Laval University.

Guba, E. G. 1990, "The Alternative Paradigm Dialog," in *Paradigm Dialog*, ed. E. G. Guba, Newbury Park, CA: Sage.

Hage, J. 1972, *Techniques and Problems of Theory Construction in Sociology*, New York: John Wiley and Sons.

Hempel, C. 1966, *Philosophy of Natural Science*, Englewood Cliffs, NJ: Prentice-Hall.

Herzberg, F., B. Mausner, and B. Synderman. 1959, *The Motivation to Work*, New York: John Wiley and Sons.

Hospers, J. 1967, *An Introduction to Philosophical Analysis*, 2nd ed., Englewood Cliffs, NJ: Prentice-Hall.

Kerr, C., F. H. Harbison, J. T. Dunlop, and C.A. Myers. 1964, *Industrialism and Industrial Man*, New York: Oxford University Press.

Larson, S., and B. Nissen, eds. 1987, *Theories of the Labor Movement*, Detroit: Wayne State University Press.

Lazarsfeld, P. 1959, "Problems in Methodology," in R. K. Merton, ed., *Sociology Today*, New York: Basic Books.

Lerner, S. 1967, "The Impact of Technological and Economic Change on the Structure of British Trade Unions," paper submitted to the First World Congress of the International Industrial Relations Association, Geneva, 4-9 September 1967 (dec. IC-678-3, mimeograph).

Marx, M. H., and W. A. Hillix. 1963 and 1979, *Systems and Theories in Psychology*, New York: McGraw-Hill.

Meehan, E. J. 1968, *Explanation in Social Science*, Homewood, IL: The Dorsey Press.

Meyer, A. G. 1963, *Marxism, The Unity of Theory and Practice*, Ann Arbor, MI: University of Michigan Press.

Nachmias, D., and C. Nachmias. 1988, *Research Methods in the Social Sciences*, 3rd ed., New York: St. Martin's Press.

Parsons, T., and E. A. Shils. 1962, *Toward a General Theory of Action*, New York: Harper and Row.

Price, R. 1991, "The Comparative Analysis of Union Growth," in *Comparative Industrial Relations, Contemporary Research and Theory*, ed. R. J. Adams, London: Harper-Collins.

Ritzer, G. 1988, *Contemporary Sociological Theory*, 2nd ed., New York: Alfred A. Knopf.

Rosenberg, A. 1988, *Philosophy of Social Science*, Boulder, CO: Westview.

Roth, P. A. 1987, *Meaning and Method in the Social Sciences*, Ithaca, NY: Cornell University Press.

Stinchcombe, A. L. 1968, *Constructing Social Theories*, New York: Harcourt, Brace and World.

Toulmin, S. 1962, *The Philosophy of Science*, London: Hutchinson.

Windmuller, J. P. 1987, "Comparative Study of Methods and Practices," in J. P. Windmuller, et al., *Collective Bargaining in Industrialized Market Economies: A Reappraisal*, Geneva: International Labor Organization.

Teaching and Building Middle Range Industrial Relations Theory

Thomas A. Kochan

Frustrated with what he perceived to be an impasse in sociological research, Merton (1949) formulated the notion of middle range theory to promote the development of logically interconnected explanatory models that are intermediate to minor working hypotheses of day-to-day research and the grandiose attempts to formulate integrated conceptual structures. Merton defined what he meant by middle range theory in his own work. He showed that by generating relatively specialized theories applicable to limited ranges of social problems and data, researchers could test hypotheses that would contribute to the consolidation and progress of social science theory and research. This contrasted with the broad, all encompassing efforts at social theory illustrated in the works of Marx, Weber, or Durkhiem. Indeed, Kurt Lewin could very well have had theories of the middle range in mind when he expressed his oft-quoted adage that "there is nothing so useful as good theory."

Merton's definition and Lewin's description of useful theory are especially appropriate for the field of industrial relations. Ever since John R. Commons established the role model for the practitioner/academic, the goal of industrial relations researchers has been to produce and empirically test theories that are not only useful to policymakers and the labor and management communities but are also valuable to researchers concerned with understanding complex social processes. While the twin goals of producing socially relevant and academically substantive research can conflict, this need not be the case. By summarizing the approach I use in teaching and developing theories of the middle range, this chapter illustrates how the divergent requirements of industrial relations research can be constructively reconciled to further both public policy and academic inquiry.

Industrial Relations' Niche in the Social Sciences

Middle range theories cannot stand alone in a field of inquiry. Instead, they must be embedded in some unifying theoretic orientation that provides the defining features of the field. Thus, in this section, I suggest what I see as the secondary and primary features of industrial relations research. These analytic foundations provide us a way to proceed with the development of middle range theory without an all-encompassing integrated framework and, at the same time, distinguish industrial relations from the competing disciplines of law, economics, the behavioral sciences, history, and political science which all share an interest in, and offer alternative perspectives on, various aspects of the employment relationship.

Secondary Features of Industrial Relations

The most enduring and prominent feature of industrial relations research has been its problem-centered orientation. Indeed, although as Adams' chapter ("All Aspects . . . ")in this volume points out, the origins of industrial relations can be traced back to the late nineteenth century, Kaufman (1991) argues that the field established itself as an area of scholarly inquiry and teaching by addressing the key "labor problem" of the early part of this century. Following the bombing of the Los Angeles Times office, concern for violent labor conflict led to the creation of the 1911-13 Commission on Industrial Relations. John R. Commons, the father of U.S. industrial relations research, was a member of that Commission, and Kaufman lists as research assistants to the Commission a veritable "Who's Who" of early industrial relations scholarship in the United States—Selig Perlman, William Leiserson, Sumner Slichter, Leo Wolman, David McCabe, and Edwin Witte (Kaufman 1991, 14, footnote 3). The exposure of these early scholars to the first-hand issues of the day left an indelible imprint on the field in the U.S. It established the scholar-practitioner as the model for future researchers in industrial relations, or as Commons called it, a researcher capable of producing practical theory.

This tradition carried over to the next generation as well. Witness, for example a similar list of "Who's Who" in post-World War II industrial relations research from those involved in one way or another in the War Labor Board: George Taylor, Clark Kerr, John Dunlop, Robert Livernash, Sumner Slichter, Richard Lester, Charles Myers, Douglas Brown, Nathan Feinsinger, Arthur Ross, Milton Derber, and many others. The emergence of labor problems in the public sector in the 1960s and 1970s saw a repeat performance with governors and state legislatures from New York and Pennsylvania, to Illinois, Michigan, and Wisconsin, to California turn to ideas and experience of industrial relations researchers in designing their public sector collective bargaining statutes. Thus, the problem-centered nature of industrial relations theory and research is clearly one of the distinguishing features of our field.

A second feature of industrial relations research is that it draws on multiple disciplines in an effort to conceptualize the problem under study in its holistic dimension. Because of the problem focus, industrial relations researchers do not have the luxury of pursuing a narrow piece of a labor or employment problem. This leads industrial relations theory and research to be more holistic in definition of the research question and multidisciplinary in perspective.

Unlike colleagues who define their primary intellectual mission as the deepening of a discipline, there is little opportunity for exploring in depth what a discipline, such as economics, has to offer to the understanding of a complex phenomenon. A disciplinary perspective can offer sharp, deep, and rich insights into a problem but seldom can provide a complete or practical solution or approach to solving the problem. This does not, however, imply that industrial relations researchers should not be well grounded in some established discipline. Recall that most of the leading scholars of this early generation came from a strong disciplinary training either in economics (Commons, Dunlop, Kerr, etc.) or history (Perlman, Brody, Gutman, Taft, etc.) or one of the behavioral sciences (McGregor, Whyte, etc.) Yet each of these scholars tended to go beyond the boundaries of their discipline to examine the broader contours of the problems of interest to them and borrowed from other disciplines and from their own experiences. Thus the value of the multidisciplinary perspective found in the best industrial relations research is not that it *denies* or minimizes the contributions and insights of the various disciplines that also speak to the issue, but that it builds on and integrates prior and current work from these fields and does so at a sufficient depth to gain the respect of those working on the same issues within the discipline. This is a tall order, especially for graduate students in our field, but one that is the price of admission.

One implication of this multidisciplinary perspective is that the best industrial relations teaching and research programs are ones that mix scholars trained in multiple disciplines with those trained directly in industrial relations. In this way the diverse theories and insights from the disciplines are brought to bear on research problems, teaching, and intellectual debates along with the specific perspectives of those trained directly in industrial relations. What should bind this diversity together is not a single effort to homogenize their research interests or perspectives but a shared interest in employment problems and an interest in enriching their own disciplinary and theoretical perspectives from interaction with colleagues from other approaches.

A third feature of industrial relations research is its reverence for and appreciation of history. Commons and the Webbs, not to mention Karl Marx, all demonstrated through their work the importance of putting any contemporary problem or theoretical insight in its proper historical perspective. Indeed perhaps Common's most enduring theoretical work—the paper in which he develops his proposition about the effects of the expansion of the market on employment conditions—is his essay on the history of shoemakers' (Commons, 1919). Moreover, the multivolume history of labor produced by Commons and his students and colleagues between 1918 and 1935 is a lasting tribute to the importance attached to the study of history for its insight into the problems of the day.

The value of history provides another important lesson to industrial relations researchers. It suggests that the problems that we study are enduring and not simply transitory features of either an early stage of industrial development or something so new that there is nothing to learn from a look at prior experience.

A fourth feature of industrial relations theory follows from its multidisciplinary character—it must be multimethod as well. Being trained in social sciences in the late 1960s at Wisconsin meant that we were expected to become competent in social science theory, quantitative methods, and experimental designs. Campbell and Stanley's (1963) primer on quasi-experimental designs was treated as a standard to evaluate the quality of the design of any research project or published paper; methodological questions on Ph.D. preliminary examinations could be expected to range from critiques of the Coleman report to questions about times series versus longitudinal designs for studying labor force participation rates to questions about construct validity, alternative tests for reliability of behavioral measures to the relative merits of path analysis verses two-stage least squares equations for testing models that were amenable to structural equations. The emphasis on methodology was designed to bring home two central points: 1) it was time (indeed overdue) for industrial relations researchers to enter the realm of the quantitative social sciences, and 2) neither econometricians nor psychometricians had a monopoly on the best way to design and conduct quantitative analysis.

This was appropriate since industrial relations was slow to take up quantitative analysis and because of this the field lost ground to other disciplines that had added quantitative analysis to their tool kit at an earlier date. Indeed, it became quite obvious that one could not effectively study many of the most interesting and important issues of the day, such as the effects of unions on wages, the determinants of inequality at the workplace and in society, or the effects of alternative employment and training policies and institutions on labor market outcomes without a sound preparation in research design and quantitative methods. It was concern over the latter issue, again a public policy concern, that led researchers like Glen Cain, Lee Hansen, and Gerald Somers—very different labor economists, one a Chicago-trained econometrician, another a policy-oriented economist who approached labor market policies from human capital and cost benefit analysis perspectives, and the third a Berkeley-trained institutional economist interested in "manpower" problems—to cooperate in the training of a cohort of students capable of evaluating the costs, benefits, and policy implications of various employment and training policies of the 1960s and early 1970s.

Yet, while recognizing the indispensable value and necessity of quantitative analysis, the respect for the insights of institutions, history, and case study research was never and should never be lost on industrial relations. Unlike some of our more pure disciplinary colleagues, we cannot afford to dismiss as "pseudoscience" those who choose to use exclusively qualitative or exclusively quantitative methods. Both, and indeed variations of both, such as case studies and ethnographies or econometric analysis of large scale surveys and narrowly focused but tightly designed laboratory experiments with student subjects, all can offer insights to industrial relations problems and need to be taken seriously rather than dismissed as lacking scientific rigor. Again, this places a greater methodological burden on students of industrial relations than it does on their colleagues within disciplines such as economics, psychology, etc., but, again, this is the price of admission to the field.

Primary Feature of Industrial Relations

While the above aspects all capture important distinguishing aspects of industrial relations research, I believe the primary feature that distinguishes the field from its counterparts lies in the normative assumptions and perspectives that underlie our conceptualization of the employment relationship. Ever since the work of Marx, the Webbs, and Commons we have accepted what later (Walton and McKersie 1965) became known as the mixed motive nature of employment relationships. That is, the parties to the employment relationship are tied together in an enduring web of partially conflicting and partially common interests or objectives. The task of industrial relations theory and research therefore is to deal with this phenomenon. Carried to the its logical conclusion, this means that industrial relations scholars are equally concerned with goals of equity and efficiency in employment relations (Barbash 1987, 1989; Meltz 1989).

This normative assumption sets the work of industrial relations scholars apart from neoclassical economics models and much of the managerialist organizational behavior or human resource management research. In neoclassical economics, competitive markets are assumed to eliminate conflicting interests by producing optimal labor market outcomes, whereas ever since the Webbs used the concept of the "higgling of the market" industrial relations researchers recognized that perfect competition poses a competitive menace to worker interests. This is why strategies for "taking wages out of competition" have played such an important role in industrial relations models. While few organizational behavior theorists would argue with the general concept that conflict is a feature in employment relationships, most theories in this field take a managerialist perspective; that is, it is management's job to coordinate and manage these divergent interests. Conflict is viewed more as a pathological or undesirable state of affairs than as a natural feature of employment relationships. Thus, the task of organization theory is to explain why conflict occurs so that managers can resolve, reduce, or eliminate it. Organization theorists, therefore, tend to look at the employment relationship from the standpoint of those who control and manage it. Thus, both neoclassical economics and most organization theory either deny or minimize the legitimacy and enduring nature of conflicting interests in employment or assume market forces or appropriate managerial behavior will obviate the need for institutional (legal or collective representation) regulation in employment relationships.

While I see the acceptance of conflicting interests in employment relationships as the primary defining characteristic of our field, there remain lively, and to some extent unresolvable, normative debates among different schools of thought regarding the *sources* of this conflict of interests and the *prescriptions* for dealing with it that flow from these different schools. Marxist or labor process scholars (Hyman 1975), for example, view the structure of capitalist society and modes of production as the basic source of conflict and thus feel any policy prescriptions short of fundamental replacement of capitalism with a socialist state and ownership structure as failing to address the root cause of the problem. Others (Fox 1974, 1990) agree with the theoretical perspectives of modern labor process theory but not its ultimate prescriptions. In contrast, those operating within what some label a pluralist perspective see the conflict as endemic to the structure of all employment relationships regardless of who owns or controls the means of production (Barbash 1984). These scholars see the primary task of industrial relations as contributing to an understanding how conflicting interests can be resolved periodically and how the parties can expand the frontier of joint problem solving (Cutcher-Gershenfeld 1991).

Since these different views reflect deep normative assumptions about the nature of society and economic relations, there is little

likelihood that some common ground can be found between them—
see for example the exchange between Richard Hyman and myself
over the approach taken in *Collective Bargaining and Industrial
Relations* (Strauss 1982). Thus, rather than attempt to force students
to accept a single normative perspective regarding the sources of
conflict in employment relationships or the appropriate policy
prescriptions to advocate for addressing these conflicts, we need to
encourage each individual student to come to grips with this issue
for him or herself. This objective should feature prominently in the
teaching of industrial relations theory and the training of graduate
students. Unfortunately, as our students are quick to point out,
sensitivity to the norms implicit in one's research often gets ignored
or suppressed in published empirical studies.

Implications for the Teaching of Industrial Relations

Theory

The defining features of our field outlined above have influenced how I try to teach industrial relations theory, as well as the
types of theory and empirical research projects I've engaged in to
date. In this section I will review how these considerations inform
my teaching of industrial relations theory, and in the next section I
will review how these perspectives have informed some of my past,
current, and future research.

Industrial relations theory cannot be taught in a semester or
even a year-long seminar or course. Instead, what we seek to do in
a formal semester course is to start the long process of acquainting
students with the history and basic theoretical and methodological
traditions and perspectives in our field and encourage students to
explore these works in more depth on their own in ways that help
them formulate their own perspective on these issues and identify
their own conceptual, disciplinary, and methodological niche from
which they will choose to work in the field. For this reason, the
teaching of industrial relations theory works best when we have a
mixture of students from mainstream industrial relations and students from different disciplines such as political science, economics, and organizational theory. The multidisciplinary knowledge
and perspectives create the debates that provide an important part

of the learning and training for debates that students will encounter over their work in the future. Diversity within the student body also reinforces the expectation that works from these different disciplines cannot and should not be ignored, devaluated, or discounted as irrelevant to industrial relations.

We start the course in a traditional fashion by reading samples of the classics or the works that might pass for grand rather than middle range theories in our field from Marx, to the Webbs, to Commons, Perlman, and Barbash, to Dunlop (1958). But these are counterpoised with the work of Milton Friedman, March and Simon, Gary Becker, Douglas McGreger, and others who take fundamentally different normative, theoretical, and disciplinary approaches to the study of employment and labor issues. Thus, the first task of an industrial relations theory course is to provide a rich appreciation of the classics in the field and the historical controversies over how to study employment problems, and the different disciplinary approaches to the field.

One device that I've used to gain a historical perspective on the field is to ask students to write a short comparative book review of an "old" and a "new" classic that addresses a similar set of questions or problems in order to examine differences in theoretical and methodological perspectives. An example of this comparison would be Slichter's 1941 book on *Union Policies and Industrial Management* or the 1960 classic Slichter, Healy, and Livernash *The Impact of Collective Bargaining on Management* with the 1984 *What do Unions Do?* by Freeman and Medoff. The goal of this exercise is to get students to appreciate both the enduring nature of basic questions in our field and to critique the extent to which recent research has made progress in methodology, conceptualization, and insight into the problem compared to the earlier work.

Another approach used is to emphasize the social *context* in which the theory and research we read was generated. For example, students not only read a sampling of Commons' work but we also read Kenneth Parson's (1963) insightful essay reviewing Commons' progressive perspectives on the social and labor problems of his time. Students are also encouraged to read Commons' entertaining autobiography *Myself* (1934). Also, we read Antonio Gramsci's *Selections from a Prison Notebook* (1971) to understand the political context of the debates over Marx, Lenin, Luxemburg, and other socialist thinkers in the early part of the century. Students tend to take great fascination in learning more about the personalities and careers that lie behind the works of more recent scholars such as Dunlop, Whyte, Kerr, Shultz, McKersie, etc. I believe this serves an important purpose, since as Ronald Schatz recent essay (1992) and Kaufman's (1991) historical treatise on the field point out: the framing of the problem and the intellectual debates that evolve cannot be entirely separated from the environment of the times and the personal experiences of the authors. This is a lesson again in introspection that bears repeating for all of us—we are influenced by our environment and this is both inevitable and positive. But at the same time we need to insure that we are not unconscious victims of events so that we bounce from issue to issue or embrace the "politically correct" thinking of the moment at the expense of a longer run perspective and set of values. Recall that Commons and his students labored on their research for more than twenty years before state and eventually national legislators would take their ideas seriously and translate them into policy and then only because of a social and political crisis rather than because of the pure power of their theories and empirical evidence.

Throughout the course we seek to move across levels of theory and research—from the grand ideas and theory of Marx to the middle range models of Walton and McKersie (1965) to the empirical tests of theoretical ideas such as the work of Freeman and Medoff or more recently our own colleagues and former students involved in the *Transformation* project (Cappelli 1983, Ichinoiski 1986, Verma 1983, Cutcher-Gershenfeld 1991). This is one way to demonstrate that each of these levels of theory and empirical research contributes to our cumulative body of knowledge and that different people, at different career stages, have comparative advantages at different levels of theorizing and empirical analysis. The point to be emphasized is that one need not produce another *Communist Manifesto* or *Industrial Democracy* or *Industrial Relations System* or *Behavioral Theory of Labor Negotiations* to contribute to industrial relations theory!

The final objective of the industrial relations theory course (sometimes we don't get this far in a single semester) is to acquaint students with the current debates and theoretical challenges facing the field. Given the problem-centered tradition of the field, there is no shortage of contemporary topics and debates to fill up this part of the course. But it is interesting to see how the topics have evolved over the twenty years of studying or teaching industrial relations theory.

As a graduate student the major debates in industrial relations theory centered over grand questions such as "what's the appropriate definition, scope, and focus of the field? Is there a single dependent variable that brings focus to the field? Is Dunlop's system's model a theory or simply a useful collection of concepts tied together in an analytical framework?" (See Somers 1969.) The problem with these debates is that they made little headway in advancing theory or speaking to critical issues of the day. The critical issues were how can we end the Vietnam War or what can be done to deal with the racial conflicts in the cities and at the workplace? Thus, there was a backlash against grand theory or broad definitional issues about the nature of our field as most of us in the U.S. turned to more narrow empirical research pursuits that, we hoped, could produce more tangible and concrete insights into tractable problems.

By the time I began teaching the pendulum slowly began to swing back to linking theory and empirical research, largely with the help of the laboratory of problems and empirical opportunities offered up by the growth of public sector collective bargaining and its attendant problems and debates. Thus, in the mid-1970s, we spent considerable time reviewing and critiqueing various studies of the effects of public-sector bargaining laws and impasse procedures on strikes and bargaining outcomes. This was the most important policy debate of the time and many of us were deeply emersed in empirical research on this topic.

In the late 1970s and early 1980s, research on the rise of nonunion personnel practices, the role of employee participation, and the relationship between unions and workplace innovations became a central topic that allowed us to debate deep normative questions as well as critique the adequacy of the various experiments, case studies, and behavioral science surveys and models for improving the quality of work. This took us to a more micro level of theory and research and away from some of the deeper and grander theoretical debates of the past.

It was not until the tumultuous events of the early 1980s that most of us in industrial relations became reconnected to debates over basic theory and current events. The conditions for a paradigm shift suggested by Thomas Kuhn (1962) existed. There were too many anomalies between what we were observing in practice and the explanations offered by our received theories and empirical evidence. Union membership had been declining for a long time but had yet to be taken seriously by industrial relations scholars. Nonunion employment systems had grown up but continued to be viewed by industrial relations researchers as exceptions to the traditional collective bargaining relationships. Efforts to reform collective bargaining by introducing various forms of employee participation were seen as interesting (or perhaps naive) behavioral science fads that failed to adequately understand the mixed motive nature of employment relationships and collective bargaining institutions. But in a series of works involving colleagues and students at MIT—see, for example, a collection of papers in *Challenges and Choices Facing American Labor* (Kochan 1984), Piore and Sabel's *The Second Industrial Divide* (1984), Katz's (1985) *Shifting Gears,* Cappelli's (1983) early empirical studies of concession bargaining—the shape of a reinterpretation of industrial relations theory and events began to unfold and to spark a debate. The debate centered on whether we were, in fact, experiencing a set of fundamental changes that required an equally fundamental rethinking of our analytical frameworks and models or simply were experiencing another in a long history of cyclical or transitory losses of union power that would result in a rebound of labor's influence in mirror image of the past. Nothing so invigorated the study of industrial relations theory and research as the power of this debate, fueled and reinforced by the fact that unions and companies themselves were engaging simultaneously in pitched debates over the same issues! Theory and practice indeed came together in this debate. One could get an audience of practitioners and researchers to take great interest in both the broad theoretical and the specific practical issues at stake in this work. *The Transformation of American Industrial Relations* (Kochan, Katz, and McKersie 1986) represented an effort to bring together the various studies that we and our colleagues and students had conducted on these issues.

While the specific features of this debate have shifted—there is now less interest in the debate over whether changes are fundamental and structural in nature or merely incremental and/or cyclical and more concern over how to cope with the changes that have occurred—the adequacy of our interpretations and the utility of our "strategic choice" model remains subject to sharp debate (Lewin

1987, Chelius and Dworkin 1990, Chaykowski and Verma 1992). We believe the next phase of this debate should take place through a comparative international context—an issue I will return to below.

Developing Industrial Relations Theory: Some Personal

Examples

How does one go about developing theories of the middle range in industrial relations? There are probably as many answers to this question as there researchers in the field. I can only offer several personal examples and attempt to use these to illustrate what I believe are some generic features.

As emphasized above, the best opportunities for developing new theory in our field are found in the critical problems or issues of the day. This is what gave birth to the field in the early part of this century and it is what will sustain the field in the future. Thus, since the explosion of bargaining in the public sector was the dominant collective bargaining problem of the 1960s and early 1970s, it is not surprising that this topic captured the attention of many of us who began our careers during that time period. The initial problem to be confronted was a very basic one: Just what was different about public-sector bargaining than collective bargaining as it was traditionally practiced in the private sector? Many experienced practitioners and scholars were offering advice on how to "improve" the conduct of public-sector bargaining based on their private sector experiences yet it was not clear that these insights generalized well to this new environment.

Interest in this basic question led me to conduct two case studies of city government bargaining (Kochan, 1972) that provided an in-depth description of how the various parties to public-sector negotiations behaved. From these case studies and a reading of various theoretical and empirical descriptions of private-sector bargaining—particularly Stevens (1963) and Walton and McKersie (1965)—emerged the concept that bargaining in the public sector was distinguished by its multilateral nature. That is, instead of a bilateral (labor versus management) process in which internal differences were largely reconciled internally prior to the bargaining deadline, bargaining in the public sector was inherently multilateral in nature since the employer was composed of multiple interests and organized based on the governmental principle of separation of powers. To turn this finding derived inductively from case study research into a formal testable model or theory required an excursion into the relevant organizational and political science theories of intraorganizational conflict and political decision-making. From this a formal model with testable propositions was proposed and survey research design and data analysis plan was constructed.

Note the sequence: the labor problem of the day helped identify and define the research question; the initial case studies provided the institutional understanding or foundation on which the question could be framed in a fashion that captured the actual practices involved; the relevant social sciences helped place the problem in a broader perspective and compare it to similar questions found in those literatures; and social science research techniques were employed to develop a formal set of propositions, a research design and measurement strategy, and a set of statistical procedures appropriate to test the model. Out of this came a rather modest "theory" of multilateral bargaining in city governments (Kochan 1974, 1975).

A second example involves a study of impasse resolution procedures that I conducted with a group of students and colleagues at Cornell in the mid-1970s (Kochan et al. 1979). Shortly after arriving at Cornell, I discovered that the State of New York passed, on an experimental basis, an amendment to its Taylor Law governing impasse resolution for police and firefighters. The new amendment that was to take effect in July, 1974, and "expire" in July, 1976, added compulsory arbitration to impasse resolution process that had previously provided only factfinding with recommendations. Thus, it appeared that a natural "quasi-experiment" was about to be created. The question, therefore, was how could we evaluate the effectiveness of the alternative dispute resolution regimes?

This project illustrates the difficulty of developing and testing theories and conducting research that speaks to public policy debates. The first problem to be encountered was the lack of any real theory to guide the research. Even identifying the key questions or criteria to use to evaluate the "success" or "effectiveness" of the alterative dispute resolution systems was uncharted territory. A review of the collective bargaining literature and especially the report of the panel of experts (John Dunlop, E. Wright Bakke, Frederick Harbison, and Chairman George Taylor) that recommended the provisions of the Taylor Law suggested that an effective dispute settlement system would avoid work stoppages, encourage the parties to settle their disputes without undue reliance on the procedures, and would not "bias" the outcomes of the process from what would have been negotiated by the parties themselves. Thus, the effectiveness criteria chosen for evaluating the procedures reflected the norms underlying the sanctity of "free collective bargaining" that had been espoused by industrial relations scholars for years.

To assess the net or independent effect of the alterative procedures on these process and outcome criteria required developing theories of the other factors shaping the probability of negotiations going to impasse and identifying other factors that influence the outcomes of public-sector bargaining. This too proved difficult, since at the time there were few theoretical or empirical studies of determinants of impasses or the effectiveness of mediation processes (mediation was embedded in both procedures as an intermediate step in the dispute resolution process). What had been written about arbitration was mainly warnings by neutrals that its presence would invariably produce a chilling or narcotic effect on the parties that would reduce the incentive or ability to negotiate settlements without dependence on the procedure.

Finally, there was a singular lack of data. It became clear that if we were to do an adequate job of assessing the two procedures we would need to collect data from the parties themselves at the level of the individual bargaining units. Thus, a massive two-year data collection effort was initiated with the help of a National Science Foundation grant and the support of an advisory committee composed of representatives of the state Public Employment Relations Board, the governor's office, the state police and firefighter unions, and New York League of Cities, and several respected and experienced neutrals. To the credit of these interested parties, they helped provide access to their colleagues for data collection and a venue for eventually discussing and debating the results of our work and our recommendations, and they left the technical research design and analysis decisions to the research team.

Note again the sequence of this project: it began with a policy question and opportunity—a change in a key law and a defined timetable for the next political debate over the law; it required hard thinking about the appropriate research design and a mix of qualitative and quantitative techniques; it required development of models of mediation and negotiations that fit the specific context of public-sector bargaining but that also drew on research from a broader array of social and behavioral sciences; it required the use of econometric techniques—indeed some that ended up being the subject of considerable debate after the fact *among* research team members (see Butler and Ehrenberg 1981, Kochan and Baderschneider 1981); and the results of the work ended up feeding into a public policy debate.

In the process a lot was learned about the effects of different types of impasse procedures, some of which could be generalized to contexts outside of New York and to procedures other than the specific ones embedded in this particular law. But whether any new fundamental theoretical breakthroughs were achieved is more questionable. We were able to offer and test a new theory of the labor mediation process (Kochan and Jick 1978) but perhaps the broader lesson of this project was that public policy evaluation studies such as this one will only generate new theory if the researchers build this objective into the design of the project on their own initiative and as a separate agenda from the policy makers and practitioners who have significant stakes in the outcomes of the research. This project also illustrates one of the strengths and limitations of our field—the involvement of the practitioners and policy representatives made for exciting and highly relevant research that could serve as input to an important public policy decision but at the same time required such intensive detailed analysis that abstract and lasting theoretical contributions were hard to produce. Moreover, in some respects, the project was premature; since its completion considerable theoretical research on arbitration, mediation, dispute resolution, and negotiations has been produced that would now be available to any industrial relations researcher who takes on a similar task.

The final example of theory development—the process that led to the publication of *The Transformation of American Industrial Relations*—was already alluded to in an earlier section of this chapter. That effort again involved multiple colleagues and students and extended (indeed continues) over six years prior to the publication of the *Transformation* book. Like the other projects, it started from a puzzle about changing practices in collective bargaining and industrial relations. Soon after arriving at MIT it became apparent to many of us on the faculty (Robert McKersie, Harry, Katz, Michael Piore, Charles Sabel, and myself) that something important was changing or likely to change in the way companies were approaching labor relations. Moreover, it had been clear to many of us that the *pressures* for change on collective bargaining were building up for a number of years without a significant response from the parties (Kochan 1980, 506-11).

But it was not until we went into the field to conduct a number of informal interviews and case studies of contemporary management policies that we came away with a deeper hunch or grounded hypothesis that the change process was already underway in many companies. What we observed was a break with the past—the acceptance of the traditional norms of collective bargaining had given way to a more aggressive managerial posture toward unions and toward an effort to bring individual and small groups of employees more directly into the problem solving process at the workplace. Moreover, we observed significant power shifts within the management structure. Industrial relations professionals had lost power, line managers had taken control of what had previously been industrial relations policy decisions, and human resource professionals without deep knowledge of, or appreciation for, unions and collective bargaining were ascending in influence. These initial exploratory interviews led to a series of substudies conducted over the next several years by a our students and colleagues. The *Transformation* book served as an interim summary of the strategic choice framework that is still under development. Whether this amounts to a new "theory" of industrial relations will have to be judged by others, presumably at some time in the future.

What is clear is that this project shares several features with those described above and with predecessor projects in our field. It seeks to address the critical questions of our time—namely, is the U.S. industrial relations system able to transform itself in ways that can meet the efficiency and equity interests (Barbash 1987, 1989; Meltz 1989) and requirements of the parties in a world that has changed in significant ways. It uses multiple methods: historical analysis, case studies, and quantitative analysis of published and new survey data. It involves close interactions with the parties themselves, ranging from panels of management, union, and gov-

ernment representatives who supported our case studies and surveys, to leaders of the AFL-CIO who shared data and included us
and some of our ideas in their deliberations over future directions
and strategies, to debates with our research colleagues over our
interpretations and the utility of the theoretical framework that
emerged out of the project. Moreover, the framework itself is a joint
product that was influenced greatly by those involved directly in
the research and the work of close colleagues such as Piore and
Sabel's *The Second Industrial Divide*.

Thus, these three different attempts to develop theories of the
"middle range" in industrial relations illustrate the diversity of
approaches to theory construction and different levels of abstraction
and generality that theory can take in our field. Each, however, was
grounded in what was felt to be a critical problem; each required
drawing on insights from different disciplines; each required multiple methods and more than a one-shot study; each started with
case study and historical analysis to provide the institutional detail
needed to speak to the basic issues; and each attempted to generate
results that spoke both to theory and to the needs and interests of
policy makers and/or practitioners. Such, I believe, are the defining
features of middle range industrial relations theories and empirical
research.

Future Challenges for Industrial Relations Theory

While it is often common for researchers to claim there is a
crisis at hand only so they can propose a solution, I believe the field
of industrial relations is indeed under siege if not in a state of crisis
that will test once again the viability of our paradigm. This time the
crisis revolves around the very normative premises that, as I argued
above, provide the field its primary identity or niche in the social
sciences. Stated most directly: Is the mixed motive perspective still
viable?

Alan Fox (1974, 1990) is perhaps one of the most influential
yet underrecognized industrial relations theorists of our generation.
His 1974 book *Beyond Contract*, while somewhat dense and ambiguous, continues to pose one of the most basic challenges to
contemporary industrial relations theory and research. Fox raises
the question of whether a pluralist industrial relations system, one

based on institutions that legitimate and institutionalize conflicting interests at the workplace, is capable of developing and sustaining a high trust relationship. He appears to be rather pessimistic about this and hints at his gradual disillusionment with the pluralism built into British and Anglo-Saxon industrial relations institutions. Recently this same theme has been developed, albeit in very different ways, by Charles Sabel (1991) and by Wolfgang Streeck (1991). Sabel argues that developing and sustaining trust relations is essential to rebuilding local and macroeconomic institutions capable of managing the industrial restructuring that needs to occur to implement economic development programs. Streeck (1991) argues that unions that continue to be built on an assumption of adversarial workplace relationships are doomed to experience further declines in membership and inhibit economic progress in their societies. Instead he advocates union strategies that seek to improve worker welfare not through simply distributive bargaining but through strategies that promote and enhance the full development and utilization of skills in organizations and across the economy.

The concept of trust is also central to the authority relations in Asian economies that grow out of Confucianist cultures. Industrial relations systems (such as found in Singapore, Korea, Japan, Taiwan, and Hong Kong) have combined both authoritarianism and personal trust in ways that Western scholars would be wise to neither ignore nor interpret solely through our traditional pluralist or social democratic lenses. Something is different about the trust and authority relations in these countries that has yet to be fully understood by those of us who look in from the outside. Also, these relationships have yet to be explained satisfactorily by those who experience and write about them from within the cultures. Thus, there may continue to be a cultural gap in industrial relations scholarship that needs to be closed if we are to fully exploit the opportunity to learn about how trust is developed and maintained in different cultural, legal, and institutional settings.

What seems to bind together all those interested in this concept is the proposition that high trust (or avoidance of what Fox described as a high conflict/low trust syndrome) is essential to achieving high levels of economic performance and worker welfare—or the twin goals of efficiency with equity at the workplace and in society. If, as I believe, these continue to be the critical objectives of an industrial relations system, and therefore serve as the ultimate normative goals of industrial relations theory, then the study of trust relationships from the level of informal work groups to the interactions of labor, government, and business at the macro levels of society deserves a prominent role on our theoretical and empirical agenda in the years ahead.

The 1980s were very hard on labor organizations around the world for a very simple reason that goes back to the Commons' proposition on the expansion of the market. Unions gained power in national industrial relations systems as they developed structures and institutions for "taking wages out of competition." With the increase international competition, the ability of unions within any country to take wages out of competition by developing *national* institutions weakened.

While this has posed significant challenges to unions it also has challenged industrial relations theorists to understand what the equivalent of Commons proposition is for economies where low-wage competition from outside, if not inside, the country is a constant threat. This has sparked a surge in theoretical debate in our field that has yet to be resolved but offers considerable room for more focused model building and empirical research. One broad theoretical answer to this debate is found in the theories of flexible specialization put forward by Piore and Sabel (1984) and Kern and Schumann (1985): Workers and unions will gain greater leverage as markets become more specialized and technologies demand greater flexibility, thereby creating an environment where skills need to be upgraded and worker trust and motivation maintained. The result is a high value-added, high-wage economy.

In our own work (Kochan, Katz, and McKersie 1986), we have modified this view somewhat by offering a strategic choice perspective. This perspective accepts and builds on the basic premise that a high value-added competitive strategy for individual firms and nations is necessary if workers and unions are to avoid the type of wage competition that leads to a deterioration of working conditions and living standards. But it goes on to argue that there is no natural set of market or technical forces that will automatically produce the high value-added, high-skill, high-wage outcomes. Instead, we offer the hypothesis that the strategic choices of business, government, and labor influence the outcomes. Some firms will stay committed to low-cost competitive strategies, while others may move more quickly and fully to the high value-added strategies. We argue that the parties at the individual firm and perhaps (although this is not well developed in our original work) at the industry or national levels have some discretion over how they choose to compete. Thus we emphasize the need to look at the *interactions of market and technical forces with the strategic choices* of business, labor, and government.

A third argument critiques both of the above views for failing to adequately consider the role of the state and national institutions in shaping the environment in which firms and worker organizations compete and labor. The regulation school (Boyer 1988), the neocorporatists (Goldthorpe 1984), and other models argue that in Europe, for example, state policy, and in the case of the Economic Community, perhaps eventually regional trading blocs, will influence the social conditions of work that firms must meet and this is eventually what will provide the counterpart to Commons' expansion of the market hypothesis. This school of thought would argue that the Webbs foresaw correctly the rise of "legal enactment" as the key regulatory force in industrial relations, following the era of mutual insurance and common rule through collective bargaining.

This is more than a small debate over the appropriate analytical model to use to reinterpret contemporary industrial relations. The different models have significantly different implications for industrial relations theory and policy analysis and institutional development. The flexible specialization models suggest that market and technological forces will force firms to take worker interests into consideration regardless of whether workers are represented by effective unions or other institutions that provide voice in strategic decisions. The strategic choice models suggest that the key decisions lie in how firms respond to conflicting market pressures— niche markets may not be big enough to go around for all firms, technology is not deterministic in how firms deploy it or its impacts on skills and employee control, and other competing environmental pressures (such as pressures from financial markets and institutions, political factors, and the values and traditional strategies of the parties) all play important roles in shaping the response and the results of efforts to transform tradition practices. Thus, organizational governance arrangements and employee voice in strategic decision-making become important in these models. The regulation or state-institutions' view elevates the level of analysis farther by arguing that we need to examine the role of state policy, culture, and values as determinants of the response to global competition and differentiated markets and new technologies.

What all three of these models have in common is a view that the traditional institutional lens of industrial relations research that focused on personnel policies and/or collective bargaining needs to expand and look more closely at developments at higher levels of the management, economic, and political system in order to understand contemporary events. Moreover, all three of these models point to the need for more comparative international research that provides us with a wider variety of institutional and political responses to changing markets and technologies. Thus, this set of theoretical challenges should serve to rekindle interest in the field of comparative industrial relations research.

As Adams ("All Aspects . . . " in this volume) argues, industrial relations has laid claim to the study of "all aspects of people at work." Yet over time, too much of industrial relations research (including my own) has focused on the narrower set of topics and issues associated with collective bargaining and formal institutions of worker representation. This left the field of personnel, now human resource management, to others who often operate within a managerialist or what Fox called a unitary perspective or set of normative premises and that take the individual organization or firm as the boundary for their analytical models. Human resource management research has exploded in recent years as management became a more dynamic actor or catalyst for change in employment relations. Yet, there are significant intellectual limitations to the current human resource management literature that industrial relations researchers could fruitfully address.

The first major limitation stems from the firm-level focus of attention. Human resource management theory has yet to move beyond its individual firm boundaries. This limits its utility as an analytic device in settings where the probability of adopting and sustaining investments in human resource practices depends on whether other firms in one's product and/or labor markets adopt complementary innovations. Moreover, the movement to strategic human resource management research called for by both academics and practitioners in recent years has yet to bear fruit in terms of significant theory or evidence on the extent to which human resource considerations influence strategic decision-making within the firm.

Despite these limitations, the separation of human resource management research from industrial relations poses an important intellectual and practical challenge to industrial relations researchers.

One of the most obvious labor market developments of recent years has been the increase in the diversity of the work forces found in modern employment relationships. Labor force participation rates of women have steadily increased in most industrialized countries and, perhaps more importantly, the career orientations of women have correspondingly broadened and risen making all issues of equal opportunity and gender relations at the workplace a more prominent part of workplace relations. Part-time work, immigration, the growth of the internationalization of management in transnational corporations, the increased use of contract and temporary workers, all contribute to greater diversity in employment relationships. This increased diversity challenges traditional institutions and the views of the employment relationship and institutional arrangements that seek to conceptualize or manage employment as a bilateral, employee versus employers or a bilateral partnership between collective agents of workers and employers. Whether one focuses on the distributive or the integrative dimensions of the employment relationship, diversity challenges the utility of bilateral models. This, perhaps, is one reason that unions and collective bargaining have experienced difficulty in small establishments and in the faster growing service, white collar, and nontraditional employment relationships. To continue to be relevant as a field of study that encompasses "all aspects of the employment relationship" will require that we devote more attention to the study and the design of institutions capable of capturing and addressing the critical features of these more diverse employment settings. Again, collective bargaining, as it has been traditionally structured, seems ill suited to the task of addressing this diversity. In the absence of a significant body of theoretical or empirical work, little regulation and even less direct or indirect employee representation has been brought into these relationships.

In summary, industrial relations researchers need to carry on the tradition of addressing the critical problems facing the parties to contemporary employment relationships. As in the past this will require us to conduct historically well-grounded multidisciplinary, multi-method research that conceptualizes the problem in its full complexity or holistic dimensions at multiple levels of analysis. It will also require giving a prominent place on our agenda to the study of issues such as diversity in the workforce and in employment settings, developing and sustaining trust, the role of human resource policy and employee voice in organizational governance, and the comparative analysis of industrial relations and human resource management institutions and policies.

Finally, perhaps we should revisit the point made at the outset of this chapter, namely, has the problem-centered, scholar-practitioner role model for industrial relations researchers served us well or held us back in the task of developing theory? Schatz (1992) recently suggested that this orientation has both deepened and limited the intellectual development of the field. Such arguments have been made before. For example, one of the most prolific of the institutional labor historians of the Wisconsin School, Phillip Taft, was often criticized by other labor historians for being too close to the labor movement. This closeness to practice, and to the practitioners, in his critics eyes, caused Taft to lose his objectivity; more importantly, it led him and others in the Wisconsin School of labor history to focus too narrowly on the study of the official institutions of labor rather than to examine workers's cultural, social, and political environments and behavior (Gutman 1976, Grossman and Hoye 1982). Derber, likewise criticized industrial relations researchers of the 1960s for being too willing to "follow the headlines" rather than staying committed to a more enduring set of problems and issues over time. Dunlop once criticized those who sought to project the future of unionism based more on their wishes or hopes than on hard analytical thinking and evidence. His predictions turned out to be more correct than those who either predicted labors demise in the 1960s or a major wave of union growth fed largely by expected gains among white collar workers. And, in a personal bit of advice, Clark Kerr—one of the most preeminent scholar-practitioner-national figures of our time — cautioned against efforts to be all things to all people. He noted that the development of industrial relations and labor economics theory suffered in the 1960s as leading industrial relations scholars of the day—Dunlop, Kerr, Shultz, Weber, Seigel, Fleming, McKersie, etc., were called upon to put their considerable policy and administrative skills to work in various public service or policy positions. This has been an important legacy of our field and, I believe, it has both deepened and limited theoretical development. But I believe industrial relations is addicted to this affliction, perhaps by the very self-selection of those who find the field attractive. For I can think of no other field that provides more opportunities and challenges to implement the Wisconsin Idea that the task of a true scholar is to combine theoretical research with commitment to teaching and public service. That is what the field has been about in the past, and I believe it will continue to be one of its most attractive traits in the future. Whether it proves in the long run to be a liability or an asset will have to be judged by those whom we seek to serve through our work.

Works Cited

Barbash, J. 1984, *The Elements of Industrial Relations,* Madison, WI: University of Wisconsin Press.

_____. 1987, "Like Nature Industrial Relations Abhors a Vacuum, *Relations Industrielles,* vol. 42, pp. 168-179.

_____. 1989, "Equity as Function: Its Rise and Attribution," in J. Barbash and K. Barbash, eds., *Theories and Concepts in Comparative Industrial Relations,* Columbia, S.C.: University of South Carolina Press, pp. 113-22.

Boyer, R., ed. 1988, *The Search for Labor Market Flexibility: The European Economic Community in Transition,* Oxford: Clarendon Press.

Butler, R. J., and R. G. Ehrenberg. 1981, "Estimating the Narcotic Effect of Public Sector Impasse Procedures," *Industrial and Labor Relations Review,* vol. 35, pp. 3-20.

Campbell, D., and J. Stanley. 1963, *Experimental and Quasi-Experimental Design for Research,* Chicago: Rand McNally.

Cappelli, P. 1983, "Concession Bargaining and the National Economy," in *Proceedings of the Thirty-fifth Annual Meetings of the Industrial Relations Research Association,* Madison, WI: Industrial Relations Research Association, pp. 362-71.

Chaykowski, R., and A. Verma. 1992, *Canadian Industrial Relations in Transition,* Toronto: Holt, Reinhart, and Winston.

Chelius, J., and J. Dworkin, eds. 1990, *Reflections on the Transformation of American Industrial Relations,* New Brunswick: IMLR Press.

Commons, J. R. 1919, "American Shoemakers, 1648-1895: A Sketch of Industrial Evolution," *The Quarterly Journal of Economics.*

_____. 1934, *Myself,* Madison, WI: University of Wisconsin Press.

Cutcher-Gershenfeld, J. 1991, "The Impact on Economic Performance of a Transformation in Workplace Relations," *Industrial and Labor Relations Review.*

Dunlop, J. T. 1958, *Industrial Relations Systems,* New York: Holt.

Fox, A. 1974, *Beyond Contract: Work, Authority, and Trust Relations.* London: Macmillan.

_____. 1990, *A Very Late Development: An Autobiography,* Coventry: Industrial Relations Research Unit, University of Warwick.

Freeman, R. B., and J. L. Medoff. 1985, *What Do Unions Do?* New York: Basic Books.

Goldthorpe, J., ed. 1984, *Order and Conflict in Contemporary Capitalism,* London: Oxford University Press.

Gramsci, A. 1971, *Selections from the Prison Notebooks,* Q. Hoare and G. Smith, eds. New York: International Publishers.

Grossman, J., and Hoye, "Labor History," in T. A. Kochan, D. J. B. Mitchell, and L. Dyer, eds. 1982, *Industrial Relations Research in the 1970s: Review and Appraisal,* Madison, WI: Industrial Relations Research Association.

Gutman, H., ed. 1976, *Work, Culture, and Society in Industrializing America,* New York: Vintage Books.

Hyman, R. 1975, *Industrial Relations: A Marxist Introduction.* London: Macmillan.

Ichinoiski, C. 1986, "The Effects of Grievance Activity on Productivity," *Industrial and Labor Relations Review,* vol. 40, pp. 75-89.

Katz, H. C. 1985, *Shifting Gears,* Cambridge, MA: MIT Press.

Kaufman, B. 1993, forthcoming, *The Origin and Evolution of the Field of Industrial Relations in the United States,* Ithaca, NY: ILR Press.

Kern, H., and M. Schumann. 1985, *The End of the Division of Labor,* Munich: Beck Publishers.

Kochan, T. A. 1972, *City Employee Bargaining with a Divided Management.* Madison, WI: Industrial Relations Research Institute, University of Wisconsin.

_____. 1974, "A Theory of Multilateral Collective Bargaining in City Governments," *Industrial and Labor Relations Review,* vol. 27, pp. 525-42.

_____. 1975, "City Government Bargaining: A Path Analysis," *Industrial Relations,* vol. 14, pp. 90-101.

_____. 1980, *Collective Bargaining and Industrial Relations,* Homewood, IL: Irwin.

_____, ed. 1984, *Challenges and Choices Facing American Labor,* Cambridge, MA: MIT Press.

Kochan, T. A., and J. Baderschneider. 1978, "Dependence on Im-

passe Procedures: Police and Firefighters in New York State,"
Industrial and Labor Relations Review, vol. 31, pp. 431-49.
_____. 1981, "Estimating the Narcotic Effect: Choosing Tech-
niques that Fit the Problem," *Industrial and Labor Relations Review,*
vol. 35, pp. 21-28.
Kochan, T., and T. Jick. 1978, "The Public Sector Mediation Pro-
cess: A Theory and Empirical Examination," *Journal of Conflict
Resolution,* vol. 22, pp. 209-40.
Kochan, T. A., H. C. Katz, and R. B. McKersie. 1986, *The Transforma-
tion of American Industrial Relations,* New York: Basic Books.
Kochan, T. A., M. Mironi, R. G. Ehrenberg, J. Baderschneider, and T.
Jick. 1979, *Dispute Resolution under Factfinding and Arbitration,*
New York: American Arbitration Association.
Kuhn, T. 1962, *The Structure of Scientific Revolutions,* Chicago: Uni-
versity of Chicago Press.
Lewin, D. 1987, "Industrial Relations as a Strategic Variable," in M.
Kleiner, R. Block, and M. Roomkin, eds., *Human Resources
Performance of the Firm,* Madison, WI: Industrial Relations
Research Association, pp. 1-41.
Meltz, N. M. 1989, "Industrial Relations: Balancing Efficiency and Eq-
uity," in J. Barbash and K. Barbash, eds., *Theories and
Concepts in Comparative Industrial Relations,* Columbia, SC:
University of South Carolina Press, pp. 109-113.
Merton, R. 1949, *Social Theory and Social Structure: Toward the Codi-
fication of Research,* Glencoe, IL: Free Press.
Parsons, K. H. 1963, "The Basis of Commons' Progressive Approach to
Labor Policy," in G. G. Somers, ed., *Labor, Management,
and Social Policy,* Madison, WI: University of Wisconsin Press,
pp. 3-24.
Piore, M., and C. Sabel. 1984, *The Second Industrial Divide,* New
York: Basic Books.
Sabel, C. 1991, "Studied Trust," unpublished manuscript, Cambridge,
MA: MIT Department of Political Science.
Schatz, R. W. 1991, "From Commons to Dunlop: Rethinking the Field
and Theory of Industrial Relations," in H. Harris and N. Licthten-
stein, eds., *Defining Industrial Democracy: Work Relations in
Twentieth Century America,* Cambridge: Cambridge University
Press.
Slichter, S. 1941, *Union Policies and Industrial Management,* Washing-
ton, DC: The Brookings Institution.
Slichter, S., J. J. Healy, and E. R. Livernash. 1960, *The Impact of Col-
lective Bargaining on Management,* Washington, DC: The
Brookings Institution.

Somers, G. G., ed. 1969, *Essays in Industrial Relations Theory,* Iowa City: Iowa University Press.

Stevens, C. 1963, *Strategy and Collective Bargaining Negotiations,* New York: McGraw Hill.

Strauss, G., ed. 1982, "Review Symposium," *Industrial Relations,* vol. 21.

Streeck, W. 1991, "More Uncertainties: German Unions Facing 1992," *Industrial Relations,* vol. 30, pp. 317-49.

Verma, A. 1983, "Union and Nonunion Industrial Relations at the Plant Level," Ph.D. Dissertation, Cambridge: MIT Sloan School of Management.

Walton, R. E., and R. B. McKersie. 1965, *A Behavioral Theory of Labor Negotiations,* New York: McGraw Hill.

Integrative Theory Building: A Personal Account

Hoyt N. Wheeler

When asked to give a personal account of some theory building that I have done, my first (foolish) response was that it sounded like great fun—a chance to wallow in narcissism. Unfortunately, like the theorizing itself, once the glow of the original notion faded a bit, it dawned upon me that I might have to do some serious work in order to make the exercise of any use to anyone. What follows is an attempt to indulge myself a little in the joy of telling about the most interesting experience in my intellectual life, while mapping out a path that others might wish to follow. That experience was the writing of *Industrial Conflict: An Integrative Theory* (Wheeler 1985). The path is one to cobbling together integrative theory, and perhaps theory in general, in the field of industrial relations.

Why Bother?

Aside from the intrinsic satisfaction of doing it, why would anyone want to engage in building integrative theory in our field? After all, by tradition industrial relations is a highly practical field, arguably needing no theory. If a theory is needed, one might think that it could be borrowed from one of the traditional disciplines, such as economics, that have historically concerned themselves with such esoteric matters.

However, just a bit of reflection suggests that the reason that we should bother building some kind of theory is that without theory it is difficult, if not impossible, to conduct scientific research in industrial relations, and frameworks for organizing instruction are absent. Without rigorous scientific research as a basis for action, practice must be based upon unsystematic anecdotes and rough analogies. The reason that theory in industrial relations needs to be integrative, in my view, is that no one theory derived from any of the related fields is adequate to the task of aiding understanding and prediction as to the central concerns of industrial relations, and to use more than one theoretical perspective at a time requires at least some degree of integration.

There is in fact a great deal of theory being used in industrial relations, as this book demonstrates (see also, as to support for unionization, Wheeler and McClendon 1991). As one might expect, much of it is borrowed directly from other disciplines. What is less usual is the combination of theories from diverse disciplines. It is this process that I would like to describe and analyze.

How I Spent My Summer Vacation (and other time)

The path that I followed in doing theory generation was somewhat convoluted and took several years to traverse. As I suspect that this is necessarily the case with such an exercise, it may be of some use to indicate what one might expect in a pursuit of integrative theory making by recounting what I did.

Inspiration, or the Fall of the Apple

Isaac Newton had his famous apple. In my case the initial stimulus for theory was reading a few pages of Carl Sagan's *The Dragons of Eden* (1977) which I had picked up at the University of Wisconsin bookstore after conducting an exercise in the resolution of industrial conflict—an arbitration hearing—sometime in 1978. Sagan's description of the operation of social dominance hierarchies among Japanese macaques (monkeys) produced a "Eureka" experience. I suddenly saw what I thought were clear parallels between the social behaviors of these close relatives of humankind and a number of industrial relations phenomena. This insight furnished both the fundamental idea and the motivational starter for pursuing the development of this idea.

I mulled over this notion, talked to some colleagues at the University of Minnesota (who were kind enough not to advise me that I was demented which I am confident some of them believed). I also did a little reading of the basic sociological literature on authority relations (e.g., Simon 1976).

The occasion for my putting something in writing on this theory was an invitation by Richard Petersen and Gerard Bomers to attend a meeting at the Netherlands School of Business, Nijenrode, the Netherlands, in 1979, and present a paper on the subject of industrial conflict. It seemed to me that a theory paper would fit this meeting, that it would be a good opportunity to get some feedback from a diverse group of good scholars, that an original creation would be a good way of thanking Richard and Gerard for a free trip to Europe, and that it would be an assured publication of a paper that would probably otherwise languish unpublished and unread. All of this worked out except the publication, as my paper did not end up being included in the volume of papers published at the conclusion of the meetings. Also discouraging was that, to the extent that anyone noticed this nascent theory at all, it drew some penetrating criticisms that might have led a more rational person to abandon such an apparently hopeless pursuit. I went on from the Netherlands to England where I presented a paper on the theory at Durham University and received a similar response.

But I had stepped onto a slippery slope toward theory building. I kept on reading different literatures in the field. Some of the criticisms led me into the classic work in industrial relations and other social sciences. I also continued what I still consider to be a fascinating journey into biological ideas. In browsing the shelves of the University of Minnesota library I had run across Edward O. Wilson's *Sociobiology* (1980), and by further reading got caught up in the debate over this controversial work and the related work in ethology. In the course of this exploration I firmed up my opinion that this stream of work was not only exciting and interesting, but had implications for industrial relations, and especially industrial conflict.

As I talked with others in the field about this set of ideas, the usual response was that what I was doing sounded at least mildly interesting, but that I really should consider a whole body (or bodies) of literature with which I was unfamiliar. George Strauss, at Berkeley, who suffered through several versions of my theory,

was an excellent source for a number of references but kept annoying me by telling me that I should look at yet one more set of
references, and (even more annoying) that I should think about how
this supposedly brilliant set of theoretical notions might be actually
used for anything. John Lawler, a colleague at Minnesota, directed
me into the sociological literature in collective behavior. Leonard
Berkowitz, at Wisconsin, whose social psychological work on
aggression had caught my fancy, was kind enough to talk with me
at some length, give me a copy of his book (Berkowitz 1962) and
suggest some areas of reading. I dutifully read everything suggested
to me. In the course of this, I produced a number of versions of the
theory in the form of various short papers, which I sent to friends
in the field for their criticism and help. I received plenty of both.

As I worked along on the development of these ideas, I must
admit to developing an increasing need for closure—and for a
publication to result from all of this. The problem was that the
project kept growing and getting farther from completion. Although
some time to work on it was provided by my continuing failure to
get funding for additional empirical work (which might have produced some coin of the U.S. academic realm—journal articles), my
inclination (and need) for material resources had led to the development of an arbitration practice that was more and more threatening to make me, once again, a practitioner of industrial conflict
rather than a theorist about it. The temptation to abandon the quest
became very strong. After all, although some of my colleagues
found the project interesting, no one said that it was exactly brilliant,
and the amount, and validity, of criticism was sometimes overwhelming. It was fun, but more than two years had produced
nothing. In addition, much of the criticism seemed to be driving me
to a book-length manuscript in order to be able to make the
arguments in sufficient detail to be convincing. That meant a lot
more work.

Towards the end of 1980, I decided that I would give in to my
compulsion to theorize and commit to writing a book. This was
based in part on sheer stubbornness and perverseness, characteristics with which I believe that I have long been liberally endowed.
It was also based on my notion that I should do what I liked to do,
as this was the chief reason that I had changed careers (from law
practice) several years before. I do believe that my preference for
doing theoretical work had been helped to grow by the intellectual

hothouse of the University of Wisconsin, where as a graduate student in industrial relations in the early 1970's one could hardly avoid developing a taste for trying new approaches to the broad questions in our field. At about the same time, in looking around on the job market, I began considering a position, which I eventually accepted, at the University of South Carolina. One of the attractions of that position was having the academically derived income to make arbitration unnecessary and thereby provide the time to finish this project.

It was indeed the case that South Carolina was conducive to the birth of this work. I presented several versions of the theory at seminars at the university and received comments and suggestions from colleagues there while continuing to receive support and criticism from friends from Calgary, Canada, to Tilburg, the Netherlands, and points in between. As the book began to take shape, I was able to publish some of the ideas in it. A book chapter presenting the theory in capsule form in a JAI Press volume, *Research in Personnel and Human Resource Management* (1985), and a comment in *Industrial and Labor Relations Review* (Wheeler 1984) critiquing the macro-level strike literature, helped me not only to focus my thinking, but also to get a feeling of having actually produced something. One of the problems with book writing is that the gestation period is even longer than that for a journal article from a major empirical project. Patience is required. Unlike perverseness, that is a trait with which I am less than well endowed. So it helped to get some sense of having a finished product.

Once I had a completed manuscript, there was the inconvenient necessity of finding a publisher. After some struggling with the decision, I finally ended up with the University of South Carolina Press. This decision was based on my being favorably impressed with their operation, the idea of starting a series in industrial relations theory at South Carolina, and the convenience of working with a local publisher. The reviews during this process were, finally, very favorable, at last confirming my hope that if I could only make the argument at enough length and in enough detail it would seem more plausible. One of the pitfalls in work of this kind is that your preliminary statements are almost bound to offend everyone and convince no one. When you approach traditional questions from a perspective with which no one else in the field is familiar, you have to not only make a persuasive argument for the particular ideas that you want to apply to your field, but also for the basic theory on which you are building. This requires ink. In a field such as ours in the United States which unlike, say, history, thinks in terms of (and rewards) relatively short journal articles, there are few practical incentives to build new theories. This is especially true when the most prestigious journals have a strong preference for empirical work, and academic departments count publications in these journals above all other proofs of scholarly achievement (read promotion, tenure, pay).

The Ideas

Having given an account of what I did in a practical way to put together this combination of ideas, it might be useful to say a bit about the ideas themselves. As this theory is an amalgam of the thoughts of others, it is necessary to consider these notions and how I chose to use them. I grouped these basic thoughts together in sets that are seen as forming the five "pillars" of the theory.

The first pillar is the existence of innate human predispositions. This is the notion that there is such a thing as human nature and that this nature influences what we do. That is, we are inclined toward and away from certain behaviors because of what we are. And, what we are is in part a product of our evolution as human animals. This is a biological model of humankind. It differs from economic man and other models.

The basic idea of biological man has, of course, been around for a long time. It is highly controversial, and has been since Charles Darwin's time. It has been the subject of the "either—or" style of reasoning which I find offensive, but which is quite common inside as well as outside of academia. That is, one is supposed to choose whether it is nature *or* nurture that motivates human behavior. It has long seemed fairly obvious to me that it must be both. Yet the debate goes on, with the particularly unfortunate result that attempts to explore what natural inclinations are, and what their effects are, are met with automatic opposition from people who are true believers (to the point of irrationality) in the rationality of human behavior, upon which neoclassical economics is founded (see Bentham 1967, Schumpeter 1954) and Marxists pursuing what Midgley (1978) has described as a "bizarre tactical aberration" in opposing the idea that human behavior is anything other than infinitely malleable (see Gould 1978).

For me, using a biological model has several appeals. Perhaps the primary one is that it permits one to link knowledge in our field to that of the general body of scientific knowledge. Also, it draws theory from a broader area than that of the organism whose behavior is being analyzed. Following Marx's example, one must start with some very basic philosophical assumptions in order to build a general theory that can compete in the marketplace for ideas. This particular approach has the additional advantage of being framed and tested in such a way as to leave room for the operation of forces deriving from other sources, such as rational calculation of advantage. Finally, I am convinced that it is scientifically valid, with the arguments and evidence in support of it being stronger than those against it.

The second pillar consists of identifying particular root causes of industrial conflict—the subject of my concern. It seems to me that there is a clear intersection between natural predispositions and two central elements of the employment relationship—social dominance and material resources. That is, a human relationship where obedience in a social hierarchy is exchanged for pay is a place where one would expect to find natural inclinations for dominance and obtaining material resources to come into play. With respect to social dominance, I found that I could draw upon bodies of literature in psychology, sociology, and even industrial relations to build this part of the theory. As to material resources, economic theory supplied this need. Perhaps the greatest challenge in this process, at least in terms of sheer hard work, was absorbing enough of these literatures to feel reasonably comfortable making use of them.

For the third pillar—a gap between employee expectations and achievements (relative deprivation)—there was an existing argument in industrial relations having to do with the conflict-inducing effects of rising expectations. Also, I had written an historical paper on the West Virginia mine wars (Wheeler 1976) in which I used Davies' (1962) "J-Curve" theory, which operates in a deprivation framework. Political scientists such as Ted Robert Gurr (1970) had used relative deprivation as an explainer of social conflict. Perhaps the neatest fit with an existing literature in industrial relations came at this point, with a conjunction between this and the literature on the effects of dissatisfaction on support for unionization (e.g.,

DeCotiis and LeLouarn 1981). What was different about the deprivation formulation, however, was that it posited a gap between what a person perceived that he or she *deserved* (was justly entitled to) and what was achieved, not merely what was *desired* and what was achieved. This seemed a stronger construct, and one more likely to motivate action of this type, than dissatisfaction. It also fit quite well with the next pillar in providing a basis for frustration.

The path to the fourth pillar, the three paths to readiness for aggressive action, was strewn with difficulties. First, there was the underlying assumption that what was being analyzed was aggressive action against the employer. This had to be arrived at and justified. Second, if it were indeed an aggressive action for which individuals had to become ready, how would one expect for it to come about? The primary answer, I came to believe, was through the operation of a frustration-aggression dynamic. This meant adopting and adapting frustration-aggression theory—a social-psychological theory that is highly controversial. My reading of the literature proposing and attacking frustration-aggression theory persuaded me that the version of it enunciated by Leonard Berkowitz (1962) was valid and useable. Even its most severe critics seemed to agree that severe and unjustified frustration was likely to lead to anger (defined as a readiness to take aggressive action) toward the frustrator. By definition, deprivation is unjustified in the eyes of the person who is deprived. It is only relatively severe instances that I would expect to pack motivational wallop. Therefore, it seemed that, even with the restrictions imposed by its detractors, the theory was useable. It also was appealing in terms of what I knew in terms of occurrences of industrial conflict often taking place after employees had peacefully pursued their objectives, been denied this by the employer, and then turned to unionization or striking only as a last resort. It appeared that the political science literature (Gurr 1970), while speaking in terms of frustration, was really only measuring deprivation. Frustration, it should be emphasized, requires a person being in motion attempting to close an expectations/achievements gap, being blocked, and then (and only then) becoming angry.

Although the frustration path appeared to be the most interesting, I became convinced that it was not the whole story. Some of the aggression research indicated that the experience most likely to produce aggression was an attack upon the potential aggressor.

While this can be put in frustration-aggression terms, it seemed confusing to do so. So, this path, the "threat" path, became a second path in this stage of the model.

One more path seemed to reveal itself. This was the path of purely rational calculation. I was prepared to say that industrial conflict did not always, or even usually, occur because of cost-benefit calculations. However, I was also convinced that, at least in some cases, readiness for this type of aggressive action could be reached by means of a calculation and that this did not necessarily require the presence of an expectations/achievements gap. So, a third, calculative, path was posited.

All of this led to a readiness for some kind of aggressive action against the employer on the part of an individual employee. It was modeled in much the same way as a frustration-aggression model for individual aggressive action. This was all well and good, but left remaining the problem that the phenomenon with which I was concerned was *collective* aggressive action.

The fifth and final pillar of the theory is comprised of the conditions for *collective* aggressive action. The first requirement, I believe, is that a substantial proportion of a group of employees reach readiness at about the same time. The second is the absence of conditions inhibiting collective action. Drawing from frustration-aggression theory, these were posited as fear of punishment for engaging in the action, and the presence of norms militating against it. The third requirement is the presence of conditions facilitating the action, which I obdurately insisted upon calling *"love, hope and saliency"* (like faith, hope and charity). Love is akin to solidarity. The idea is that people will be more likely to act together if they care about one another. Calling it "love" brought down upon me a torrent of criticism similar to that which I received from talking about "status sex" in my analysis of social dominance. The arguments that the term "love" was inappropriate for use in scientific discourse, and that it was somehow inappropriate to talk about sex, I must confess to finding more amusing than convincing. Is it Puritanical discomfort with talking about love and sex that prompts these criticisms? Or is it just that in our field we have traditionally excluded these fundamental aspects of our humanness in favor of abstract rationality? It is probably the latter, but this in itself argues for the necessity of taking a hard look at the connections between human nature and social scientific theorizing.

Hope is a positive estimate of the probabilities of success in achieving what is believed to be deserved. This fits very well with the literature which finds perceived instrumentality of the union a predictor of support for unionization. Saliency is collective action being made to seem appealing, either through the occurrence of a dramatic event or the actions of leaders.

The model tying all of this together has been through many incarnations. It has been tentatively stated, made more complex, simplified, combined, and cut in half. If I took a hard look at it today, I would probably make even more adjustments in it. I do believe that the motto KISS (Keep It Simple, Stupid) applies to models, but it is very difficult to follow.

The last part of my book consists of attempts to apply it. (As indicated above, this was primarily to satisfy the whims of George Strauss.) Somewhat to my surprise, my analyses, which I strived to make objective, did show that it actually worked out pretty well. In a further attempt in this direction, I am, along with some colleagues, currently engaged in the last stages of a major empirical project in an attempt to test this theory as it applies to unionization in the United States.

Hints from Hoyt

For those who have not been dissuaded from pursuing integrative industrial relations theorizing by now, I do have a few bits of (more or less sage) advice. I suppose these are best described as my beliefs as to the requirements that one has to meet in order to do this with some degree of success. By the way, I would consider successful any attempt that resulted in the statement of a new approach that has reasonable prospects of being useable as a guide to research and understanding.

The first requirement is a to have a strong inclination (natural predisposition?) for the activity of theorizing. One has to not only believe that it is important, but also have something more than merely a tolerance from the painful task of thinking—particularly in drawing together diverse strands of research. Getting a kick out of ideas helps.

The second requirement is to somehow have an insight (inspiration?) that is both a bit different and personally exciting. Without this "Eureka" experience it is difficult to set off in a new direction. I'm less sure of how one makes a Eureka experience more likely to occur. Perhaps reading theoretical literature, particularly outside one's field, is a way to do this. Wide reading in general is probably helpful.

A third requirement may be to care a good deal for the field and about the importance of theorizing about it. Without this, the fourth requirement—grinding it out—is probably not possible. There is, particularly in integrative work, a large amount of drudgery. Simply locating materials in unfamiliar fields can be difficult. Then mastering the rudiments of a set of unfamiliar fields demands both time and patience. The fun of the work is mainly in the original inspiration and the eventual integration. Along the way, it can be very exciting to find a piece to the jigsaw puzzle of a theory. However, to find that piece often takes much patient searching.

A fifth requirement is a thick skin. Even more than in the doing of empirical work, integrative theory building invites attack. I would argue that this is as it should be. Usually an interesting new approach appears to be interesting only until it is thoroughly examined and new only until a thorough literature search has been made. There is indeed little new under the sun. Where multiple disciplines have dealt with an area of concern, it is especially likely that one will discover something, only to find that scholars in another field discovered it long before. In my case, it was Ted Robert Gurr's *Why Men Rebel* (1970) that almost did me in. I discovered it relatively late in my reading, quite by serendipitous accident. At first glance it appeared to me that, ten years previously, Gurr had already done what I was attempting to do. To my great relief I found, upon careful reading, that Gurr's work was sufficiently similar to be of considerable assistance to me, but had not pre-empted the field. Among other differences, my formulation's biological foundations, use of collective behavior literature, and different conceptualization of frustration, distinguish it from Gurr's.

The last requirement is a lot of help from one's friends. The introduction to my book is mainly a long list of names of colleagues from many universities in several countries, reflecting the number of people who made very significant contributions to the work. This is not merely a matter of form. It is truly the greatest thing about our field that so many of us are willing to spend time and effort assisting the work of our comrades. There is no reward for this except the intrinsic satisfaction of having made a contribution, yet it is probably what distinguishes the scholar who really cares about the growth of knowledge in his or her field.

A Final Word

Upon reflection, I must confess to having had more fun out of this one venture into theorizing than anything else I have done as an academic, at least outside the classroom. It also served as an escape for me during some very difficult times. I recommend it as an experience. I do believe that it is important for our field. So, come on in, the water is fine, and those of us who are in it would like to have more company.

Works Cited

Barbash, J. 1970, "The Causes of Rank-and-File Unrest," in J. Seidman, ed., *Trade Union Government and Collective Bargaining*, New York: Praeger Publishers.

Bentham, J. 1967, *A Fragment on Government and an Introduction to the Principles of Morals and Legislation*, Oxford: Basil Blackwell.

Berkowitz, L. 1962, *Aggression: A Social Psychological Analysis*, New York: McGraw-Hill.

Davies, J. 1962, "Toward a Theory of Revolution," *American Sociological Review*, vol. 73, no. 1, pp. 5-19.

DeCotiis, T., and J. LeLouarn. 1981, "A Predictive Study of Voting in a Representation Election Using Union Instrumentality and Work Perceptions," *Organizational Behavior and Human Performance*, vol. 27, pp. 102-118.

Gould, S. J. 1978, "Biological Potential vs. Biological Determinism," in A. S. Caplan, ed., *The Sociobiology Debate*, New York: Harper and Row.

Gurr, T. 1970, *Why Men Rebel*, Princeton, NJ: Princeton University Press.

Midgley, M. 1978, *Beast and Man*, New York: New American Library.

Sagan, C. 1977, *The Dragons of Eden*, New York: Ballantine Books.

Simon, H. 1976, *Administrative Behavior*, 3rd ed., New York: Free Press.

Schumpeter, J. 1954, *History of Economic Analysis*, New York: Oxford University Press.

Wheeler, H. 1976, "Mountaineer Mine Wars: An Anaylsis of the West Virginia Mine Wars of 1912-13 and 1920-21," *Business History Review,* vol. 1, no. 1, pp. 70-91.

_____. 1984, "Determinants of Strikes: Comment," *Industrial and Labor Relations Review,* vol. 37, no. 2, pp. 263-69.

_____. 1985, "Toward an Integrative Theory of Industrial Conflict," in K. Rowland and J. Ferris, eds., *Research in Personnel and Human Resources Management,* vol. 3, Greenwich, CT: JAI Press.

_____. 1985, *Industrial Conflict: An Integrative Theory,* Columbia, SC: University of South Carolina Press.

Wheeler, H., and J. McClendon. 1991, "The Individual Decision to Unionize," in G. Strauss, D. Gallagher, and J. Fiorito, eds., *The State of the Unions,* Madison, WI: Industrial Relations Research Association.

Wilson, E. 1980, *Sociobiology,* abgd. ed., Cambridge, MA: Belknap Press.

Index